# BLACK TENTS of BALUCHISTAN

# SMITHSONIAN SERIES IN ETHNOGRAPHIC INQUIRY

William L. Merrill and Ivan Karp, Series Editors

Ethnography as fieldwork, analysis, and literary form is the distinguishing feature of modern anthropology. Guided by the assumption that anthropological theory and ethnography are inextricably linked, this series is devoted to exploring the ethnographic enterprise.

# BLACK TENTS of BALUCHISTAN

*Philip Carl Salzman*

SMITHSONIAN INSTITUTION PRESS

WASHINGTON AND LONDON

COPY EDITOR: Vicky Macintyre
PRODUCTION EDITOR: Duke Johns
DESIGNER: Amber Frid-Jimenez

Library of Congress Cataloging-in-Publication Data
Salzman, Philip Carl.
    Black tents of Baluchistan / Philip Carl Salzman.
      p.   cm.
    Includes bibliographical references and index.
    ISBN 1-56098-810-X (alk. paper)
      1. Baluchi (Southwest Asian people)—Social conditions.
    2. Baluchi (Southwest Asian people)—Economic conditions.
    3. Baluchi (Southwest Asian people)—Domestic animals.
    4. Herders—Iran—Sarhad Plateau.   5. Sarhad Plateau
    (Iran)—Social life and customs.   I. Title.
    DS269.B33 S37   2000
    305.891598—dc21                99-088316

British Library Cataloguing-in-Publication Data available

Manufactured in the United States of America
07  06  05  04  03  02  01  00   5  4  3  2  1

∞ The paper used in this publication meets the minimum requirements of the American National Standard for Information Sciences—Permanence of Paper for Printed Library Materials ANSI Z39.48–1984.

# CONTENTS

# ACKNOWLEDGMENTS

The first acknowledgment must be offered to my hosts, friends, and acquaintances among the Baluch of the Sarhad. It is obvious that without their support, cooperation, and assistance nothing could have come from my efforts to learn about their life. To have accepted total strangers, who frankly at first appeared to be rather odd and who initially could hardly communicate, into the bosom of their intimate community, was a principled act of great hospitality. For the kindness, graciousness, and delicacy with which they subsequently offered their help and friendship, and the underlying humanity and decency that these qualities reflected, I shall always be an admirer of the Baluch and shall always be grateful. My closest friend, Shams A'din; his mother, Zarbonu, who loaned us her tent and shared her wisdom; calm and moderate Ja'far, the camp headman, and the fine woman, Monas, who was his wife; Id Mahmud; and the many others who shared their community and their lives with my then wife Joan David and myself, will always be a valued part of my life. The masterful Sardar of the Yarahmadzai, Haji Han Mahmud, accepted our presence in his tribe, and his charming half-brother Nezar Mahmud took us under his wing and recommended us to Ja'far's community. I intend that this partial record of their lives stand as a tribute to all of them.

Joan Alice David shared life in Baluchistan with me during 1967–68 and 1972–73, as well as the complex preparations for going and the subsequent processes of writing and publishing. She provided intellectual support, emotional comfort, and practical assistance throughout. Our shared memories of our experiences and friends in Baluchistan were deeply valued by us. Writing this book, I often wanted to consult her; but we parted long ago.

My parents, Leonora and Norman Salzman, directly assisted my Baluchistan research in a variety of ways. But, more important, they facilitated everything I have ever done by their unconditional love and acceptance, confidence and pride, and un-

The author with Nezar Mahmud Yarmahmudzai (left) and Shams A'din Dadolzai (right), at Gorani, Mashkil, 1973. (Photograph by Joan David)

stinting support. Although we have lost my father, my mother continues to be my greatest fan and has with relish revisited the Baluch in chapter drafts of this work.

I must also say something of my teachers. Everett K. Wilson and Raymond Gordon taught me sociology at Antioch College in Yellow Springs, Ohio. After I was introduced to social anthropology by Kennith Little, Michael Banton, and Malcolm Ruel at the University of Edinburgh, I pursued anthropology with Victor Ayoub at Antioch. At the University of Chicago, my supervisor Lloyd A. Fallers and other committee members, Nur O. Yalman and Robert McC. Adams, supported me and encouraged my Baluchistan research.

At McGill University, where I began teaching after my first stint in Baluchistan, my department and its chair Richard F. Salisbury, and the university authorities cooperated in advancing my research. While many of my colleagues were supportive, I want to mention particularly Dan R. Aronson, now with the World Bank, who constantly encouraged my work and stimulated my thinking, and Donald Von Eschen of the Department of Sociology, who repeatedly championed my accomplishments and insisted on the importance of ethnographic accounts of tribal peoples for the enrichment of comparative sociology.

While anthropologists may be paradigmatic "lone adventurers" in spirit and methodology, they in fact rely on a multitude of large institutions to make their adventures possible. In addition to our universities, we usually depend upon granting agencies to fund our not inexpensive research. Fieldwork in Baluchistan during 1967–68 was funded by a National Science Foundation doctoral research grant, during

1972–73 by the Canada Council, and during 1976 by the Social Science and Humanities Research Council of Canada. McGill University provided a number of small grants for various phases of the research. In the field, research permission was gained through the good offices of the U.S. Embassy in 1967–68 and the Canadian Embassy in 1972–73. Residence in Tehran and various other resources and aid were provided by the British Institute of Persian Studies during 1967–68 and 1972–73 and the American Institute during 1976. The then assistant director of the British Institute, Brian Spooner, long since of the University of Pennsylvania, guided my first steps into Baluchistan.

I wish also to express my gratitude to Lois Beck, Brian Spooner, and an anonymous reviewer for Smithsonian Institution Press, who have read this work in manuscript and provided their expert advice, both general on anthropological matters and specific to Iran and Baluchistan. These colleagues provided, at length and in detail, thoughtful and valuable comments and suggestions. This is a further example of the way in which ethnography is a collective rather than individual enterprise. I have responded in my revisions as best I could, although I fear that on many points they will remain unsatisfied. For whatever improvements I have been able to incorporate in the text, the reader will have these expert advisers to thank.

Lisa Marlene Edelsward, herself an anthropologist and author of ethnographies on Finland and Sardinia, with whom I have shared my life and family responsibilities for the past decade, has encouraged the writing of this volume, provided helpful advice, and done more than her share of supervision of our children, Joshua and Leah, to free me to write.

# INTRODUCTION

*Black Tents of Baluchistan* is an ethnographic account of the Baluch, particularly the Yarahmadzai Baluch, of the Sarhad Plateau of southeastern Iran. While inevitably selective due to my own interests and limitations as an observer, it touches on various aspects of detail and pattern in Baluchi life. I have tried to convey a sense of the Baluch as complex human beings involved in multiple relationships, pursuing a range of purposes, their lives multilayered. In order to present a grounded account of Baluchi life, I have focused on a specific group of individuals that I knew fairly well and have recounted events and series of events in their lives. Attention has been given to everyday activities as much as to more dramatic events, so as to represent Sarhadi life as the Baluch themselves experienced it.

Intending to convey Baluchi life in its complexity and richness, I have in my descriptions tried to avoid global labeling of Baluch—as, for example, "nomads," "Muslims," "desert dwellers," "tribesmen," or "pastoralists"—in order to refrain from characterizing them as a specific type of people or society or culture, to abstain from reductionistically limiting their humanity and lives to some conceptual essence. This, it seems to me, is the first responsibility of the ethnographer, to be true to the people being described, to present them in a way that does justice to their particular experience, their reality, and their humanity.

Nonetheless, the Sarhadi Baluch are of interest beyond the particularistic enterprise of the ethnographer. Most ethnographers, in our complementary role as social anthropologist, strive to go beyond our ethnographic accounts in order to elicit insights from which to build more general understandings as part of a comparative sociology or cultural studies. The Sarhadi Baluch are of interest in this regard because their society and culture are similar to and different from a range of others. However, in order to compare the Sarhadi case with various others, we cannot avoid abstracting certain features of Baluchi life to place them, along with other ethnographic cases, on analytic continua. This abstraction, while inevitably losing particularity, advances our general understanding, which in turn enriches our appreciation of the significance of particular cases. Even ethnographic description itself rests upon general knowledge, for perception and description are only possible through a cognitive framework of general concepts. It is for these reasons that there are also appropriate moments for abstracting, as we must do in the following discussion, and for speaking of the Sarhadi Baluch as "nomads" and "tribesmen," and "desert dwellers."

This more general relevance of the "case" of the Sarhadi Baluch is the primary basis for any interest beyond the limited ranks of Baluchophiles, students of the Iranian periphery, and aficionados of peripatetic peoples. What, then, are the features of Sarhadi Baluch life that are of general or even "theoretical" interest?

## MULTIPLICITY

We anthropologists commonly use simple concepts to represent complex phenomena, especially when we are speaking generally and at a high level of abstraction. We have often used sets of terms—such as "hunters and gatherers," "horticulturalists," "pastoralists," and "agriculturalists," or "bands," "tribes," "chiefdoms," and "states"—to represent different types of production systems or kinds of sociopolitical organization. It is difficult to think at a general level without such concepts. However, in generalization and comparison, as well as in description, we must always be on guard against essentializing, against taking one identified feature or pattern and crowning it the central characteristic of a population, society, or culture.

Reality is of course always very complex, and any population, society, or culture has many features, aspects, and dimensions, no one of which can stand for the others. The closer we get to observations "on the ground," to the particulars of specific societies and cultures, to the ethnographic case study, the more likely we are to see plurality and multiplicity rather than unity and coherence. Consequently, characterizing a population or a society by identifying its "essence" is usually reductionistic; that is, by reducing a complex reality to a single, central feature or pattern, we distort and oversimplify and thus misrepresent reality. As Geertz (1979:123) puts it, "Characterizing whole civilizations in terms of one or another of their leading institutions is a dubious procedure. . . ."

Observing and trying to understand the Sarhadi Baluch with the crude conceptual tools "nomadism" and "pastoralism," I had to come to terms with the fact that the Baluch could not be reasonably characterized simply as "pastoral nomads" because they were deeply engaged in a variety of productive activities—both large- and small-stock pastoralism, runoff cultivation, *qanat* irrigation cultivation, arboriculture, gathering, selling their labor, smuggling, trading, in the past predatory raiding, and, as the future would develop, guiding illegal émigrés—and were conspicuously busy trying to manage their many related activities. Their nomadism was as much moving between the sites of different forms of production as it was for strictly pastoral purposes. Trying to capture this committed and ongoing multiplicity, I coined the phrases "multi-resource economy" (1971a) and "multi-resource nomadism" (1972), arguing that this pattern was widespread among peoples often labeled "pastoral nomads." This observation and conceptualization have long been accepted and continue to be a reference point (Fratkin, Roth, and Galvin 1994:1; Lancaster and Lancaster 1996:393). The full details of the multi-resource Sarhadi economy, previously only briefly described, have awaited this account.

The multiplicity of Baluchi economic life was not a sport in an otherwise integrated, unitary social life and culture. Rather, plurality was apparent in other spheres, such as political life and identity. Baluchi political organization was mounted on two distinct, sometimes complementary, sometimes contradictory principles, rather the way a tent stands as a result of both the lifting tent poles and the adhering stakes:

- Among these Baluch, patrilineal descent, *rend,* on the one hand, organized people horizontally, into equivalent, contingent lineage groups of smaller or larger magnitude, thus manifesting the political tendencies of egalitarianism, decentralization, and democracy.
- On the other hand, political seniority, *master,* in every setting organized people vertically, into relative seniority and juniority, into leaders and followers, thus manifesting the political tendencies of authority, hierarchy, and centralization. Both internal and external political relations tended to reflect the complicated and uneasy interplay of these two tendencies. Were the Yarahmadzai, Gamshadzai, and Ismailzai "segmentary tribes," or were they "chiefdoms"? The first answer is that this is too simplistic a question.

Baluchi identity, too, was plural, reflecting a number of quite distinct conceptions, stances, roles, and predispositions. Sarhadi Baluch prided themselves on being "hardy survivors," "fearless warriors," "devout Muslims," "territorial tribesmen," "substantial livestock owners," "loyal lineage mates," "tent-dwelling nomads," and in the 1970s added "astute entrepreneurs."

- As "hardy survivors," the Baluch were able to walk great distances without stopping, sleep with their heads resting on a rock, and work without regard to heat or cold.
- As "fearless warriors," the Baluch were ready to put themselves at risk in violent confrontation to fight for their property and their honor, for their lineages and their tribes, and for booty and profit.
- As "devout Muslims," the Baluch followed the Sunni way in their surrender to God, informing themselves from the advice of their learned mullas, disciplining themselves, and observing their obligations to follow His instructions.

- As "territorial tribesmen," the Sarhadi Baluch asserted their most encompassing political loyalty and their control over the territory of their tribe.
- As "substantial livestock owners," the Baluch followed a dignified calling as responsible supervisors, managing a rich source of livelihood, and able to establish self-sufficiency.
- As "loyal lineage mates," the Baluch exhibited solidarity in supporting the members of their lineage in both conflict and misfortune and placed the unity of the lineage above narrower interests.
- As "tent-dwelling nomads," the Baluch used spatial mobility to pursue their goals, defend their interests, and contingently inhabit the totality of their territory.
- As "astute entrepreneurs," the Baluch exploited new opportunities, activities, and relationships to gain and import income back to the Sarhad.

These self-concepts and identities—not of course a complete and exhaustive list—show the multiplicity in the way Sarhadi Baluch thought of themselves, spoke of themselves, and acted out. The social category *baluch*, designating tent dwelling, multi-resource primary producers, encompasses some of these self-concepts—survivor, livestock owner, nomad—but not all. (When I refer to the indigenous population of the Sarhad as an ethnic category, as distinct from Persians or Euro-Americans, I will use the form "Baluch" and "Baluchi." When I refer specifically to the social category of nomadic, tent-dwelling, livestock-rearing, indigenes, as opposed to the small groups of agriculturalists, blacksmiths, or elite rulers, I will use the form *baluch* and *baluchi* or the phrase "Sarhadi tent-dwellers" [Spooner 1969]. Of course, the ethnic category Baluch includes the members of the social category *baluch*.) The multiple identities of the Sarhadi Baluch cannot be seen as merely facets of a general identity, tidily ordered into a unitary whole. Some were complementary, or at least not in conflict. Most were contingent, relevant only in certain circumstances. Some were to a degree contradictory, such as herd owner and lineage mate, or warrior and Muslim, and had to be repeatedly negotiated and rationalized. The rhetorical assertion of one identity over another was a constant strategy of ordinary and extraordinary negotiation.

Does the multiplicity of the Sarhadi Baluch in their economic and political life and identity indicate that they are unusual or even unique among societies and cultures, or does it rather suggest that our conceptions of society and culture have too often been essentialistic, have overemphasized and exaggerated structural integration? The tendency to seek the cultural essence has been exacerbated in modern anthropology by the rise of the configurationalist school, the distinguished proponents of which have been Ruth Benedict (1935), Claude Lévi-Strauss (1963, 1966), Clifford Geertz (1968, 1980), and Marshal Sahlins (1976, 1981). After its ascendancy during the 1980s, configurationalism in its modern guises, and particularly its abstraction of cultural essences, came under attack by postmodernists (Clifford and Marcus 1986; Clifford

1988), postmodern radical empiricists (Jackson 1989), and neo-empiricists (Barth 1994; Kottak and Colson 1994; Vayda 1994), alike.

This account of the Sarhadi Baluch reports frankly the multiplicity found. But it is also true, as we shall see, that the multiplicity was limited, not infinite, and that there was a significant degree of integration among the elements, and not myriads of cultural contradictions or a chaos of randomness. While it might be attention getting to present an alternative extreme theory and christen it with a catchy slo-gan—"random culture" or "postcultural chaos"—this is not what I found in the Sarhad of Baluchistan.

## CHANGE AND ADAPTATION

The culturally embedded multiplicity found in the economy, politics, and self-concept of the Sarhadi Baluch did not result from an unusual love of elaboration or a particular inability to integrate lives into a coherent, unitary whole. Rather, the multi-plicity developed from and was a response to the complexity of life processes that ex-ist almost everywhere, but also to the especially unstable conditions of Sarhadi life. One of the few constants in Sarhadi Baluchi life was the instability and unpredictability of the Sarhadi physical, political, and economic environments. From one year to the next, conditions could and often did change radically: between rain and pasture one year and drought and famine the next; between peace and quiet one year and conflict and vio-lence the next; between possibilities of local income one year and of external income the next. The multiple ways of producing income, organizing political life, and con-ceiving of themselves provided the Baluch with alternative patterns of response that could be selected according to the circumstances of the moment. Baluchi cultural mul-tiplicity was thus not so much an untidy disorganization as it was a form of organized flexibility used to adapt to the ever changing conditions of the Sarhadi milieu.

Of course, the entire range of Baluchi multiplicity was not likely to be exploited to the fullest or even manifested at any given moment. One mode of organization may, at a particular time, have been in play, while another was dormant, just as cer-tain sectors of production might have been active while others appeared to have lapsed. People may have spoken of and acted out certain identities, while other iden-tities did not seem to be present. But that some orientations or activities were not evi-dent at a given moment could not be taken to mean that they were not present. The prominence or dominance of a particular orientation or stance may well have been contingent on the conditions of the moment (Salzman 1978a, 1980). Other orienta-tions and stances were embedded in Baluchi culture and available for activation when desired. These inactive or unimplemented orientations and stances were maintained in a variety of ways in the repertoire and thus were available for activation. These "maintenance mechanisms" included the following:

- "Asserted ideology" refers to the widely repeated verbal expression among the populace that a particular social pattern is in general practice in the society, although in fact practice differs markedly from the expressed pattern. For example, among the Sarhadi Baluch, the ideal that all members of a tribe are brothers and sisters and do not fight with one another was constantly repeated, even though everyone knew that violent conflicts sometimes erupted between lineages. But the ideal of tribal solidarity was constantly expressed and served as an alternative stance to segmentary opposition.
- "Operational generalization" refers to the existence in general practice of a range of variations, of a variety of activities, none of which is dominant but any of which could provide a pattern for broader or even exclusive usage. For example, the *baluchi* multi-resource economy maintained in existence a number of different types of production, any one of which was thus available for either expansion or contraction, as seemed opportune according to the circumstances.
- "Ritual enactment" is the representation in formal ritual of values, orientations, modes of interaction, and bases of association that may not at any moment be put into practice outside the ritual context. For example, the tying of the turban, the "crowning" of a new tribal chief, was done by the *hakom*, ruler (from the Persian Qajar dynasty title of "governor"), of the Kurds of Kuhi Daptan, even though the tribes had long been effectively independent from and militarily stronger than the Kurds. This ritual, however, maintained as a model a hierarchical patronage that contrasted with the strong, egalitarian, and independentist ethos of the segmentary organization.
- "Literary validation" is the enshrinement of modes of organization, norms, and identities in texts having a sacred or otherwise authoritative character. For example, the Qoran and its local interpreters provided a set of organizational forms, social regulations, and values that, not always corresponding to tribal norms or practice, provided alternatives upon which, as "devout Muslims," the Baluch could always draw.
- "Minority deviance" refers to the existence among a particular subgroup of activities and practices distinct from those of the population at large. For example, a minority of Sarhadi Baluch were members of sufi orders, and their participation maintained as a model alternative to the tribe the organization and norms of the orders.

Each of these embeddings of multiplicity maintains in the repertoire of the population alternative values and orientations, modes of organization, and activities and practices that may remain inactive, in reserve, but are available for activation by the population as opportune.

The Sarhadi Baluch were always on the alert for what was opportune as one set of conditions superseded another, as a variety of unpredictable multiyear cycles brought new environmental, political, and economic circumstances and challenges. In responding, the Baluch were able, unconsciously or purposely, to draw from their cultural repertoire, to select from their multiplicity those practices that appeared to serve them best in the changing conditions. Because of the constant arrival of cyclical change, not to mention cumulative change brought about by transformations in the wider world, Baluchi life at any particular moment was only a partial exposé of Baluchi culture. To understand Baluchi society and culture in their full multiplicity, we must observe the flexibility of the Baluch as they adapted and readapted to the constant changes of their world.

For this, the typical anthropological fieldwork carried out during a brief period, usually one year, providing little more than a synchronic snapshot, often hazy at that, was not adequate (Colson 1984; Kottak and Colson 1994; cf. Marcus 1994:52, n. 1). I was fortunate in being able to carry out research in Baluchistan over a 10-year period, 1967–76, for a total of 26 months. I was unfortunate thereafter in losing research access to Baluchistan as a result of the upheavals of the Islamic Revolution and the restrictions of the regime (although some Western anthropologists have been able to return to Iran). Had these difficulties not arisen, I would certainly have continued research in Baluchistan and would probably have expanded my purview; Zahedan, the increasingly Baluchized provincial capital, seemed to me a promising research site. But as I have said, circumstances are constantly changing, and the anthropologist is not immune to those shifts that transform local life.

## COMPARISONS

The Sarhadi Baluch are of interest not only because they exhibited a particular way of life, but because that way of life was similar to and different from that of other people elsewhere. This is important for three reasons. First, the Baluchi case may be placed among others to exhibit both the commonalities and the range of variations among human societies and cultures. Second, the Baluchi case may be placed among others to illustrate and document a stage in the cumulative evolutionary changes in human society and culture. Third, the Baluchi case may be placed alongside of others on analytic continua in order to determine patterns in the association of cultural features. A similar exercise can be based upon examination of the Baluchi case during different historical periods.

### Ecology and Demography

The Sarhadi Baluch were a small, mobile population thinly spread over a large area of desert. In this they contrasted with denser mobile populations in richer lands, such as the plains Turkmen (Irons 1975), and the mountain Basseri (Barth 1961) and Qashqai (Beck 1986, 1991), and with sedentary populations.

The pastoral nomadism of the Sarhadi Baluch was mainly an adaptation to microenvironmental variations, rather than seasonal or altitudinal macroenvironmental variations. In this respect they were similar to the Turkmen (Irons 1975) and contrasted with the Zagros mountain nomads (Barth 1961; Beck 1986, 1991), who migrated long distances between winter lowlands and summer highlands.

## Production and Economics

The production system of the Sarhadi Baluch was diversified, drawing upon multiple resources, rather than being specialized in one form of production. In this regard, they contrast with the Basseri (Barth 1961), who were highly specialized in pastoralism.

The Baluch were subsistence oriented, producing primarily for their own consumption, rather than for exchange or sale. In this respect they differed from the Basseri and other Zagros tribes, which were more heavily market oriented. Emanuel Marx (1996) argues that all pastoralists have been market oriented, and that it is impossible for pastoralists to be subsistence oriented. The Baluchi case would appear to challenge this theory.

A major economic strategy of the Sarhadi Baluch during the Baluch Period, prior to 1935, was predatory raiding of livestock, goods, and slaves outside of the Sarhad, a highly lucrative endeavor. A similar pattern was found among the Turkmen (Irons 1975). This contrasts with the more political occupations of cities by Zagros tribes such as the Bakhtiari and the Qashqai (Avery 1965), the more subtle extortion of oases by Rwala Bedouin (Lancaster 1981), the less confrontational rustling by peasant pastoralists of highland Sardinia (Caltagirone 1989), and the peaceful face of more integrated pastoral nomadic peasants such as the Komachi (Bradburd 1990).

## Social Organization

Local, residential groups among the Sarhadi Baluch were based upon one-year contracts and were thus formally reconstituted annually. Within residential groups, the spatial arrangement of tents was easily changeable, and each migration provided an opportunity for repositioning. This contrasts with sedentary populations whose residential groups are more fixed and immutable.

As is common among tribal peoples in the Middle East, marriage is preferentially endogamous among the Sarhadi Baluch. This leads to an overlapping of ties of descent, kinship, and affinity, and affects gender relations. This marriage pattern contrasts with that of other tribal peoples, such as the Nuer (Evans-Pritchard 1940) and Somali (Lewis 1961), who follow exogamous rules that require marriage outside of a person's own lineage.

Among Baluchi tribesmen, there was no vertical, social class distinction. All were tribesmen; all were deemed brothers and sisters, descended from a common ancestor. All belonged to the social category *baluch* and were free to associate with, reside with, and marry one another. There was no social distinction between leaders and followers. Regarded as lower social classes were slaves, and, after slavery was abolished, descendants of slaves, and also the small bands of smiths. This general egalitarian pattern among Sarhadi tribesmen contrasts with the hierarchical pattern of a separate ruling class above distinct classes of tent dwellers and oasis cultivators, and an underclass of slaves, typical of southern Baluchistan (Spooner 1969; Salzman 1978b). It contrasts also with stratified desert societies such as the Tuareg (Nicolaisen 1963; Keenan 1977; Bernus 1981), while being similar to egalitarian tribal systems such as the Somali (Lewis 1961) and the Turkmen (Irons 1975).

The question of equality among tribesmen in general and pastoral tribesmen in particular has been a focus of debate in anthropology. Through the 1960s, anthropologists tended to regard tribesmen as egalitarian (Sahlins 1968). With the upsurge of Marxism in anthropology during the 1970s and increased attention to inequality, and among some researchers what seemed to be an enthusiasm for inequality and for identifying people as victims, a revisionist view of all tribesmen as always unequal was strongly advocated (Asad 1970, 1978; Bradburd 1980; Meloni 1984; Black-Michaud 1986; Bonte 1990; Fratkin, Roth, and Galvin 1994). Following the decline of Marxism in anthropology, a less formulaic approach, in which the degree of equality or inequality is seen as primarily an empirical question, has become more acceptable. In consequence, a counterrevisionist position assumes that, as cultures and societies vary, and tribal peoples and their circumstances vary, the degree of equality and inequality is also likely to vary among the many tribes (Schneider 1979; Irons 1994; Salzman 1999a) and over time (Rao 1995). The following counterrevisionist account of the tribes of the Sarhad of Baluchistan, which finds the Yarahmadzai and other Sarhadi tribes substantially egalitarian in both principle and practice, suggests that the interesting and useful question is not "Are nomadic tribesmen equal or unequal?" but "What are the ecological, social, and political conditions within which tribesmen tend to be more egalitarian and those within which one or another degree of inequality is manifested among tribesmen?"

## Politics

The political system of the Sarhadi tribes combined segmentary lineage systems and tribal chiefs, instituting an interplay and a tension between the contingent, decentralizing, democratic tendencies of lineages with the permanent, centralizing, hierarchical tendencies of a chiefship. The detailed accounts of conflicts described below, especially in chapter 10, illustrate this interplay, as in the shift from segmentary to unitary politics as the political process shifts from conflict and confrontation to reconciliation and resolution. Particularly noteworthy, because it has not been described in other ethnographic accounts, is the contribution to blood money by individuals near to and far from the injured party, irrespective of structural position and segmentary affiliation, as part of the unitary politics of reconciliation and resolution.

The balance in the Sarhadi tribes between the segmentary lineage system and the chiefship places the Sarhadi Baluch between the lineage-dominated political systems of the Nuer, Somali, and Turkmen, on the one hand, and the strong chiefdoms of the Basseri (Barth 1961; cf. Salzman 2000), Qashqai (Beck 1986, 1991), and Bakhtiari. The Sarhadi tribes were perhaps more similar in political structure to the Rwala Bedouin (Lancaster 1981) than these great Zagros tribal chiefdoms and confederacies.

The place of lineage systems in tribal politics has been a subject of great debate in anthropology. After Evans-Pritchard's publication of *The Nuer* (1940), in which he explained the "ordered anarchy" of the Nuer partly in terms of what came to be called a "segmentary lineage system," which is a set of rules about descent affiliation and political allegiance (see also Sahlins 1968), an orthodoxy developed among social anthropologists that segmentary lineage systems were widespread if not universal among tribal peoples. This orthodoxy was rejected in the 1960s by revisionists such as Peters (1967; for a critique, see Salzman 1978c), who argued that even among those people who claimed to have a segmentary lineage system, they did not really follow it, and so as a theoretical framework the "segmentary lineage system" explains nothing. The counterrevisionist position to which I subscribe is that tribal peoples vary, and that it is an empirical question whether segmentary lineage systems are or are not important in any particular society. The following account of the Sarhadi tribes demonstrates the importance of the segmentary lineage system in the lives of the *baluch*. This *baluchi* case, along with others, such as the Nuer (Evans-Pritchard 1940), the Somali (Lewis 1961), and the Turkmen (Irons 1975), in which the segmentary lineage system is a basic element in people's social and political maneuvers, puts to rest finally the question of whether segmentary lineage systems do or do not exist and raises the more interesting and important questions of the specific circumstances and conditions in which segmentary lineage systems arise and play an important part, the contrasting situations and contexts in which such lineage systems do not arise and are not part of the social and political lives of tribal peoples, and the social, economic, and political changes that tend to strengthen political lineage systems and those that weaken them.

The membership of each of the Sarhadi tribes—the Yarahmadzai, Gamshadzai, Ismailzai—numbered in the few thousands. They were thus substantially larger than groups of peasant pastoralists such as the Komachi (Bradburd 1990), but considerably smaller than the Basseri and minuscule compared with the great confederacies of the Bakhtiari (Garthwaite 1983) and Qashqai (Beck 1986), the populations of which were closer to a million in number.

The independence of the Sarhadi tribes during the Baluch Period was similar to that of the Yomut and other Turkmen tribes (Irons 1975) prior to the Iranian Period.

These cases raise doubts about Emanuel Marx's (1996) assertion that a "tribe" is always an administrative unit of the state. It is true that later Sarhadi and Turkmen tribes were "pacified" and "encapsulated" by the Iranian state. In contrast to the Sarhadi and Yomut cases are the great Bakhtiari confederacy (Avery 1965; Garthwaite 1983), which was a serious force in Iranian national politics, and the Komachi peasant pastoralists (Bradburd 1990), integrated at the bottom of the state system.

## The Relevance of the Sarhadi Baluch

These selected and necessarily oversimplified illustrations are meant to suggest the interest of the Sarhadi case in a comparative context. I cannot in this ethnographic account pursue these compelling comparisons, but as a prerequisite to their development, a detailed account of the Sarhadi Baluch is required. This is the purpose of the following ethnographic report.

## ORGANIZATION OF THIS WORK

In order to assist the reader in approaching this ethnographic account, I would like to make explicit my intentions in the organization of chapters and topics, and in the presentation of Iranian languages (*baluchi* and *farsi*, i.e., Persian).

## The Logic of Part and Chapter Organization

The descriptive chapters of this volume, chapters 1 through 12, are divided into three parts: "Tent Living," "Making a Living," and "Living in Order and Conflict." The first of the 12 chapters is about living in black tents, and the final chapter is on religion, with intervening chapters on daily living, local groups, the economy, social organization, and politics. The logic of presentation is to begin from the smallest spatial entity, the tent, and move through increasingly larger entities—the community, tribe, region—to the largest, the universe.

There is also to some degree, as the reader moves through the chapters, what might seem a corresponding progression from the concrete to the abstract. This distinction between the concrete and the abstract is in fact somewhat illusory, for apparently concrete entities, such as tents and food and households, rest on abstract cultural conceptions such as values and goals, and environmental and technological knowledge, while abstractions such as the tribe, the state, and religion influence, guide, and sometimes compel concrete behavior with great human consequences. Nonetheless, beginning with the apparently concrete may ease the entry by the reader into the lives of the Baluch dwelling in the deserts and mountains of the Sarhad of Iranian Baluchistan.

The organizational structure of chapters and parts is like a skeleton or a house frame or a trellis, a coherent frame upon and through which a complicated, interrelated, and somewhat incoherent body grows. Description of the life of many people, of their society and culture, must always be a bit untidy and also somewhat artificial, because the elements and flows of people's lives intertwine and interweave, while description is linear and must artificially begin with one thing and go to another and then another. There is no single or correct way to organize a description of people's lives. As a matter of necessity and convenience, I have chosen a structure, but I readily admit that this particular organization—beginning with the smallest entity and moving through ones of ever increasing scope, to the largest—is as arbitrary as any other. The reader should not, however, imagine that the structure of description used here implies or imposes some underlying theory, such as that tents and material culture are more "basic" than social organization and politics, and that religion is just superstructure, or, conversely, that the progression from tents to religion is a procession from the trivial to the sublime. My substantive discussion throughout, including explicit theoretical assertions, should refute any such presumption of a structurally infiltrated, hidden theoretical agenda.

## Iranian Languages

There are a number of reasons that I have included many *baluchi* terms in the text (and have provided a glossary for easy reference). The most important is to identify *baluchi* concepts for which there is no equivalent English term (e.g., *baluch,* a social category referring to nomadic, tent-dwellers who raise livestock and engage in small-scale cultivation; *pas,* sheep and goats, or small stock; the many terms for livestock of different types; the many terms for different kinds of dates; *wasildar,* livestock owner; *master,* political seniority; *rend,* line of descent; *sawab,* religious merit; and the many terms for ritual acts). In other cases, the reporting of a term or phrase verifies the use of certain important *baluchi* conceptions for which there are equivalent terms or phrases in English (e.g., *topak,* solidarity; *haj,* pilgrimage; *dasti huda,* literally: "the hand of God," meaning "it was done by God").

The Baluchi language is recognized as a distinct Western Iranian language, sharing this category with Kurdish and Persian (*farsi*); however, until very recent times Baluchi was exclusively a spoken language, not a written one. Furthermore, there are many dialects of Baluchi, and the Baluchi of Iranian Baluchistan is different to a greater or lesser degree from other dialects. For example, it is more influenced by Persian (*farsi*) than Baluchi dialects to the east, which are more influenced by Urdu. There is no standard way of writing Baluchi, especially in the Sarhad of Iranian Baluchistan, where state education is in Persian and where Baluch who are capable of writing do so in Persian. Thus the Baluchi language that I present here is a representation of a spoken, not written, language. My transcriptions of Baluchi words are an attempt to convey what these words sound like when they are spoken. (In some cases, for comparison, I present related Persian words in the standard transcriptions of their written forms. Systematic differences of pronunciation between cognates in *baluchi* and Persian have been indicated in the introductory comments to the glossary.) Not being a linguist or an expert in Iranian languages, I am at a disadvantage in transcribing *baluchi* terms. So while I have tried to formulate a clear and consistent representation of *baluchi* terms, I would advise the reader to take my transcription of *baluchi* terms as indicative, rather than definitive.

To end, I want to specify a few details of grammar and my representation of them. Possession and adjectival qualification are often indicated in *baluchi* by the addition of "i" as the end qualifier, which I have transcribed by adding the "i" at the end of the word, as in *baluchi labs,* the Baluchi language. (In contrast, in Persian [ *farsi*] this possessive or adjectival "i," called *ezafe,* is attached to the noun being qualified, and while usually not written in Persian, is commonly transcribed as "-i," e.g., *zaban-i farsi,* in the Persian language.) In my narrative, I use "Baluch" to mean individuals or groups, and "Baluchi" as an adjective indicating such things as Baluchi language, customs, practices, dress, cuisine, and so on, and follow the same grammatical convention with "Sarhad" meaning the geographical region, and "Sahardi" meaning things pertaining to the Sarhad.

# PART ONE
*Tent Living*

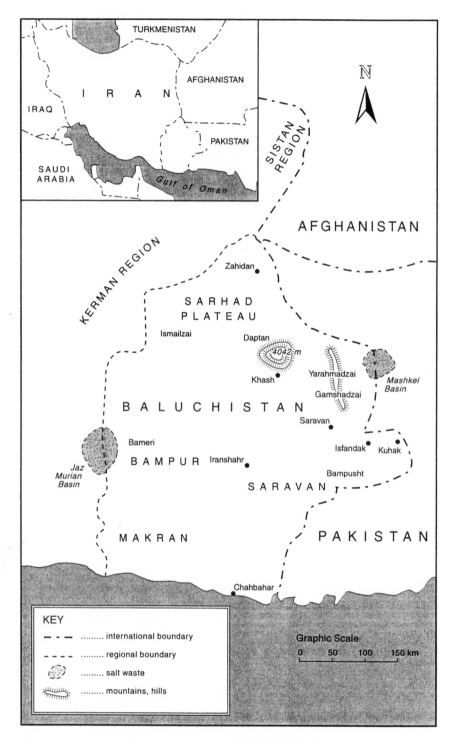

Figure 1.1. Iranian Baluchistan. (Inspired by Spooner 1964:56, fig. 1).

# I.

# BLACK TENTS OF PUSHTI KAMAL

The fourteen, black, goat-hair tents were strung out in a line on the rocky plain called Pushti Kamal. All around, in the middle distance, were jagged, craggy, volcanic hills and small mountains, jutting up unannounced from the plain. In the far distance, to the east, was the vast Morpish mountain range, running north-south, marking the southeastern edge of the high Iranian plateau, leading down to lands of lower elevation in the east. Dominating the northern view was the majestic volcano Daptan (Persian: Kuh-i Taftan), from which continually arose the smoky evidence of its still burning fires.

The dramatic high desert landscape, severe at all times, was wearing its austere winter cloak of tan, brown, and black. No green cast from grass or bushes was visible to soften the treeless expanses and rocky outcroppings. Daptan, at 4,042 meters (13,262 feet), was capped with snow, and, on the high plains at 1,698 meters (5,570 feet), the daytime warmth of the sun dissipated quickly, leaving the nights freezing. This was a characteristic winter scene in the Sarhad, the northern, highland region of Iranian Baluchistan.

It was the last day of 1967, the day I set up my tent in a Baluchi herding camp and began what I felt to be my proper ethnographic fieldwork. From the start, Baluchistan had been my goal, my chosen setting for the research that would bring me, I imagined, a profound understanding of Baluchi nomadic tribesmen and insight into nomads more generally, and consequently a Ph.D. from the University of Chicago, validation as an anthropologist, and, in those halcyon days of burgeoning student demographics and expanding universities, a guaranteed academic position.

I had selected Baluchistan as a field site for a number of reasons, not least practical ones such as the accessibility of Iranian languages and the friendliness and apparent stability of the Iranian political regime. The intellectual basis for my choice of Baluchistan was its contrast as a resource-poor desert region with the comparatively rich environment of the Zagros Mountains of Western Iran, and thus the likely con-trast between the ways of life of the Baluchi tribes and those of the famous Zagros tribes such as the Bakhtiari, Qashqai, and Basseri (Barth 1961; Salzman 1967). I had hy-pothesized that, as a result of environmental differences, the Baluchi tribes would be more like the scattered, egalitarian, decentralized, desert tribes of Somalia (Lewis 1961) than like the relatively demographically dense, hierarchical, centralized Zagros tribes (Salzman 1995b). Research in Baluchistan would put my hypothesis to the ethnographic test and provide a basis for more general understanding through com-parison of the Baluchi case with others.

My hypothesis defined the Baluch as pastoral nomads and thus emphasized their nomadic mobility and raising of livestock. But, as I was to discover during my field research, the Baluch did many more things than these and thought of themselves in many other ways. So I shall try to present a balanced picture of the Baluch, placing nomadism and pastoralism into ethnographic context, and thus avoid a theoretically driven essentialism and reductionism that oversimplify and distort the complexity of people's lives.

My trip to the Sarhad had been a lengthy one, with numerous delays, neither in-tended nor desired, along the way. I set out with my then wife, Joan David, in the summer of 1967, our first stop being the Land Rover factory in England, where we picked up a new, blue and white, short-wheelbase, four-wheel drive Land Rover, with spare on hood, paid for partly by a dissertation research grant from the National Sci-ence Foundation. We then drove, the Land Rover packed to the ceiling with personal and camping gear, through Europe to Turkey, where we had our first taste of the Middle East at Edirne, arriving quite exhausted from Bulgaria at dusk to see, stand-ing out against the sky, the outline of mosques and minarets. Joan perked up imme-diately, exclaiming, "Look at the mosques!" I had seen them too, but my heart dropped into my stomach, and I thought, keeping it to myself, "What am I—a not very adventurous Jewish boy from Baltimore—doing here?"

A long, dusty trip across Turkey followed a short and luxurious stay in Istanbul and brought us to Azerbaijan in northwestern Iran, at the far opposite tip of Iran from Baluchistan, which is the southeastern region bordering Pakistan. The next step was to Teheran, where we were put up at the British Institute of Persian studies, took more Persian language lessons, and tried to get research permission. But there was no established procedure for awarding a research permit, and gaining support from Iranian authorities proved difficult as the American Embassy officials had a policy of not helping scholars. After a long and tedious round of futile office visits, wearing a suit in the sweltering Tehran summer, I came to understand the genius of a truly an-cient bureaucratic system. As the ministry gateman said to the hopeful arrival, "No point coming in the morning, they don't do any work in the morning; but don't come back in the afternoon, they are not even here in the afternoon."

Finally, as a result of an intervention by the U.S. Embassy's science attaché, who was new and did not understand that he was not supposed to help, I was given Iranian government permission to go to Zahedan, the capital of the province of Sistan and Baluchistan, but only to Zahedan. There was apparently considerable reluctance to allow me to enter "darkest" Baluchistan because—to identify one of perhaps several reasons—of the harm I might come to and the repercussions for the Iranian government by what would be a presumably concerned U.S. government. It is true that a few years before I arrived a minor U.S. official was shot and killed in Baluchistan when he tried to resist robbers with a handgun.

But there was a general sense among Persians, which perhaps applied equally to all of the surrounding tribal regions, that harm would befall you if you dared to leave the security of Persian civilization and enter the lands of the wild and savage tribesmen. I was repeatedly told in Teheran that if I went to Baluchistan, "they," the Baluchi tribesmen, would kill me. These comments reflected not a realistic prognostication of the likelihood of my impending demise but a culturally instituted and historically based fear of the many and powerful non-Persian tribal peoples whose territories surrounded the Persian heartland of the Iranian Plateau and its cities, towns, and villages, and who for many centuries until the "pacification" conquests of Reza Shah in the 1930s engaged in wholesale extortion and robbery, raiding and banditry, kidnapping and killing, and even the conquest of Persian populations. My proposed ethnographic project among the Baluch was, for Persians, colored by this fear.

Having little specific knowledge of Baluchistan, I was fortunate to be able to draw upon Brian Spooner, assistant director of the British Institute, who had recently done his dissertation research on politics in southern Baluchistan and who maintained ongoing contacts with his informants, especially members of the ruling stratum, the *hakomzat*, who came to Teheran from time to time. Spooner and I discussed my project, and he suggested research in the Sarhad of Baluchistan, which was primarily pastoral, a cold, highland region lacking the agricultural oases of southern Baluchistan. He mentioned the Yarahmadzai as one of the important tribes. To ease my way, Spooner gave me an introduction, via a letter that I carried, to a member of the chiefly family of the Ismailzai tribe who lived in Zahedan, the recently constructed town that served as the capital of the Province of Sistan and Baluchistan. This man gave me a letter to a Sarhadi *sardar*, who some months later I met in Khash, and he then introduced me to Sardar Han Mahmud of the Yarahmadzai.

After several months in Teheran we were glad to finally be on our way to Baluchistan, although the 2,000-kilometer (more than 1,200-mile) drive along the edge of the central desert of Iran proved to be dusty and somewhat harrowing, especially when the road seemed to disappear and we accidently strayed into the desert. Zahedan, to which we had been assigned by the government, was disappointing for me, because in the fall of 1967 it was a totally Persian town, largely bureaucratic in intent and personnel, and drably colorless. The few Baluch to be seen were, literally, in trenches digging. In the evolution of Zahedan, this was a brief moment, as I was to see in subsequent visits in 1972–73 and 1976, for Baluch rapidly flooded into this town, some setting up residences and businesses, others coming for temporary business, and yet others flowing through on their way elsewhere. By 1976, Zahedan was much expanded, and was as colorful a tribal town as any community in Pakistan or in Afghanistan.

For the couple of months that we were in Zahedan, where we rented a room in the home of a Persian family, we continued, with the help of the teenage daughter, to study Persian. In December, not exactly with anyone's permission, we left Zahedan for the small town of Khash (Baluchi: Washt) in the Sarhad, where we met two U.S. Peace Corps teachers, who apparently had not been killed by rampaging Baluchi tribesmen, even though they were trying to teach the Baluch English.

The Yarahmadzai Sardar Han Mahmud was camped at Garonchin, in the southern part of Yarahmadzai tribal territory. When we arrived to meet the Sardar and ask his permission to reside with the Yarahmadzai, we found an evocative setting of black tents nestled among small sand dunes. After the spicy dinner we were hospitably offered, and from the tent made over to us for the night, I had—for gastrointestinal reasons—repeatedly to exit quickly to the outside and found a dramatic scene with the strong moonlight throwing dark shadows across the curves of the tents and sand dunes, as I wove along in search of a private place.

Aided by my Peace Corps friend, whose Persian was then somewhat more fluent than mine, I conversed with the Sardar about my request. That I wanted to reside with a camp that was purely pastoral and had no agriculture—a wish stimulated by my seeing unexpectedly at Garonchin an irrigation pump driven by a large diesel engine and associated agricultural fields—seemed to make no sense whatever to the Sardar. My ideal-typical, conceptual purity played no part in the productive schemes and adaptive strategies of the Baluch, and the Sardar could not imagine why I would have such a preference. Nor could he imagine about such things for very long, for he was a very practically minded man, and such questions did not keep his attention much longer than could the inarticulate, uninteresting stranger whom he accepted as a guest of the tribe and, after making an appointment for two days later to place this stranger in a herding camp, quickly dismissed from his mind.

When we arrived at Gorchan, the small settlement of mud-brick huts and gardens occupied by the chiefly family during the winter, located in the north-central part of the tribal territory on the highland plain, some 65 kilometers (40 miles) north of Garonchin, we found not Sardar Han Mahmud, but his half-brother, Nezar Mahmud, a smaller man with a warmer expression. My disappointment at being "stood up" by the Sardar quickly dissipated as I conversed with Nezar Mahmud, for he seemed a more interested, thoughtful person who enjoyed engaging with others. Nezar Mahmud said that he had chosen the Dadolzai, that is, the descendants of Dadol, a lineage group, for us to reside with. Not only were the Dadolzai primarily tent-dwelling pastoralists, but they were respected people with a good reputation. We then drove, with Nezar Mahmud guiding, a few miles to the west, to the plain of Pushti Kamal and the Dadolzai camp led by Ja'far.

We drove off the track and across the plain to the line of black tents clinging to the sandy soil. The distinguished-looking man who approached our car was Ja'far himself. He apparently had not been informed that there was going to be an exciting new addition to his camp. But Ja'far soon became excited, in a dignified way, after Nezar Mahmud had explained his intentions, or so we surmised, for they were speaking Baluchi, which, although an Iranian language, is distinct from Persian and not intelligible to Persian speakers, a category to which we were in any case barely more than honorary members. After 20 minutes of intense discussion, Ja'far relented and accepted our presence. I suppose I should have later asked about that discussion, but I always felt that such an inquiry would be a violation of the hospitality we were offered, particularly in the light of the consideration and kindness with which Ja'far and all of the Dadolzai treated us during our many years of association.

The four of us, who had remained at the car, now approached the camp. Joan, who was wearing blue jeans with a large denim work shirt hanging loose outside, and whose hair was braided, was ushered into a tent where a number of women had gathered. Apparently acting on behalf of this assembly, one young woman felt Joan's breasts, which were purposely not prominent visually, in order to affirm that she was indeed a woman. When we left, after a half hour or so, Joan, of somewhat timid disposition, appeared a bit shaken by this experience. I myself did not undergo such close scrutiny, saved perhaps by the testimony of my beard.

We returned to Khash and for the next couple of days, collected supplies, packed, and prepared as best we could for our entry into Baluchi tent life, which began on the last day of 1967.


## THE MAKINGS OF A TENT

At Ja'far's suggestion, because we were to a degree deemed to be his responsibility, we set up our aluminum-exoskeleton, baby-blue canvas tent at the eastern end of the camp's line of tents, next to Ja'far's tent. But, in the interests of privacy and quiet, I chose a spot some distance away, about the length of three Baluchi tents, thus leaving a substantially wider gap than there was between the other tents in the camp. Ja'far did not protest too much; perhaps neither of us was quite ready for total immersion.

Joan and I had had no experience camping, even in North America, and, having both grown up in eastern cities and having studied in the midwest, had never lived in or near a desert. Nor had we experienced a setting in which the basic necessities of life could not be conveniently purchased. So it was with some trepidation mixed with excitement that we celebrated the New Year by sharing our last European chocolate bar before slipping into our double sleeping bag and somewhat nervously waiting for sleep.

If Joan and I did not know very well how to live in a tent, we were in a good position to learn from experts. The Baluch of "our" camp lived in their tents year-round, as had their parents and grandparents before them. They valued their tents not only as shelter, but as a representation of their way of life. One woman said to me with much feeling, using the Persian terms to make a play on words, that she loved her *chadur*, tent, as much as her *chadur*, veil.

The word in the Baluchi language for the black, goat-hair tent is *gedom*. The same word was used to refer to the goat-hair cloth panels that make up the ceiling of the tent.

Goat hair, *mud* (pronounced "mood"), is a "raw material" drawn from the black goats of the tribal flocks. The first step in making a tent was shearing the hair from the goats. This was usually done on a tent-by-tent basis by a senior male of the household, and not coordinated with other households. Shearing was not conceived of as a special occasion and was done according to the convenience of household members. There was no collective shearing or ritual manifestation. Goats were sheared one by one, each temporarily immobilized by tying the legs together and laying the animal on its side. Amid the bleating, shears—*dokarch* (literally: two knives), consisting of two blades on stems, the stems joined at the end by a wooden peg, held by the user in the middle and at the tip of the blades—were used to cut off the hair, which was long and coarse. The underwool, *kork*, of the goats was not used for making tents. The *dokarch*, together with many metal and wood tools and implements used by Sarhadi tent dwellers, was made by local craftworkers and blacksmiths, called Luri, who made up a small, low-caste population that lived separately from the tribesmen in family groups and moved around offering their services to the tribesmen.

Once enough hair, from 40 to 50 kilos, was accumulated for making a tent panel, whether totally from a household's own animals, or from borrowing, exchange, or purchase (in 1967 at 5 toman per kilo in Khash), the next stage of cleaning and separating the hair was undertaken, usually by a number of women, who sat around the large pile of goat hair, each with a thin, wandlike stick in each hand, beating for an hour or two the pile of hair. The spinning of the hair into yarn with a wooden spindle, *jalak*, was a slow process, usually undertaken by a senior woman of the household and carried out over a number of months whenever time was available. Once spun, the yarn was rolled into large balls, sometimes 2 feet across.

Weaving, which usually took place in late spring, was done on a wooden, horizontal loom, *mehudar*, commonly made by Luri, the construction of which was based upon a "frame" of four large pegs stabilized by being driven deep into the ground. The pegs functioned as the corners of a rectangle of some 1.5 meters (5 feet) by 9 to 11 meters (30 or 35 feet). Substantial wooden rods were placed across the short ends of the rectangle, and the warp yarn was strung out from one end to the other and

Figure 1.2. Zarbonu, on the right, and her daughter Shams Hartun, weaving goat hair on a horizontal loom to make a tent roof strip, 1968. The strong sun on the horizontally strung warp threads throws a clear shadow on the sand. (Photograph by author)

back, looping around the rods, providing the foundation for the cloth to be woven. There was in addition a framework with a double cross bar above the center of the loom, each bar tied with twine to alternate rows of warp yarn. The weaving began when the weavers, usually two women sitting side by side, shoved a weft, or cross, yarn through the two layers of warp yarn. The enclosed weft yarn was then beaten tight with the claw-like beater consisting of a wooden handle holding thin, sheet metal claws. The person working the crossbars then raised the one that had been lowered and lowered the one that had been raised, crossing the two layers of warp thread over the single weft yarn that had been inserted, and opening a place for the next weft yarn. As the weaving slowly progressed, the weavers moved forward, sitting on the completed cloth and weaving at its expandable end. Weaving a tent panel took four days of continuous work.

Tent panels, also referred to as *gedom,* the strips of woven goat-hair cloth, were around 1 meter (3 or 4 feet) wide and between 6 and 9 meters (20 to 30) feet long. The shape and dimensions of panels were determined by the technological limitations of the horizontal loom. The width was limited by the need for each weaver to reach halfway into the two layers of warp thread in order to pass the weft yarn through. The length was limited by the capability of the crossbars to separate the layers of warp thread enough to allow the weft yarn to pass. These limitations of the loom were partly a function of its portability, a necessary characteristic of any tool playing an important part in nomadic life.

Mobility was obviously the primary raison d'être for the use of the tent as a shelter. The tent's portability allowed the transport of shelter as part of nomadic movement. Displacement of residence in this case did not mean the loss of shelter and the necessity of finding materials and constructing new shelters, an unlikely possibility in a desert environment. Rather, tents were taken apart, packed on camels—or in the Land Rover, in the case of this anthropologist—and carried along on the migration to the new settlement site. Other impedimenta, such as clothes, bedding, cooking utensils, and tools, were kept to a minimum, and any equipment requiring heroic efforts was likely to be left behind, or, more likely, not acquired in the first place. The entire household and technology were geared toward mobility, and only a loom that met the criterion of portability could be included in the corpus of household equipment.

The smallest tent required two of these goat-hair cloth tent panels, stitched together, while larger tents usually had at least three panels, providing greater width to the tent. I have never seen panels stitched lengthwise or tents of a length beyond the slightly variable one-panel standard. Panels were used as the ceiling of the tent, held up in the center by two or three stout wooden tent poles between 2 and 3 meters (around 7 and 9 feet) high, topped with rectangular wooden crowns to distribute the weight and keep the pole end from poking a hole in the cloth, and held up along the edges by a half-dozen small, wooden poles 1 to 1 1/2 meters (around 3 to 5 feet) high, although additional panels were occasionally used as front and/or back walls of tents.

Most commonly used as tent walls were mats, *gwerpat*, woven from the long, thin leaves, *pish*, of the fronds of palm trees. These were much cheaper than goat-hair cloth panels because of the availability or low cost of the materials. They were often made by women of the black tents from frond leaves gathered from family date palms. Flat strips about 6 inches wide were woven and stored in large rolls; later, the strips would be stitched together with a thin string, *baragin chiluk*, made of palm frond leaves, into these large, long mats, *gwerpat*, for use as tent walls. Purchased *gwerpat* were usually imported from southern Baluchistan, where they were woven from the leaves of the wild palm, *daz* or *pork*. Mat siding was not only less expensive than goat-hair panels, but it was also lighter and easier to transport. The upper edge of the wall mats was held onto the edge of the ceiling tent panel by large, iron pins, *gedom shake*, made by Luri. The side poles were held in place by tent ropes, *tanabi*, usually *chiluk*, of woven palm frond leaves, made by the tribesmen at their date groves, attached to heavy wooden pegs driven into the ground. *Chiluk* was made by weaving two strands of thin, fresh, green, palm leaves together, softening the leaves by hammering the rope between rocks, and then drying the rope in the sun. Customarily, the weaving of palm leaves into flat mats, *gwerpat*, was done by women, while the making of rope, *chiluk*, was undertaken by men. At the date groves, any free time, including during conversational chats with others, seemed to be accompanied by the weaving of *pish*, rather the way, in the West, some people knit.

Ja'far's tent in the winter of 1968 was a large, three-panel and three-pole tent, with *pish* mats serving as the two walls. It was 5 × 8 meters (around 17 × 26 feet), or 41 square meters (442 square feet).

This outer shell of the tent provided partial protection from the elements and a modicum of privacy for its occupants. The heavy goat-hair cloth ceiling was full of natural oils that repelled water, protecting those dwelling within from rain. Now it did not rain very much in Baluchistan, some years not at all. But when it did rain, the rain fell in the winter, and not infrequently it all came in a heavy downpour. During the winter of 1967–68, there was substantial rainfall, most arriving in a three-week period in February. It poured and poured, but little water entered the tents. After the rains, it also took quite a while for the tents to dry, before they were not too heavy with moisture to pack onto camels for migration.

During the winter of 1967 there were also sand storms of several days' duration due to high winds, and the tents weathered these storms well also, effectively protecting the habitants. Because of the high altitude, the winters were fairly cold by Middle Eastern standards. The temperature dropped to freezing at night. To get a drink from my canteen early in the morning, I had to break through a layer of ice. The tent did not provide much insulation against the loss of heat, but it did provide some. When a fire was lit against the cold, as it usually was on winter evenings, the tent was noticeably warmer than the outside.

So, too, did body heat maintain a somewhat higher level of temperature. For it was not only people who inhabited the tent during the winter, but also animals. As we shall see, in this camp, the flocks, *galag*, of small stock, *pas*—including both sheep, *sepid pas* (literally "white small stock"), and goats, *sah pas* (literally "black small stock")—were not large, at most no more than several dozen. During the winter, the tent was divided into a portion for the *pas*, called the *gwash*, and a portion for the people. In Ja'far's tent, his 42 adult *pas* were confined in an area not quite 2 × 6 meters (around 6 × 17 feet), a bit more than 10 square meters (around 100 square feet). Inside the tent, the *pas* were thus protected from the elements and, packed together behind a rope webbing barrier, *tat*, provided warmth for one another. At the same time, their body heat raised the temperature of the tent somewhat, to the benefit of

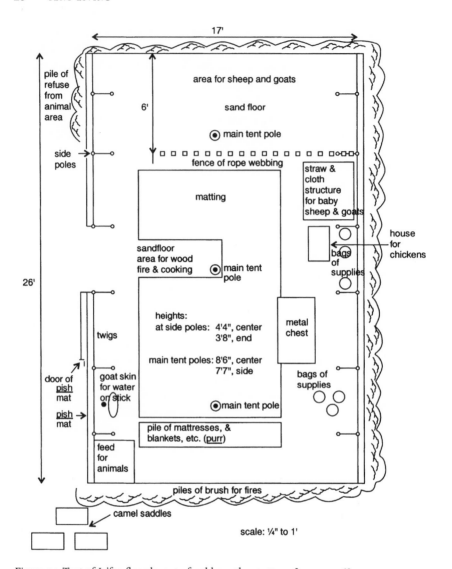

Figure 1.3. Tent of Ja'far, floor layout of cold-weather pattern, January 1968.

the human occupants. Recently born lambs and kids were placed within the tent, in small shelters dug out from the earth and closed with cloth, straw, or other handy material; those more like caves were called *kuhd* and those more like huts *dramshuik*. So, too, chickens were provided with a small shelter inside the tent.

Other seasons provided other challenges. The strong sun of spring, summer, and fall in the Sarhad of Baluchistan beat down unimpeded. There were no trees to provide shade, and no shade other than that offered by tents. The thick, black, goat-hair tent roofs blocked the sun's rays, providing those within a respite from the unrelent-

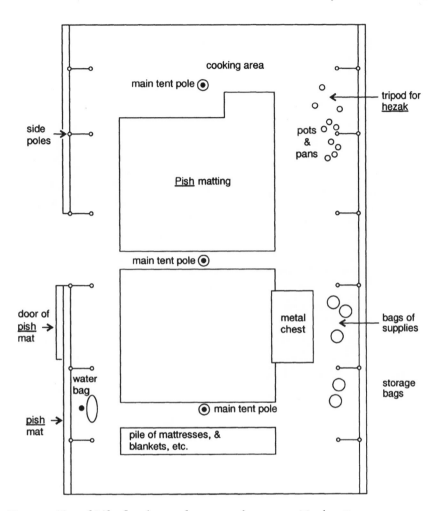

Figure 1.4. Tent of Ja'far, floor layout of warm-weather pattern, March 1968.

ing heat of the sun. Our baby-blue, canvas tent roof did not block the sun and thus offered us poor protection from its rays. But conditions in our tent were even worse, because, in spite of the tent's two windows and door, ventilation was not sufficient to keep the sun from turning it into an oven. In contrast, the sides of the Baluchi tents were either raised onto the roof or detached and removed, leaving both long sides of the tent totally open and the tent accessible to even the smallest, refreshing breezes. Under the sun and in the heat, black goat-hair tents are oases.

The tent also provided a modicum of privacy. When it was closed, what was going on inside could not be seen. This physical barrier was enforced by conventional etiquette, which required that one never approach a tent from the back, but rather circle around and approach from the front, where the door opening in the mat was

Figure 1.5. Lashkar Han standing in front of black tents, 1973. In hot weather, the side mats of tents are opened to provide good ventilation under the shade offered by the tent roof. (Photograph by author)

located. Nor did one approach a tent silently and unannounced, but rather made some sound to alert those inside that someone was coming. One did not enter a tent if the door opening was closed.

Sound, however, was not blocked by the tents, and it was difficult not to hear what was going on in nearby or even more distant tents. Noises from the surrounding environment, such as the bleating of the sheep and goats and the grating calls of the camels, penetrated the tent walls without difficulty. Once we had guests, a distinguished academic Islamicist and his wife, accustomed to urban life, who found, in this camp out in the middle of the Baluchistan desert, that it was too noisy for them to be able to sleep. I saved the day by providing ear plugs (an indispensable aid to ethnographic fieldwork). The passage of sounds through tent walls was not always inadvertent; sometimes it was intentional. While I was inside a tent interviewing a man about kin connections, his mother piped up from two tents away to correct some information that my informant was providing.

Privacy, being separated from other people, "keeping oneself to oneself" as the English expression goes, was not a general value among the Baluch. There were of course strong norms about not interfering with people in their own spheres of decision. And there was an etiquette about not intruding on people's privacy in a narrow range of specific situations. For example, Baluch did not flock around someone engaged in urinating or defecating. If a Baluch was outside of camp and came across someone behind a sand dune engaged in a personal function, they "did not see" this person, as they put it, and continued on their way. Similarly, Baluchi males did not expose their genitalia in the presence of others, and would avoid intruding upon someone who might be exposed, for example, while shaving pubic hair. Baluch, like Persians, regard body hair as rude and shave it.

Privacy was thus regarded by Baluch as appropriate in a restricted set of specific contexts. But privacy in the sense of solitude was undesirable, despised, and even feared. For Baluchi desert dwellers, "life is with people," to borrow a book title, and sociability was the normative mode. To spend time with others was the desirable thing. Baluch liked to stand around together and to sit together, to work and to rest together, to chat and to be silent together, inside or outside their tents. Mutual visiting was a constant activity, and there was quite a bit of "hanging out" together among Baluch of all ages.

Not to leave someone alone was a moral imperative. Ideally, no one should be left alone in his or her tent. In particular, a sick person should have company at all times, and so there was a constant flow of visitors into any tent where someone was ill or convalescing.

Baluch regarded the desire for sociability as normal. Conversely, the desire for solitude was regarded as a sign of psychic pathology. Someone who wanted to be alone was, on those grounds, regarded as mentally disturbed, crazy. On those grounds alone, and aside from the multitude of our other bizarre behaviors, Joan and I were definitely strange, if not crazy. We, of course, growing up only children in reasonably well-off middle-class American families, had spent most of our lives with considerably more solitude and less sociability than dictated by the Baluchi norm. Furthermore, sociability was much more tiring in a new language that we were in the course of acquiring. We really did not want to spend all of our time with people. We needed time to write notes and think things over; we wanted time to read. We felt we needed to be alone with ourselves and to be quiet. We were not being very human by Baluchi standards.

Of course, the other side to this was the virtually unlimited openness and availability of Baluch to our visits and interrogations. The unstinting hospitality and kindness shown to us by our hosts and neighbors facilitated greatly our ethnographic inquiries and also our comfort and contentment in this, to us, initially alien and difficult land. In other words, we exploited Baluchi sociability for our professional and personal needs, while being largely excused by the Baluch from living up to their standard of sociability.

## INSIDE THE TENT

Space inside the tent was allocated to a variety of uses. The center-peaked, sloping roof of the tent provided height up to around 3 meters (9 feet) in the center of the interior, while at the edges of the space, by the wall of the tent, the roof was only 1 to 1½ meters (4 feet or so) high. Consequently, in general the center of the interior was reserved for living and activity space, and the margins around the walls were reserved for the storage of equipment and supplies.

The most important storage area was at one end of the tent, where an ordered stack of bedding, rugs and carpets, cushions, eating and covering cloths, and luggage bags, resting on a low wooden platform—the entire stack called a *purr*—both stored and displayed the collective textile wealth of the family. The tent provided basically one room for all living activities.

There was a rare and exceptional disposition of the *purr,* across the middle of the tent and perpendicular to the two long sides, which divided the tent into two rooms. This is done only to signal two distinct living spaces for two separate families. The necessary corollary is two hearths, one on each side of the *purr,* one for each family. I have seen this a couple of times, used by parents and married, adult children who had to share a tent temporarily but who maintained separate households. For example, when Ja'far's recently acquired son-in-law, Id Mahmud, returned in April 1968 from Abu Dhabi on the Arab side of the Gulf, where he had been working as a construction laborer, Ja'far's tent was divided by placing the *purr* in the center of the tent and rearranging the siding to make separate doors for each section. Ja'far had a three-strip tent roof, but one strip was, at the time of Id Mahmud's arrival, being used as siding for the back of the tent. It was agreed to expand the size of the tent, so as better to accommodate two households, by using all three tent strips, *gedom,* as the roof when setting up after the next migration, and adding palm matting for the back siding. Such arrangements were most common for recent marriages, especially when the husband was away working. However, it was expected and usual for each nuclear family to have its own tent; this was one of the highest material imperatives of adulthood. So the sharing of a tent was a temporary expedient, and not continued for long.

In tent life, activity space was not only spatial but temporal, in that the sleeping area became an eating area at a different time of the day, and a food preparation area at another time, and a yarn-spinning area at another time. So the bedding could occupy the living space only during the sleeping period, after which it had to be restacked on the *purr,* just as the prayer rug was set out in the living space during prayer and then refolded for deposit on the *purr.*

The textiles making up the *purr* were the main furniture, containers, and baggage of the Baluchi tent dwellers. Most were hand sewn or woven and were mainly heavy enough to take rough wear. But both volume and weight were important. These textile items could be folded into relatively small packages, taking little space, and were much lighter in weight than wood, leather, or metal furniture, containers, or baggage. Textile household goods could thus be stored in a small area, could be taken for use and returned to storage easily, and could be transported during migration easily.

The collection of textiles on the *purr* reflected the wealth of the household. The quantity, quality, and condition of the textiles were heavily conditioned by the disposable income, including raw material such as wool and hair, as well as the effective female spinning, weaving, and sewing labor pool of the household. To a considerable degree, the textile household goods available for use determined the amount of hospitality a family could offer, for overnight hospitality required bedding that had to be provided for guests sleeping over. So by reflecting the wealth of the family and the amount of hospitality they could offer, the *purr* was a crude index of the prestige of the family.

While the *purr* displayed the household textile goods for all to see, at the same time it concealed, in two different ways. One was that the *purr* functioned as a bureau, the folds of the less-used, lower layers serving as undrawable "drawers." Any small object or material of value—documents, money, jewelry, articles of clothing—could be secreted in a fold, with no one the wiser. The second way that the *purr* concealed was that, 3 meters (10 feet) across and piled high with dense textiles, the *purr* functioned as a screen. The area behind the *purr* was, in effect, a small, hidden room, useful as a private retreat for engaging in personal tasks not suitable for public display. Often women bathed, washed their hair, and engaged in other activities of their toilette there. Clothes could be changed without fear of public exposure. This constricted area behind the *purr* was the most private area within the living quarters of the Baluch. Thus the open display of the *purr* concealed the hidden.

As previously mentioned, an area in the tent was often, particularly in winter, allocated to livestock. This area was at the opposite end of the tent from the *purr* and when used in this fashion reduced the amount of living and working space for the human inhabitants of the tent. Even when the animals were out of the tent during the daytime, as was the case except in extreme weather such as snow accumulation, the animals' area was not usable, as there was always a thick layer of animal feces. In fact, the feces accumulated so rapidly that it was necessary to shovel it out regularly or the space would have shrunk as the ground rose toward the sloping gradient of the roof; so shoveling out feces was a common winter chore.

Around the perimeter of the tent, where the sloping roof is joined to the low walls, was ranged a variety of structures and equipment. Near the animal pen, at the back wall of the tent, were the small enclosures for the lambs and kids and for the chickens. Then moving toward the end of the tent with the *purr*, there were lined up bags of supplies such as grain, flour, dates, and oil, and a sheet metal chest with pots, dishes, glasses, and the like. Ranged along the front wall of the tent, with its door flap in the middle, were, beginning in the corner next to the *purr,* feed for the animals, then a forked stick that served as a stand for a goat-skin water bag, and then a pile of twigs for use as fuel. These were the exact arrangements in Ja'far's tent in the winter of 1967–68, and details varied from tent to tent, but the general pattern was representative.

In the middle of the tent, by the central tent pole, was an area of uncovered sand used for the hearth. There fires made from the twigs of bushes would provide heat for cooking and warmth. Frequently the ashes would be removed and the area replenished with fresh sand. Around the hearth was a large area, the central living space, covered with open-weave, strawlike matting, *tagert.* These were sometimes made by Sarhadi Baluch, with *pish,* palm frond leaves, from their date palms. During the summer of 1967, Sazien, Shams A'din's wife, made two *tagert* for use in their tent. *Tagert* that were purchased were usually woven in southern Baluchistan from wild palm leaves, *pish,* like the side walls of the tent.

## TENT LIVING

In the Baluchi tent, as is true generally in tents and houses throughout the Middle East, the living surface was at ground level. There was no vertically oriented furniture to provide a place to sit, lie, cook, eat, or work above ground level. The customary furniture of the Baluchi tent was textile, to make the ground level clean and comfortable.

There were rugs to sit on, either locally made, flat-woven, floating weft rugs, *kunt,* or purchased, knotted pile carpets, *gali,* usually of a "Baluchi" design, made in Sistan to the north. Sometimes large, heavy-gauge, striped, cotton cloths, made in Pakistan, were used for sitting, and sometimes people sat directly on the floor matting. Cushions of the bolster type, often cylinder shaped, would be placed on the rugs, sometimes against a tent pole or the *purr,* to give the back comfortable support.

Chatting and drinking tea with company, lounging comfortably in the tent, was the main leisure activity of Baluch. Company in this case was usually casual visitors from among camp neighbors and fellow residents. And of course lounging and chatting with family members was common during work breaks. On winter evenings after the sun went down, lounging around the fire to stay warm, either with family members or with neighbors as well, was a pleasant after-dinner occupation. In the winter, lounging in a physical sense was necessary, for the smoke from the wood fire accumulated from the tent roof down, and the lower one was, the easier it was to breath. The characteristic smell of the smoke from the wood fire impregnated the tent cloth, clothes, cushions, rugs, and bedding, and to me was the smell of Baluchi tent life. Even today, when I smell wood smoke, I get an olfactory flashback to

Figure 1.6. Ja'far, Monas, with two of their children, conversing with a campmate inside their tent, 1968. Ja'far leans casually against a tent pole, while Monas nurses her infant daughter. (Photograph by author)

Baluchistan. In summer, as mentioned, the shade of the tent was the only refuge from the searing rays of the sun, and the most likely source of a quenching drink of cool water from a goat-skin bag. Resting in the tent during the high heat of the summer day was an established strategy, with many work tasks put off and scheduled for cooler periods.

During winter, cooking equipment and dishes were brought into the central tent area, used, and removed, as were bedding for sleeping, rugs and cushions for lounging, work materials and equipment, and small animals for various attentions. In this multipurpose area, the impedimenta for various activities were set up and then returned to their storage areas. We can see the mobility of nomadic life replicated in miniature in the movement of things into and from the bare central space of the tent. As with the packing and transport burden of nomadism, the constant bringing and removing of equipment and material in the single space of the tent required equipment that was relatively small, light weight, and easily stored.

For many kinds of work at floor level, such as sifting flour, preparing dough and making bread, shearing sheep and goats, and "washing" pots with sand, the conventional position was squatting, with knees at one's sides, a position at which Baluch were very adept and in which they were quite comfortable.

## THE PERSONAL TENT

The concealment, protection against the elements, and working space of the tent was replicated in miniature in the dress of the Baluch. Most obviously, the veil, *chadur,* of the women, is a tentlike garment, and thought of as such by Baluchi women: a large, semicircular cloth, worn with the center of the straight side at one's forehead, the circular side hanging down one's back and at one's sides, to the ankles. The veil could be worn to cover the front part of the hair or to expose the front of the hair; it could flow open, covering only sides and back or could be held closed covering most of the face and the entire body. In the desert camp, surrounded by kin and coresidents—categories that included, in this endogamy-oriented community, potential and even preferred marriage mates, and even potential illicit lovers, although I saw little evidence that extramarital love was a major preoccupation—women, whether married or unmarried, rarely closed their veils to cover their faces and bodies. Coresidents were commonly livelong acquaintances and almost always kinsmen of some degree. Modesty was more a matter of comportment and interaction than visual blocking, at least as far as the veil was concerned.

At the same time, Baluchi clothing was modest, in the sense that it covered most of the body and limbs. Anyone showing a bit too much skin, as Joan did sometimes when her jeans would ride up to expose her lower shin, would be rebuked, often by the older ladies, with a cry of *"pust, pust,"* "skin, skin," and would likely experience an old lady's hand tugging downward on the pant leg.

Sarhadi women wore full, loose trousers, *shalwar,* which hung to the tops of their feet. On top of their bodies hanging over the trousers, they wore full, loose dresses, *jamag,* that began at the base of the neck and went to the wrists and ankles. The top of the sleeves, where they attached to the body of the dress, were very wide. Over this, as mentioned, they wore a veil, *chadur.* The men wore even looser trousers, also called *shalwar,* with a waist four times the size of their body waists, so that when it was drawn tight with a drawstring, cloth hung not ungracefully in multiple, large folds down the inside of the legs. Above was worn a full shirt, also called *jamag,* which hung outside of the trousers and over them to midthigh or even down to the knee. Usually men wore a head covering of some kind, the most conventional being a turban, consisting of a long cloth wrapped around a cylindrical or rounded skull cap.

To the Western eye, Baluchi clothes may appear to be exotic and colorful—I certainly found them so—but acquaintance with local conditions drives home to the observer that these outfits were highly practical and eminently appropriate to the environment in which they were used. Clothes were thus another example of Baluchi design being better adapted to Baluchistan than items based upon extrinsic design, such as the Western, casual clothes I brought with me.

Baluchi outfits allowed Baluchi men and women to maintain their modesty and avoid offending others when engaging in various personal functions, by not exposing to other people parts of their bodies that they felt were meant to remain covered and by not exposing for public scrutiny various bodily processes and leavings. Baluch must engage in various personal tasks, depending upon the task, either in a one-room dwelling with a number of other people or else outside, at a distance from the camp, at best partly out of sight behind a sand dune.

For excretory functions, urination and defecation, both men and women would usually squat. And for both men and women, the long, loose *jamag* shirt and dress fell around them to the ground and totally covered their bodies and their leavings. The women's veils provided a further layer of obstruction from view. It was as if a set of Baluchi clothes were a small tent that every Baluch constantly carried with him or her.

The looseness and freedom of movement provided by Baluchi clothes contributed to their coverage. Garments have so much cloth that they could be repositioned to expose a small part of the body while continuing to cover the rest; it was not necessary to remove a Baluchi garment to gain access to parts of one's body. For excretory functions, clothes could be disposed so as to expose only the private parts and only to the ground, while other parts of the body remained covered. Or to work in wet or muddy conditions, for example, while watering camels or making mud bricks, the upper part of the *shalwar* could be hiked up and stuffed in the waistband, pulling the bottom cuffs up to the knee or above.

Changing clothes was often done with others present in the vicinity, such as in a tent. This was possible because it was not necessary to remove the clothes one had on as a prelude to putting on other clothes. The procedure—which would be admired even by those Europeans adept at undressing and slipping on a bathing suit under cover of a beach towel—relied on the looseness of Baluchi clothes. The wearer inserted the new pants or shirt/dress into the pants or shirt/dress being worn, pulled in the feet from the trouser legs or the arms from the sleeves, slipped on the new pants or shirt/dress inside the old clothes, and then removed the outside layer of old pants or shirt/dress, without a square inch of *pust* having been shown.

This looseness of Baluchi clothes and the freedom of movement it made possible facilitated many forms of activities. Squatting as one of the basic working postures was made possible by the nonbinding freedom of the clothes. Anyone who has tried to squat and work in blue jeans will recognize their limitations. Jan Mahmud once returned to camp from working outside the territory wearing tight jeans, generating considerable mirth that rapidly evolved into hilarity as he tried to sit, urinate squatting, and do various odd jobs, none of which were very comfortable. He was back in his Baluchi clothes the next day.

Another example of ease of adjustment combined with maximum coverage was the way the looseness of women's dresses facilitated nursing. The vertical seam of the dress under the sleeve would be opened six inches or so for the period of nursing. The baby would be held horizontally across the body, with the baby's head at the far side of the breast. The dress was pulled toward the front, opening the seam and pulling the hole toward the breast, allowing the baby to nurse. Little of the mother's body was exposed. Mothers did not seem shy about nursing in mixed company and did not appear to be embarrassed about the brief exposure of their breast and nipple.

The coverage of Baluchi clothes also protected wearers from the elements. Little of the strong sun of these equatorial latitudes reached Baluchi skin, as little was exposed. The looseness of the clothes also provided an air layer that helped to keep out both the heat and the cold. Sand, too, was kept off the body and out of the hair by the cover of clothes. For me personally, perhaps the most annoying physical consequence of living in the desert was having sand in my hair and on my scalp most of the time. But I foolishly did not wear a hat, although my Baluchi friends were wiser. Nor was I as accustomed as they were to washing my hair in a basin of water.

It was not a folk-fashion conceit or expression of ethnic solidarity that led me to adopt Baluchi wear. If anything, I was reluctant to wear Baluchi clothes on such grounds because I felt it inappropriate to pretend I was Baluch. Furthermore, I did not particularly wish to signal the Persians of Khash and the provincial bureaucracy that I was identifying with the Baluch as distinct from them. Rather, it was the practical advantages of Baluchi clothes that led me to adopt them, at least in part. While I satisfied myself with light and loose western pants, I had several Baluchi shirts made that I regularly wore. They were loose and comfortable, protected me from the elements, and provided coverage when I needed it.

## MARKERS

Clothes have social functions as well. Most notably, they mark off, through similarity and difference, membership in common or different social categories.

In Iranian Baluchistan, Baluchi clothes signaled Baluchi ethnicity—other elements of which included Baluchistan origins, capability in Baluchi language, affiliation with a Baluchi tribal or village community, and, for most Baluch, Sunni Islam—in distinction from Persian or Sikh or other ethnicity. But, certainly from the 1960s on, not all Baluch wore Baluchi clothes all of the time. Those Baluch working in urban settings (for example, in Zahedan), in offices and shops, sometimes adopted Persian clothes, just as they used the Persian language, *farsi*. On the other hand, members of other Iranian ethnic groups virtually never wore Baluchi clothes.

Within the community of Baluch, characteristics of clothes could signal membership in status groups. For example, the clothes of adult male Yarahmadzai tribesmen were usually white, grey, or khaki in color. That is, colorless clothing was deemed appropriate for adult males. Color was a form of decoration regarded as unmanly. Thus it was with disdain and disparagement that Yarahmadzai tribesmen described the loud colors of the clothes of the Ghulamzai, literally "the descendants of slaves," a lower-status group of former slaves and their descendants attached to the Yarahmadzai tribe. For the Yarahmadzai, the spectacle of the Ghulamzai, in their flashy, unmanly clothes, riding their donkeys—for they were never allowed to own camels—was both risible and disgusting, and appropriate to their slave origins and status. When Ghulamzai came into view, Yarahmadzai would point them out to me, ridiculing their bright clothes. And it was a good thing they did point them out to me, because the pale and muted hues of blue and dusty rose of their clothes appeared to me so unspectacular that I certainly would not have noticed on my own. To me, the difference seemed much more conceptual than perceptual, but it served well as a diacritic between the two status groups.

To a degree, we can say, in Baluchistan and elsewhere, that "clothes make the man [and the woman]," in that clothes made evident what the man and woman are signaling about themselves. In the West, the signaling can be social, indicating membership in groups, such as motorcycle gangs or fraternities, or in status groups, such as wealthy or working-class, or in age groups, such as teen-age or adult, or in lifestyle categories, such as gay or neo-Nazi. But clothes are equally likely to be expressions of individuality, of self-expression, lifestyle, or identification, or simply style. In the West, a Palestinian scarf is no predictor of ethnic background, nor is a motorcycle jacket a reliable indicator of means of travel. Furthermore, people may change their clothes and their styles as the mood hits them. In general in the West, type and detail of clothes are not mandated socially, and the limits of tolerance are fairly wide, and have become increasingly wide from the 1960s. Uniforms and uniform dress have become rare in the West.

In contrast, in Baluchistan, the standard for clothes was largely set by social group membership. In addition to affiliation to larger ethnic categories and to status groups within those categories, gender and age were also marked by clothes. The differences between men's and women's clothes have already been described. There were no unisex clothes among the Baluch and no cross-dressing that I saw.

Sex differences in clothes were marked right from the start. Boy toddlers wore little shirts and girl toddlers wore short little dresses; neither wore pants, for they urinated and defecated at will on the ground, thus demonstrating that sand does have its good points. Both female and male toddlers wore little, tied-on skull caps, to keep their heads clean and protected; but the caps of the female toddlers had attached a rectangle of cloth hanging down behind, covering the neck, rather like one sees in films of the French Foreign Legion in the Sahara. But why should girls need their necks protected more than boys? Of course they did not, and the hanging cloth was not about sun block. Rather, the hanging cloth together with the cap was deemed to be a proto-veil, introducing the child to the veil, and signaling, as if it were not clearly signaled by what was or was not hanging below, that this was a female child.

The clothes of post-toddler boys and girls corresponded increasingly closely to those of young adult males and females. The boys' clothes were colorless, while the girl's dresses and pants were brightly colored, made of purchased, printed cloth of bright red and green, with small or large figures of flowers prominent, the veils somewhat less extravagant. As if the colored prints were not sufficiently decorative, elaborately hand-embroidered cloths, *abreshum* (named from the silky thread used; the term also means "silk," as it does in Persian), in bold primary colors, were sewn onto the bodice, *abreshumi zi*, the large front pentagonal pocket, *abreshumi goptan*, and the cuffs, *abreshumi astunk*, of the dress. Men's clothes, with the exception of the "traditional" wedding shirt, were not embroidered.

Embroidery was regarded as an appropriate activity of girls and young women prior to marriage. It was a skilled activity, with much need for precision work within the narrow conventions of this particular form of nonrepresentative stitching, but also left room for creativity, especially in overall design. The embroidery on one's clothes displayed one's skill and devotion to work, and it enhanced beauty at a phase of life when the girl herself was her most important product. Once women married, began running their own households and having children, self-enhancement and display were regarded as inappropriate, for the quality of a woman at this phase of her life was seen in her contributions to her household. Weaving for the household, rather than embroidering for herself, was the appropriate craft priority. So as women became responsible for their households, this was reflected in a muting of their clothing; the colors were more muted and the designs less bold, with smaller elements. As women aged, this process continued, until in their fifties or so, or as a result of bereavement, they took up plain black dresses, trousers, and veils.

Men's clothes, austere from the beginning, did not change with age. Rather, a man's phase of life was visually reflected in facial hair. Boys had hairless faces. Young men, before marriage and until they had children, wore moustaches. Young fathers added full beards, but cut them short. As the older children grew and more children appeared, and the father became responsible for a maturing household, he began to let his beard grow. By full middle age, men had large beards and moustaches. When a man began to fail, no longer capable of engaging in productive activities, and the children had established their own households, or those who remained took increasing practical responsibility for the household, the declining male would shave his moustaches and wear only a beard.

There were of course also nonvisual indicators of age status. One was the form of a person's name; until a person was regarded as an adult, she or he was called by a diminutive. For women, the change in name came with puberty and marriage, which were usually close together. For men, the change of name also came with marriage

**Table 1.1.** Diminutives and Adult Names among Sarhadi Tent Dwellers

| Pre-adult Diminutive | Adult Name |
| --- | --- |
| *Male* | |
| Shahuk | Shah Mahmud |
| Mahmuduk | Mahmud |
| Abdulluk | Abdulla |
| Gam Dad | Jan Mahmud |
| Shamuk | Shams A'din |
| Shiruk | Shir Mahmud |
| Janguk | Jangi Han |
| Jomuk | Jome |
| *Female* | |
| Bibuk | Bibi Nur |
| Laluk | Lal Malik |
| Nuras | Nur Bibi |
| Mariumuk | Marium |
| Shamsuk | Shams Hartun |
| Mahdaruk | Marium |

*Note:* Diminutives were also used among adults to express affection. Close kin and spouses sometimes continued to use diminutives when others exclusively used the adult name.

but was usually long after puberty. The change to an adult name and growing a beard often went together.

Baluchi outfits and their variations were largely dictated by custom supported by public opinion. Type of clothing among tent dwellers in the deserts of Baluchistan was compulsory rather than voluntary, categorical rather than individual. People wore the clothing of their group and their category, and they wore it all the time. Social placement was the main message of clothing; room for personal expression was very limited.

Although mandatory and categorical, local fashion also had an aesthetic dimension. Baluch felt and said that their clothes were beautiful. They drew particular pleasure from the way their clothes flowed gracefully and fluttered in the wind as people moved.

## FASHION

Baluchi clothes had clear functions in the local setting and were well adapted for practical and social living. But it would be wrong to suggest that practical considerations were the only influence on Baluchi clothes. They were also influenced by fashion and aesthetics.

During the first half of the twentieth century, Sarhadi dress was simple and standardized. The plates in *Raiders of the Sarhad* by General R. E. F. Dyer (*passim*, but especially "Surrendered Raiders," opposite p. 89) show men in *jamag*, *shalwar*, and turban similar to those worn when I was in Baluchistan fifty years later. But in these black and white plates most of the clothes and turbans appear to be white. Most of the men are wearing cloths around their necks and some have knee-length coats of perhaps a tan color. The only women to appear in plates ("Raided Slaves on the Way to Their Homes" and "A Persian Girl Captured by Juma Khan, and Who Escaped to Khwash," opposite p. 165) seem to be wearing a short, waist-length *chadur* and a *jamag* of a tan color, while the *shalwar* cannot be seen. But whether these captives' clothes were the same as those of local women cannot be known, for no local women appear in photos.

It was reported to me by elderly informants that simple cotton cloth was imported to the Sarhad from Sistan in the north, Kerman in the west, or Pakistan in the east, and clothes were made by the Sarhadi women. White cloth was brought for the men, and then dyed tan with plants gathered in the mountains. Tan cloth was used for the women's *chadur*, but their *jamag* and *shalwar* were made from black cloth that was imported along with the white cloth. The neck hole of the men's shirt was like that of the women's dresses: a hole with a vertical slit at one side of the neck, buttoned at the top to slip the garment on and off. The bottom hem on men's shirts and women's dresses was a large circle. There was no decoration on men's or women's clothes. By the late 1960s, with urban styles creeping in via Persians who had come permanently or temporarily to Baluchistan, and most of the men's clothes made by tailors for payment, men's shirts had collars and buttoned openings part way down the front, and the bottom hem was shaped into front and back tails.

Embroidery was primarily an aesthetic enhancement. It evolved from an earlier simple, red decorative embroidery, when Sikh shopkeepers arrived in northern Baluchistan after World War II with the establishment of the train from Quetta to Zahedan and brought manufactured sewing materials, including the brightly colored thread, *dasag*. Baluchi women adopted this thread and elaborated their embroidery to take advantage of the greater potential of this fine, brightly colored thread. Embroidery became more and more elaborate and required greater and greater skill, reaching an efflorescence in the 1960s. At that point, the standard of embroidery had surpassed what many women could or were willing to do. Then some tailors began decorating dresses, on the bodice, pockets, and cuffs, with sewing machines. By the late 1970s, some Baluchi women in the camps were purchasing handmade embroidery to sew on their dresses, others were buying machine-decorated dresses, and yet others were downplaying the necessity of embroidery.

In 1968, in the camp of Ja'far, women's dresses fell to the top of the foot. By 1976, the dresses were a good 4 to 6 inches shorter, showing for all to see the bottom 4 inches or so of the trousers. The men grumbled about this; they did not like it at all, preferring the dresses to cover the trousers totally. The women, however, were all agreed that this new dress length was fine and would be the new standard. When I asked them about it, the men complained but said, "What can we do about it? The women have decided and will not listen to us." And so things stood when I was last there, the matter apparently decided.

While the standard of dress is collectively rather than individually determined, collective opinion is affected by exposure to other forms of dress and the arrival of new materials, and thus local fashion changes could be seen in the adoption of external modes and in the shifts in the internal standard that could be considered local fashion.

## WONDERMENT AND HABITUATION

The visual impact of the Baluch, with their distinctive clothes and characteristic dwellings, was quite strong. Visually, I found the Baluch and their dwellings quite wonderful. The austere and striking landscape was of course an impressive setting for the Baluch. For me, as a neophyte anthropologist, the cultural distinctness of my subjects was delightfully blatant; I felt validated as an anthropologist just by being there.

It did not hurt the strength of the impression that I found the Baluch quite attractive. At every age, the men seemed handsome and dignified, and the women beautiful and graceful. But visual impressions quickly become distorted by other factors, and the kindness and gentleness with which we were treated by the Baluch undoubtedly warmed my vision.

While the Baluch were silently if not undiscernibly not much impressed with our clothes—except my shoes, which were objects of envy—we, too, were judged favorably aesthetically because of our fair skin and also because of our slimness. We were young: Joan was 24 and I was 28. Neither dark skin, associated in the minds of the Baluch with slaves from southern Baluchistan, nor portliness, in fact rather rare in the rigors of desertic Baluchistan, were regarded by the Baluch as attractive.

More important in the attitudes of our Baluchi friends and coresidents toward us was that we continually and in a virtually unique fashion demonstrated respectful interest in them. We did this first of all by taking up residence with them, a commitment never before seen in the Sarhad by a non-Baluch. No Persian or anyone else had ever set up their household and lived with Baluch in a herding camp or elsewhere. I believe that this was eventually if not initially regarded as a serious show of respect. We wanted to and did interact with our Baluchi coresidents as coresidents, and at that level at least as equals.

For the most part, my demands upon our Baluchi campmates were for information about themselves, a clear and ongoing sign of interest. And I made efforts to reciprocate their kindness and support by offering things that I had at my disposal that they did not have. For example, when we weekly drove to Khash to pick up mail, go to the bathhouse, and buy supplies, I offered rides, 32 kilometers (20 miles) each way over a dirt track, in my Land Rover, which was much faster and more comfortable traveling than the other available ways: by foot, camel, or bicycle. And while I did not offer people money or goods in exchange for information, I did on various ritual occasions buy an animal and rice to provide food for everyone in the camp. I passed on to an elder my due portion as contributor, the head of the beast.

I came to think, later during this first residence and also during my longer second and shorter third stays, of this herding camp as a social unit in some ways similar to the Department of Anthropology with which I was affiliated. Both units were small ongoing communities, in which people were dependent upon one another, although the camp was residential as well as occupational while the department was occupational but not residential. I was close to some people and less to others in both the camp and department. I found life to be stressful and demanding in both, partly because of my own needs and goals, but also enriching and rewarding in both. In camp, I would think of the physical quadrangle of offices that made up my department, and of the professional reenforcement and enrichment, and, yes, status, that I found so satisfying. In the department, I would think of the camp and the tents and my friends, and the seemingly limitless opportunity to do anthropological research rather than talk about it. I repeatedly wondered, imaging in my mind one group and the other, whether I liked better my Baluchi campmates or my departmental colleagues. I tended to feel that I liked my campmates a bit better, but then it was easier to like them because I was less dependent upon them, for both material things and my self-definition, while I was more dependent upon my colleagues.

# 2.
# THE CAMPING GROUP

Having been introduced in the first chapter to the author of this report and to the black tents, the reader might be justifiably impatient to meet the people themselves, as it is the people who live in the tents who are the main subjects of this ethnographic account. But how exactly can we go about meeting the people through the medium of the printed word? This question raises the problem, among others, of where, at what level of organization, can we best meet "the people." When we say we want to meet "the people," what is the entity to which we are referring? Is it preferable to begin with the largest possible entity, such as the ethnolinguistic category, in this case all "Baluch"? Or with the smaller political entities, in this case tribes and hakomates? Or perhaps it is better—because it seems more "concrete"—to introduce people at more intimate levels of organization, the family, the work team, or even the individual. Where exactly can "people" be found?

Anthropologists often talk about people as carriers of a "culture," which usually means a "way of life." But "a way of life" is a process lived by people, not an entity. In fact, we study "a culture" primarily by engaging in ethnographic field research with a number, usually a few, of "the people" living in a limited locale, who to some degree share a way of life, and, on the basis of the information collected, we try to abstract basic patterns. "Culture" is thus a fairly high-level abstraction from the ideas and activities of a collection of people.

This approach to culture has been criticized on a number of grounds, one of which, as I have suggested above, is that in striving to establish a tidy overall pattern, it abstracts and reifies an "essence," thus misrepresenting the diversity, multiplicity, and vitality of life within any population and any set of ideas and activities (Barth 1994; Vayda 1994). Other critics go even farther, arguing that if we stick to the actual evidence that we collect, we cannot go much beyond reporting what people say to us (Jackson 1989; Marcus 1994). These arguments raise serious doubts about "the culture" as the focus of description, doubts not alleviated by the position of the advocates of the study of culture, who say that the basic information we collect can be no more than our interpretations of our subjects' interpretations (Geertz 1983).

At the same time, the idea advocated by the "dialogical" approach—that all we can honestly do is report what people say to us—seems rather extreme for a number of reasons. To begin with, it focuses upon one method of collecting information, interviewing, whereas in fact fieldwork anthropologists usually collect information in a variety of ways. One important way is through direct observation of what people do, of their activities and practices, and direct observation of the remains of what people have done in the past, such as the houses they have built, the fields that they have tilled, the cheese that they have made, the pictures that they have painted, the books that they have written, and so on. Another important way is to observe what people say, not to us in interviews, but to each other in the course of their real lives. Furthermore, if one is so skeptical that one dismisses the information collected by direct observation in "natural" settings as unreliable, there is no justification, in my view, for arguing that what people say to us in interviews is more reliable, for if anything it is less reliable, not being a part of the people's lives in their own social context. Furthermore, the "dialogical" approach surrenders a great strength of anthropological method, of long-term field research, namely, the checking and cross-checking of information collected from a variety of sources using a variety of methods.

The "dialogical" position that we can report only what people say to us in interviews is extreme also in that it privileges the individual as the "unit of analysis"—assuming that the individual represents the only, or the main, or the most important organizational entity—and tends to neglect the many collective levels of organization that make the existence of "the individual" possible. This would be equally true of an exclusively biographical approach to ethnography, although most advocates of biography and autobiography in ethnography do not recommend them as exclusive sources of information.

Now "the individual" may seem, at first glance, the most "basic" unit of human life and society, especially to those of us accustomed to a considerable degree of "individualism" in our personal lives in our Western, industrial, home societies, noting of course that "society," like culture, is also a reified concept. And while the individual in Western societies, which of course are not all the same, does have considerable freedom of movement and decision and does not usually share a destiny with others by virtue of being a member of a corporate group, I would be reluctant to say that the individual is the "basic unit" of society, or, perhaps better, of the social milieu. The reason for this is that the freedom of the individual in Western societies depends upon the security, constraint, and support given by powerful, overarching institutions, such as governments with their bureaucracies, courts, and enforcing agents, industrial production and distribution systems, educational institutions, transport and communication networks, and so on. Individuals are free not because they are "basic," but because social, economic, and spatial flexibility and mobility—in short, "freedom"—are required for an industrial system to function successfully.

For similar reasons, it makes no more sense to identify one particular collective entity at one level of organization, such as the family or the local community, as the "basic unit" of society. In all people's lives, different situations and moments call into play social ties of a lesser or greater range as well as signal reliance upon conceptual and emotive orientations that range from idiosyncratic to those shared locally, supralocally, and even beyond on a vast scale. So to my mind the important thing is to identify all of the levels of engagement relevant to the lives of people and to specify the particular circumstances under which different levels become relevant, rather than erroneously granting privileged status to one entity, whether "individual," "family," "community," "tribe," "ethnic group," or "civilization." The notion of "basic unit of society" obscures rather than advances these goals and so should not be used as a guide for identifying a focus for an ethnographic account. Starting a description with a particular kind of social group does not mean that that type of group is more basic than the others, both more and less inclusive, which must also be described.

But we must start somewhere, even if we recognize that the starting point is arbitrary and that the social entity serving as the entrée to our account is not more important than others that together with it serve as the framework of social life. The particular point of entry is perhaps more a matter of convenience than anything else. We will begin "meeting people" as members of a camp, a residential community of black tents, focusing on the camp of Ja'far, as it existed in the winter of 1967–68 and over the next 10 years. This was the community in which I lived for most of my stay in the Sarhad and that was the focus of my collection of information.

From November 1967 to late February 1968, this camp, the Ja'fari Halk, was located in south-central Pushti Kamal, in the center of the Sarhad plateau. The camp consisted of 14 tents and had a population of 26 adults and 17 children, a total of 43, although some were away from camp for extended periods. Let me begin with a brief introduction to a few of the individuals who are important in the narrative to follow:

Ja'far was the most politically senior, *master,* man of the camp and as such was headman. Probably around 40 in 1967, he had a half-dozen, mostly young, children and a flock of livestock that was a good size by local standards. Ja'far, a dignified man with a pleasant expression, was our official host in the camp. He was a thoughtful, even-tempered, gracious individual, who enjoyed the company of others, liked a quiet laugh, and was perceptive about people. Monas, married to Ja'far, was an attractive, dignified woman in her early 30s, with a half-dozen lovely and lively children. She was gracious and gentle, combining these characteristics with a high competence in household matters. Monas was always ready to step in and help whenever we had a household problem, and we depended upon her in numerous ways, not least for the daily baking of our bread. Id Mahmud had a few years before our arrival married Monas and Ja'far's daughter Bibi Nur, making him their son-in-law. Ghulam Mah-

Figure 2.1. Ja'far, headman of the Dadolzai camping group with which the author resided, 1968. (Photograph by author)

MUD, the son of Ja'far's dead brother, was raised by Ja'far and Monas and in 1970 married their second eldest daughter, GOL PERI.

GULAP was in 1967–68 a retired elder in his 60s or beyond with failing capabilities, no longer active. He had fathered four children who had lived to adulthood and who themselves had produced or were soon to produce children. Gulap died before our return to the Sarhad in 1972. ZARBONU, Gulap's wife and mother of the four children, looked frail and worn, but was active, effective, and still as sharp as a tack. She proved to be a good friend and helpful informant. In 1972–73 Zarbonu generously loaned us her tent and moved in with SHAMS A'DIN, her youngest son, who was my closest friend and an ongoing informant. In his mid-20s when we first arrived, recently married and without children, Shams A'din was an energetic and pleasant individual, ready and able to pitch in and help his fellows, and us as well. Shams A'din was married to SAZIEN, daughter of IDO (or AIDO), the brother of Zarbonu and the shepherd of the camp during the 1970s. The eldest son of Zarbonu and Gulap was MAHMUD KARIM,

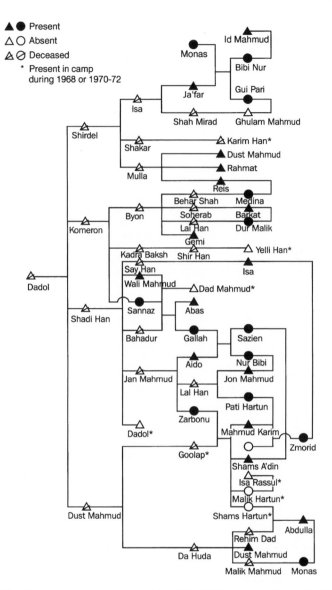

Figure 2.2. Close kin ties among members of the Ja'far-i Halk, 1972–73. Part A. Dadolzai members.

who was a decade older than Shams A'din, and recently married in 1967 to PATI HAR-
TUN, sister of GAM DAD (by the time of our return in 1972 called by his adult name
JAN MAHMUD), after having earlier divorced his first wife. Both SHAMS HARTUN and
MALIK HARTUN, the elder and younger daughters of Zarbonu and Gulap, lived in
camp in 1967–68, the twice-widowed Shams Hartun with her children, ABDULUK and

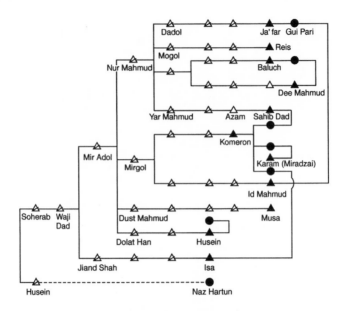

Figure 2.3. Close kin ties among members of the Ja'far-i Halk, 1972–73. Part B. Non-Dadolzai members.

ALUK, and Malik Hartun with her young husband ISA (son of) RASUL. By 1972, Shams Hartun had remarried and was living in Zahedan, the provincial capital, with her husband, although her children remained in the camp. And in 1972 Isa Rasul moved with Malik Hartun and their children to a camp of his kinsmen.

All of the people mentioned so far were members of the patrilineage Dadolzai, the descendants of Dadol, with the exception of Monas, Id Mahmud, and Isa Rasul. Ja'far and his children belonged to the Dadolzai sublineage Shirdelzai, while Gulap and his children belonged to the sublineage Dust Mahmudzai, and Zarbonu and Ido belonged to the sublineage Shadi Hanzai. Monas came from a different tribal group, Isa Rasul from a different section of the Yarahmadzai tribe, and Id Mahmud from the same Soherabzai section of the Yarahmadzai as the Dadolzai.

YELLI HAN, of the Komeronzai sublineage of the Dadolzai, and his wife ZAR MALIK, the sister of Monas, lived in the camp when we were there in 1967–68 but lived elsewhere in 1972–73 and 1976. KARIM HAN of the Shirdelzai, a poor man who had no livestock, was a member of the camp during the 1967–68 year, but had died before we returned in 1972. REIS, DUST MAHMUD, and RAHMAT, all sons of Mulla of the Shirdelzai and thus close cousins of Ja'far, joined the camp in 1972–73. They had larger than average herds and were strongly livestock-oriented. DUST MAHMUD (son of) Da Huda, of the Dust Mahmudzai sublineage, a poor man in late middle age who was not very capable, lived on and off in the camp, sometimes working as a substitute shepherd, but also spent some time away working as a shepherd for another camp.

In 1967–68 the strongest non-Dadolzai contingent of the camp consisted of PATI MAHMUD and three other members of the Mehimzai, MORUD, NAWAB, and HEROLA. Pati Mahmud, in middle age in 1967, with both grown and young children, was both bright and devious, and not a very trustworthy person. In 1972 the strongest non-Dadolzai contingent was KOMERON of the Mirgolzai and his three sons-in-law: SAHIB DAD, KARAM, and ISA. Komeron was a very exacting herd owner and tended to demand a lot from his fellow herd owners and to lean hard on shepherds.

Quite a bit more about these individuals will be presented as the account proceeds, for they were the people I lived with, conversed with, and observed on a daily basis. Many of the "examples" of aspects of Sarhadi life and the "cases" of activities and events come from their lives.

## CONSTITUTING A CAMP

Many things happened in a camp, and a camp was many things to its members. But the formal constitution of a camp, *halk,* was based upon an annual herding contract, *karar,* thus making a camping group, in an official sense, a herding group. The contract was made between all livestock owners, *wasildar* (*wasil* = property, livestock; suffix *dar* = owner or "head" of), or those representing them, and a shepherd, *shwaneg,* for the herding of the collective flock of small stock, *pas,* goats and sheep, for one year, spelling out terms of work and payment. There was, as a matter of principle, one flock only per camp; in a formal sense, a camp was an epiphenomenon and the human manifestation of a flock of *pas.*

The making of an annual herding contract took a lot of thought and often considerable negotiation, not only between the herd owners and the shepherd, but among the herd owners themselves. Discussion, debate, and negotiation often went on for the several months leading up to the herding agreement. There were many factors to consider.

One important constraining factor was the total number of *pas,* sheep and goats, in the camp herd. If there was too large a concentration of *pas,* pasture and water in a given area would not sustain the animals for very long, and too much movement would be required for the herd, which would wear down the animals, and more frequent migration of the camp would be required, which would wear down the human members of the camp. This placed an upper limit on the number of *pas* it was desirable to have in the herd in a given year, depending upon the environmental conditions that year. At the same time, there was a lower limit of number of *pas* in a camp herd, because with too few, the animals would feel insecure and not graze, and because the shepherd either had to take lower pay, which made it difficult to find a good shepherd, *shwaneg,* or the cost per animal of the shepherd increased for the *pas*-owning employers, *wasildar,* and thus reduced income.

A second factor was labor. There had to be enough active adult men and women in camp to carry out the various tasks likely to arise, such as cleaning wells, searching for lost animals, and the heavy packing associated with migration.

A third factor was security. There had to be men in the camp, not only to oversee the herds, but to supervise the women and children, who were not to be left alone without protection. This consideration had to take into account traditional activities that drew men away from camp, such as pollinating the date palms in the spring, working on the limited grain cultivation, going to market or mill, and, in the past, predatory raiding, and more recent activities, such as smuggling, trading (i.e., physically importing goods in bulk for sale, usually in an urban market), and migrant labor outside of the tribal territory.

A fourth factor was cooperation. With repeated decisions being made about herding and migration, decisions that bore directly upon the movement and location of the community itself, as well as upon the welfare of a major economic resource, the herds, the human constitution of the group and the procedures for decisionmaking had to facilitate collective agreement or compromise. The alternative to satisfactory collective decisions, in a collectivity of mobile, economically independent households, was not inaction, which would have led to the economic loss of productivity and of capital resources, but fission, the splitting of the group. And this would have had detrimental side effects, for whatever balance had been established in herd size, labor resources, and security provision in the *halk* as a whole would have been reduced or lost as tents left or the camp fissioned.

With these considerations in mind, male household heads in the deserts and mountains of the Sarhad had to take on the role of *wasildar*, livestock owner, or, more precisely, the individual with prime responsibly for the household flock. As *wasildar*, a man had to associate and cooperate with other *wasildar* in the management of the collective flock of the camp, and, as employer, had also to hire and work with a *shwaneg*. Being a *wasildar* meant controlling capital wealth in livestock, wealth that had the potential for expanding through the reproduction of the animals. And having this animal wealth meant having products that could be allocated to human consumption and thus to the support of oneself and one's family. Consequently, the more production one had, the more one could draw on livestock products to advance the economic self-sufficiency and independence of oneself and one's family.

Being a *wasildar*, or a *maldar* (*mal* = property in general, but also livestock; suffix *dar* = owner of) as Baluch sometimes say, was more than just a role to be played, an activity that had to be carried out. Being a livestock owner, a *wasildar* or *maldar*, was one of the ways that tent-dwelling Baluch thought of and defined themselves. In other words, being a livestock owner was one of the strands that was woven into the complex tapestry of Baluchi identity. However, it is worth noting at the outset that, just as Baluchi weavings vary one from another as more natural color or more dyed yarns are used, as floating weft designs are incorporated more freely or more sparingly, as shapes are repeated or varied, so too the overall pattern of Baluchi identity changed through space and time as some elements became more pronounced and others less, and even as some elements became dominant as others became minor and marginal.

So far, I have been using the word "Baluch" as a proper name. It was used as a proper name in a number of ways. It was a formal political term of the state of Iran, used as the name of the province of Iran: the Province of Sistan and Baluchistan. Sistan was a geographically, historically, and ethnically distinct region north of the provincial capital of Zahedan. Baluchistan, which made up the rest of the province, meant "the land of the Baluch" (suffix *istan* = "the land of"). "Baluch" was also occasionally used as a proper name for individuals, who were called "Baluch" the way others were called "Nur Bibi" or "Mahmud." The term also entered into local usage as an ethnic category, to distinguish "Baluch" from "Persians." Several criteria marked the boundary between Baluch and the Persians in Baluchistan: language (Baluchi versus Persian); religion (Sunni versus Shi'a Islam); habitation (nomadic camp dwellers versus sedentary village and town dwellers); dress (loose, flowing clothes versus tighter clothes); and affinity to the wider Iranian society (minimal for the Baluch versus substantial for the Persians). All of these criteria did not work in all cases—some Baluch were traditionally oasis dwellers and some had switched from tents to stable dwellings, and a minority of Baluch were Shi'a—but there are sufficient elements of difference to make the boundary quite clear in particular cases. Sometimes, especially when they were away from home in towns or cities of Iran, or Pakistan, or the Persian/Arabian Gulf Emirates, tent dwellers of the Sarhad thought of themselves as Baluch in the broad ethnic sense, in contrast to Persians, Sindis, Punjabis, Pathans, Arabs, and so on.

However, the word *baluch*, of long-standing use in Baluchistan, represented not so much an ethnic category as a social category, defined by criteria of occupation, affiliation, and way of life. In conventional usage, *baluch* meant a nomadic, tent-dwelling, livestock-herding, rainfall-runoff micro-cultivating, lineage-affiliated inhabitant of the desert and mountain. This concept *baluch* was contrasted with *shahri*, sedentary, hut-dwelling, irrigation cultivators who lived in oases, and with *hakomzat*, members of the ruling class, as well as with *ghulam*, slaves. On the high plains of the Sarhad, there were descendants of *ghulam*, the Ghulamzai (suffix *zai* = descendants of), but no oases and no *shahri* or *hakomzat*. However, as was well known to the desert dwellers, in the nearby mountain chain of Daptani Kuh (Persian: Kuh-i Taftan), there was a Kordish *hakom* and *hakomzat*, and agriculturalists who were considered *shahri*. And, as was also well known, to the south of the Sarhad, in Saravan, and in the regions beyond, the many oases were cultivated by *shahri* and ruled by *hakim*.

Returning now to the constitution of the camping group, *halk*, we may note that the contractual and short-term nature of *halk* formation allowed careful consideration of the constraints mentioned above in constituting and reconstituting the group.

Each and every year, prior to a new, annual, contractual agreement between *wasildar* and *shwaneg*, camp residents reviewed previous years and anticipated the coming year, in order to consider factors relevant to decisions shaping the new contract. Which combinations of what size household herds would form a good camp herd? What activity commitments were likely to conflict with what others? Who would be available for what tasks and who would have to be covered for? And who would get along together and who not? As a result of these various calculations, certain sets of *wasildar* were seen as forming a more viable *halk* than other sets. Various measures were taken, explicitly and implicitly, actively and passively, by the people involved to put together a viable set of *wasildar*.

The herd owners, *wasildar*, were through the herding contract bound together as coresidents during the year term. Although from a formal standpoint the herding aspect had primacy over the residence aspect of the *halk*, and although the interests of the residents as *wasildar* were weighed heavily, the residential dimension was extremely important, for both short-term and long-term reasons. Who one resided with involved much more than the size of the camp herd and the number of active adult men and women in the camp to assist in heavy labor. It involved, in the short term, trust in people who had access to one's family and property, and dependence upon people in the face of ordinary and extraordinary obstacles that would arise during the course of daily life and the biological cycle. It involved, in the long run, ties built upon exchange, generalized and other, that defined, to a degree, personal obligations.

The camp was the center of the social universe for a resident, and so the importance of the *halk* was greater than the undeniably major interests of the *wasildar* in his *pas*. There were thus more general social constraints in *halk* formation. People preferred to reside with those with whom they had long-term commitments and in whom they had long-term interests. And this fed back to the short-term interests as well, for insofar as coresidence ties were part of broader multiplex relationships, dependability and thus trust were increased.

## MULTIPLEX RELATIONS

The camp, *halk*, once constituted, became a residential community, in that all *wasildar* "signatories" to the herding contract had their tents in the camp, for, if they did not, they would have been cut off from their livestock and would have had no access to the products of their livestock. The camp was a community in that all of its members knew each other individually. Within this community, the members had, to a greater or lesser extent, multiplex ties; that is, the ties among camp members were based upon several or many different roles and relationships. In other words, relationships were not defined and organized in terms of one kind of activity or one type of motivation. Rather, two people related to one another according to one set of concerns and norms at one moment, and another set of concerns and norms at another. To serve as an example, let us look at two members of the Halki Ja'far who had a thickly stratified layer of multiplex ties: Shams A'din and Ido.

Shams A'din—the name (usually transcribed from Persian or Arabic texts as Shams ad-Din or Shamsu'l-din) means "sun of religion"—was, in early 1968 when I met him for the first time, in his mid-20s (he did not know his age exactly) and recently married, but so far without children. At the time, I too was close to his age, about to be 28, and was recently married, without children. Shams A'din, around 1.7 meters (5 feet, 5 inches), average for these Baluch, and about my height too, and naturally muscular, with an open, friendly facial expression, was an active young man energetic in his work and always willing to pitch in helping others.

Shams A'din also knew some elementary Persian, which in the initial stages of my research made it easier for me to converse with him than with others who knew only Baluchi or Urdu, the latter from travels and perhaps work in Pakistan. Quite early, but after a brief period when members of the camp, Shams A'din included, had a bit of time to "feel us out," to see what we would act like and what kind of people we seemed to be, Shams A'din became a regular informant and an informal assistant helping me, as he helped other members of the community with their tasks, in understanding what was going on, by translating what other people said in Baluchi and by explaining what, in his view, was happening. He quickly became my closest friend in Baluchistan and remained so during my subsequent field trips, and I continue to think of him warmly and wish we had the opportunity to meet again.

One of the reasons that I was accepted as readily as I was into the Ja'fari Halk and was welcomed as a resident and as a visitor in people's tents, that is, their homes, was that I was not an unrestrained male stranger, an obvious potential sexual threat to the honor of the women and consequently the men and the entire community. On the contrary, while I was a stranger and an adult male, and, although I did not publicize the fact, was quite attracted to women and found Baluchi women very appealing, I was, in Baluchi eyes, not unrestrained because I was accompanied by my wife. The fact that Joan and I were together, spent time together, and were obviously attached to one another, and that we had our own household, made me appear domesticated to the Baluch, restrained by the marital tie and ordered by domestic life, and thus somewhat less a sexual threat to Baluchi women. I had anticipated that Joan's presence would be very important for me for reasons of companionship. But I had not very clearly appreciated how much I would depend upon her for new and arduous forms of domestic labor, such as bringing water from the well, cooking on a kerosene stove, and hand washing clothes, that freed me to carry out my research. Nor had I appreciated how much her presence would legitimize me in the eyes of the Baluch, gaining me freer access to Baluchi homes and to Baluch, male and female, as informants.

During fieldwork in 1968 and 1972–73, Joan was with me, and we maintained a separate tent and domestic establishment. In 1976, I came to the Sarhad without Joan and stayed with Shams A'din and his family as a guest in their tent. The day after my arrival, Shams A'din said that he had something to discuss with me and suggested that we go for a walk. As we were walking, not far from camp, he said that he regarded me as a great friend, and he wanted me to know that he was very happy that I was staying with him and that everything he had was mine. Everything, that is, but one: his wife, Sazien. She was forbidden to me. I replied that I understood and agreed completely. And, drawing on Baluchi extended kin terminology, I said that as far as I was concerned, Sazien was my sister, *gohar*, and so there was no question of any sexual interference on my part. Confidence in me as a sexually safe coresident depended upon credit built up during previous trips; but this time, without the restraint of a wife's presence, even my closest friends were a bit nervous and did not want me hanging around with womenfolk, *jeni adam*.

Ido (or Aido), in 1972–73, when I first shared a residence with him in the camp of Ja'far, for he had been living in another camp in 1968, was in his late 40s, compact in body but a bit worn, grizzled with a lined face. He was what one might call a professional shepherd, for he had worked as a shepherd on and off throughout his adult life. In 1968, he had been a shepherd for another camp, which is why he had not been resident in the camp of Ja'far. I did, however, meet him, for he was Shams A'din's father-in-law. When the recently married Shams A'din and his wife had a fight because she would not bring Shams A'din something when he asked, he slapped her. She then left and returned to her father's, Ido's, tent, located conveniently at that moment in an adjacent locale. Shams A'din asked me to act as intermediary, *wasta*, to intervene on his behalf, to apologize and ask for Sazien to return—a task for which I felt ill-equipped and carried out awkwardly, probably generating as much mirth as reconciliation. Sazien did return to Shams A'din, and thereafter Shams A'din showed a bit more patience and forbearance. Ido himself had rejoined the camp of Ja'far around 1970 and had taken on the job of *shwaneg* of the camp herd, and continued as shepherd at least through 1976, when I was last there.

What, then, were the multiple relationships between Shams A'din and Ido?

Once Ido had returned to the camp of Ja'far, Ido and Shams A'din became once again *coresidents*, or fellow community members. Their tents were thus spatially close by and they would have run into each other frequently, often several or more times a day. Campwide activities would involve both of them, as both decisionmakers and actors. For example, migration of the camp from one place to another involved both of them in a decisionmaking process to determine the timing and goal of migration and each of them in moving their tent and goods. As representatives of independent households, each had a say, and the views of each had to be considered in the final decision about whether and when and where to migrate.

When there was a prayer leader, as there was during parts of 1972–73, men from the community prayed together, in unison, as is recommended, for in Islam praying as a member of the community of believers is preferable to praying alone and received strong approbation. Those praying together, which would sometimes include Shams A'din and Ido, were *co-congregationalists*, sharing the experience of devotion.

Both Ido and Shams A'din were members of the Dadolzai descent group, the descendants of Dadol, Dadol being the apical ancestor from whom they traced common descent, and were thus *lineage mates*. The Dadolzai was a descent group, *rend*, which considered itself a functioning, corporate, support group, *brasrend*, in which members were obliged to come to the aid of one another, whether in conflict or in other material need. Ido and Shams A'din thus had an obligation to assist each other and a common obligation to help other Dadolzai. One criterion by which a *brasrend* was judged was whether its members were solidary, *topak*, standing together and supporting each other. By virtue of the values they held, Ido and Shams A'din were obliged to be solidary.

Ido was older than Shams A'din, and by reckoning from the present generation, but not by descent, was in the ascending generation from Shams A'din's. Ido was thus senior, *master*, to Shams A'din, and Shams A'din was junior to Ido. This meant that Shams A'din owed Ido respect by virtue of *seniority*.

Ido was not only Shams A'din's father's father's brother's son's son, making Ido and Shams A'din descendants of a common great grandfather, Dadol, and thus lineage mates, as indicated above. At the same time, Ido was Shams A'din's mother's brother, making the Ido and Shams A'din closer kin through this matrilateral tie than through the more distant patrilineal tie. The *mother's brother/sister's son tie* is a relationship of presumed closeness, emphasizing relaxed nurturing rather than authority.

Shams A'din was married to Sazien, Ido's daughter. Another way to put this was that Ido gave his daughter, Sazien, to Shams A'din in marriage. However, by emphasizing Ido as father here, I do not want to give an incorrect impression. In general, mothers had a great deal of say about who their children would marry. Decisions about betrothals were usually taken jointly by the parents. Shams A'din and Ido were thus *son-in-law/father-in-law*. This is a relationship requiring some formality, distance, and delicateness. Both the parents and husband had interests, obligations, and rights in the daughter/wife, and she had rights, obligations, and interests in relation to both her husband and her parents.

Ido and Shams A'din were, along with a half dozen or so others, members of an informal work "team," sharing labor with one another to increase the efficiency of the multifarious tasks that needed to be done. Some tasks of one individual, such as searching for a lost sheep, benefited from the help of many people, each of whom could go in a different direction. Other tasks for a number of individuals, such as transporting grain to a mill, could be done by one person, thus saving the others the time and effort. Shams A'din and Ido were thus *coworkers*, repeatedly cooperating in various work tasks.

Shams A'din and Ido were *coemployers,* along with five other camp residents, of a camel herder, *bakjat (bak* = camel herd), one of the young sons of another man in the group. Together with the other employers, they had to instruct, supervise, and compensate the *bakjat* and make decisions about subsequent contracts.

From the time that Shams A'din was married, set up an independent household, and had his own household flock, he was a *wasildar,* livestock owner and *employer* of shepherds. When Ido became the *shwaneg,* shepherd, of the camp of Ja'far, he was an *employee* of Shams A'din, herding, caring for, and responsible for Shams A'din's *pas,* goats and sheep. Shams A'din, together with the other *wasildar,* had to instruct, supervise, and compensate Ido for his work.

Both men were affected by the activities of the same *female work team,* which included among other women Galla, who was Ido's wife and Shams A'din's mother-in-law; Sazien, who was Ido's daughter and Shams A'din's wife; and Nur Bibi, who was Ido's daughter and Shams A'din's sister-in-law.

Thus Shams A'din and Ido were, at the same time, coresidents, co-congregationalists, *brasrend* lineage mates, junior/senior, sister's son/mother's brother, son-in-law/father-in-law, coworkers, coemployers, and employer/employee and were affected by the same work team of women. Shams A'din's and Ido's relationship was, in this sense, very dense, with many layers and dimensions.

Let us take one more example to illustrate the many layers of multiplex relationships in the camp. Sazien, whose husband was Shams A'din and whose father was Ido, had multiple ties with, among others, Pati Hartun.

Sazien and Pati Hartun were members of the same *brasrend,* the Dadolzai. And they were members of a smaller segment, the Shadi Hanzai, Shadi Han having been one of the four sons of Dadol. As well, they were members of an even smaller segment, the Jan Mahmudzai, Jan Mahmud being one of five sons of Shadi Han. Patrilineally, they were descendants of Jan Mahmud, who was the grandfather of both of them, through two of Jan Mahmud's sons, Lal Han and Ido. This made them *lineage mates,* close patrikin, with strong obligations of solidarity, *topak,* and mutual assistance, *kumak.*

Sazien and Pati Hartun were, patrilaterally, *fathers' brothers' daughters,* that is, patrilateral first cousins. As such, both were members of families unified by the solidarity of siblings. Each had the other's father as father's brother.

Sazien and Pati Hartun were, for considerable periods, *coresidents,* living in the same herding camp, both when they were growing up and later, when they were female heads of independent households.

Sazien and Pati Hartun became *sisters-in-law* two different ways. Sazien's sister, Nur Bibi, married Pati Hartun's brother, Jan Mahmud, who was named after his grandfather. And Sazien and Pati Hartun married two brothers, Shams A'din and Mahmud Karim, respectively. So the two cousins became, through marriage, sisters.

Sazien and Pati Hartun were also *coworkers,* members of an informal, work "team," in which a half-dozen women shared and divided tasks, such as getting water from well or stream, washing clothes at a distant water source, cleaning goat hair, cooking for feasts, and the like.

The two women were, somewhat less directly, implicated in the *cooperation of their husbands* and, in the case of Sazien, her father Ido, and, in the case of Pati Hartun, her brother Jan Mahmud, whether in their work team, camel herding, *pas* herding, or defending the lineage. What their close male relatives did in their activities affected each of them and the other. Nor were they without opinion about such matters, or always hesitant to express themselves, especially to their husbands, about any issues that might arise and decisions to be taken.

Sazien and Pati Hartun were thus lineage mates, close cousins, coresidents, sisters-in-law, and coworkers, and both were affected by the same work team of men.

In the multiplex ties of Ido and Shams A'din, and of Sazien and Pati Hartun, each specific relation, as set out above, had its own norms and pressures, but each existed in a complex setting of the totality of relations, along with numerous other ties, each with its norms and pressures. Perhaps a tapestry would be a more apt metaphor than stratigraphy, for each relation does not exist in a layer separate and discrete from the others, but is woven around and through the others, and the total effect is the result of the interplay among all of the different "colors" and all of the combinations and patterns that they make.

Some relations between Ido and Shams A'din were hierarchical, such as Ido's being *master*, senior, to Shams A'din, and being Shams A'din's mother's brother, or Shams A'din being Ido's *wasildar* employer. In other cases, Shams A'din and Ido collaborated as equals, as in being lineage mates, co-congregationalists, and informal coworkers. Some ties promoted intimacy, such as mother's brother's/sister's son, lineage mates, and coworkers, while others required distance, as in *wasildar* employer/*shwaneg* employee, and father-in-law/son-in-law. Their entire complex of ties could not in practice be easily disaggregated, and so interaction on one level, in regard to one relation and its set of roles, was always colored to a greater or lesser degree by the other relations and roles. One problem that arose for each actor was how the expectations and demands, satisfactions and stresses of one relation affected the other relations in the dense, multiplex tie with the other.

For Sazien and Pati Hartun, too, the interplay among lineage, kin, affinal ties, residential membership, their work ties and their male relatives' work ties, had to be managed. Did stresses in their work relations affect the work relations of their male kin? Did severing of employer/employee ties lead to change in coresidential status? How much adjustment of expectation in one relation would be justifiable in terms of the overall multiplex tie?

The many layers of relationship of Shams A'din and Ido and of Sazien and Pati Hartun did not come all at once, in a package, but rather accumulated over time. Some were permanent and immutable while others were voluntary and changeable. For example, lineage membership based upon descent and patri- and matrilateral kin ties were given and unchangeable. These ties, which to a degree were open to interpretation and negotiation by individuals as regards substantive content, were also recognized, defined, and responded to by the broader public. Other relationships, such as marriage and the affinal ties that flowed from these, were not strictly immutable and were occasionally broken, but for the most part were maintained over the long run. Residence, cooperation in work, and employment were formally short-term, based upon contracts of limited duration. But even these, with their built-in opportunities for change, often exhibited, at least for a number of individuals, considerable continuity.

The social relations between individual camp members reflected decisions taken by individuals, for a variety of reasons, which resulted in denser or thinner ties. The decision to live with or not to live with one's lineage mates, to marry with close or distant kin, to work with kinsmen or affines, or neither, resulted in either a tendency toward accumulation of ties with a particular set of individuals or a dispersal of ties more widely.

Sarhadi herding camps were not homogeneous entities. There were larger and smaller knots of dense social relations, and the ties between the knots were often shallow. This social landscape was manifested spatially, in the layout and distribution of tents in the camp, and in the presence and absence of tents in the camp over time. In the layout of camps, the proximity of tents was a sign of social closeness, while the distance of tents was a sign of social distance.

## SOCIAL RELATIONS AND SPATIAL ARRANGEMENTS

The nomadic mobility of Sarhadi camping groups, the movement of the camps from one site to another, is described in detail in chapter 7. These changes of site, commonly a dozen times a year, required the establishment, after each move, of a spatial arrangement of the tents that made up the camp. Consequently, each migration to a new site provided an opportunity for reaffirming the previous spatial order and arrangement of tents in relation to one another or for initiating a change and readjustment into a new spatial arrangement of tents. As the spatial propinquity of tents was conventionally deemed in Sarhadi society to reflect social closeness, reaffirmation or readjustment of spatial relations was taken to be one index of social relations among particular individuals and families.

Examining the spatial arrangements of tents of the Ja'fari Halk at 14 sites—7 during the period January–June 1968, 6 during the period from October 1972 through July 1973 (Salzman 1992:90–102), and 1 during the spring of 1976—we can identify repetition and change in the spatial arrangements and also the underlying patterns that are reflected in both.

## Lineage Mates, Kinsmen, and Affines

There was a strong tendency for individuals bound by common descent to cluster together. During 1967, the only two members of the Shirdelzai sub- or microlineage of the Dadolzai, Ja'far and Karim Han, tended to have their tents close by, even though the two men had little in common as individuals, Ja'far being relatively well-to-do and the leader of the camp, in short, successful and influential, Karim Han being quite poor and without great weight.

At some sites, however, although Ja'far's tent and Karim Han's tents were nearby, the tent of Yelli Han of the Komeronzai sublineage was closer to Ja'far's, sometimes interposed between the other two tents. Why was a Komeronzai separating two Shirdelzai? The answer is that the location of Yelli Han's tent was not a result of his or Ja'-far's microlineage affiliation, but rather of the relationship of Monas and Zar Malik, respectively, Ja'far's and Yelli Han's wives, but also sisters, and, as Ganguzai, foreigners to the Yarahmadzai to which most everyone else belonged. So here it was the kin ties between women that determined the spatial arrangement. In this case, it is worth noting, Yelli Han was the only member of the Komeronzai sublineage and so himself was not pulled in another direction by the presence of his sublineage mates, which would have created a contrary attraction to that of his wife toward her kin.

Five years later, Karim Han had died and Yelli Han and Zar Malik were living elsewhere. But three other members of the Shirdelzai—Reis, Rahmat, and Dust Mahmud—were sometime members of the camp, and they were always spatially closest to Ja'far in a compact cluster, usually a line of tents. In this way, the Shirdelzai of the camp—some of them brothers, others cousins—expressed their solidarity.

Together with these Shirdelzai in every instance was Id Mahmud, a Mir Golzai who by descent was moderately distant from all of the Dadolzai. Id Mahmud's presence was a result of his affinal tie to Ja'far: he had married Ja'far's daughter Bibi Nur and was thus son-in-law to the Dadolzai and the Shirdelzai in general, and of course Ja'far in particular. The presence of a son-in-law's tent adjacent to that of his parents-in-law is often in the Sarhad a temporary arrangement resulting from the continuing dependence of a young wife on her mother and family. In this case as in the others, the tie of Id Mahmud's wife to her family was important, but in addition Id Mahmud, whose father was deceased and who had no brothers, and who did not get along with his uncles, attached himself to Ja'far, treating him rather as a surrogate father, and planned to remain with him and the Dadolzai.

The tendency for microlineage mates to cluster could also be seen among the Dust Mahmudzai sublineage of the Dadolzai. The core members of the Dust Mahmudzai cluster were Gulap and Zarbonu and their children, Mahmud Karim, Shams Hartun, Shams A'din, and a cousin, Dust Mahmud, and they would always place their tents next to one another. There were three other tents that, when part of this camp, always clustered with the Dust Mahmudzai.

One was that of Gam Dad, the Shadi Hanzai Dadolzai young man, later known as Jan Mahmud, and his mother, whose sister/daughter, Pati Hartun, was married to Mahmud Karim. So the kin tie to Pati Hartun and affinal tie to Mahmud Karim brought this tent to the Dust Mahmudzai, even when there were occasionally other Shadi Hanzai present. Jan Mahmud's presence with the Dust Mahmudzai tended to pull the other Shadi Hanzai, such as Dad Mahmud during spring and summer 1968, spatially close to the Dust Mahmudzai. But as well there were many close kin and affinal ties between the Dust Mahmudzai and Shadi Hanzai, so their social and thus spatial closeness was "natural."

The second tent was that of Isa Rasul, of the distant Rahmatzai section of the Yarahmadzai, who was married to Gulap and Zarbonu's daughter Malik Hartun and was thus son-in-law to the Dust Mahmudzai, as well as the Dadolzai in general.

Finally, there was the tent of Husein of the Dolat Hanzai Yarahmadzai, whose wife Gol Sim was matrikin to and a friend of Zarbonu.

During 1972 and 1973, more tents of the Shadi Hanzai joined the Ja'fari Halk, including those of Ido, Abas, Walli Mahmud, and Isa. With so many Shadi Hanzai lineage mates present, where did Jan Mahmud place his tent? At some locations, when the Dust Mahmudzai and Shadi Hanzai were close by one another, Jan Mahmud was able to place his tent between that of his sister and Mahmud Karim, on one side, and the tent of his Shadi Hanzai father-in-law Ido and his other lineage mates, on the other. But at the sites that saw the Dust Mahmudzai and Shadi Hanzai somewhat separate, Jan Mahmud now gravitated to the Shadi Hanzai. The pull of his wife's parents and his own Shadi Hanzai lineage mates was greater than that of his and his mother's desire to be near their sister/daughter. Another factor was that previously Jan Mahmud had depended upon his older and more experienced Dust Mahmudzai brothers-in-law to guide and assist him, but as he became older and had his own senior in-laws and other lineage mates to count on, he was no longer tied so strongly by practical concerns to the Dust Mahmudzai.

During this same time that Jan Mahmud was shifting the location of his tent from his brothers-in-law of the Dust Mahmudzai to his parents-in-law and lineage mates of the Shadi Hanzai, the tent of the young Shadi Hanzai Isa was pulled spatially away from his Shadi Hanzai lineage mates into the orbit of the Dust Mahmudzai. For Isa had married Zmorid, the daughter of Mahmud Karim, and from then on placed his tent next to that of his father-in-law, joining, in effect, the Dust Mahmudzai cluster. Of course, as the Dust Mahmudzai and Shadi Hanzai tended to set up their tents close together, those with very strong ties in both groups, such as Isa and Jan Mahmud, had the opportunity to place their tents between and thus close to members of both sub-lineages, and thus to exhibit their ongoing ties with both groups.

Camp members from lineages other than the Dadolzai also tended to cluster. During the 1967–68 period, there were usually three or four tents of members of the Mehimzai, of which Pati Mahmud was the most senior. These tents were always located in a cluster at one or the other end of the camp, usually at the opposite end from Ja'far, but never in the middle of the camp. This location at the far end, away from the camp *master*, headman, indicated a degree of marginality. The same spatial arrangement could be seen during the fall and winter of 1972–73 with Komeron of the Mirgolzai and his sons-in-law Sahib Dad and Karam.

In sum, social ties and solidarity drew people together in the spatial placement of their tents. As we have seen, tents often clustered because mature men tended to gravitate toward their closest lineage mates. Immature and young men, especially those lacking fathers and brothers, could be found located near their mature brothers-in-law. The tents of recently married men were often located next to their fathers-in-law, even though this sometimes placed the men far from their own lineages. These patterns must also be expressed looking at the same arrangements from the point of view of women. Thus the tents of girls recently married were commonly located next to their mothers', fathers', and/or brothers' tents. The tents of women who were close kin were sometimes adjacent, notwithstanding, in effect overriding, the lineage affiliation of their husbands. We can conclude that the placement of a tent at any camp site depended upon the conjunction of three main factors: the stage of family cycle; the particular lineage, kin, and affinal ties between the tent members and those of other tents; and the relation of the tent to the predominant lineage of the camp.

## The Camel Meat Incident: Conflict and the Spatial Arrangement of Tents

The possibility of changing the spatial propinquity of tents meant not only that people could move close to express solidarity, but also that people in conflict were not tied to one another spatially but could move apart and separate from one another. Here, as in other contexts among nomads, retreat, in the form of spatial rearrangement, was an attractive alternative to continued and intensified conflict.

We can see this in the spatial arrangements of the tents of Gemi and Barkat. Both members of the Komeronzai, Barkat and his wife Dur Malik were children of Gemi's brothers. During the fall and winter of 1972–73, they were the only members of the Komeronzai in the Ja'fari Halk, and their tents were adjacent at no less than three separate sites. Then an argument broke out.

On January 30, there was a lot of yelling in camp. Initially, this consisted of cursing between Gemi and Gol Sim, in the vicinity of Barkat's tent. Then Gol Sim moved across camp, back to her tent at the other end, continuing to yell all the time, and continuing for a half hour once she got back to her tent.

The problem arose over a portion of camel meat that was Barkat's and Dur Malik's share of a camel sacrificed for *tuhean aid*, the big religious festival of the year. This meat was somehow turned over by Dur Malik to Gol Sim. Gemi called Gol Sim a thief and a devil, and Gol Sim's mother and father the same, and Gol Sim responded in kind.

One version of the story was that Dur Malik was not feeling well one night and did not want to stay in her tent alone, so she went and stayed with Gol Sim. Gol Sim then took the opportunity to ask for camel meat, and Dur Malik gave it to her.

Another version of the story was that Dur Malik, who some characterized as a bit *harab,* messed up, in the head, could not stand to have fresh meat around, because it made her dizzy and upset. The share of meat that came to her for *aid* was too much for her to have in her tent. So she asked Gemi to keep it in his tent, to which he agreed. Later, she asked Gemi's wife Naz Hartun to get her a small piece of meat for herself and her children. But Dur Malik did not like the piece of meat that Naz Hartun brought and asked for another. Another was brought, but she did not like that one either. At this point, Gemi and Naz Hartun were so irritated that they said they would not keep the meat and put it outside of their tent. Then, Dur Malik, still not wanting to keep the meat in her tent, took it to Gol Sim to keep for her. Gol Sim agreed. Later, after Barkat returned to camp, Gol Sim brought the meat to Barkat's tent. It is then that Gol Sim and Gemi had their run-in, with Gemi, as well as cursing her, accusing her of speaking against him and his wife.

This exchange certainly got the attention of the camp. In fact, the yelling, especially after the disputants were so far apart that they could not hear one another, was really directed at the camp at large, that is, at public opinion. It was as if other people were being invited to join in the dispute. What usually happened was that someone would intervene to calm the disputants down and begin a process of reconciliation. After Gol Sim had sat in front of her tent yelling about the distant Gemi, Zarbonu went to her and quieted her down.

The reaction in the camp to this dispute was not primarily directed against Gol Sim, although it was widely thought that she was not a good person, but was rather a scrounger, and was perfectly capable of taking unfair advantage. I can attest that Gol Sim came around to our tent unusually frequently to ask for things. But mainly there was disapprobation of Gemi for making such a loud, unseemly display, for bringing a conflict into public, and for cursing a woman. The next day, January 31, Ja'far and several other men, including myself, were sitting around Ja'far's tent drinking tea and chatting. When Gemi came in, Ja'far said in a joking tone that the predatory *dal morg,* eagle, had arrived, and that from now on we would call him *dal morg* and not Gemi. After some repetitions of this theme, there was a mock tussle between these the two bearded elders, Ja'far and Gemi. Of course none of this was a joke. Ja'far was, in the nicest possible way, ridiculing Gemi's behavior by saying that Gemi had acted like a predatory bird in attacking Gol Sim, and telling him that his fellows disapproved. Ja'far was trying to shame Gami into more discrete behavior.

But Gemi was probably not the best student that Ja'far could have chosen to teach discrete behavior. Tall and gaunt, of grave demeanor, Gemi was nonetheless recognized as someone with a *sobaki del,* a light heart, who had to say everything he felt. It was much better, I was told, to have a *garoni del,* heavy heart, that could keep its feelings to itself. People with *sobaki del* were always in a *holikoni,* in a hurry, but life was not such that things could advance in a hurry. It is much better to wait, to be slow, I was told. It was deemed ill-mannered to rush about or to rush other people.

It was particularly undesirable for *kom,* kinsmen, to be having a public fight. This was deemed very unseemly and reflected badly on the Dadolzai as a whole. Good people did not fight with one another. Difficulties should be resolved through *wasta,* intermediaries. Gemi, I was told, should have gone to Ja'far, who was after all a *hamsaru* and *hamzat,* contemporary and elder, and complained to him. It was always better to resolve disputes indirectly rather than through noisy, unseemly, and counterproductive confrontations.

Furthermore, Gemi had violated a general principle of gender relations by arguing with a woman. Men should not argue and fight with women; it is unsuitable and inappropriate. One of the rationales for this prohibition, it was explained to me, was that women have less *yakl,* reason, than men. The implicit point of this argument seemed to be that men were lowering themselves if they argued with women.

(Now let me say immediately that this statement about women being less rational than men is not my personal viewpoint, but what my male Baluchi informants told me. By repeating this statement, I am not endorsing it; I am merely trying to inform readers about the statements of some Baluch. I would, however, like to make it clear that I refuse to take responsibility for the ideas of the Baluch. I mention this because my undergraduate students, especially my female students, always seem to think that if I report this cultural fact, I am announcing my personal concurrence. So I wish to be explicit that I am not advocating the view that women are less rational than men. I am merely trying to convey the understanding that in certain contexts Baluchi men will take this view, or at least make the statement.)

On further inquiry, in response to my probing questions, my informants admitted that some women did indeed have *yakl* and some men did not have *yakl,* and they were prepared to say that such and such a particular man from the camp was not very rational and that such and such a particular woman from the camp was indeed rational. But they still held the general principle to be true, as was its corollary, that men should not fight with women.

Two days after the original incident, Ja'far went to Gemi and told him he was in the wrong for making such a public display and for cursing, and convinced him to come alone with Ja'far to apologize to Gol Sim and to make peace. Gemi agreed and went along, and apologized. Ja'far gave little consideration to what Gol Sim had or had not said. As far as he was concerned, the important point was that a man must not fight with a *jani adam,* a woman—although, it was granted that a man could argue with his wife; marriage had some privileges after all. Ja'far said that he had to settle this dispute, because it was necessary to have peace in the camp. Otherwise,

Figure 2.4. Three women and a child, 1968. (Photograph by Joan David)

one or the other of the enemies would feel that he or she would have to leave the camp. But even after the peacemaking, Gol Sim could be heard complaining that Gemi was a *dal morg*.

After the next move of the camp on March 12, while setting up at Kamil Han Chah, Barkat pitched his tent at the opposite end of the camp from Gemi. Relations between Gemi's wife, Naz Hartun, and his wife, Dur Malik, had deteriorated after the camel meat incident, so Barkat said. Of course, Barkat may have been overcommunicating the conflict between the wives and undercommunicating tension between himself and Gemi, as a way of minimizing damage to his relationship with a close kinsman and micro–lineage mate. Barkat mentioned, among other things, that Naz Hartun had been complaining that he, Barkat, did not do his share of the grazing of the camels and *pas*, sheep and goats. Undoubtedly there were other issues, probably issues of long duration, between these two families. So Barkat decided that separation through spatial distancing of the two tents would avoid further disputes. This arrangement was maintained at later sites. Three years later, in 1976, Barkat's and

Gemi's tents remained separated, and their camels and lambs and kids were being herded separately.

Sarhadi tent dwellers, not being tied to particular locations, were able to adjust their spatial relations with others according to social exigencies. The spatial consequences of the camel meat incident exemplify the way that difficulties in social relationships could be managed by putting some distance between the conflicting parties. The reduction of interaction among those whose tents were separated reduced the occasions for disagreement, dispute, and conflict. The removal or reduction of tension arising from everyday interaction between the parties by means of spatial separation allowed other binding relationships between them, such as generalized mutual aid and collective responsibility among lineage mates, to be more easily maintained and respected.

## VARIATIONS IN SIZE OF CAMPING GROUPS

There was considerable variation in the size of camping groups in the Sarhad. Individual camping groups varied substantially over time and different camping groups differed in size. The usual range was from 1 to 20 tents. The overall average of 22 *halk* (not a systematic sample) was 6 tents.

In examining individual camping groups, it is clear that the size of camps was far from static over time; households left and joined camps every year, and sometimes more frequently, with a resulting variation in camp size over time. For example, the Azami Halk during the three years 1970–71, 1971–72, 1972–73 shifted from 5 tents to 9, to 4, and finally 3. Tents of the Ja'fari Halk were split in 1970–71 into two camps of 7 and 19, and combined into one camp of 13 with the others tents scattering; in 1971–72, formed a camp of 13, then 19, and finally 21; in 1972–73, began with 17, increased to 21, broke into two camps of 14 and 4, reunited in a camp of 21, and then shrunk to 16. This was not exceptional flux for a large camp. The same camp, during the six-month period of active migration in the winter, spring, and summer of 1967, changed size frequently; the numbers at each new migration site were 14, 18, 18, 22, 18, 17, 17. And the shift in personnel was greater than is reflected in the number of tents; for example, the continuity of size at the last two sites conceals a shift of 6 tents: 3 tents left and 3 new tents joined the camp.

There was not only variation over time in particular camps, but also variation over space. One geographical pattern that emerges from examination of the 22 cases is the difference between camping groups located in the mountains and those located on the plains. The mountain camps averaged 2.8 tents; the plains camps averaged 9.8 tents. Several factors jointly contributed to the difference in size between mountain and plains camps.

One factor was the ideal size of a herd (Swidler 1972). In general, the ideal size of a herd on the plains was larger than the ideal size of a herd in the mountains. On the plains, a herd could range more widely more quickly in search of pasturage than in the mountains, where terrain was a considerable constraint. Thus, on the plain, a larger herd could be more easily accommodated in the daily round with the shepherd than in the mountains. Of course, this assumes that other factors remained equal. A good year on the plains and a bad year in the mountains would have increased this differential; the reverse would have decreased it. Differences in ideal herd size would be reflected in different-sized camps insofar as camps were able to approach the ideal and insofar as each household herd was equal in size. In other words, with equal-sized household flocks, fewer tents were required to form a mountain camp with a small collective flock than were required to form a plains camp with a larger collective flock.

Here, however, is the second factor, for household herds were not equal; rather, they were larger in the mountain camps than in the plains camps. This contributed to the differential in camping group size, for fewer households were required to make up the ideal size herd. The average number of *pas,* sheep and goats, per household in the mountain camps was 39; the average number in plains camps was 17. This difference would suggest either that mountain camps were better off, had a higher standard of living, or that the plains camps were less dependent upon pastoralism for a livelihood. It is the latter that was the case: the plains camps, closer to towns and transportation routes, depended more than the mountain camps upon income from market activities, including migrant labor and smuggling. The mountain camps were more self-sufficient, producing directly more of the consumption goods they needed. But the plains camps had a higher total income, and a correspondingly higher material standard of living, as indicated by material possessions and regular consumption patterns.

This leads to a third factor: supervision and protection. Women, children, flocks, and property had to be supervised and protected when men left the camp for long periods of time during migrant labor or trading. This requirement led to tents gathering in larger camps, to ensure that some responsible adult males would be present for supervision and protection even when many others were away. In the plains camp of Ja'far, for example, in the fall of 1972, 10 of the 16 male household heads and 10 sons and sons-in-law were away from camp for periods of several weeks to several months while engaging in market-related activities. In contrast, less than half, 46 percent, of the Gamshadzai mountain camp household heads were away, and none among the Siahani camps. This factor has been pointed out for another area of Baluchistan:

> The camp is an economically cooperative unit, containing a mixed labor pool, each segment of which is reliant on the others. Thus, for example, people who are absent for extended periods of time scouting for new pastures or working in the villages can only be free to pursue these activities if others remain behind to tend the animals or, in the case of migratory married males, to watch over their women and children. . . .

[Thus] nomads with small household herds may combine into fairly large camps to form a large and diversified labor pool for the simultaneous exploitation of a variety of economic opportunities, both pastoral and non-pastoral, without at the same time abandoning the nucleus of animals which could provide the basis for future herd increment. (Pastner 1971:175, 179)

## CAMPS AND LINEAGES

What was the social makeup of these camps? Who came together to form them, and who joined and left camps? In general, the majority of male household heads in a *halk* were members of the same shallow lineage, *brasrend*. In 15 *halk*, 76 percent of household heads were members of the same *brasrend*. Even in one of the largest and most mixed *halk*, over 21 periods, 62 percent of household heads were from one *brasrend*. Furthermore, the household heads from other *brasrend*, making up 38 percent of the total, were split among four different *brasrend* on average. Thus, although there were small blocs from other lineages on occasion (e.g., the Mehimzai among the Dadolzai of the Ja'fari Halk), and small blocs based upon nonlineage kin connections (e.g., Komeron and his sons-in-law, Isa, Sahib Dad, and Karam, in the Ja'fari Halk), for the most part, the tents affiliated with lineages other than the dominant one were not closely related to one another and were in effect socially fragmented.

The sheer numerical dominance of one lineage in a *halk* was, however, not the only consideration. Another factor was continuity of membership. This is important because it indicated continued commitment to the *halk* and ongoing responsibility. Here, too, members of the dominant lineage of camps were much stronger than members of other lineages; they stayed members of a *halk* longer and were members more frequently. In order to specify this more precisely, I have calculated the number of sites at which various camp members were present. The results can be summed up by what I call "the continuity of residence index" or CRI (Salzman 1992). Looking at this CRI for the Ja'fari Halk, we can see a substantial difference between tents with Dadolzai males and those without. The CRI for the tents with Dadolzai males was .57 (of a maximum of 1.0), while the CRI for tents with male members of other lineages was .21. Similarly, the CRI for the Yarmahmudzai members of the Azam-i Halk was .71; the CRI for members of other lineages was .33. We find, thus, in herding camps, that members of the numerically dominant lineage tended to stay members of the camp much longer than members of other lineages.

Given single lineage dominance within *halk*, what patterns of relationship did this reflect? No single pattern was characteristic, but frequently, especially in small *halk*, there was a cluster of close ties. One such pattern that frequently formed the core of a *halk* was a father and his adult sons. A second was based upon the descendants of two brothers. A third, somewhat less usual, was a lineal pattern of three generations. But these patterns were not determined by the kin ties; sons do not always belong to the same *halk* as their father, and brothers do not always belong to the same *halk*. Members of camps are selected, or select themselves, from much larger universes in which individuals have equal claims for membership, insofar as lineage membership justifies a claim to camp membership.

The Dadolzai Ja'fari Halk usually contained no more than a dozen male Dadolzai household heads, on two occasions rising to 14 and on one to 16. These Dadolzai were drawn from a larger group of 26 adult Dadolzai males resident in Yarahmadzai tribal territory, leaving aside the 13 residing elsewhere. No principle of descent or lineage membership determined or defined which Dadolzai individuals would reside in this or another Dadolzai camp. Certainly there was never an instance when all Dadolzai, or even most Dadolzai, resided together in a camp. Nor were the Dadolzai neatly distributed according to microlineage affiliation. Each of the four populous Dadolzai microlineages were represented during most periods, and none resided in one to the exclusion of other camps.

Of course, mere presence in camp did not determine an individual's role in the camp. Individuals with large numbers of animals played a more important part in certain crucial aspects of camp life, such as relations with the shepherd and decisions about migration, than those who had few or none. Some microlineages were more heavily represented than others, for example, the Dust Mahmudzai in Ja'fari Halk, but not to the extent that the camp could be said to be their camp. In sum, the lineage was the primary universe from which camp members were drawn, but lineage membership alone did not determine camp membership.

Although each *halk* was a socioeconomic entity in its own right, it was not necessarily a social isolate. When the requirements of good herding practice did not allow those who wished to remain in proximity to belong to one camping group, the goal of proximity and social access was achieved by a compromise strategy. This was for two or more *halk* to camp nearby, thus becoming *hamsaheg*, neighbors.

Often, *hamsaheg halk* consist of members of the same lineage. An example of this was the two Dadolzai *halk* that camped close to one another in 1967–68 for several periods. Another example, this time of a small number of close kin, was three Siahani *halk*. But not all *hamsaheg halk* consisted of lineage mates. Dinari Halk of the Mohammedzai and Jangi Halk of the Dorahzai were *hamsaheg*, although of different lineages, and with no affinal ties. Likewise, Azami Halk of the Yarmahmudzai and Ja'fari Halk of the Dadolzai were *hamsaheg* for a time. As with the latter case, the proximity was sometimes fortuitous, and short-lived. Most frequently, it was *halk* with lineage or multiple affinal ties that consciously tried to stay together, if herding and other strategic factors allowed.

This social factor, the desirability of camping close to another *halk*, was a significant one in the equation of multiple considerations that decided migration policy.

However, the proviso "if herding and other factors allow" was crucial, for separation of *hamsaheg halk* as a result of divergent migration patterns could and did take place when decisions in the two camps about herding and about the husbanding of other resources diverged and overrode social considerations of maintaining proximity.

# 3.
# EATING AND DRINKING

What people need to live, and what they need to eat and drink, is to a large extent culturally defined and spelled out in local standards and local people's expectations and hopes. In the deserts and mountains of the Sarhad of Baluchistan, cultural standards of "need" were mostly local in derivation and were closely adjusted to the local environment. Patterns of consumption and production both followed and informed these standards.

## FOOD AND DRINK

Sarhadi cuisine was relatively simple, and its material elements were largely produced locally or within neighboring regions of Baluchistan. The centerpiece of local cuisine was the *hatuk* ("tuk" pronounced as "took"), the ideal type of dish for daily midday and evening meals and festive occasions alike. *Hatuk* consisted of an edible liquid into which bread was broken and that the bread would absorb. There were five main kinds of *hatuk:*

*Shiri hatuk,* or milk *hatuk,* was a basic, everyday dish consisting of bread broken into a bowl of milk, usually a mix of half-soured, half-fresh milk, sometimes flavored with a pinch of turmeric, *darzard,* or *masale,* a simple curry powder, with a small amount of oil, *rogan,* preferably *rogani pas,* clarified butter, floating on the top.

*Gushti hatuk,* or meat *hatuk,* commonly made on festive occasions, consisted of bread broken into a bowl of thin gravy made from meat (whether lamb, mutton, goat, camel, or, even more rarely, deer), tomatoes, perhaps onions, one or more curry spices, and hot peppers, with pieces of meat served separately on a plate.

*Morghi hatuk,* or bird *hatuk,* often served to guests, had gravy made from chicken or game birds and was prepared and served similarly to *gushti hatuk.*

*Adassi hatuk,* or lentil *hatuk,* was prepared for family eating.

*Abi hatuk,* or water *hatuk,* characteristic of great poverty and of times of extreme drought, was a meal in which bread was broken into a bowl of water, flavored perhaps only by hot peppers.

To those without experience of *hatuk,* bread soaked in liquid might not sound very palatable. Indeed, at the beginning of my residence among the Yarahmadzai, I would dunk my bread into the liquid but not let it soak. However, once again the local folks were right and I was wrong. When I finally tried *hatuk—shiri, gushti,* and *morghi* only, for I was never served *adassi* or *abi*—the way it was eaten locally, I found it delicious. This should not have surprised me, long an avid consumer of Indian, Chinese, and other national cuisines from around the world. And it should surprise few readers, for many of us in wealthy countries have in the past several decades expanded our consumption and appreciation of cuisines from many countries. And before in Greece and Turkey, and since in India and Sardinia, I have on numerous occasions found rural, "peasant" food delicious. Sometimes, though, a bit of time is required to become accustomed to the food for full appreciation, especially when the food is, or appears to be, rather different than what one is used to.

A single portion of *hatuk* can be eaten by an individual, and *hatuk* was often eaten this way. But *hatuk* was also often consumed collectively, by a number of people, eating out of a common bowl. In a family, at home in their tent, a wife and husband, and children, would share a bowl of *hatuk,* the babies, if any, being fed out of the bowl by the parents.

At feasts involving gatherings of individuals, such as weddings, religious holidays, and political negotiations, communal eating was the norm. Men and women were separated and located in different spaces, without visual contact. A group of six or eight guests would sit around a large bowl of meat gravy, and, each having been supplied with bread and most likely a side plate with pieces of meat, would break his or her own bread into the liquid, striving to use only the space in the bowl that represented his or her appropriate share, and removed only the bread that she or he deposited. All were "breaking bread together," and all were sharing the common bowl and its offering of sustenance and pleasure. From this sharing arose a sense of commonality, of collectivity, and of unity.

In a family, of course, there was a strong sense of community, for, whatever the variation in interpersonal tone from one family to the next, all family members depended upon common, family resources. At a feast for a religious holiday, all participants were present as members of a religious community, a concept strongly advanced in Islam. At a feast for a life cycle passage, all participants were present as guests of the hosting family and were all formally equivalent and unified as celebrants, guided by the guest/host rules of etiquette. And at a feast for political negotiation, the commonality and unity of the guests would be the goal of the event, and the rhetoric often explicitly stressed precisely the solidarity of the participants. The sharing of the communal meal both expressed and advanced social commonality. Even this anthropologist must confess repeatedly experiencing an unexpected frisson of emotion in communal feasting reflecting an extraordinary sense of communion.

## Bread

One reason that *hatuk* did not a priori appeal to me was my preconception of soggy bread. The bread made in Baluchi tents is, however, quite substantial and maintains consistency even after having absorbed milk or thin gravy. The bread, *nan*, most commonly made in the camp of Ja'far was *galfach* (with "ch" pronounced as in "church"), which, like all Baluchi breads, was round and flat, in this case about 38 centimeters (15 inches) across and a bit less than a centimeter (3/8 inch) high, relatively light, leavened, made of wheat. The bottom of *galfach* was smooth, while the top was bumpy and also marked with what appeared to be a triangular brand. *Galfach* was baked in a characteristic fashion. After the dough, *hamir*, was prepared, had risen, and was ready to bake, the amount appropriate for one *galfach* was placed on a large, very shallow, concave iron disk, *tin* (pronounced "teen"), was spread across the disk, and was pressed down and flattened with the fingertips, leaving indentations. Meanwhile, a small hearth fire had been started—in the center of the tent in the winter, toward the end of the tent or outside in warmer or hot weather—and the twigs had been allowed to burn down to hot ashes. On top of the hot ashes was placed a small, iron, triangular stand, *padink*, and on top of this the disk with the dough, the dough facing down, about 4 inches from the hot ashes. After 5 or 10 minutes, the bread, triangularly seared from the hot iron stand, was removed from the *tin* with a spatula, *nan gwag*, and was ready to eat. *Galfach* was eaten on a daily basis, plain or with clarified butter, *rogani pas*, or with yogurt, *bastag* (Persian: *mast*), together with other foods, such as onion, or in a liquid *hatuk*. *Galfach* was too airy to hold well and was usually eaten fresh.

A wheat bread even more delicate than *galfach* was the very thin, 3-millimeter (⅛-inch), unleavened *lawash*, also around 38 centimeters (15 inches) across. *Lawash*, too, was cooked on a *tin* and *padink*, but in a different manner. The *tin* sat on the stand, heated up, and the *lawash* dough was dramatically punched into a disk as the baker, rather like a showy pizza crust baker, flipped it in the air and flopped it onto the lightly greased *tin* for 10 seconds on one side, then on the other. It was then ready to eat. *Lawash* was the bread of choice among Baluch, invariably provided for guests and featured at feasts, and eaten alone, in *hatuk* or with pieces of meat or eggs. *Lawash* had to be eaten immediately, for in the dry air of the desert, its staleness arrived in minutes rather than hours; and stale *lawash* had a consistency and taste like nothing so much as old cardboard. Both because of the extra work in baking and its poor storage quality, *lawash* was thus rarely made for daily, household consumption.

The most hardy wheat bread was the dense, heavy *wari* around 5 centimeters (2 inches) thick and around 38 centimeters (15 inches) across, with a tough crust. To bake *wari,* the fire was burnt down to hot ashes, some of the ashes were swept aside, the dough was placed on the remaining layer of hot ashes, and then it was covered with the other hot ashes. The hot ashes thus acted as an oven, providing both the heat source and the heat container. After a half hour, the now baked *wari* was removed from the ashes, brushed off with the hand, and was ready to eat. However, *wari,* unlike *galfach* and especially *lawash,* would hold its moisture and remain edible for quite a few hours, up to a whole day. So *wari* was favored for times when bread had to hold for a period, such as overnight for eating at breakfast, but especially for occasions such as meals during migration, when food preparation had to be kept to a minimum, and so people depended upon ready-to-eat food that had been prepared ahead of time.

In the camp of Ja'far, women household heads commonly prepared bread twice a day, a lengthy process that included sifting the flour, making the dough, preparing the fire, and baking. By the grace of modern technology, from the mid-1960s on, women almost never used their millstones for arduously grinding grain into flour; motor-driven mills were accessible in a few desert locations and in the town of Khash. Making bread was one of the major activities and responsibilities of adult women of the camp. Bread was the most common foodstuff and a basic staple of the Baluchi diet. In terms of calories and bulk, bread was the main food. The conventional phrase for inviting someone to a meal was, *Be-all, nan bur,* "come and eat bread."

## Milk and Milk Products

After bread, dairy products were the most important staple, providing a significant portion of calories and being the main dietary source of proteins, fats, calcium, and other nutrients and vitamins, as well as providing to the palatability of the local diet a wide range of tastes and textures. Dairy products came primarily from a mixture of the milk of the small stock, *pas,* including both sheep and goats, which were milked indiscriminately into the same pot. The milk of camels, *hushtair* (Persian = *shotur*) was much savored, usually drunk fresh, but most owners had no more than one camel in milk, and they were loath to deprive the vulnerable nursing young camel of its mother's milk. There were a number of commonly used dairy products from the milk of small stock, *shiri pas:*

*Tajag* was sweet milk, as it came from the animals. It was drunk straight, and for breakfast was sometimes added, along with sugar, to tea, making a nourishing drink similar to the South Asian style of tea brewed in milk rather than water, with sugar and spices added.

Soured milk, *shiri turoshp,* made by adding root of the *sagdanton* plant, was much favored. *Shiri hatuk* was almost always made with half-sweet and half-soured milk.

*Bastag,* yogurt (Persian = *mast*), was made by adding soured milk to fresh, sweet milk and storing the mixture in a sheepskin bag, *hezak,* for several hours. *Bastag* was eaten with bread for a quick meal.

Figure 3.1. Milking, 1968. Males and females, and young and old, bring family animals from the herd, hold the animals steady, and do the milking. (Photograph by author)

Clarified butter, *rogani pas,* was made from *bastag* by shaking a *hezak,* hanging from a wooden tripod, for several hours. The characteristic, repeated slush/thump, slush/thump of buttermaking was a frequent sound in the spring. Clarified butter was eaten with bread, used as cooking oil, as in the frying of eggs, and for combining with other ingredients, such as grain for making halva, *halwa,* and with dates for making preserve, *shirag.* Unlike the above-mentioned dairy products, which had to be eaten fairly quickly before they went bad, *rogani pas,* while taking considerably more labor to produce, lasted indefinitely and so could be consumed in a regulated way and conserved for future weeks and months. This ability to store and preserve *rogani pas* was particularly welcome given the seasonal variation in the availability of milk.

Unclarified, white, sour butter, *meska,* could not be stored and was rarely eaten. When made it had to be eaten immediately. Most commonly it was eaten with fresh dates.

Seasonal unavailability of milk was the reason for the production of dried milk solids, *shilanch* (Persian = *kashk*), which, in its final dried form, could be kept indefinitely. It was prepared by storing sour milk in a *hezak* for 20 days, during which it separated. With the liquid whey poured off, the remaining curds were cooked to evaporate further remaining liquid. Then, for final drying, the solids were shaped into walnut-size pieces and placed on a clean cloth on a tent roof, out of reach of *pas*, to be dried in the sun. *Shilanch* was usually saved until periods scarce in milk and then ground into powder, mixed with water, and served as reconstituted milk; it was used primarily for *shiri hatuk*.

## Dates

The third most important staple food of Baluchi tent dwellers was dates, *hormag*, of which there are at least 19 local varieties, each substantially or somewhat different from the others. Dates, rich in fruit sugars (over 50 percent by weight) and minerals (2 percent by weight), with small amounts of protein and fat (each around 2 percent by weight) (*Encyclopaedia Britannica* 1975, Micropaedia III:389), play an important part in the Baluchi diet. The date harvest began at the first ripening in midsummer and continued for six or eight weeks. During this period, fresh dates were eaten in abundance and with relish. However, the bulk of the harvest was packed for storage: modest quantities of certain types of dates were packed fresh in sheep- or goatskin bags, *hezak*, while most dates were dried and the pits removed, and the date meat, *jatk*, packed tightly and stored in large, heavy, wool sacs, *gwal*. These packed dates could be stored and eaten throughout the fall, winter, and spring, until the next date harvest approached. This availability of dates—depending in practice upon the initial quantity and rate of consumption—throughout the food-sparse fall and winter seasons, allowed the Baluch to span the gap of less productive periods and maintain a reasonable diet throughout seasonal variations.

Fresh and dried dates were eaten on their own. The different varieties of dates had distinctive tastes, and some were regarded as tastier than others. The most favored date for eating fresh was the *rabi*, red when growing, black when ripe. The larger, yellow *shingishkan*, was the next most prized, followed by the yellow *kalut*, large black *dandari*, black *yakmushtu*, yellow *baranshahi*, and yellow *huskitch*, although various individuals might rank them slightly differently, especially lower in the list. There was among Baluch a well-established awareness of the many varieties of dates and their qualities, as well as careful discrimination among them.

For immediate consumption, fresh dates were occasionally dipped in white, sour, whole butter *meska*, combining the candy-like sweetness of the date with the sourness of the butter, a superb combination. Dried dates were commonly mixed with *rogani pas* to make a date preserve, *shirag*, which could be stored for some time, to be eaten with bread, usually by dipping a piece of bread into some preserve served in a bowl.

## Meat, Eggs, Vegetables, and Fruit

I would estimate that between 80 and 90 percent of the Baluchi diet was made up of bread, milk products, and dates. Most of the other foods that they ate regularly contributed few calories, although they were important for taste and some for vitamins and minerals. The remaining foods were eaten rarely, with long intervals.

Vegetables were few in the desert. Tomatoes were a common cooking ingredient, especially for rare meat dishes, largely because dried tomatoes could be purchased, stored, and transported without difficulty. Onions were the other common vegetable, and, once purchased, could be stored for some time. Wild onions, *pimazi kuh,* were seasonally gathered by women of the camp. Dried hot peppers were used to flavor food, especially the *hatuk* dishes.

Rice was eaten mainly as a medicinal dish, when people were ill. Rarely, it was served to guests or as a festive dish.

Chicken eggs fried and served in a pool of oil and eaten with bread were consumed once or more a week by those minority of tent dwellers who had chickens and could find the eggs.

Animal blood, forbidden, *haram,* to Muslims, was not eaten and not extracted from animals for consumption.

Meat, *gusht,* was eaten rarely, on average perhaps no more than once a month. The livestock, both *pas* and *hushtair,* were primarily capital resources, treated as renewable rather than consumable. That is, the milk, hair, and wool of the sheep and goats and of the camels were extracted and used, and the riding and burden services of the camels were used, while all efforts were made to conserve, reproduce, and increase the animal capital. Killing a productive animal would have, for the Baluch, been like killing the "golden goose." But there were two classes of animals that, in the management of flocks, were "disposable," and these were most male *pas,* other than the few kept as studs for reproduction, and dry, postreproduction females. These animals, it was judged, should not be maintained permanently as part of the herd and were butchered for consumption or sold for butchering. In the Baluchi deserts, animals were slaughtered and meat was eaten primarily when there were guests and during religious and life cycle feasts. Baluch did not expect meat on a day-to-day basis, and would have looked askance at anyone who slaughtered their animals to eat meat. Only when productive animals fell sick and were likely to die, were they ritually slaughtered—the throat cut while the knife-wielder intoned "Bi'smi'llah al-Rahman, al-Rahim," In the name of God, the Merciful, the Compassionate—so that the meat could be eaten.

Fruit, other than dates, was rare in the desert. Fresh fruit, seasonally, and preserves could be purchased in Khash, and fruit was sometimes available in a few irrigation-based orchards and in oases to the south but was rarely bought by tribesmen and seldom seen in camps.

Tea, however, was consumed daily, at breakfast often as a sweetened milk drink, at other times, as a snack, after meals, and as an offering to visitors, made with water and drunk out of glasses through hard pieces of compacted sugar, *gand,* held in the mouth, in the Persian and Russian style. The so appropriate and seemingly eternal custom—sitting on carpets in tents, chatting, and drinking tea—was in fact quite a recent development. Tea was not used in the deserts of the Sarhad until after World War II, when the new train line was established between Quetta—in what was then British Baluchistan, now part of Pakistan—and Zahedan, the newly established provincial capital of Iranian Baluchistan. At that time, commercial traders began to come to Baluchistan, bringing, among other things, tea from India. In more remote places in Baluchistan, such as the Siah Kuh, Black Mountains, north of Isfandak, during the early 1970s, the nomadic, tent-dwelling *baluch* did not drink tea and did not have kettles or sugar.

## Snacks

Some of the staples—bread, dates, date jam, and tea—were also consumed as snacks, small amounts of food taken between meals to curb hunger, for pleasure, or as a social ritual. But there were also a variety of foods that were regarded strictly as snack and pleasure rather than meal foods.

*Danku,* roasted grains of wheat, was eaten like peanuts.

*Kuhal,* made of wheat and milk, cooked, dried, ground, and was consumed cold with oil.

Fruit was rare, but according to availability and season, apricots, apples, and watermelon were enjoyed.

There were several types of *halwa,* halva sweetmeat, all eaten warm: *baht,* made with flour, dates, and *pasi rogan,* clarified butter; *sauzek,* made with green wheat, cooked, dried, milled, wetted, and mixed with clarified butter; *madar,* wetted flour and clarified butter; *galam,* rough ground wheat, wetted and eaten with clarified butter; *zarati baht,* ground corn, wetted and eaten with clarified butter.

## TOOLS OF CONSUMPTION

Food storage, portage, preparation, and serving required an elaborate set of containers and tools appropriate not only for the task but for tent life. Most of those in use during the 1960s and 1970s were produced locally.

The traditional, locally made container for potable and edible liquids was the skin bag.

A *mashk* was a skin bag for storing and carrying water. It was made from a goatskin, the thickest and toughest of skins, cured with local plants. A large *mashk* was kept for water storage in tents, hanging by a rope tied to the ends of the skin from a forked stick stuck into the ground. These skin bags were porous, and the skin itself remained wet and pliable—when dry and hard the skins easily cracked—and the moisture on the surface of the skin slowly evaporated in still air, or quickly evaporated in a breeze, cooling the water inside. This indigenous water refrigeration system was much appreciated in the hot weather. Medium-size *mashk* were used for transporting water, on a daily basis bringing water from the well to the tent, and less regularly on migration from one camp site to another. Small *mashk* were used for short trips away from camp, for example, when searching for a lost camel, rather the way we use a canteen.

A *hezak* was a skin bag for storing and carrying milk. Made from either a sheep- or goatskin, it was cured with different local plants than *mashk* specifically for holding milk. Large *hezak* were used for storage and treatment of milk and milk products, such as making *bastag* and *rogani pas*. Smaller *hezak* were used for transport. When a *hezak* was old and no longer held liquid well, it was used to store *rabi* dates.

The *zek* was a small skin, of either sheep or goats, used for the storage and/or transport of *rogani pas* or *shirag,* neither of which was ever produced or used in large quantities.

There were a variety of iron implements and containers, made by the local Luri blacksmiths and purchased by the Baluch, for the preparation of food and drink.

The *padink* was the triangular stand on short legs, to be placed over a fire, which served as a stove.

The *tin* was the slightly concave, sheet metal disk used especially for making bread.

The *nan gwagh* was a long, thin spatula used for removing bread from the *tin* griddle.

*Ablagon* were handleless pots with tight-fitting covers for dough, *hamir,* or *rogani pas.*

*Galas* were large bowls for cooking and for serving. They were used for communal *hatuk* consumed by a half-dozen or so people.

A *honsag* was a ladle.

The *shiri pala* was a funnel used for pouring milk in *hezak,* sometimes with a clump of straw as a filter for straining milk and removing animal hair, and for pouring water in *mashk, rogani pas* in *zek,* and so on.

General tools also used in cooking included the *karch,* knife, and *kolang,* pick.

All of these implements and containers were simple, crude, and hardy. They were handmade by local blacksmiths and were not as refined as those produced by specialized craftsmen in urban bazaars in Persian cities, or as finished as goods manufactured in the West. However, they fulfilled local needs very nicely: their price was modest and could often be paid in kind, for example, with dates, and they were made tough to survive the literal rough-and-tumble of nomadic life.

A cooking and baking alternative to an open fire or hot ashes with a *padink* standing over was the *tandur,* a dried-mud oven in the shape of a cylinder sitting on one end, with the other end open toward the sky. Around a meter (3 feet) high and ⅗ meter (2 feet) wide, the *tandur* was always constructed outside of tents and used most often in summer, especially for occasions when large quantities of bread had to be baked. Unlike the fire and *padink,* which could be used to cook only one flat bread at a time, a number of breads could be stuck in different places on the inside wall of the *tandur* and baked together.

Textiles, woven locally in a flat weave, sometimes with floating weft designs, were also used for containing and serving food.

The *gwal* was a large bag, woven with a wool warp and either a wool or cotton weft, used for storage and transport of bulky foodstuffs, such as grain, flour, and dates. The cruder wool of camels was sometimes used, alone or together with sheep's wool, for the yarn.

A *shiakin* was a small, folding textile with a large pocket for flour and was used for preparing bread and for keeping bread fresh once it was made.

The *mesakin* was a small rug used exclusively for serving food. It was placed on the floor in front of the eater, and the food was placed on top of it.

These textiles were thick, tightly woven, and heavy. The yarn contained the natural animal oils. Consequently, these rugs and bags lasted a long time even in the rough conditions in which they were used.

## THE MAKINGS

According to my informants Ido, Gami, Yelli Han, and Shams A'din, their households and most other tents consisting of two adults and several children and routinely baking bread twice a day required between 15 and 20 *man zaboli,* or 75–100 kilos, of grain each month. On a daily basis, this would have been around 3 kilos per tent, on average a half kilo per person. On an annual basis, each tent would have used 900–1,200 kilos of grain. The monetary value in 1968 based on the sale price in Khash of 4 toman per *man* would have been 60–80 toman a month and 720–960 toman a year, although in the countryside grain was selling at the higher price of 5 toman a *man,* presumably because of smaller supply and greater convenience, in that transport of the grain from town was unnecessary.

From the date harvest in 1967, Yelli Han filled 10 *gwal,* each carrying 15–20 *man* (75–100 kilos) of dates, of which he sold 2 *gwal* and kept 8 for his family, at 90 kilos per *gwal,* a total of 720 kilos of dates. Divided over the nine-month season away from the date palms, for during the date harvest people ate fresh dates as they were harvested, 80 kilos of dates were available per month for Yelli Han's family, or a bit less than 3 kilos per day. For six persons, this worked out to around a half kilo of dates per day. Shams A'din during the same season got 120 *man* (600 kilos) of dates in 8 *gwal.* These

**Table 3.1.** Equivalences of Foodstuffs, Goods, and Services in Iranian Toman

| Foodstuff, Good, or Service | Price (toman) | Chapter[a] |
|---|---|---|
| Monthly supply of wheat for family of 6 | 60–80 | 3 |
| Adult male goat (*trusht*) | 50 | 4 |
| Adult female sheep (*mish*) | 120 | 4 |
| Adult male burden camel (*dachi*) | 600 | 4 |
| Adult female burden camel (*lira*) | 600–700 | 4 |
| Dates, per *man* (5 kilos) | 5½ | 5 |
| Clarified butter, per liter | 18 | |
| Mattress | 80 | 6 |
| Quilt | 38 | 6 |
| Tea kettle | 10 | 6 |
| Shirt and pants for male ( *jamag* and *shalwar*) | 60 | 6 |
| Used sport coat | 10 | 6 |
| Long veil (*chadur*) | 30 | 6 |
| Tea, per kilo, retail | 20–25 | 6 |
| Profit from a month of trading | 1,000 | 6 |
| Savings from a month of manual labor | 500 | 6 |
| Adult passenger fare on truck between the Sarhad and Mashkil | 10–12 | 7 |

*Note:* Sarhadi tent dwellers were both purchasers and sellers of certain foodstuffs, goods, and services, such as grain, dates, and livestock, and only purchasers of others, such as tailored clothes and metal goods.

[a]Relevant chapters in this volume.

dates spread out over the nine months away from the date groves provided 67 kilos per month, or 2.2 kilos per day. Divided among the members of the two households that shared capital resources, Shams A'din and his wife Sazein, who as yet had no children, and Shams A'din's parents Gulap and Zarbonu, there were 0.55 kilos, more than a half kilo per person per day.

The amount of milk from the *pas*, sheep and goats, that could be taken for human use after the young lambs and kids had nursed depended upon the age and health of the individual animals and the seasonally and annually variant state of the pasturage. Productive animals feeding on good spring pasturage could produce between a half liter and a whole liter of milk at each milking. Adults and adolescent children—drinking milk with tea in the morning, drinking milk straight for a snack, and eating *shiri hatuk* twice a day for the main meals—could each easily consume 4 liters of milk a day. For a family of two adults, two adolescent children, and two smaller children who we will consider to need half portions, daily consumption would be 20 liters of milk, which would be the produce of between 20 and 40 milking animals with a single daily milking, or between 10 and 20 milking animals with two milkings a day. In addition, making butter took at least several liters of milk, and any surplus of butter could also easily be sold. Furthermore, a considerable amount of milk was needed for the preparation of dried milk solids, *shilanch,* to provide reconstituted milk during the long summer, fall, and winter seasons when milk production was low or nil.

## ALLOCATION AND DISTRIBUTION OF FOOD

In principle and in everyday practice, each tent with its single hearth provided, prepared, and consumed food as an independent entity. Occasionally tents contained two living areas and two hearths, usually on an exceptional and short-term basis, such as when a recently married couple did not yet have a tent of their own and shared the tent of the bride's parents. But most commonly a nuclear family in its own tent prepared and shared food together. At meal times, especially for *hatuk* at midday and in the evening, the parents and children would sit and eat together, often out of a common bowl.

While food was thus the preserve of the nuclear family in its tent and hearth, there were more than a few circumstances and occasions in which food was shared beyond the tent. These could be described in terms of their intent: religion, social solidarity, and hospitality.

### Ritual Distribution

In order to reinforce a motivated prayer for a particular end, whether to bring about a good event or to forestall a bad event, or to give thanks for a hoped-for result that had come about, Sarhadi tent dwellers would sometimes distribute food.

In the *patir,* requesting help from God (see chapter 12), foodstuffs, such as bread, dates, or candy, would be distributed gratuitously and without distinction to members of the camping group community.

For the *hairat,* asking God's assistance (see chapter 12), an animal was sacrificed and portions of the meat distributed gratuitously and without distinction to other tents.

### Social Solidarity

An important value and virtue for the Sarhadi Baluch was *topak,* social solidarity, which could be manifested in a number of ways, one of which was sharing food. The most obvious kind of sharing was the giving of food by the more well-to-do to the less fortunate or elderly poor, *beawus.* This tended to be done by kinsmen and was carried out very informally and discretely. Such acts were conceived as reflecting solidarity rather than charity, the carrying out of a duty rather than the exhibition of largesse. But here, too, there was a complementary religious element, for doers of good deeds received religious merit, *sawab*, for their acts.

Another form of food sharing was, in effect, the sharing of a loss through the division, *wond konag*, and purchase of meat from an animal that had died inadvertently. In this case, most or all of the tents of the camp were obliged to receive a portion, *wond*, of the meat and to pay a set fee for each portion. In this way, the owner of the animal, the *wonddar*, was compensated for at least part of the value of the animal.

On May 10, 1973, Ja'far's *lira*, male camel, went blind and crazy and could only be subdued by the combined efforts of a half-dozen men, and it was clear that the animal would have to be put down. Even if the animal had been calm, it could no longer see to graze. And there was no knowing how the illness would progress and whether the animal was in danger of dying. If the *lira* had died a natural death, it could by Islamic law not be eaten; only an animal ritually slaughtered may be eaten. When Ja'far returned to camp several days later, the camel was ritually slaughtered. Reis performed the ritual, saying the appropriate Islamic formula and cutting the camel's throat. Shams A'din, Ido, Shiruk, Bahadur, and Id Mahmud pitched in to skin and butcher the carcass. Then all of the meat, excepting the head and the neck, was divided into 15 equal parts, with an audience of most of the men of the camp sitting around and watching. Those who had slaughtered and butchered the camel were given the head and neck for their efforts. All of this was done on behalf of and overseen by Ja'far, the owner of the camel.

Each portion, *wond*, was priced at 20 toman, for most tent dwellers a fairly high layout for a luxury foodstuff. The sale of the 15 portions had a total value 300 toman, around half the monetary value of a healthy *lira*. Each individual representing a tent picked a number from 1 to 20, and someone counted through the portions until that number came up, thus randomizing the selection of that individual's portion. The *wond* were distributed among 13 tents.

The members of the camp were happy to have meat to eat, although many could not really afford it and would not have spent the money for it if they had not felt the obligation to do so. Most Sarhadi tent dwellers did not eat meat very frequently, and, as the meat in each portion was substantial, most people salted and dried what they did not eat the first night so that it would last for several days.

The point of this division of meat was to spread the loss and keep the owner of the animal from bearing the entire cost of the loss. Thus distribution of foodstuffs with financial compensation was meant to benefit the person distributing, the *wonddar*, who then did not have to carry the full financial weight of the unexpected and unintended loss of the animal. Of course, one day's seller of *wond* would another day become a purchaser, not out of preference but out of *topak*, solidarity, which in this exercise was manifested in a kind of insurance against animal loss. Those who could

**Table 3.2.** Distribution of Camel Meat Portions (*Wond*) from Ja'far's Camel

| Name | Wond | Comment |
|---|---|---|
| Ja'far | 2 (1 + ½ + ½) | Including 2 returned half-portions |
| Id Mahmud | 1 | |
| Reis | 1 | |
| Reis and Baluch | 1 (½ + ½) | |
| Rahmat | 1 | |
| Dust Mahmud | 1 | |
| Barkat and Gemi | 1 (½ + ½) | 2 poorer tents |
| Ido | 1 | |
| Isa | 1 | |
| Abas | ½ | —[a] |
| Jan Mahmud | ½ | —[a] |
| Shams A'din | 1 | |
| Abdul | 1 | |
| Philip (ethnographer) | 2 | Portions divided among poorer tents |

[a]Full portions were allocated to the tents of Abas and Jan Mahmud, but since both men were away from the Sarhad working, their wives each returned half a portion.

not possibly afford the cost of the meat were not expected to pay and were excused from accepting a *wond*. But if kinsmen who were deemed able to pay did not accept, the *wonddar* was expected to be angry, and others were expected to raise questions about whether those who did not accept were *beatopak,* lacking in solidarity. Two of the women felt that they could not commit the requested amount of money, especially with their husbands away and not able to enjoy the meat, and returned half of their portions. The return of the half portions saw the usually placid Ja'far, the *wonddar,* visibly annoyed.

The obligation to purchase *wond* was not limited to unintentional losses of livestock. The call for solidarity, *topak,* also was heard when an individual in need of money slaughtered an animal. In this case, too, kinsmen and campmates were expected to purchase a *wond.*

## Hospitality

If solidarity was for the Sarhadi Baluch the value and virtue that should guide one in relations with one's kinsmen, lineage mates, and campmates, hospitality was the value and virtue that should guide one in relations with outsiders with whom one is in a state of peace. It was accepted as a great obligation to welcome and provide for "strangers," people whose tents or houses were elsewhere. To provide hospitality and provide food for others was to be a *nandeh,* literally a "bread giver." It was not only an obligation but an honor for the hosts, because guests, *dawati,* honored their hosts, *wasildar,* by coming to them and by so doing acknowledging their hosts as people of substance. Providing hospitality was at the same time a gracious act for which one received credit, *sawab,* from God.

The better off a tent dweller was, the more able he was to provide the food, especially luxury food, for guests. "Strangers" away from home visiting a camp would commonly go to their kinsmen, if any, or, lacking kinsmen, to the politically senior, *master,* individual in the group. The hosts would be obliged to provide attention, space, food, and, in the case of an overnight stay, bedding. In a host/guest relationship, the cultural expectations were high and the etiquette demanding.

Whether campmates or strangers, visitors to a tent were usually offered tea. Two refusals were customary before acceptance after the third offer. The tea ritual usually included the removal of the large, hard, pressed sugar blocks or cones from their embroidered storage bags and the splitting of them into smaller chunks by the use of a small hammer designed for that purpose, and the further breaking of the sugar into smaller chunks using metal shears also made for that purpose. The tea, meanwhile, was made by boiling water in a kettle over a small open fire and pouring the boiling water into a small teapot with loose tea, generally tea imported or smuggled from Pakistan. When the water had colored with the liquor of the tea, it was poured into small glasses, usually of the Duralex variety, the guest or guests first, others next, and the host, if at all, last. With the pieces of hard and slow-to-melt sugar placed directly in the mouth, the hot tea was drunk through the sugar, releasing some of the sweetness. It was not uncommon for two or three rounds of tea and sugar to be offered. The effect, in both taste and calories and satisfaction, was a little more like tea and cookies than plain black tea as Joan and I drank it in our tent.

In general, host/guest relations were kept within gender boundaries, men hosting men and women hosting women. For example, when Shams A'din was away and a male guest came to his tent, his wife Sazien called Shams A'din's brother, Mahmud Karim, to act as host. And when Nezar Mahmud, the brother of the Sardar, was away and male guests came to his tent, his wife Mah Bibi called, in the absence of other senior males, the Sardar's oldest son, who, at 11 years of age, performed the role of host in a dignified fashion.

At a formal host/guest meal, where the guest was not related to the host or was of high prestige, the etiquette was fairly strict. First, tea was offered while the meal was being prepared, which often required two hours or more, especially if an animal was being slaughtered. Meals were never prepared until guests arrived, for the arrival of guests, even if expected, was inevitably highly uncertain, there being so many unforseen exigencies that might delay a visit. Thus the exchange of news, the chatting, the discussion of business—all took place before the meal. Once the meal arrived and was eaten, that segment of the visit was deemed completed and guests were free to move around or leave.

Prior to the meal, water for washing hands was brought around. This was particularly important as the Sarhadi tent dwellers eat with their hands rather than with flatwear. A bowl was placed below the hands of the guest and water was poured from a pitcher, allowing the guest to rinse his or her hands. Some households accustomed to entertaining had pitcher and bowl sets made especially for hand washing. In the winter, the water was heated so that the guests could rinse their hands with warm water.

On the most formal occasions, the host, no matter how high in status, did not eat with the guests, but, standing, moving around, or sitting facing the guests, attended them, ensuring that they were well served, that the food was satisfactory, that the guests were able to converse with the host as much as they liked.

The host always apologized for the poor quality of the food, no matter how sumptuous and extraordinary by local standards. He apologized for the meager quantity of the food, no matter if it was, as it was supposed to be, six times what an ordinary mortal could eat. The host would repeatedly urge the guests to eat more and castigate the guests for eating so little, even if they had eaten vast quantities and felt as if they were splitting, saying that the food must not be very good or else the guests would eat more. (This standardized hosting drill, which I have experienced and observed numerous times in the Sarhad, was the best evidence I could find—I joked to myself—that the founder of the Baluch was an Italian or Jewish mother, or more likely a Jewish Italian mother.)

After the meal, the hand washing apparatus returned so that the guest could clean his or her hands of the remains of the food. Tea was once again brought, and two or three rounds presented.

In the spring of 1973, the Sardar of the Yarahmadzai tribe, Haji Han Mahmud, entertained Sardar Halil Han of the Gamshadzai tribe in Han Mahmud's tent at his camp, then located at Garonchin. Han Mahmud himself slaughtered and butchered a goat in Halil Han's honor. Halil Han was of course a guest of great stature, but he was also an affinal kinsman and long-time acquaintance of Han Mahmud, as well as the uncle of Gran Bibi, Han Mahmud's Gamshadzai wife. So while honor was appropriately given, the formalities were not at their most stringent. Han Mahmud, Halil Han, and the other guests, sitting in the place of honor in front of the *pur*, ate together, sharing a common, large bowl for their *gushti hatuk*, cooked by Gran Bibi. After the guests had been served, Gran Bibi sat with her children by the fire and ate out of a common bowl. Following common practice, Gran Bibi turned and adjusted her *chadur* so that she could not be seen eating by the male guests, for eating was deemed an intimate act, and women would have felt embarrassed if men outside of their immediate families had observed them eating.

# PART TWO
*Making a Living*

# 4.
# HERDING AND HUSBANDING

"Making a living" is the activities people undertake to acquire the things they need to live. "Need" in the sense that I am using it here refers to what local people feel they need. In this sense, "need" is heavily influenced by local culture as well as by local circumstance—ecological, economic, and political—and individual idiosyncratic and family particularities and peculiarities. This sense of "need" thus slides into expectation, and desire. But it is always there, a tensed spring pushing, as the hoped-for fruits of production pull teleologically, in the many demanding tasks of production.

With need and desire supplying the motive, and the fruits of production supplying the goal, the means meant to connect motive and goal within the Sarhadi environment is a general strategy that incorporates capital resources, individual effort and skill, technology, and social cooperation. This strategy is multiple-resource exploitation directed toward subsistence consumption.

## PASTORALISM AS PART OF A
## MULTI-RESOURCE ECONOMY

Multiple-resource, or multi-resource, exploitation is drawing upon many aspects of the environment in order to produce and extract a variety of different products. This diversification, involvement in many different types of production, found in the Sarhad of Baluchistan contrasts with specialization, the concentration on one kind of production directed toward one main kind of product. The Sarhadi multi-resource economy thus provided both a diversity of products and at the same time provided insurance in case of failure in one or another productive sector.

The Sarhadi multi-resource economy was oriented toward providing the necessities of life for the producers and their families. That is, it was primarily a subsistence economy, each individual and family producing for the purpose of direct consumption. The consumption-oriented economy of the Sarhad can be contrasted with market-oriented economies, in which production is directed toward market exchange, toward barter or sale.

In providing an overview of how the Sarhadi Baluch made a living, in reviewing the various productive sectors in which they were involved, it is useful to distinguish two historical periods, divided by a significant shift in Sarhadi society: the period from 1850 until 1935, during which the Sarhadi Baluch were largely independent politically, can be referred to as "the Baluchi Period"; the period from 1935 until 1976, during which the Sarhadi Baluch were under the effective military and political control of the Pahlevi government of Iran, can be referred to as "the Iranian Period" (see chapter 11).

The productive constants during both periods, from 1850 until 1980, were major commitments to pastoralism, date palm arboriculture, and grain cultivation, with minor supplements from hunting and gathering. The difference between the two periods was not in the degrees of openness or closedness to the outside, not in the earlier period being local and the later one being extra-local, regional, and beyond. In both periods there was a substantial inflow of products to the Sarhad from outside. Rather, the main difference was in the nature of the transactions bringing that inflow. During the Baluchi Period, most of the inflow was a result of Baluchi predatory raiding of Persian villages and caravans. During the Iranian period, most of the inflow was a result of the sale of labor outside of the Sarhad or small-scale importing and trading by Sarhadi Baluch. In addition to this major change in the source of external income, both periods witnessed a gradual increase in acquiring goods through purchase, but with an increasingly rapid rate during the Iranian period. Let us examine each of these productive sectors in turn, beginning with pastoralism, considering, as we go along, how different sectors supported or undercut one another and how, or to what extent, the total profile made a coherent package reflecting an effective strategy.

Pastoralism on the Sarhad, as elsewhere, means raising livestock on natural pasture. Livestock were raised for the products they produced—hair, wool, skin, milk, meat, manure—and the services they performed—riding, burden, traction. Livestock also reproduce, thus expanding their own numbers. Because of these products and services, and the ability to reproduce, livestock were a repository of economic value and also prestige.

I am going to present here material on raising livestock. While some of it may seem unnecessarily detailed or technical, this information is necessary because the *baluch* depended heavily upon their animals for their livelihood. But as well, the *baluch* were constantly concerned about their livestock, continually thinking about their animals and making decisions about them. Being a *baluch* was, among other things, having a preoccupation with livestock and with making a living from livestock.

## CLIMATE AND ITS IMPACT

The nature of pastoralism in any particular place is greatly influenced by local conditions. In the arid Sarhad, there was little rain and this resulted in a sparsity of vegetation for livestock to eat and of water to drink. In addition to the sparsity, rain and vegetation varied from season to season and year to year, and varied in spatial distribution over the territory.

During the two periods, 1963–67 and 1971–76, encompassing 11 years, the average annual rainfall, recorded at Khash, was 131 millimeters (5.1 inches). However, the variation from year to year was huge: the driest years being 1965 with 39 millimeters (1.5 inches) and 1971 with 41 millimeters (1.6 inches), the wettest being 1972 with 212 millimeters (8.4 inches) and 1976 with 256 millimeters (10 inches), a more than fivefold variation in annual rainfall (see table 4.1). These driest years were called *dokal*, drought, whereas the wet years were called, *abadeh*, plentiful. Out of the 11 years, 4 years (1965, 1966, 1971, 1973) were drought years, whereas 3 years (1972, 1975, 1976) were years of plenty. If these two sets of years are representative, a drought year comes every 3 or 4 years.

Rainfall in the Sarhad, as is common in the arid belt stretching from the Sahara to China, fell mostly in the winter, thus providing no relief for man, beast, or plant during the torrid summers. Through the six years 1971–76, more than 80 percent of the rain fell during the months of December, January, and February, and most of the rest in November and March (see table 4.2). As a consequence, even during good years, only the long spring, *bahargah*, between winter and high summer, was a time of florescence of plants, when there was a slight green cast to the desert expanses of the Sarhad, and, during the most "plentiful" years, such as 1976, tiny flowers of many colors bloomed among the grass blades.

Aridity was thus the most prominent influence on pastoralism in the Sarhad. In addition, livestock had to tolerate a considerable range of temperatures on the Sarhad from season to season. The region's altitudes—1,698 meters (5,570 feet) in the high desert plains, 4,042 meters (13,262 feet) in the Kuhi Daptan, and 2,816 meters (9,240 feet) in the Morpish Mountains at Kuhi Gazu—brought cool winter temperatures. On the high plains, winter temperatures regularly dropped below freezing in the night, with average daily temperatures around 5 to 10 degrees centigrade (in the 40s Fahrenheit), and there was substantial snowfall on occasion, as there was in 1972–73. The types of livestock raised had to be suitably hardy in these arid and variable conditions. The animals had to be able to survive, produce, and reproduce on small amounts of pasturage and water and in both cold and hot weather.

## SMALL STOCK

As we have seen, Sarhadi pastoralism was based upon small stock, *pas*, including short-legged goats, *sah pas* (literally, black small stock), and fat-tail sheep, *sepid pas* (lit-

**Table 4.1.** Rainfall Recorded at Khash

| Year | Millimeters | Inches |
|------|-------------|--------|
| 1963 | 144 | 5.6 |
| 1964 | 107 | 4.2 |
| 1965 | 39 | 1.5 |
| 1966 | 54 | 2.1 |
| 1967 | 136 | 5.4 |
| 1971 | 41 | 1.6 |
| 1972 | 212 | 8.4 |
| 1973 | 72 | 2.8 |
| 1974 | 169 | 6.6 |
| 1975 | 209 | 8.2 |
| 1976 | 256 | 10.1 |

*Source:* Iranian Meteorological Service, Khash Station.

**Table 4.2.** Rainfall at Khash on a Monthly Basis, 1971–76 (in millimeters)

| Month | 1971 | 1972 | 1973 | 1974 | 1975 | 1976 | Average |
|-------|------|------|------|------|------|------|---------|
| Mehr (September) | 0.0 | 0.0 | 0.0 | 0.0 | 3.0 | 0.0 | 0.5  (=0.02″) |
| Aban (October) | 0.0 | 0.4 | 1.2 | 0.0 | 0.0 | 0.0 | 0.27 (=0.01″) |
| Azar (November) | 1.5 | 1.0 | 1.4 | 6.7 | 33.4 | 7.6 | 8.6  (=0.34″) |
| Dey (December) | 0.4 | 24.5 | 47.0 | 10.5 | 44.2 | 0.0 | 21.1 (=0.83″) |
| Bahman (January) | 31.0 | 72.0 | 0.0 | 69.0 | 99.4 | 46.4 | 52.97 (=2.1″) |
| Esfand (February) | 1.5 | 75.7 | 8.0 | 68.3 | 15.0 | 90.6 | 43.2 (=1.7″) |
| Farvar (March) | 2.1 | 4.6 | 7.1 | 6.5 | 5.1 | 80.0 | 17.6 (=0.69″) |
| Ordi (April) | 0.8 | 28.9 | 0.0 | 0.0 | 4.5 | 0.0 | 5.7  (=0.22″) |
| Khordad (May) | 4.0 | 0.0 | 0.0 | 0.0 | 1.8 | 0.0 | 0.97 (=0.04″) |
| Tyr (June) | 0.0 | 5.2 | 7.0 | 0.0 | 0.0 | 31.5 | 7.3  (=0.28″) |
| Mordad (July) | 0.0 | 0.0 | 0.0 | 0.0 | 2.2 | 0.0 | 0.37 (=0.01″) |
| Shahri (August) | 0.0 | 0.0 | 0.0 | 0.0 | 0.0 | 0.0 | 0.0  (=0.0″) |

*Source:* Iranian Meteorological Service, Khash Station.

erally, white small stock). Sarhadi Baluch kept more goats than sheep, which they said was because the goat is hardier, eating a wider range of vegetation.

> The chief differences between goat and sheep are in their ecological requirements. . . . The sheep is essentially a grass feeder. . . . The goat is a browser, preferring foliage of shrubs to grass. . . . The goat is probably content with even sparser food than oriental breeds of sheep, in particular it eats aromatic herbs despised by other ruminants, hence it can penetrate farther into the desert. (Zeuner 1963:130)

**Table 4.3.** Livestock in the Camp of Ja'far, November 1972

| Maldar | Sepid Pas (Sheep) | | Sah Pas (Goats) | | Hustair (Camels) |
|---|---|---|---|---|---|
| | New | Adult | New | Adult | |
| Ja'far | 2 | 6 | 5 | 11 | 2 |
| Ghulam Mah. | — | — | — | 7 | 1 |
| Reis | 3 | 11 | 6 | 22 | 2 |
| Dust Mah. | 5 | 26 | 6 | 16 | 2 |
| Shams A'din | 2 | 5 | — | 3 | 1 |
| Zarbonu | 2 | 2 | — | 3 | — |
| Mahmud K. | — | 4 | 1 | 7 | 2 |
| Jan Bibi | — | — | — | 6 | — |
| Lashkar H. | — | — | — | 4 | — |
| Musa | — | — | — | — | 1 |
| Jan Mahmud | — | — | 4 | 18 | 2 |
| Ido | 1 | 2 | 3 | 7 | 1 |
| Abas | — | — | — | — | 1 |
| Abdulla | — | 1 | 3 | 6 | 1 |
| Barkat | 1 | 1 | 2 | 5 | — |
| Gemi | — | — | — | 3 | 2 |
| Id Mahmud | 1 | 1 | 1 | 4 | 2 |
| Isa | — | — | 3 | 6 | — |
| Baluch | 1 | 4 | 2 | 7 | 3 |
| Komeron | — | — | 5 | 15 | 3 |
| Sahib Dad | 2 | 9 | 4 | 7 | 2 |

Sarhadi goats produced more milk than Sarhadi sheep, produced needed hair, and were more resistant to disease. Sheep, on the other hand, produced milk with a higher fat content than goat milk, supplied needed wool, had more desirable meat, and were worth more on the market.

In the flocks, *ramag* or *galag,* of the camp of Ja'far over a number of years, in spite of changes of resident *wasildar* and of flock numbers, the ratio of goats to sheep stayed constant (table 4.3). In February 1968, for example, there were 131 *pas,* 90 goats and 41 sheep, while in November 1972, there were 296 *pas,* 204 goats and 92 sheep. In spite of shifts of herd owners and family herds over time, these Sarhadi *baluch* maintained a ratio of roughly 2 goats for each sheep.

Household herds were not very large. In the camp of Ja'far during 1968, the average household herd was 6.5 adult *pas* plus newborn, while in 1972, with changes in the constituent households of the camp, the household herds averaged 13.5 *pas* plus newborn (table 4.4). This was far from the 40 adult *pas* that Sarhadi Baluch said is the number needed to support a family. No household herds of the 14 tents in the camp of Ja'far in 1968 approached 40 adult *pas,* while in 1972 only one household herd of

**Table 4.4.** Adult *Pas* in Household
Herds, Camp of Ja'far, February 1968
and November 1972

| Name | 1968 | 1972 |
| --- | --- | --- |
| Dust Mahmud Da Huda | 0 | np |
| Isa | 6 | np |
| Golhan | 10 | np |
| Goolap / Zarbonu | 6 | 5 |
| Hosein | 0 | np |
| Ja'far | 24 | 17 |
| Jan Mahmud (Gam D.) | 3 | 18 |
| Karim Han | 1 | np |
| Mahmud Karim | 5 | 11 |
| Morud | 7 | np |
| Nawab | 1 | np |
| Pati Mahmud | 9 | np |
| Shams A'din | 9 | 8 |
| Shams Hartun / Abdulla | 8 | 7 |
| Abas | np | 0 |
| Aido | np | 9 |
| Baluch | np | 11 |
| Barkat | np | 6 |
| Dust Mahmud Mulla | np | 42 |
| Isa G. | np | 6 |
| Gemi | np | 3 |
| Komeron | np | 15 |
| Reis | np | 33 |
| Sahib Dad | np | 16 |

*Note:* np = not present.

17 in the camp exceeded 40 adult *pas,* and only one of the others approached that number.

Not only were household herds small, but their sizes fluctuated, sometimes substantially and sometimes rapidly. Household herds fluctuated according to human intent as animals were added by reproduction and exchange and removed by slaughter and exchange. Herds fluctuated against their owners' intent through disease, injury, wandering, theft, and, above all, drought.

Reproduction of livestock was systematically encouraged by herd owners to maximize the number of new offspring. The covering of the females was timed and supervised, and the births were aided. In February 1968, the herds of the camp of Ja'far produced 13 lambs from 28 adult sheep and 29 kids from 61 adult goats. In November 1972, there were 20 lambs from 72 sheep and 47 kids from 157 goats.

**Table 4.5.**  Categories and Labels for *Pas*

| Age and Sex | *Sah Pas* (Goats) | *Sepid Pas* (Sheep) |
|---|---|---|
| <6 months | | |
| Male | Shaneg | Gwarag |
| Female | Shaneg | Gwarag |
| 6 months–2 years | | |
| Male | Trusht | Gartur |
| Female | Chati | Yibor |
| 2–7 years | | |
| Male | Pachenu | Gwarant |
| Female | Gitaj | Plat |
| >7 years | | |
| Male | Pir pachen | Pir gwarant |
| Female | Boz | Mish |

Animals were sold, traded, or slaughtered, according to specific criteria. *Pas* were categorized according to species, age, and sex (table 4.5). These categories reflected the different potentials of different animals and provided the basis for herd management, or husbandry.

During 1972–73, for example, Ja'far sold 2 *trusht* (for 50 and 60 toman) and slaughtered 2 *trusht* and 1 *boz*, the latter for a religious holiday; 1 *trusht* and 1 *chati* died, and 1 *trusht* and 1 *chati* were given in *haki shwaneg*, contractual payment to the shepherd, for a total reduction of 9 goats, 7 purposefully and 2 to unintended causes, a large number out of Ja'far's total family herd of 24 young and adult *pas*. At the same time, Ja'far acquired 1 *gitaj* and 1 *mish* in exchange for a young camel, and so added 1 goat and 1 sheep to his family herd.

What led Ja'far to sell and slaughter these particular animals? Perhaps the main consideration was the importance of milk products for the Baluch, which made female *pas* the animals of choice and male *pas* expendable. (Among other pastoral peoples, in other productive regimes, where wool or meat is the main product, female and male animals are more equally valuable.) Furthermore, in addition to the lactation of female *pas*, their particular role in reproduction, the carrying of one or two young, requires many females, whereas the male role in reproduction, the supplying of semen, requires no more than one or two males. Thus Ja'far disposed of five young male goats, *trusht*, whose main use among the Sarhadi *baluch* is in being allocated for meat or exchange. The one young female *chati* died unintentionally. The female *boz* was past reproduction and lactation and thus expendable. The young female *chati* given in exchange was specified in the shepherd's contract, a necessary clause to allow shepherds to build their own flocks, and without which no one would agree to be a shepherd. We can see that Ja'far was disposing of the least productive *pas*, males and postproductive females, and keeping the productive fe-males.

During the same period, Id Mahmud disposed of four *pas*, three *trusht*, two by sale (50 toman each) and one slaughtered, and one *mish*, by sale (120 toman). Id Mahmud thus disposed of one female sheep, but an old one, at or close to a postproductive age. Shams A'din slaughtered a *boz*, one *gwareg* and three *shaneg*, sold one productive fe-male *gitaj* (100 toman), and gave one male *gartur* in payment to the shepherd, *haki shwaneg*.

That these kinds of decisions were general among all *wasildar* was indicated by the population profile of the camp *ramag*. Looking at the category of adult *pas*, those that have been kept and allowed to live to adulthood, we find 122 female goats, *gitaj*, and 1 male goat, *plachen*; 63 female sheep, *plat*, and 1 ram, *gwarant*.

Maintaining household herds and camp *ramag* of only the productive animals re-duced labor and, even more important, reduced grazing on the pasture, thus con-serving the sparse pasturage and consequently reducing the daily movement of the camp flock and the need for migration of the camp to new locations. Limiting the *pas* to productive female animals and thus an overall lower number was an effective way of adjusting to the limited pasturage available.

The population profile of the camp *ramag* of 1972 reveals what appears to be an anomaly: there were virtually no young female *pas*. If the 63 *plat*, ages two to seven, are reduced by one-fifth, or around 13 animals, every year as the six-year-old *plat* be-come seven years old and less productive *mish*, they would have to be replaced by two-year-old *yibor*. But in 1972 there were only 2 *yibor* to fill the place of 13 retiring *plat*. Similarly, the 116 *gitaj* would need 23 replacements annually as one-fifth of the *gitaj* approach retirement and become *boz*. But in 1972 there were only 10 *chati* in the flock ready to take their place as *gitaj*. In short, the adult *pas* were (as always) aging, but there were not enough young *pas* to replace most of them.

The reason for this is quite clear. The previous year, 1971, had been a drought year, *dokal*, with a rainfall of only 41 millimeters (1.6 inches). There had been inadequate pasturage to support the *pas* and many had died, but especially the newborn and young, that is, those that would have been *yibor* and *chati* in 1972. Figures from six of the largest family herds indicate that in 1971, of 92 young *pas*, 55 died from lack of nourishment due to the drought, leaving 37, of which around half, 18, would have been female. With some given to the shepherd or otherwise exchanged, the 18 female *pas* became the 10 *chati* and 2 *yibor* in the flock in 1972.

Adult *pas* were also down in 1972 as a result of the 1971 *dokal*. In the same six large family herds, out of a total of 204 adult *pas*, 70 died from poor nourishment due to the drought, leaving 134 adult *pas*.

We must note also that the number of newborn *pas* in 1972—20 lambs from 72 sheep and 47 kids from 157 goats, for a total of 67 newborn *pas* from 226 adult *pas*—reflects quite a low level of productivity at 3 young for every 10 adults. In 1971, before the drought, in the six largest family herds there were 92 young from 204 adult *pas*, a substantially higher level of productivity at 4.5 young for every 10 adults. The reason for this was the poor condition of the surviving adult female *pas* after the 1971 drought in which many adult *pas* died of inadequate nourishment. With many of the surviving *pas* in poor condition, successful pregnancies carried to term were fewer than those produced by a healthy flock.

The drought, *dokal,* of 1971 was a disaster for the livestock and pastoralism in the Sarhad, but it was not an unusual or even unexpected disaster. Droughts were recurrent and *dokal* years were not infrequent. In 1965, after two average years, the area received only 39.2 millimeters (1.5 inches) of rain, even less than in 1971, and that *dokal* year was followed by one not much better, with 54.3 millimeters (2.1 inches) of rain. During these years, Ja'far lost more than half his 40 *pas*, and Yelli Han sustained a loss of similar magnitude. In an even more severe drought in the late 1950s, Goolap lost most of his *pas,* said to be a herd of over 100, as did most other tribesmen.

Drought and plenty were part of a fairly regular multiyear cycle in the Sarhad. *Dokal* years seem to have come around once every four years, but not infrequently two *dokal* years came together or were broken by one average or good year. Living and surviving in the Sarhad meant adapting to this multiyear cycle. Adapting to this cycle meant being able to get through the bad, drought years in a condition to flourish during the good years of plenty. Coping with drought involved a wide range of special, drought-oriented strategies for dealing with livestock, and it involved drawing strategically on other sectors of the multi-resource economy.

## MANAGEMENT OF SMALL STOCK

While the pastoral was only one sector of the Sarhadi multi-resource economy and the livestock were few in number, the animals were a constant source of concern and object of energy investment on the part of the tent dwellers. In fact, the small numbers of livestock accentuated the value of each animal and allowed a degree of attention to individual animals not possible with a larger number. The attention was with good effect, for the needs of the animals, given this environmental setting, were great. The most noteworthy patterns of animal care had to do with the provision of sustenance and protection from cold.

The primary strategy for providing the *ramagi pas* of adolescent and adult small stock with sustenance was herding the animals to an area of good pasture, *bahar,* and giving them an opportunity to graze and browse, and also to drink. This strategy presumed access to pastureland. Access to pastureland did indeed exist for the members of the camp of Ja'far, because all were members of the Yarahmadzai tribe and by virtue of that membership had access to Yarahmadzai territory. The control of territory was one of the features of Sarhadi tribes, and the Yarahmadzai territory, an area of at least 100 kilometers by 200 kilometers, or 20,000 square kilometers (7,806 square miles)—ranging from Washt/Khash in the west to the Hamuni Mashkil in the east, Kuhi Daptan in the north to Garonchin in the south—was clearly delineated and recognized by other tribes.

Within Yarahmadzai territory there was an "open access" policy, affirming that all Yarahmadzai tribesmen had a right to go anywhere within the territory to reside and pasture their animals. Tribesmen said that the land and natural pasture were made by God and, thus belonging to no particular individual or group within the tribe, were available to all. And if it was a good year, and pasture was plentiful, the Yarahmadzai had an obligation to admit outsiders, from other tribes, who occasionally would apply to reside on Yarahmadzai territory to share God's bounty. Cultivated areas were, of course, excluded from this general principle.

Similarly, the strategy of grazing on natural pasture presumed access to water. Natural water sources, such as streams, runoff channels, and rain ponds, also deemed made by God and owned by no man, were available to any Yarahmadzai who wished to use them. In contrast, constructed water sources, such as wells, qanat (underground irrigation tunnels), and irrigation channels, belonged to the Yarahmadzai lineage or individual who constructed them and could be used by other Yarahmadzai only with permission of the owners.

Daily herding of the flock to pasture (figure 4.1) and returning to camp for milking and sleep, was carried out according to plans arising from detailed consultation among the *wasildar* and *shwaneg*. During 1967–68, the shepherd of the camp of Ja'far was a 13-year-old boy, Abdulluk (Little Abdul), who was hired because of his availability rather than ability. The *wasildar* were not pleased with his performance in getting the *ramag* to pasture, especially when he refused, because he was afraid of the dark, to take the *ramag* out at night. The hiring of a mature and experience shepherd, Ido, in 1972, led to more adequate herding of the *ramag* and more satisfaction among the *wasildar*. In addition to the daily herding strategy, the availability of pasture in the vicinity of the camp was a major factor in considerations—always lengthy, detailed discussions among all herd owners—about whether to move camp and migrate elsewhere.

Herding schedules varied closely with the season. The cold winter of the Sarhad was a threat to the animals. Official records from Zahedan (125 miles north, but 800 feet lower in latitude) give mean monthly temperatures of about 3 degrees centigrade (43, 41, and 45 degrees Farenheit) for December through February (Naval Intelligence Unit 1945:591) In the Sarhad, temperatures dropped below freezing at night during these months, with substantial frosts from time to time. By midday, under the sun, the temperature rose to a comfortable 60 degrees Farenheit, or even a bit higher.

During the coldest part of winter, December and January, the *ramag* was taken out for the warmest part of the day, from 6–7 A.M. to 4–5 P.M., the *hort,* nursing lambs and kids, being allowed to nurse, after milking by the owners, when the *ramag* returned.

Figure 4.1. Abdulluk, shepherd of the Dadolzai camp led by Ja'far, 1968. The kid in the foreground is stealing a last suck before his dam returns to the herd. (Photograph by author)

By 6 P.M., the *pas* were inside their owner's tents, in their designated compartment, the *gwash*. Tents and mats were patched and the tents made as secure as possible from the cold. Rags were stuffed into the cracks and piles of brush for firewood were heaped around the sides and backs of tents for added protection from the wind.

In early February, with the weather a bit warmer and a bit of pasturage, *bahar*, coming up, the herding day was somewhat extended, with the *ramag* going to pasture an hour earlier, 5–6 A.M., returning for milking and nursing at 3–4 P.M., and then going out again for three hours, before returning at 7 P.M. to spend the night in the tents. As February progressed, so did the time of return, extending to 10 P.M. later in February. By March, the adult *pas* were back in camp at night but sleeping outside, their unfenced area called *dara*.

In April and May, in full spring, *bahargah*, the *pas* were away early and back late, but returned in the morning and afternoon for milking. In summer—June, July, and August—the *pas* stayed out all night to graze in the more comfortable temperatures without the burning heat of the sunshine.

Providing the *ramag* with water, which involved moving the animals to a water site—well, rain pond, or stream—also followed a seasonal cycle. In winter the *pas* were watered once every two days, in late spring once a day, in early summer twice a day, in late summer three times a day, and in the fall once a day. The availability of water and its ease of access became a matter of increasing importance in herd management and camp location as the year turned toward the hot, dry summer.

Special provisions were made for the newborn *pas*, called *hort*, until they were weaned at several months. During the first two or three weeks, the *hort* were tethered inside their owner's tents, and sometimes allowed to wander through the camp. During winter nights, to protect the newborn from the cold, they were placed in miniature huts, *dramshuik*, or small caves, *kuhd*, covered with sticks and palm matting or cloth, often covered with soil, located inside the tents near the animals' pen. After the first several weeks, the *hort* of a number of tents were combined in a flock, *abzeh*, and were taken, by an old man or by small children, for pasture in the area immediately surrounding the camp.

The relations between the *hort* and the adult *pas*, particularly their mothers, had to be regulated in order to control the disposition of milk, which was needed by both these nursing lambs and kids and the human members of the camp. The goal, of course, was to regulate the taking of milk so that (1) the *hort* were properly nourished, and (2) the maximum amount of milk was available for human consumption. One aspect of regulation was restricting nursing, usually through spatial separation of the young from their mothers, and their coming together and nursing only under the supervision and control of the herd owners. During the first few months of life, when the *hort* was either tethered in a tent or out with the *abzeh* and separated from their mothers, which were herded away from camp with the rest of the *ramag*, the *hort* and their mothers came together only when the *ramag* returned to camp for milking and nursing, in that order (although the presence of the *hort* was used to stimulate the mothers and free the milk flow).

When the *hort* reached three to four months, were developed enough to survive on pasturage, and were strong enough to keep up with the *ramag*, a problem arose, because some would continue to nurse given the opportunity. This problem was usually resolved by placing these young *pas* in the *ramag* of another camp, where no female would allow them to nurse. Commonly two camps temporarily exchanged these young animals. In this way, young animals could go out with a *ramag*, become socialized to *ramag* routines, build up physically through exercise, and gain full nourishment from grazing, while being separated from their mothers and thus precluded from drawing on the milk supply. The exchange of *hort* between camps was one illustration of the interdependence of camping groups and lack of complete self-sufficiency of any one camping group.

Some *pas* were weaned, *del sard,* after two months, some longer, and some would suckle, given the opportunity, after six months. Some were weaned by means of a stick, *alak,* inserted into the mouth such that pasture could be eaten but nursing was effectively blocked.

How milk was divided between the *hort* and the people depended upon the season and upon the age and health of the animals. In December, just after *hort* had been dropped, when the need of the *hort* was greatest and their mothers did not have much milk, the *hort* were allowed most of the milk. By February, when the *hort* were larger and grazing a bit, and, in a good year, when pasturage had begun to grow and the mothers were producing more milk, the milk was divided more evenly between *hort* and people.

Gestation of *pas* is six months, so it was possible for *pas* to be mated twice and to drop twice in a year. In good years, *pas* were mated quickly: a June mating for a December parturition and a January mating for a June parturition. But in a poor year, mating was put off until September so that the young would be dropped in spring rather than during the worst of winter, when the poor pasturage remaining from a bad year would mean little milk from the mothers.

Pastoralism is, by our definition, raising livestock on natural pasture. The Sarhadi Baluch were pastoralists not by conceptual adhesion but by productive convenience. They relied upon natural pasture when they could, but when natural pasture was inadequate, even for the modest needs of the Sarhad's few hardy animals spread thinly over the landscape, their willingness to secure and provide sustenance for their animals was limited only by their means. In fact, to some degree livestock owners, *wasildar,* irregularly provided foodstuffs to their animals. This provision was generally intended to support the animals through the worst season of the annual round and through *dokal,* drought years.

Natural pasture was scarce during the winter, for winter was the season farthest from the florescence of plentiful spring, the pasture having suffered the burning of summer and lack of rain during the fall. As well, winter added the challenge of cold temperatures. The dropping of newborn *pas* during this season made the animals particularly vulnerable.

Most vulnerable were the newborn and very young *pas,* for which a date pit gruel, *misinin,* was provided daily. Date pits were cracked and broken into small bits by being hammered with a stone on a small stone anvil. This date pounding stone provided the characteristic sound of a winter morning, as the "clunk . . . clunk . . . clunk" from one tent was answered and joined by the rhythmic clunking from the other tents. The small pieces of date pit were then soaked in water for several hours, a process that softened them so that they could be eaten by the kids, *shaneg,* and lambs, *gwarag.* When the *abzeh,* the small flock of *hort,* nursing young *pas,* returned to the camp in the middle of the afternoon, usually before the *galag* of adult *pas,* they were divided and sent to the tents of their owners, where small bowls of *misinin* were set out for them. Newborn *pas* whose mothers had little or no milk were fed dates and bread. Those herd owners who did not have an adequate supply of date pits fed their animals grain, especially barley.

For example, during the winter of 1972–73, Shams A'din was feeding *misinin* and dates to two *plat,* one *gitaj,* all three weak and thin after having given birth, and four *gwarag* and one *shaneg,* which, he said, would otherwise have been too weak to survive the cold weather. During the great snowfall of 1972–73, when considerable snow accumulated and lay for a week, the *pas* were not able to leave their pens in the tents, although in the tents at least they were protected from the snow. Everyone fed their animals whatever they had at hand, whether fodder, dates, date pits, grain, flour, in order to keep them alive and reasonably well.

Fodder, *duzi*—whether green, fresh fodder, *alef,* dried fodder, *gedag,* or dried white fodder, *kah,* hay—is sometimes acquired from areas of irrigation agriculture in the Sarhad to feed adult animals, especially vulnerable ones that are pregnant or ill. During the *dokal* of 1971, Ja'far bought for 2 toman a *man* (5 kilos) at the settlement of Gazu, two *gwal,* large bags, of *gedag* to feed his *pas* during an eight-day migration. During the winter of 1972–73, Ja'far purchased 20 *man* (100 kilos) of *duzi* at the agricultural areas of Nilagu and Shagbond. Shams A'din exchanged a *gwal* of dates in anticipation of grain and received two *gwal* of *gedag.*

The provision of cultivated foodstuffs—dates, date pits, grain, hay, fodder crops—for the livestock is one way in which the products of other productive sectors, such as date arboriculture and grain and fodder cultivation, were used to support the production of livestock. The different sectors of the multi-resource economy were thus not only additive, but were mutually supporting.

## CAMELS

In addition to *pas,* goats and sheep, the other main kind of livestock was the camel, *hushtair*—the slim, smooth, warm-weather dromedary—which played a major role in the life of Sarhadi tent dwellers. Unlike *pas,* which were valued especially for their milk, hair, wool, and meat, camels—while also appreciated for milk, hair, wool, and meat—were valued most for the services they provided in carrying baggage and riders. Burden camels able to carry the tents, equipment, and supplies made possible the displacement of camping groups from one site to another. Nomadic movement of the Sarhadi Baluch would have been impossible without a means to transport the impedimenta of life from one place to another, a means supplied by the camel.

Camels were categorized according to function and quality (table 4.6). The label *mahri rud bari* designated a fine riding camel. The label *mahri dashti* designated a good

**Table 4.6.** Categories, Labels, and Prices
for Camels

| Age | Male | Female |
|---|---|---|
| Newborn | Herruk | Herruk |
| 6 months | Herr | Herr |
| 1 year | Jird | Jird |
| 2 years | Pourap | Kowant |
| 3–8 years | Dachi | Lira |
| >10 years | Pira jurt | Pira lira |

| | Prices (toman) | |
|---|---|---|
| | *mahri rud bari* | *bari* |
| Herruk | 200–300 | 100–200 |
| Pourap (male) | 800–1,000 | 500–600 |
| Kowant (female) | 900–1,500 | 600–700 |
| Datchi (male) | 700–800 | 600 |
| Lira (female) | 1,000 | 600–700 |
| Pira jurt (male) | 300–400 | 300–400 |
| Pira lira (female) | 300–400 | 400–450 |

riding camel. The label *bari* designated a burden animal. Prices of camels varied according to category. In 1972–73, for example, Ja'far traded two *bari herruk,* one in exchange for one *gitaj* (general price, 100 toman) and one *mish* (general price, 120 toman), the other in exchange for five date palms, *mach,* and 50 toman in cash.

We should note, in reviewing the general pricing, that while for *pas,* the difference in cost between the milk-producing females and the males was great, from 50 percent to 100 percent or more, the difference between female and male camels was not that great, from 0 to 25 percent. The reason was that, although female camels carried and nursed young, male camels were larger, stronger, and faster in carrying riders or baggage. Furthermore, there was a conflict between reproduction and burden, because stressing a female camel with heavy burdens during pregnancy would have been dangerous for the fetus and the mother. So there were good reasons for wanting male and well as female camels.

In the camp of Ja'far in 1968, there were 28 adult and 4 young (*herruk, herr,* and *jird*) camels, an average of 2 adult camels per household, of which there were 14. In 1972, there were 19 adult camels and 9 young attached to 17 households, an average of 1.1 adult camels per household. This decline in the number of camels was due to two factors. One was the losses resulting from the drought, for there were no newborn *herruk,* which would have been in gestation during the drought. The other was a somewhat greater reliance by tent dwellers on motorized transport, which was becoming increasingly available, in the form of motorcycle taxis, jeep taxis, and trucks for portage, with a consequent noticeable decrease in willingness on the part of the tent dwellers to invest in camels.

Of the 28 camels—young, adult, and old, but none under one year—in the camp of Ja'far in 1972, 19 were female and 9 were male, a ratio of about 2 females for each male, significantly different from the female/male ratio among adult *pas* of more than 90 to 1. Of the 28, 24 were *bari* and 4 were *mahri dashti*, a ratio of 6 to 1, indicating that the priority of the camp members was the transport of goods.


## MANAGEMENT OF CAMELS

The herding of camels, *hushtair,* was organized differently from the herding of *pas.* Within the confines of an established camp, several sets of households organized to combine their camels into small herds, *bak,* each set agreeing to pay a boy, usually between 8 and 12 years old and commonly from one of the households of the set, to be camelherd, *bakjat,* responsible for seeing the camels to and from pasture and keeping control of their whereabouts. In the camp of Ja'far during 1972–73, there were four *bak* and four *bakjat,* each a son of one of the camel owners. The four *bak* had respectively nine, five, seven, and seven camels.

Camels did not need the close supervision that *pas* did, and *bakjat* were not expected to spend full time in the pasture with the camels. Adult camels, which were generally large and strong, were not as vulnerable to attack by wolves and were quite happy to wander and feed on their own. However, they had to be kept away from cultivation and had to be taken to be watered.

Camels were given water once a day during the winter. In good spring seasons, when there was plenty of fresh pasturage, the camels got all necessary moisture from pasturage and were not taken to water at all. In poor spring seasons, with little pasturage, the camels were watered every other day. In late spring camels were watered every other day, in early summer once a day, and in high summer twice a day, in the morning and early afternoon.

Camels were given foodstuffs by their owners in order to supplement pasturage. Pregnant, young, or weak camels were given roots, dug up and cleaned by herd owners. In 1968 one pregnant camel showed up, on her own, at her owner's tent at 5 P.M. sharp every day in order to receive her meal of roots. During an unusual and substantial accumulation of snow during the winter of 1972–73, the camels were not able to move from their sleeping places behind the tents. Everyone fed their camels whatever they had in their tents—*duzi*, dates, flour—to keep them alive until the snow melted a week later. In general during the winter, camels that might suffer from the cold, because they were weak, young, or pregnant, were covered with blanket-cloaks that were tied on, protecting them day and night from the low temperatures.

In the case of camels, reproduction could hardly be said to be "natural," for human intervention and assistance appears to have been necessary at various crucial stages. Left on their own, camels seemed to have difficulty copulating; the females were often unwilling, while the males, although enthusiastic, were inept (perhaps a pattern that applies to other species as well). In order to overcome this difficulty, camel copulation was facilitated and managed by a group of men. With the unruly male and female camels being held by ropes, salt was rubbed into the vagina, to make the female more receptive, and the sexual member of the male camel was guided into the vagina by human assistance. At the final end of the process, birth, extended human assistance was necessary to extract the *herruk* from its mother. Baluch said that without their interventions, camels would not succeed at reproducing. This may have been to a degree hyperbole, but human assistance certainly eased the process and ensured a greater rate of reproduction than would have taken place if the camels had been left to their own inclinations and abilities.

## CERTAINTY AND UNCERTAINTY
## IN SARHADI PASTORALISM

Baluch never say anything about next year, next week, or even tomorrow without saying *insha allah,* "with the will of God." At the theological level, this is a recognition of the ultimate power of God and the ultimate impotence of man. But how well the theological sentiment fit the more mundane circumstances under which the Sarhadi Baluch lived and strove to make a living. If we substitute "nature" for "God," we have a fair reading of the inability of Baluchi tent dwellers to control basic conditions upon which depended their future success in productive activities such as pastoralism.

As we have seen, droughts were recurrent and frequent. Out of every five or six years, two years were very likely to be drought years in which the little rain generated little pasture, and livestock, particularly the newborn, and the young, deprived of milk from their dry mothers, died from a lack of nourishment. Nor did the herd owners fare well, deprived of milk and its products, their main source of protein and fat. Consequently undernourished, tribesmen themselves were more vulnerable to illness and disease.

On a monthly, seasonal, and annual basis, the Baluch lived with uncertainty. At the same time, nothing was more certain than the uncertainty itself. Baluch expected it and knew that they would have to cope with it. Furthermore, in the longer term, nothing was more certain than rainfall and pasture fluctuation and the irregular alternation between years of rainfall and years of drought, between years of plenty and years of scarcity. These multiyear cycles were as basic to Baluchi life as seasonal cycles. Other common uncertainties bearing upon pastoralism were repeated but unpredictable periods of freezing weather, livestock disease, and attacks on the livestock by animal and human predators.

The certainty of uncertainty provided the basis upon which the Sarhadi *baluch* built a set of established, encultured, institutionalized measures to deal with these climatic and other variations. One specific measure, mentioned above, was providing fodder for livestock when necessary. Another specific measure, also mentioned earlier, was the storage of food, such as the preparation during good seasons and good years of *shilanch,* dried milk solids, for human consumption when milk was not available, and the preparation and packing of dates for the entire seasonal cycle. A third measure, a more general strategy, to be discussed later, was migration in search of pasture beyond the usual area, for example, into high ranges of mountains. A fourth measure was the overall strategy of diversification of productive effort into a number of quite different sectors, of which pastoralism was only one, and others of which, as we shall see, reached outside the Sarhad and even Baluchistan. This diversification of the multi-resource economy into sectors, each of which depended upon different environmental conditions, went far toward guaranteeing that, in the face of a failure in one sector, Sarhadi *baluch* could fall back upon other sectors. So while pastoralism was a major productive enterprise for the Sarhadi *baluch,* it was not the only one, and it was well understood that pastoral production would cyclically flourish and decline in response to multiyear climatic variations.

The *baluchi* response to uncertainty was not ritualism or quietism; while believers, and increasingly participants in religious activity, the *baluch* were not "otherworldly." The *baluchi* response to uncertainty in production was—within the general strategy of diversification—initiative, effort, and risk in maintaining and advancing each household economy. In order to adapt effectively to environmental conditions, Sarhadi *baluch* engaged in a constant collection of information, and, in considering a wide range of response options, they continually engaged in consultation with one another, especially regarding collective decisions, such as giving guidance to the shepherd or deciding when and where to migrate. Though the tent dwellers may not have been able to control climatic and other conditions that directly affected their lives, they constantly strove to adapt effectively to those conditions and, as we shall see, to find new ways of adapting.

The above are by no means our last words on pastoralism in the Sarhad. We shall hear much more about animals and their needs in later discussions about nomadism. But for the moment, let us turn to other sectors of production.

# 5.
## CULTIVATING

In addition to pastoralism, Sarhadi Baluch were engaged in a substantial way in several other economic sectors. Sarhadi tent dwellers had been pursuing date palm cultivation for at least a hundred years and perhaps much longer, and dates, as we have seen, were a major component of their diet. As well, date cultivation was an important source of feed for their animals, and the date palms were a valuable source of raw materials. Another sector in which Sarhadi Baluch were committed was grain cultivation, as the source for the basic staple, bread. While in the past opportunistic runoff cultivation was most typical, from the 1960s irrigation agriculture expanded. No less important in the Sarhadi economy had been the predatory raiding of caravans and villages outside of the Sarhad and often outside of Baluchistan. Since the suppression of raiding in the 1930s, engagement of the Sarhadi Baluch outside of Baluchistan increasingly took the form of migrant labor, the trading and importing of goods, and smuggling. Hunting and gathering was always an important supplement to other forms of production and continued to be important as a source of fuel and raw materials, as well as wild foods. Let us explore these sectors in turn, beginning in this chapter with cultivation.

## DATE ARBORICULTURE

The major nonpastoral resource of the tent-dwelling Sarhadi Baluch was the date groves on the western edge of the Hamuni Mashkil, the desert drainage basin to the east of the Sarhad, past the Morpish Mountains and off the Plateau. In contrast to the 1,700 meters of the Sarhadi high plains, the altitude of the Hamuni Mashkil was 457 meters (1,500 feet). There were 11 named date grove areas, each with one or more settlement areas, distinctly separated from one another by stretches of desert (figure 5.1).

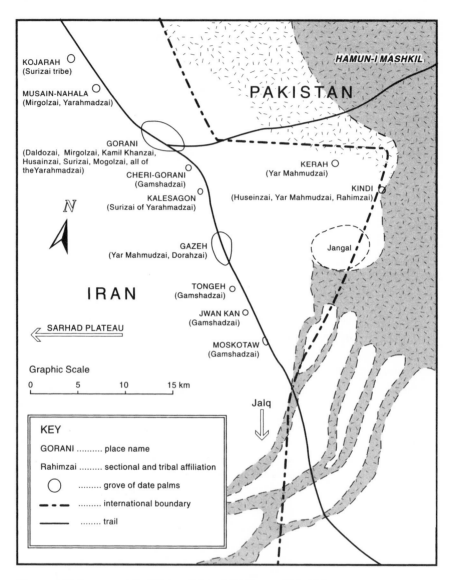

Figure 5.1. Date groves at the Western Edge of the Hamun-i Mashkil.

Each of these grove areas was identified with the tribe and tribal sections that predominantly owned the date palms at that location. Nine of these grove areas
stretched in a line from northwest to southeast: Kojarah (Surizai section of the Yarahmadzai tribe), Musain-Nahala (Mirgolzai lineage of the Yarahmadzai tribe), Gorani
(Surizai section and Soherabzai section—including Dadolzai, Mir Golzai, Kamil Hanzai, Husainzai, Mogolzai—of the Yarahmadzai), Cheri-Gorani (Gamshadzai tribe),
Kalesagon (Surizai section of the Yarahmadzai), Gazeh (Yar Mahmudzai lineage of

the Soherabzai section of the Yarahmadzai), Tongeh (Gamshadzai), Jwan Kan (Gamshadzai), and Moksotaw (Gamshadzai). East of Gorani was Raja (Rahmatzai section of Yarahmadzai), and due east of Cheri-Gorani and Kalesagon, separated by a good stretch of desert, were Kerah (Yar Mahmudzai lineage of the Yarahmadzai) and Kindi (Yar Mahmudzai of the Soherabzai, and the Hoseinzai, and Rahmatzai sections of the Yarahmadzai). Most members of the camp of Ja'far had their date palms at Gorani, the largest of the grove areas.

These date palm groves have been important to the Sarhadi Baluch since at least the mid-1800s. Their ownership by Sarhadi tribes was recognized in Western sources in the fourth quarter of the nineteenth century, when an international boundary commission was establishing the borderline between Iran and the Khanate of Kalat, a semidependency of the British Indian Empire (Persian Boundary Commission [India] 1876:63). These tribal date groves on the western edge of the Hamuni Mashkil became a matter of controversy. Sykes (1902:228–29) indicated that he "had first heard of the existence of these unimportant groves when in the Sarhad in 1893. . . . These groves, far from being 'half of Baluchistan,' are of but little value, but this did not prevent their being a source of constant annoyance." In referring to the Yarahmadzai, Sykes (1902:230, n. 1) states that "this Sarhad tribe was constantly raiding across the frontier [into British India], and it was partly on that account that we [from British India] so gladly gave up the date-groves owned by them." The boundary between Iran and Kalat, later to become the boundary between Iran and Pakistan, was drawn up by the commission with an otherwise unexplainable detour to the northeast at the western edge of the Hamun so as to include on the Persian side of the demarcation the groves owned by the Sarhadi Baluch.

The Hamuni Mashkil was about 150 kilometers (over 90 miles) east of Washt/Khash as the crow flies, and over 200 kilometers (over 120 miles) as the camels slowly wended their way through the passes of the Morpish Mountains, descending 1,220 meters (around 4,000 feet) in altitude from the Sarhadi portion of the Iranian Plateau to the lower desert plains. It was a long and arduous way from Ja'far's camp at Pushti Kamal. Why, then, did the Sarhadi Baluch have their date groves at the Hamuni Mashkil?

Most simply, the Sarhad was unsuitable for date palms. Its freezing winter climate precluded the cultivation of dates (Spooner 1967:10, 34). According to Sir Percy Sykes (1941:71), the maximum altitude for growing date palms in this part of the world is 1,200 meters (around 4,000 feet), considerably lower than the 1,700 meters (around 5,550 feet) of the Sarhad Plateau. Date-growing areas to the south, such as Saravan (e.g., Shastun at 1,180 meters, or 3,872 feet), Bampusht (e.g., Isfandak at 1,091 meters, or 3,580 feet), and Makran, are characterized by warmer climates. So the Sarhad was ruled out for date cultivation. But why select the distant and extraordinarily hot, arid, and windy Hamuni Mashkil?

The cultivation of dates in Baluchistan usually followed one of two patterns. The first was the oasis pattern characteristic of settlements such as Shastun in Saravan and Isfandak in Bampusht. In these oases (Spooner 1969; Salzman 1978b), irrigation brought water to tight clusters of date palms under which grew other cultigens, including grains, vegetables, and fruits. Regular, intensive labor the year round was required to man the irrigation canals and grow the multiseason crops. There was thus a permanent, settled population of cultivators, called *shahri*. The other pattern was the mountain pattern, in which drainage water from small runoff channels was captured at small flat areas by simple earthwork walls no more than a foot high, and a few date palms and small patches of grain and vegetables were cultivated. Unlike the dense cultivation and residence of the oases, the mountain patches of cultivation were dispersed widely, and the cultivators, tent dwelling *baluch,* moved among them.

In order to cultivate dates, the Baluch of the Sarhad had to use a location with a climate warmer than the Sarhad. They could not follow the oasis pattern, which required permanent settlement, without abandoning the Sarhad and their lives in the black tents. They could not follow the mountain pattern in the neighboring Kuhi Daptan or the Morpish Mountains, because these mountains, with their higher altitudes than the Sarhad Plain, were even colder than the Sarhad, and date palms would not grow there. And scattered sites in more southerly mountains were too distant from the Sarhad and would have required abandonment.

The Hamuni Mashkil was attractive for several reasons. First, it was certainly warm enough for date cultivation. Second, the hydrological conditions were unusual and particularly suitable to the needs of the Sarhadi Baluch. The Hamuni Mashkil was an inland drainage basin into which waters from Daptan, Morpish, and other mountain ranges ran. At the center the soil of the Hamun was saline from the evaporation of sitting water. But at the edges of the Hamun, sweet water from the mountains brought the water table close to the surface. In fact, the water was so close to the surface, no more than one meter during the spring, that date palms could sink their roots down to the water and drink without human assistance. Nothing could have suited the Sarhadi Baluch so well, for they were freed from any need to provide water for their palms or even to be present while the palm roots silently absorbed water directly from the water table. The Baluch were thus able to absent themselves from the groves and go about their other business on the Sarhad or elsewhere for most of the year, coming to the groves only for two weeks of pollination in the spring and two months of harvest in high summer.

This drainage basin pattern of date palm cultivation, as pursued by the Sarhadi Baluch at the Mashkil drainage basin, shared some features but also diverged from both the oasis and mountain patterns. First, while the groves of oases were tightly concentrated, to minimize the travel and dispersion of water, the palms of the mountains were dispersed among small plots here and there throughout the mountains. In contrast, the palms of the drainage basin were all in large groves, but the palms themselves were spread thinly over the surface, so that they would not have to compete with one another for soil and water. Second, unlike the oasis and mountain patterns, which used surface water or brought water to the surface to cultivate other crops under the palms, water in the drainage basin groves remained underground in the water table, tapped directly by the roots of the palms, and there was no water at the surface for other crops.

The drainage basin groves appeared—to my eye, at least—to be scant, unkempt, and scraggly, in comparison with the tiny perfect plots of the mountains and the rich fecund gardens of the oases. This impression resulted not only from the relatively thin distribution of the date palms over the land surface, but also from the squat bushy shape of many, almost trunkless palms, *nahal,* and the medium palms, *gwang,* with short rough trunks, so untidy in comparison with the smooth, tall, graceful, waving palms, *dahk,* of the oases of southern Baluchistan. This was not just a matter of aesthetics, for tall palms ensured that the ground level was free for other crops and that the sunlight for the surface crops would not be blocked by the crowns of the palms. But tall palms, elegant though they were, required arduous and dangerous climbing for each task of cultivation. At the Mashkil date groves, palms tended to be short. One reason was that the strong winds of the *bad-e sad o bist ruz,* the infamous wind of 120 days, blowing down from the north, tended to erode the soil around the roots of palms and put great pressure on tall palms, so that many of them were toppled by the wind. Another reason was that no surface crops provided motivation for tribesmen to expose the surface to the sun by cultivating tall palms. Sarhadi Baluch tended to prefer short palms because they were easier and safer to work.

Within each of the date grove areas, there were one or more concentrated living areas, with dwellings that were repeatedly used on a temporary basis during the pollination and harvest seasons. In some living areas, there were collections of small dwellings, *manah,* made of palm fronds, *chat* or *chart.* These did not last many years, for the frond leaves dried and became brittle, but they were relatively easy to construct. Where *manah* were prevalent, it was because the soil did not lend itself to the making of mud bricks. Where the soil was appropriate, the Sarhadi date cultivators built *ban,* or mud-brick, one-room houses with sand floors and rafters of palm trunks and with roofs of palm fronds. The brick *ban* blocked the sun and provided shade, and, with doors facing the south, blocked the constant, strong wind coming from the north. Recently built *ban* tended to be larger and higher and provided dwellers with substantially lower temperatures inside than out during the daytime. The converse was true at night, for while the temperature dropped at dusk and the night was cool, throughout the night the mud bricks gave off the heat they had absorbed from the sun during the day. While those living in *manah* may have spent the night in their dwellings, those living in *ban* invariably escaped the mud-brick heat by sleeping outside, in the open, near their houses.

At Gorani, there were four settlements, *bonend,* each identified with a particular tribe, section, or lineage: the Gamshadzai *bonend,* the Mir Golzai *bonend,* the Kamil

Hanzai *bonend,* and the *bonend* predominantly occupied by members of the camp of Ja'far and other members of the dominant Dadolzai lineage but shared with a large group of Mogolzai, a closely related lineage. The Dadolzai and Mogolzai *bonend* consisted of 46 *ban* and 2 *manah.* Seven of the *ban* were abandoned, as the owners had built new ones, larger and higher, and correspondingly more comfortable, among the 37 *ban* occupied (2 were unoccupied, but still in use). Of these, 18 were owned by members of the Dadolzai lineage, 9 by members of the Mogolzai lineage, and 10 by members of other lineages, a number of whom were sons-in-law of the Dadolzai or Mogolzai. During the late summer harvest season of 1972, some *ban* owners were not resident in the *bonend,* and some nonowners were residing in borrowed *ban;* of 31 male household heads, 14 were Dadolzai, 10 Mogolzai, and 7 of other lineage affiliation. As did a number of palm grove settlements, Gorani had a small one-room mudbrick mosque decorated with three small steeple-like additions, each topped with a beer bottle, and fronted by a mud-brick fence enclosing a porch area. Men coming together to pray did so outside, in front of the mosque.

The *ban* of the Dadolzai and Mogolzai *bonend* could not be built just anywhere; sites had to be located in close proximity both to the soil that was to be used for the bricks and to wells that would supply the water for making the bricks and later provide water for household needs. Within the built-up areas of the *bonend,* many sites were occupied, and it was not always easy to build new *ban* near certain others as the occupants might wish. But in spite of these physical inhibitions and limitations, the distribution of *ban* reflected fairly clearly distinct social patterns: the Mogolzai were clustered together, as were the Dadolzai, with no Dadolzai interspersed among the Mogolzai nor Mogolzai among the Dadolzai. Sons-in-law from other lineages had *ban* next to their affines; members of distant or unrelated lineages were located on the edges of the settlement. In short, the spatial arrangement of *ban* reflected lineage affiliation and kin ties. Even within lineages, sub- or microlineages clustered together. The Dadolzai were split into neighborhoods separated by a stand of palms, the Shirdelzai Dadolzai and the Komeronzai Dadolzai to the north, the Dust Mahmudzai Dadolzai to the south. Members of the Shadi Hanzai Dadolzai were split between the two neighborhoods, location in the north or south neighborhood being determined by affinal ties with the other sublineages.

In activities that involved cooperation or collective participation by numbers of individuals, recruitment tended to follow lineage lines. For example, in the building of *ban,* the two jobs that were done collectively were bricklaying and the hauling and placing of palm trunks for rafters. In four cases of construction activities on Dadolzai-owned *ban,* one of roof repair, one of palm trunk transportation, and two of bricklaying, involving respectively 16, 12, 14, and 17 workers, not one of the workers was Mogolzai, all of the workers having been Dadolzai, their affines, and associates. Similarly with migration between Mashkil and the Sarhad, groupings of tribesmen in camel caravans or, by the mid-1970s, in rented trucks, were always lineage groupings, the Dadolzai and their associates making their arrangements and moving together, and the Mogolzai making their arrangements and moving together. Further, even in prayer, remarkably, the separation by lineage was manifested. As was quite well known among the Sarhadi Baluch, it is incumbent upon Muslims to pray, whenever possible, as a group, as a member of the community of Islam, under the guidance of a learned prayer leader. The residents of the *bonend* had recognized this and built a mosque. Evening and night prayers were led by a mulla. But not all of the *bonend* residents participated equally in these collective prayers; quite the contrary. For the most part, it was the Dadolzai and their associated affines who prayed regularly at the mosque. The Mogolzai, with the exception of one man who attended regularly and another who came occasionally, did not come to the mosque, preferring to pray individually in their *ban*. Although the Dadolzai and the Mogolzai each claimed that it was they who had built the mosque, its location was in the Dadolzai section of the *bonend*. Distance, though, could not have been a factor, for the Mogolzai were spatially closer than the Dadolzai of the southern neighborhood who did attend the mosque regularly. In general, then, in the various *bonend* of Mashkil, the basis of cooperation and association, as well as residential propinquity, was lineage affiliation.

## Seasons of the Dates

Sarhadi *baluch* divided the year into five seasons:

- *Bahargah*, spring, began with the appearance of pasturage, *bahar*. It spanned March, April, and May and ended with *zard o bahar*, the drying of the pasture, and included *iwar*, the pollination of the date palms, usually during the second half of March.
- *Garmon*, early summer, included June and all or part of July and was divided into *gala zar o bur*, the drying of the grain, *duro*, harvest, and *juhan*, piles of grain.
- *Hamin*, high summer, spanned August, September, and all or part of October and was divided into *suzkumpk*, the period of the immature, green dates; *moksund*, the tying of date bags; *mokbur*, the date harvest; and *shawarkashk*, the transport of the dates to the Sarhad.
- *Yirat*, fall, corresponded more or less with November.
- *Zemistan*, winter, spanned December, January, and February.

For the *baluch*, as for rural producers generally, the seasons represented not only climatic variations but also specific production activities tied to the development cycles of plants and animals. Seasons were thought of not abstractly, but in terms of the activities that they represented, and were subdivided into periods of those activities.

*Hamin*, high summer, was the specific season of date production activities, because this was the period of date ripening and was divided into major phases of work. But *hamin* was, in a practical sense, consequent upon *iwar*, pollination, which took place much earlier, in *bahargah,* spring.

## Pollination

For all of the year but *hamin,* the high-summer date season, the Sarhadi *baluch* lived on the high Sarhad Plateau, occupying their tents and tending to their livestock, grain cultivation, and other activities. But for two or three weeks in the spring, *bahargah,* they were claimed by the date palms. The reason for this was that date palms, *mach* or *mok,* are either male or female, each palm growing exclusively either the male stamen, *gosh,* or the female pistil, *whush* or *hush* or *wusht.* Dates did not grow on the male palms, *narin,* but only on the female palms, *madag,* and would only form if the female *whush* were pollinated by the male *gosh.* If there were no pollination, only a small, seedless growth, *pin,* which was not edible, appeared. When the pollen of the *gosh* reached the *whush,* dates began to grow, developing from a hard, green, unripe stage, *suzkumpk,* and eventually ripening into a softer, yellow or black, ripe stage, *hormag.*

Natural pollination of the *whush* by pollen from the *gosh* was a chancy business. The carrying of pollen to its target by the wind was extremely imperfect, leaving most *gosh* unpollinated and few dates developing. For the purposes of the Baluch, what was wanted was a much surer method of pollinating, one that would lead to the largest possible crop of dates. Thus the Baluch themselves undertook the task of pollination, *iwar,* and this was the purpose of their two- or three-week excursion in the spring. There was no displacement of residence; the tents and most family members remained on the Sarhad. Not all active men went to the date groves. Perhaps a third of the active men went to the groves, to pollinate their palms and the palms of those left behind on the high plateau or occupied elsewhere. During *iwar,* the men from the camp of Ja'far who descended to the date palm groves at Mashkil lived together in one or two dwellings, sharing the simple chores of preparing their modest work-detail diet of bread, ghee and date preserve, *shirag,* and tea, the ingredients of which they carried to the groves from the Sarhad.

The pollination of the palms by the hand of man, while arduous, was not a greatly complicated procedure. The procedure could begin when the protective pods, *kur karchuk,* of the *gosh* and the *whush* opened naturally, signaling that the inner, reproductive stems, the *goshalak* and the *whushalak,* were mature and ready for pollination. If the pods were still closed when the men arrived, they had to wait for the opening. The first step was to collect the *goshalak,* cutting away the outer pod with a serrated blade sickle, *harrag,* an indispensable tool for date cultivation, and casting the pod pieces aside. The *goshalak* stems were then carefully cut and gently collected. This process would have been much easier if the palms frond stems were not lined with large, sharp spines, *kontak,* any one of which could easily stab through clothes, sandals, and flesh, causing serious injury, thus requiring supple and delicate self-placement by the Baluchi pollinators as they pursued their task. At the same time, the relative shortness of the almost trunkless *nahal* and the moderate height, up to 6 meters (almost 20 feet), of the *gwang,* the most common palms at Gorani, relieved the men of difficult climbs and the dangers of a long fall.

The *goshalak* stems with the pollen attached were then carefully carried to a female palm, *madag.* Remaining parts of the now open protective pod of the *whush* were removed with the *harrag,* leaving the *whushalak* standing exposed. The *goshalak* from the male palm were then carefully pushed down into the *whushalak,* bringing together the male stamen and female pistil and pollinating the stigma. From this point, the palm could be left to itself for three months while the dates began to grow.

## Bagging the Dates

It was only three months later, in high summer, *hamin,* that the Sarhadi *baluch*—men, women, and children, old and young—left their tents and flocks behind on the high plateau and descended to the Mashkil date groves, saying, "We are going to eat dates." The season in the date groves was seen by the tent dwellers, especially the young, as a summer vacation, a break in their normal routine, and an opportunity to enjoy fresh dates to their fill.

If *hamin* was a vacation, it was certainly a working vacation. From the time of arrival at Mashkil, bagging the dates began. The date clusters had grown on *whushalak* stalks in the crown of the palms. At this time they were not yet mature but were either still green, *suzkumpk,* or had turned color but had not yet softened, *kumpk.* These immature dates could be blown off the palms by the wind. And once the dates matured and softened, becoming *hormag,* they may well have fallen off the palm and been damaged, lost, or eaten by camels. Dates in low palms were also vulnerable to hungry camels, which were perfectly capable of eating large quantities. By placing the immature bunches of dates growing on the palms in protective bags, *sund,* the Baluch could ensure that the maturing process would continue without losses. An additional advantage was that bagged clusters of dates were easy to harvest, for all that was required was the cutting of the stem and the lowering of the bag.

The bags, *sund,* were long shallow envelopes, a meter or more long and a half meter or more high (around 4 feet × 2 feet), with open tops, woven from leaves, *pish,* of the date palm fronds. *Chiluk* rope, also made from *pish,* was used to close the top of the bag and thus enclose the dates, as well as to secure the bag onto the palm. Young and mature men did most of the bagging. It was an arduous task primarily because of the same spines, *kontak,* that made difficult negotiating the palms for pollination. Taller palms also had to be climbed. Unlike the relatively mild weather of *iwar,* temperatures during *hamin* were sizzling, up to 60 centigrade (140 Farenheit), exacerbated by the strong, hot wind, making the work draining even for hardy Baluch, although they were never in a rush to admit it.

Often men went out alone, but frequently boys went along to carry *sund,* to collect any dates that fell, to carry a small *mashk* of refreshing water, and to continue their year-round training course in learning how to be a *baluch* and how to make a living the *baluchi* way. Older boys also tried out the techniques that they had observed, developing the skills to do the job properly, and receiving not always welcome commentary on their attempts. Older men would also attend, sometimes to direct the work, sometimes to weave *chaluk* for on-the-spot use. The amount of work done on a given day depended on a number of factors: whether the *sund* and *chaluk* were ready and available or whether they had to be woven in the course of the work; whether there were many spines on the fronds, or whether they had been stripped earlier; whether the palm had been well pruned, leaving the dates open to easy access, or whether there was a jungle of fronds through which to struggle on the way to the dates; whether the palm was conveniently short or whether it was tall, necessitating a climb and various other preparations, such as support straps.

Once the dates were safely in their *sund,* the Baluch could rest easy as the dates ripened. In the meantime, there were other tasks to be done.

## Pruning and Planting

Palms grew by sending out new fronds at the top. It was among new and recent fronds that the *whush* was found and the dates grew. Superseded fronds lower down would, after some years, fall off naturally. But for the Baluch, who benefited from easy access to the top of the palm, the wait for the lowest fronds to fall off was inconvenient, and the higher but superseded fronds had also to be negotiated on the way up. Furthermore, lower fronds are "dead wood," inhibiting the growth of the palm and reducing date production. So cutting off the superseded fronds was an annual task in husbanding the palms.

Palms naturally reproduced by scattering seed, that is dates, and by sending out suckers, *jujuk,* from their roots. A grove area could thus become crowded with new palms competing with the old for water and even sunlight. Thinning groves by removing unwanted, new palms, in order to minimize competition for productive palms, was another maintenance task. At the same time, *jujuk,* like superseded fronds, drew strength from the palm, and they were sometimes removed manually, using a large metal chisel, *bubang,* and a heavy wooden mallet, *kortuuk,* and sometimes removed by burning.

Access to palm crowns and dates could be eased by stripping the fronds of spines. Here, as in the removal of old fronds, the *harrag* was the main tool.

The strong wind at the Hamun gradually blew away the soil at the roots of the palms, destroying the roots and undermining the stability of the palms, and felling the palms if no counter action was taken. Responding to this problem, the Baluch piled up soil around the bases of their palms.

A *jujuk* was not only a drain on its host palm or a threat to neighboring palms, to be removed and destroyed. A *jujuk* was also potentially a new palm to expand the grove and provide additional dates. The dates of trees from *jujuk* were of high quality, while those grown from seeds were poor. So planting *jujuk* was the preferred way to expand one's grove. *Jujuk* were, with considerable effort, cut from their host palms with the *bubang* and *kortuuk*, hauled to a new site, and carefully planted. These transplanted *jujuk* had to be provided with water and nourishment and protected from animals. They were often surrounded by low walls, *dewal*, of mud brick or palm fronds held together by rope. Similarly, small palms, *nahal*, were sometimes uprooted and, with their fronds cut off, transplanted. They were usually soaked in water near a well before being replanted. Transplanted *jujuk* and *nahal* were watered during their first *hamin* and sometimes watered in subsequent *hamin*. Some *jujuk* were placed to receive, through simple surface channels, runoff water from wells, camel watering, or household use. But it was only when the palms sink their roots down to the water table, that they could grow on their own without water from the hand of man. In the first seasons, the fronds were often bound together into an upright bundle to maintain moisture until the roots could sink down. To aid growth, fertilizer in the form of camel dung was added to the soil. At the planting, a prayer was said for the growth of the palm.

That the cultivation of date groves was a long-term investment was both attractive and unattractive to Baluch, who did not have a great deal of spare time and effort. It was unattractive because many years had to pass before a date palm began to produce substantial numbers of dates. Palms at Gorani needed 7 to 10 years before they began to bear dates, and they did not reach their maximum production until at least 12 and as long as 20 years. Thus to plant a new date palm was to look far ahead for fruition, perhaps even longer than the owner could expect to live.

Cultivation of date groves was also a happy long-term investment in that date palms, once they began producing, could produce for many years. From their initial production at 6 or 8 years and initial maximum production at 20 years, they continued at full production until they were 30 or 35 years old, when production began to decline, reaching 15–20 percent of the maximum sometime between 40 and 50 years of age. So there was from 20 to 30 good years of productivity in a date palm. This reward justified for many Baluch the effort of hammering away at *jujuk* to detach them, hauling them to new sites, digging holes and transplanting them, irrigating, fertilizing, and fencing them. We should note, however, that the date groves at Mashkil, relying on groundwater and tended only part-time, were inferior to those elsewhere in Baluchistan in productivity and quality. For example, date palms elsewhere in Baluchistan were in their prime at 100 years and produced even up to 200 years (Spooner, personal communication: January 3, 1997).

Date palms as capital resources were also exchanged in various transactions. Even palms that had not reached their most productive stages were attractive acquisitions. We have seen that Ja'far received five date palms and 50 toman in exchange for a baby camel. Date palms were also used for marriage exchanges and for contributions to new households. Palms were also passed along from one owner to another in antici-patory and de facto inheritance. Taking the family of Gulap as an illustration, let us see the transfer and distribution of palms in inheritance.

Counting both anticipatory and de facto inheritance, 182 palms, *mach,* were distrib-uted among family members from the grove of Gulap (table 5.1). Date palms were thus a major form of wealth passed from one generation to the next in this family. Of course, many of these palms would have been planted and nurtured by the two sons, Mahmud Karim and Shams A'din, even if at earlier stages under the guidance and su-pervision of their father. So the passing along may be seen not only in the legal sense from Gulap to Mahmud Karim and Shams A'din, but in an institutional sense from Mahmud Karim's and Shams Adin's family of orientation, including themselves and their parents and siblings, to their new families of procreation, including themselves, their wives, and their children. Similarly, the importance of inheritance can be seen in many other cases. To mention only one more, Jan Mahmud, a sole son, received on the death of his father 200 *mach* as well as 12 *pas,* 1 camel, and 12 hours of irriga-tion water.

## Harvesting and Packing

Because of the bagging done previously, harvesting of the dates was a relatively simple operation. One man climbed the palm, used his *harrag* to cut, *burri,* the stalk, the grown *hushalak,* connecting the bagged cluster of dates to the palm. The *sund* with the dates inside was then tied to a long goat-hair rope, *ris* (also used for tying loads onto camels during migration), and lowered to the ground, where someone else was waiting to receive it. The same process was followed for the other bagged date clusters in the palm. After coming down from the palm, the harvester and oth-ers present opened the *sund* and picked the dates off the *whush.* They picked out those dates that had been spoiled by insects, usually few, and threw them away. Those that were dried up or still hard and unripened, *kumpk,* were set aside, along with the un-pollinated *pin,* for the camels and *pas.* Then the *sund* with the dates inside were bound with *chiluk* or *ris* and carried back to the dwelling for further processing and packing.

Now while the Sarhadi Baluch said that they go to Mashkil to "eat dates," the dates harvested during *hamin* were an important foodstuff for the entire following year. The Baluch thus faced the task of packing and storing the dates so that they could be safely transported to the Sarhad high plateau and would be safely preserved for family con-sumption in three, six, or even nine months. Only two types of dates could be packed with their pits, *rabi* and *shingiskan.* These two could, after washing, be packed moist

**Table 5.1.** Inheritance of Palms among the Family of Gulap

| Name | Relationship | Anticipatory | At Decease |
|------|--------------|--------------|------------|
| Mahmud Karim | Eldest son | 40 palms, *mach* <br> 1 camel <br> (at marriage) | 40 *mach* |
| Shams Hartun | Daughter | 15 *mach* <br> (at marriage) | |
| Malik Hartun | Daughter | 15 *mach* <br> (at marriage) | |
| Shams A'din | Son | 1 camel, 5 *pas* <br> (at marriage) | 60 *mach* |
| Zarbonu | Wife | | 12 *mach*, 5 *pas*, <br> ½ camel |

in *pas* skin bags, *hezak*, although there were usually only a limited number of *hezak* available. *Hezak* were also small and relatively delicate and so were somewhat troublesome to transport.

Alternatively, the *rabi* and *shingushkan* could be put in *sund* to be dried on the roof of the dwelling, *ban*, after which they were washed and packed in large, heavy wool or wool and cotton bags, *gwal*. Moist dates were not put into *gwal*, because they would be crushed and the liquid would leak. Packing dates into a *gwal* was usually done by tying the top two corners of the *gwal* with long goat-hair ropes, *ris*, and tying the *ris* to the palm trunk rafters of the *ban*, while the bottom of the *gwal* remained on the sand floor. An adult man then climbed into the *gwal* and used his (washed) feet to pack down dates as other family members, often women, poured dates, batch by batch, into the *gwal*. Through this method, a large amount of dates could be packed tightly into a single container. A typical *gwal* would be about 1.2 meters (4 feet) high by almost a meter (2½ feet) wide, and would hold about 15 *man*, or 75 kilos, of dates.

*Rabi* was the name used for a date from a palm that had been grown from a sucker and was consequently a high-quality date. All varieties of dates from palms grown from seeds were called *koruch*. Among these, only *shangishkan* could be packed whole with their pits. All other varieties of *koruch*, and there were many, had to be pitted before storing, or else the dates would harbor worms, *kerm*. After being dried, these *koruch* were placed on a large stone serving as an anvil, *hwank*, and then crushed by a stone, *sarsang*, held in the hand. Once the date was crushed, the pit, *gardag*, was plucked out and set aside. This work was usually but not exclusively done by women. The pitless dates were then poured into the *gwal* and packed down by the foot of man. The resulting date meat was called *jatk* and served as a household staple food throughout the following year.

Productivity varied from palm to palm, from year to year, and according to each individual's palm "portfolio." Let us begin with annual variations. The date harvest at Gorani was poor in 1972, with significantly lower numbers of dates than previous years. For example—and here I rely on estimates from individuals about their individual harvests—Ja'far got 15 *man* of *rabi* and 75 *man* of *koruch* in 1972, almost a 50 percent decline from the harvest of 1971, 20 *man* of *rabi* and 150 *man* of *koruch*. Jan Mahmud got 10 and 20 in 1972, down from 25 and 25 in 1971. Gemi got 10 and 50, down from 14 and 65 in 1971.

The speculation about the decline in the date harvest attributed it to conditions during *iwar*, pollination. (The presence of a non-Muslim anthropologist and wife was not mentioned, as far as I ever heard of it, as a possible cause.) One factor was the unusually cold temperature at Mashkil, which was said to have inhibited pollination. A second factor was the unusual amount and strength of the wind at that time, which also inhibited pollination. A third factor mentioned was the lack of rain: none at Mashkil for five years and a drought year in the highlands the previous year. This latter contributed to a low water table at Mashkil, which could inhibit the development of palms and dates. But, we might ask, was the water table higher after the bad drought of 1971 with its bumper crop of dates? While the causal analyses of the Baluch might seem an exercise in a posteriori speculation, some Sarhadi Baluch had anticipated a bad harvest and skipped the trip to Mashkil in 1972.

Although fewer people than usual may have come to Mashkil in 1972, in general more people came to Mashkil during the 1970s than previously because more people had date palms. During the 1960s and 1970s a lot of time and labor had been invested in planting new palms. In 1972 Jangi Han transplanted 10 *nahal* and 70 *jujuk*, Dust Mahmud 45 *jujuk*, Id Mahmud 5 *nahal* and 20 *jujuk*, Jan Mahmud 3 *nahal* and 20 *jujuk*, Reis 4 *nahal* and 60 *jujuk*. Most people were planting only or mainly *rabi jujuk* or *shingishkan*. *Rabi* and *shingishkan* were deemed better tasting than *koruch*, had more meat per date, and thus were preferred for consumption, and as well had a higher market value. Furthermore, for storage it was not necessary to crush these dates and remove the pits, an arduous process that people preferred to avoid.

Each owner as harvester had to make strategic decisions about long-term investment in new palms for harvests in the distant future. A given was that each harvester would be collecting his own dates, so additional time had to be set aside for planting new palms. But competing with the possibility of investing time and labor in planting new palms was a different possibility for investing labor, one with an immediate payoff: this was harvesting the palms of other people for a share, usually 25 percent. The problem was that, on top of harvesting one's own palms, it was difficult to both harvest other people's palms and at the same time plant *nahal* and *jujuk* to expand one's own palm holdings. Id Mahmud, for example, saw in his own experience a clear negative relationship between harvesting the dates of others and transplanting his own new palms.

On the basis of his experience and analysis, which indicated that he could, in ad-

**Table 5.2.** Work Allocation of Id Mahmud, 1970–72

| Year | Number of New Palms Planted | Man Dates Harvested for Others | Dates Harvested for Self |
|------|------|------|------|
| 1970 | 35 | 0 | 16 |
| 1971 | 6 | 35 | 20 |
| 1972 | 40 | 7 | 17 |

dition to harvesting his own dates, harvest for others or plant new palms to expand his holdings, Id Mahmud decided to stop harvesting for others, and instead to invest his efforts and energy into planting new palms (see table 5.2). He saw this as an investment in the future that would be crucial for his security in his old age and for his children.

Individual palms produced earlier and better when the water table was high, the soil was good and not salinated, and there was no competition from other palms nearby. Shams A'din's efforts to grow new palms had foundered on the salty soil into which he had transplanted. This discouraged him, and in 1972 and 1971 he invested his energy in harvesting for others, receiving respectively 15 *man* (75 kilos, or 165 pounds) and 26 *man* (130 kilos, or 286 pounds) dates for his 25 percent share, while producing 72 *man* (360 kilos, or 792 pounds) and 84 *man* (420 kilos, or 924 pounds) from his own palms.

How many dates did producers receive from a harvest? On the basis of estimates from a few individual producers at Gorani, the total amount of dates harvested per producer (13 in this sample) in 1972 was 249 kilos (548 pounds), in 1971 (12 in this sample) it was 345.4 kilos (760 pounds), and in 1970 (6 in this sample) 342 kilos (752 pounds). While these are based upon reports and are thus not totally reliable figures, and are also not necessarily representative of the larger population, they do give some idea of the magnitude of the harvests and of annual variations. If we divide the harvest by weeks in a year, the 1972 harvest provided Sarhadi date-producing families with 4.8 kilos (10.6 pounds) of dates, mainly date meat, per week, the 1971 harvest provided 6.6 kilos (14.5 pounds) per week, and the 1970 harvest 6.6 kilos (14.5 pounds) per week. Once again, these are not precise figures, being calculations based on estimates. But I think it would be safe to conclude that most Sarhadi Baluch date producers provided their families with several kilos of dates per week for the entire year.

However, not only dates were provided. As well, large amounts of date pits, *gardag*, were collected. In the settlements at Gorani were small structures consisting of low, circular, mud-brick walls, and these were the receptacles for collecting, storing, and drying date pits while the Sarhadi Baluch were resident. As we have seen, date pits were used as fodder and were an important contribution to the nutrition of livestock.

Thus, while *hezak* and *gwal* of dates may have taken pride of place in the baggage carried back to the highlands, no one neglected to bring as many *gwal* of date pits as they could fill. Damaged dates and *kumpk* for fodder were also transported.

## Date Production in Relation to Other Productive Sectors

Whereas date production was good in 1971 and 1970 and poor in 1972, pastoral production was very poor during the drought years of 1970 and 1971 and much better in 1972. So when in 1970 and 1971 there was a sparsity of pastoral products available for consumption or exchange, the supply of dates and date pits was, by local standards at least, plentiful. In 1972, when the supply of dates declined somewhat because of a poorer harvest, pastoral production had increased in response to the, by local standards, substantial rainfall. Thus in 1970 and 1971 bumper production of dates made up, to a degree at least, for the shortfall of pastoral production, while in 1972, successful pastoral production made up for a shortfall in date production.

The balance of productive and unproductive sectors throughout the three-year period 1970–73 illustrates the benefits of productive diversification. Sarhadi Baluch counted on their own primary production for the food to fill their stomachs and keep them alive and healthy. To oversimplify, for we are looking at two sectors only, during 1970–73, the Sarhadi Baluch had dates to eat when they had little milk or meat, and when dates were scarcer they had more milk and meat.

Levels of production in different sectors were independent because the factors that affected production in different sectors were different and did not vary together. Wind and cold were not critical factors in pastoral production, as they were in date production. Rainfall, so essential to pastoralism, was more detrimental than helpful to date production, which is why in California date producers cover their dates to keep the rain off. Annual and local rainfall variation was rather less critical for date palms, which depended on runoff from distant mountains to feed the drainage basin water table.

So there was a good possibility, as in the case of the years 1970–73 just reviewed, that a decline in one productive sector would not be accompanied by a decline in any other or all other sectors. Thus each sector acted as a backup for each other sector, and the entire diversified multi-resource economy had a substantial built-in insurance component. Sarhadi Baluch were unlikely in any given year to be totally wiped out economically and left without anything to eat. Their productive strategy was a conservative one; they were not as concerned about gaining new heights of maximum production as about guaranteeing a secure, minimum production. It was their lives and well-being that they were trying to conserve, and to do this they had to have something to fall back on in response to inevitable and uncontrollable cyclical shortfalls in one or another production sector. What they were able to fall back on when one productive sector failed was the other productive sectors.

## Nonedible Products

Foodstuffs were not the only products to come from date palms. As we have seen, the thin leaves, *pish*, of the palm fronds were the raw material for making many articles used by the Baluch. Much of the equipment used in date production itself was made of palm frond leaves: the *sund* to bag the dates; the rope, *chiluk*, to close the bags and hold them securely in the palm; thin cord to repair *hezak* and *mashk*; heavy rope, *garaband*, for securing workmen to palms; and *kapat*, small loose-weave bags with small openings, for the storage of small amounts of dates. *Chiluk* used for suspending and transporting *mashk* and *hezak* was called *mashkband*.

As well, many items used in other spheres of Baluchi life were made from material supplied by date palms. The mats for tent flooring, *tagert*, and tent siding, *gwerpat*, and the ropes, *tanabi*, that held up the tent, were woven from *pish*. Transport bags of various sizes and shapes are woven from *pish*: the *katel*, smaller than *sund* and more tightly and elegantly woven, and the *kach*, similar to the *katel* but larger. Products woven from *pish* were used for animals: *kayd* was a camel hobble, made from several strands of *chiluk*; the *barband*, like the *garaband* heavier than *kayd*, was used for tying loads, especially *gwal* on camels for migration; the rope fence, *tat*, that separated people from *pas* in tents, was woven from *chiluk*. *Pish* even served religious ends, as a woven mat with directional shape, *nomazi*, was used for prayer.

## GRAIN AND GARDEN CULTIVATION

During the Baluchi Period, and even until after World War II, agriculture was very limited on the Sarhad high plateau. There was some grain cultivation at Washt/ Khash, with labor supplied by a small, dependent *shahri* population, earlier under the control of the Daptan Kordish Hakomate and later controlled by the Yarahmadzai tribe, and a very limited amount of cultivation along the western slopes of the Morpish Mountains. The total agricultural production was very modest and contributed only a small amount of grain to a few tribesmen (Dyer 1921; Spooner 1967:7–8).

The climatic factors of low rainfall and cold temperatures contributed to limited cultivation. The "oasis complex" of southern Baluchistan, in which date, grain, and vegetable cultivation were combined in small, intensively cultivated areas, could not serve in the Sarhad where the freezing winters precluded date palm arboriculture. At the same time, the low and erratic precipitation made impossible a more extensive form of rainfall cultivation.

In the oases of southern Baluchistan, the irrigation systems were commonly based on shallow mother wells of a meter or two in riverbeds, the water being carried by relatively short primary channels to the garden areas. This was not possible on the plateau area of the Sarhad, where the water table was quite deep, no less and often more than 10 meters below the surface, making it very difficult to tap water and bring it to the surface for purposes of irrigation.

## Opportunistic Agriculture

The simplest kind of cultivation on the Sarhad, more common in the Morpish Mountains than on the high plateau, was runoff gardening. In this pattern, a flat area at the bottom of a runoff channel, a gully, running down from an area of higher elevation, a hill or mountain, would be enclosed by a simple retaining wall, *gwarband,* of soil. After the melting of snow or after a rain, the water would run down the gully to the flat area and be contained by the retaining wall and absorbed by the fenced-off patch of soil. This can be considered opportunistic gardening, in that it depended upon an unreliable water source; the crop was successful only in a good year, when runoff water was adequate, but in a drought year there was little or no runoff water and consequently no crop. The Baluch considered the water *api huda,* God's water, because it was natural rather than from a source constructed by man and so was deemed to be neither controlled nor owned by men. Such opportunistic cultivation was viable because the investment of labor and seed was very modest. There was little preparation of the soil and only a small amount of seed to be planted. In a good year, there is a nice little crop; in a bad year, there is no crop but not much investment is lost. In the winter of 1968, for example, two men from the Halki Ja'far, Padi Mahmud and Ja'far himself, sowed barley at the bottom of a runoff channel in eastern Pushi Kamal. They waited to see if there would be rain and then sowed the patch, spending only one day on the initial cultivation. More rain followed during that slightly better than average year, and the two men had a good crop of barley to harvest.

## *Kan* Irrigation

The cultivation at Washt and along the western slopes of the Morpish was based upon *kan* irrigation. The *kan,* known in Persian as *qanat,* an underground irrigation tunnel carrying water from a higher elevation to a lower cultivation area, was the traditional technology of the Persian irrigation system (Wulff 1966:249–54). The *kan* was particularly suited to desert environments because the water was closed in an underground tunnel and loss of water by evaporation was minimal. In some other areas of Iran, *kan* were 10 to 20 kilometers (6 to 12 miles) long, and even longer (English 1966). Both initial capitalization and ongoing maintenance costs were, however, quite high.

Sir Percy Sykes, who had been in the Sarhad in the 1890s, reported (1904:130) that around Khash there were "ruins of numerous kanats." General Dyer (1921:74–75) reported that in 1916 he had counted the remains of 73 *kan* bringing water to the Washt/Khash Plain, but that only two were in operation when he was there. Prior to the

Baluchi Period, there had been on the Sarhad an efflorescence of irrigation cultivation, probably by a Persian-speaking population, an offshoot of the major settlement area in Sistan. It appears that this irrigation-based colony declined before the expansion of pastoral nomadism in the Sarhad, and this decline, opening the area for exploitation, was probably a precondition of the establishment in the Sarhad of the *baluch* and their multi-resource economy.

During the nineteenth century, when the Sarhad was effectively politically autonomous and economically based largely on local resources, the remains of the *kan* system were of little use to the local Sarhadi Baluch population. There was neither the expertise to repair and reactivate the *kan* nor the surplus to invest in doing so. Furthermore, dependence upon irrigation agriculture was not economically practical nor culturally attractive to the Sarhadi *baluch*, for it involved stationary residence and onerous physical labor. Dyer (1921:164) says that the Yarmohammedzai (i.e., the Yarahmadzai) "maintained it to be a gross indignity for a fighting man to be made to work with his hands, and contended that all manual labor should be performed by lower caste people such as the Khwashis." Perhaps there was also a strategic consideration, for irrigation cultivation is a valuable sedentary resource that cannot be removed, as can flocks, during a military retreat. Heavy commitment to sedentary capital resources made the population more vulnerable to attack and control than a mobile population that could escape with its livestock wealth intact. Whatever the balance between strategic considerations and occupational identity, the tent-dwelling tribesmen did not see themselves as cultivators and did not pursue the expansion of irrigation cultivation in the Sarhad.

## Agriculture in the Iranian Period

With pacification in 1935, which I have designated the end of the Baluchi Period, and increasing military and administrative control of the Sarhad by the Iranian government, agriculture became increasingly attractive to the tent dwellers. In part, this was due to the decline in income from predatory raiding by Sarhadi Baluch and the need for new sources of income to replace it. Grain cultivation based upon irrigation was one option. At the same time, some of the inhibitors of irrigation agriculture declined. The military vulnerability of immovable resources lost, to a degree at least, its relevance. The specialized skills required for *kan* became more readily available as Persians were drawn to a Baluchistan now under Iranian state control. The capital needed to fund expensive *kan*, while still not easily drawn from the indigenous economy, was to some extent provided through Iranian government institutions and from private Persian sources, as well as from new market engagement through migrant labor, trading, and smuggling.

The result of these changing conditions was a significant development of irrigation agriculture throughout the Sarhad during the postwar period, especially in the

1960s. Some 15 small villages, each with several seasonally occupied mud-brick huts, were scattered primarily north/south along the western edge of the Morpish range. Most were under the control of tribesmen, although some were controlled by Persians and a few had Persian agricultural workers. For example, Gorchan, Gwanich, Shagbond, and Garonchin were locations of irrigation agriculture controlled by local Baluch, except for Gwanich, which was controlled by the Kords of Daptan. While most areas were irrigated by *ganat*, some, such as Gwanich, south of Pushti Kamal and owned by the Kord Sardar, and Garonchin, financed by the Iranian provincial government of Baluchistan and controlled by the Sardar of the Yarahmadzai, used motorized pumps. In some areas of irrigation agriculture, such as Gorchan, permanent mud-brick dwellings had been constructed and walled orchards developed, while at others, such as Garonchin, there was only the structure housing the pump motor, and anyone staying at Garonchin lived in black tents. Of course, even those tribesmen owning or with access to permanent structures lived in them, if at all, only seasonally or periodically and the rest of the time lived in tents as members of camping groups, while using the brick structures for storage.

## Persian Agricultural Villages

As well, a number of *kan*-based agricultural villages, run and occupied largely by Persians originating in Yazd in central Iran, sprang up in the Sarhad in the late 1950s and 1960s. One of the earliest ones was Ismailabad, to the northwest of Washt/Khash, established in 1956 through the initiative of a Yazdi resident in the provincial capital of Zahedan. At first occupied only by Yazdis, its uncultivated areas were by the late 1960s seasonally occupied by Baluchi herding camps, one of which was Yarahmadzai. These tent dwellers were in a partly symbiotic and partly dependent relationship with the Yazdi peasant cultivators. The tribesmen herded livestock owned by the peasants and provided labor to the peasants when it was needed for various agricultural tasks. And the tent dwellers' livestock could feed on the remains of the harvested fields and leave behind their droppings as fertilizer. On the tent dwellers' return from the date groves at Mashkil, they were able to sell dates to the peasants at 5½ toman a man. By the late 1960s, a few Baluch had bought rights over fields and house space in the village as some of the Yazdis had moved away. Thus beyond the division of labor and exchange between tribesmen and peasant, at least some tribesmen associating with these well-versed agriculturalists learned new skills and found new economic and occupational opportunities in irrigation cultivation.

## Tribal Two-Crop Irrigation Cultivation

Among the Yarahmadzai tribesmen, irrigation agriculture was usually a two-crop, grain, *gandom*, system. The primary crop was winter wheat, *gala*, which was favored because it was the more desirable grain for consumption and more valuable on the market. More winter wheat was planted and the return was greater than for other crops. Wheat alternated in the annual agricultural cycle with barley, *jo*. Together the two grain crops accounted by far for the greatest percentage of the agricultural produce and consequently were the primary focus of the tribesmen's agricultural concern. Wheat was sown in plowed fields in late November and December, irrigated throughout the winter and spring, and harvested in early summer, in June. Barley was sown in July, irrigated throughout the summer, and harvested in late October and November. Grain was grown in open fields, but most other crops were grown in walled gardens, *bagh*. The cultivation of other edible grains (corn), vegetables (beetroot, onions), fruit (apples, apricots, grapes, pomegranates, watermelon), nutmeats (pistachios), and other crops (alfalfa, cotton) was very limited and irregularly distributed throughout the areas of cultivation.

Rights to agricultural land were determined by rights over the water that irrigated it. This was general tribal practice but also seemed to receive support from the local Iranian courts. In the summer of 1968, Sa'mard, a Rigi of Afzalabad, made an official complaint to the Persian authorities that men from Shagbond had encroached on his land. The case came before the court at the provincial capital, Zahedan, with Boinyad, Cherag, and Mulla Rustam as defendants. The judgment of the court was that the charge could not be sustained because the land in question was being irrigated from the *kan* at Shagbond, and thus the right of use fell to the men of Shagbond. In this case, the government courts supported the norms of tribal tenure. Both state and tribal practice arose from and recognized the desert environment in which dry land is plentiful but water is very scarce.

For both legal and environmental reasons, the control of *kan* and more recently pumps was crucial for access to agricultural resources. Shares were specified in irrigation hours within a temporal sequence. For example, Yelli Han owned 24 hours out of the 11-day sequence of the *kan* at Shagbond. The volume of water produced by a particular water source determined the amount of land that could be irrigated and thus cultivated and consequently determined the value of that water source. Both *kan* and pumps varied in this respect, according to the water source they tapped as well as their initial construction and state of repair or deterioration. In general, *kan* irrigated from a few to a score of acres, with diesel engine pumps serving up to several scores of acres. In Yarahmadzai tribal territory, shares were usually small, the chiefly family excepted. At Garonchin, irrigated by a large diesel motor contributed by the government of the Province of Sistan and Baluchistan, there was a total of 336 hours of irrigation, a 14-day cycle. The chief of the Yarahmadzai, Sardar Han Mahmud, who had negotiated this contribution, took 150 hours, giving his two brothers 24 hours each and two nephews 12 hours each, a sum of 222 hours, or two-thirds of the water, for the chiefly family. The other third of the water was distributed, mostly in amounts of 2 to 6 hours, among 26 members of lineages, particularly the Dorahzai and Rushanzai, customarily associated with the neighborhood of Garonchin.

Why did the Sardar have 45 percent of the irrigation water? What he said to me was that he had planned to keep 48 for himself and give the rest of the 150 hours to members of his lineage, the Yarmahmudzai. But they did not come to claim and use this water, so he kept it for himself. The Sardar also said that previously he had only 48 hours, with the rest allocated to the Yarmahmudzai, but they did not pitch in to repair and keep up the irrigation system. He also said that, for the cultivation of watermelon, 150 hours of irrigation was needed.

Construction and maintenance of *kan* in Sarhadi tribal territory has frequently been a lineage-based collective endeavor, although with allocated shares and individual rights of alienation. The *kan* at Shagbond was controlled by the Dadolzai, the dominant lineage in the Halki Ja'far, but some individual members of the lineage sold their shares, and members of other lineages have taken their places. Those members of the Dadolzai who owned water rights had them at Shagbond, and the Dadolzai, including members of Halki Ja'far, associated with the men from Shagbond in both agricultural and pastoral pursuits.

Throughout the Yarahmadzai tribe, only a modest percentage, perhaps 10 percent, of tribesmen had rights, by ownership or rental, to irrigation water. This does not mean that only a small portion of the tribesmen had an interest in irrigation agriculture, for regular or harvest labor contributions provided many more individuals with a direct return of wages, usually in kind, from this sector, as well as increased access to grain from the agriculture of kinsmen and from local agriculture generally.

## Sharecropping

The division of labor in cultivation depended upon household resources in both labor and water. Harvest excepted, a large household could usually supply enough agricultural laborers for the usual, ongoing agricultural tasks, irrigation included. Few households had more cultivation than could be handled through the crop growth cycle by family labor. However, the labor picture was complicated by the absence of young and adult men who were away from tribal territory and engaged in more remunerative activities such as migrant labor or trading. The demands of the agricultural cycle, combined with the absence, temporary or otherwise, of household members who might have provided the labor, led to sharecropping. The usual arrangements among tribesmen in the Sarhad was for labor to receive 3 of 10 parts of the crop, water to receive 6 of 10 parts, and the plow animal, ox or camel, to receive 1 of 10 parts. Each sharecropper, *sharik,* had also the use of a small area of land, and the water to irrigate it, for his own cultivation. In the winter of 1968, two members of the Halki Ja'far, Mahmud Karim and Shams A'din, were working as *sharik* at Shagbond, "on the water" owned by their lineage mates. Shams A'din worked on the land of Halil, who was at that time absent from tribal territory importing cloth from the Persian Gulf to Iran. The summer harvest brought about 60 *man* (300 kilos, or 660 pounds) of grain, of which Shams A'din's share was 18 *man* (90 kilos, or 198 pounds) of wheat. The other small plot brought Shams A'din 2 additional *man* (10 kilos, or 22 pounds). For those who did not ordinarily work as *sharik,* labor at harvest time brought 1 of 25 parts of the harvest crop, which in the case of Halil's land was 2.4 *man* (12 kilos, or more than 26 pounds).

## Maintaining Irrigation Systems

A necessary type of labor in *kan* irrigation was maintenance. A *kan* was after all an underground tunnel with soil walls, through which water flowed, so the erosion and breakdown was fairly rapid. The unskilled *kan* workman, *muzur,* cleaned out sediment and did minor repair and was remunerated at 5 toman a day. This job was frequently done by tribesmen with no pretense of special skills. The skilled *kan* workman, *kakian,* with his wooden, crane-like rig, *chaharag,* which was made locally by Luris, was indispensable in maintaining *kan* in operating condition for any period at all. For their work, these specialists, most of whom were Persian, received 25 toman a day, a quite high wage, which was indicative not only of the demand for the work and special skills required but also of the dangers of *kan* work, especially construction and major repair, for a *kan* cave-in could easily take the life of a *kakian* and was not that infrequent. With the new engine-driven pumps, operator-mechanics were the equivalent to the *kakian,* in that they were skilled, well paid, and necessary for the operation, although in the case of motor-driven pumps, they were obliged to attend to daily operations in a way that the *kakian* was not for daily operations of the *kan.*

The precariousness of a *kan* irrigation agriculture was illustrated by the development at Nugju, located just to the south of Shagbond. Dependent upon a *kan* were grain fields and a few accompanying mud-brick dwellings. The community consisted primarily of Rushanzai. Pati Mahmud, a member of the Halki Ja'far during 1967–68, grew up there, his father having a house and cultivating there, and lived there himself until the early 1960s, when the *kan* deteriorated and fell into disrepair. The funds necessary to hire the *kakian* were not available, proper repairs could not be made, and in due course the volume of water declined, and finally the flow ceased altogether. The Rushanzai, some 15 families, abandoned the site and moved elsewhere, to herding camps and to other agricultural areas. In 1968, there were plans to reclaim Nugju by exchanging rights for water with a *kakian* in return for labor to bring the *kan* back into service.

## Use of Agricultural Products

The return from agriculture varied from season to season, from holding to holding. Income in agricultural products ranged from the few *man* of grain gained by laboring during the harvest to the hundreds of *man* of grain coming to the few larger owners. Most of the agricultural products, mainly grain, were consumed within the households producing them, and in the case of large owners, at least some substantial amount was distributed through hospitality. While there was a small amount of exchange of grain for other products among tribesmen, on the whole the exchange and sale of grain and other agricultural products was quite limited, and usually a result of circumstantial necessities rather than the availability of a surplus much beyond household needs.

# 6.
## RAIDING AND TRADING

Predation has played a crucial part in making a living on the Sarhad, more during the Baluchi Period than since. One additional sector of the tribal economy was hunting and gathering, preying on wild, nondomesticated species and collecting naturally found minerals in the Sarhad and at Mashkil. Another major economic sector was predatory raiding of people and their property, typically outside of the Sarhad and often far from the home territory.

## HUNTING AND GATHERING

The collection of wild, undomesticated species of plants and animals and of minerals was a regular part of the yearly, seasonal, and in some instances daily round of activities. In most cases, what was collected was a useful supplement, in terms of either quantity or variety, to the rest of the economy. In certain cases, however, the resource was an essential pillar of the economy.

The clearest example of a critical contribution to the economy was firewood, *dar*, gathered from bushes and trees in the vicinity of the camp. *Dar* was the major household energy source, after human muscle power, providing heat for cooking and for warmth in the winter, and light after dark. The gathering of *dar* for the household was a prime responsibility of the females of the family, allocated to younger girls whenever possible, and a considerable amount of time was invested in this activity. There was no economically viable substitute for *dar* as a source of energy. Kerosene, available in Khash beginning in the postwar period and used among the Sarhadi tent dwellers very occasionally in small amounts for lanterns, was far too expensive for cooking and heating. Kerosene also required relatively expensive equipment, such as manufactured metal stoves, for its use, and that equipment, even if purchased, was not well suited for Baluchi cooking technology. I know this from personal experience, because Joan and I, rich foreigners that we were, used kerosene stoves. Joan, admittedly learning Baluchi cooking from scratch, struggled to make Baluchi bread on top of a kerosene stove, with sad results. We finally gave up, much to Joan's relief, and contracted out our bread needs to a sympathetic neighbor, the splendid Monaz, Ja'far's wife.

Firewood was also occasionally collected for sale, in this case by men. A number of the members of the Halki Ja'far would, from time to time, especially in winter when local productive activities were at a minimum, spend a day collecting a camel load of *dar,* which could be sold for 5 toman 30 miles away in Khash, primarily at the brick kiln. The work, especially the transport, was arduous, and total income from such sale was small, no one distant from Khash doing this more than three or four times in a winter.

The other essential element was salt, gathered at the Hamuni Mashkil. Large chunks of salt were dug out of the deposits in the central Hamun areas and transported by camel back to the Sarhad in the spring after *iwar,* pollination of the date palms, and in the autumn after *mokbur,* the date harvest. Most of the salt was consumed within the household, including provision for the animals, but some was sold or traded with other households, at the equivalent of 2 toman a *man* (5 kilos). In the case of salt, purchase from outside sources would not have been as prohibitive as would have been the case with fuel. On the other hand, unlike firewood, salt took little time and labor to collect, a half year's supply being collected in a half day at the most.

From mid-February in any good year, the women and girls gathered wild onions, *pimazi kuh,* and other edible grasses, thus making gathering one of the few sources of vegetable intake. Wild pistachio nuts were gathered from the groves on the Yarahmadzai-Gamshadzai border, south of Garonchin, although with the expansion of cultivation these became less important. Also gathered were various herbs and roots used for curing the leather of *mashk* and *hezak.*

In winter, roots were dug up by men and women to feed vulnerable camels. Up to 5 kilos (11 pounds) of root might be fed per day to an adult camel. Given the quantity used, gathered roots would be expensive to replace by a more valuable foodstuff.

For men, hunting was a sport as well as a source of luxury meat. The favorite game was gazelle, *ahouk,* fowl, especially quail, *kapt,* and rabbit, *harguisht.* Gazelle was usually hunted with firearms, fowl could also be trapped in nets, and rabbit could be caught by sight hounds, whippet-type dogs, trained for this purpose. Wild boar, found in a few riverbed areas, was also hunted for sport, using firearms, but could not be eaten because for Muslims pork was forbidden, *haram.* The Sarhad, according to reports, was earlier in the century filled with game, but had since been largely hunted out, although I once saw a young *ahouk* that had been captured alive and was being kept in a camp, to what end I did not care to speculate. For the ordinary tent dweller, the income from hunting was negligible.

I did not see or hear much about hunting prizes but did once find myself caught in a hunting dilemma. Accompanied by Nezar Mahmud, brother of the Yarahmadzai Sardar, we were driving our Land Rover to Mashkil to visit with the men doing *iwar*. We had taken the longer route, the only one possible at that time to negotiate by motor vehicle, around the southern end of the Morpish Mountains then east through Jalq, and back north again into the great desert waste between the Morpish Range and the Hamun. I was driving along the rough dirt track somewhat nervously, feeling the isolation, hours away from the nearest settlement and more from the nearest auto mechanic, when Nezar Mahmud, having spotted a gazelle 200 yards off the road, burst into excitement. "There, a gazelle, go get him." "Huh?" I said. "The gazelle, chase him with the car and hit him." Oh my god, I thought. Simultaneously I feared for the springs of my car, envisioning being stranded with a hulk of a Land Rover wrecked on the small dunes and rocks of this desolate plain, and for the poor gazelle, nonhunter that I was (and am). To me, it would have been foolish and nasty to drive off the road to chase that gazelle. To Nezar Mahmud, it was unintelligible why anyone would waste this God-given opportunity, and miss the chance of arriving triumphant at Gorani with enough meat to treat everyone. I expressed my reservations. Nezar Mahmud insisted. I refused. He was the Sardar, well, the brother of the Sardar, and had done much for us. But I was the driver and I got my way. We drove the rest of the way to Mashkil in a funk. Nezar Mahmud fumed silently the whole way. At least he recouped a few credits with the men at Mashkil when he recounted, in his lively, dramatic, rhetorical style, the story of our trip, his championing of the hunt, and our opportunity lost. Nezar Mahmud was a good-natured man, and after a time he forgave me and continued to be a close friend.

## PREDATORY RAIDING

The picture of Sarhadi life during the late nineteenth and early twentieth centuries is consistent among European observers. Curzon (1892:262–63) reports as follows:

> This remote and inaccessible district had long baffled the zeal of European explorers, Pottinger and St. John having both tried in vain to enter it. At length in 1885 Captain R. H. Jennings, an officer deputed by the Indian Government, was the first to penetrate its mysteries, and to give to it an existence on the map. Its local name, not inappropriately, Yaghistan i.e. the country of the Yaghis, our outlaws of Baluchistan. Captain Jennings found Serhad [*sic*] to be inhabited by Beluchi, Kord, and Brahui tribes. . . . All were Sunnis, all detested the Persians, all subsisted upon rapine; and the Persian authority amounted to little more than a prudent recognition of local chieftains and an occasional armed expedition for the collection of revenue. Serhad produces an unlimited supply of sheep and goats, and grows an immense amount of tamarisk, camelthorn, and asafoetida. Its principal place, and indeed the only place which has hitherto figured on the map, is Washt, a large village inhabited by Kords.

Percy Sykes (1902:93), having visited in the 1890s, is quite explicit about the "Sarhad, until a few years ago a nest of robbers, and now but little better." As for the Yarahmadzai tribe in particular, "This Sarhad tribe was constantly raiding across the frontier" (Sykes 1902:230, n. 1). General R. E. H. Dyer (1921:42–43), who had campaigned against them in 1915, states baldly that "the [Sarhadi] tribes literally live by raiding":

> [I] learnt of a great raid that had recently been made into Persia by a section of the Yarmahommedzais, under a leader called Izzat. As an outcome of this raid hundreds of Persian ladies and children had been dragged from their homes and brought by Izzat into the Sarhad, there to be bartered as slaves. (1921:78)

Dyer undertook to send these and other slaves back to their homes in Narmashir, a district of Kerman Province to the northwest of Baluchistan. He also forced Jiand Han, the Yarahmadzai Sardar, to "return . . . all Government camels seized when he had raided the British lines of communication, and also the four hundred Afghan camels which . . . his men had seized on the caravan route from Nushki to Robat" (Dyer 1921:142).

A decade later, Coleridge Kennard (1927) saw Sarhadi raiding from the receiving end. At Darzin, between Kerman and Bam,

> the only living souls in the place appear to be six men from Fahrej who are constructing a fort. There is nothing whatever to be obtained save great dishes of white mulberries. The Baluchis in their last raid appear to have carried off everything, inhabitants included. . . .
>
> Just as we are preparing for the night a *jambaz* rider arrives from over the desert to announce that a Baluchi raiding army—"a very powerful one; a thousand men ride in it"—is close to his heels, marching from Kwash under Shasavar Khan [Yarahmadzai], against Kainat and Neh. We are directly on the storm track. It is soon reported that they will arrive here during the night and that they are at present passing Buzgird Kuh. The news and its elaboration spread like wildfire through the camp and Djevand and Abdullah are ready to panic. There is nothing to do but to pack up in haste and try to gain the Nung plain. (Kennard 1927:140, 185)

Rosita Forbes (1931:137–38) says that "throughout the ages Kerman has suffered from locusts and Baluchis. The former destroyed the crops and the latter carried off the women. There is a Persian proverb which affirms that 'Isfahan will be destroyed by water, Yazd by sand and Kerman by horsehoofs.'" Nor did the "wild Baluchi marauders" do much for trade, especially along the caravan route between Kerman and India: "Although . . . the ancient route continued to be used, for many years . . . it had been considered dangerous, owing to the constant depredations at the hands of Baluchi raiding parties" (Forbes 1931:142).

My Baluchi informants confirmed the reports by the Europeans. They said that from the earliest times through the 1930s, raiding was customary and regular. It was not unusual for raiding parties to ride out once a month. Usually there were two large excursions each year, led by the Sardar and consisting of up to a hundred men. Pakistan and Kerman were favorite targets. One of the main purposes, they said, was the capture of livestock, a point not stressed by European reporters. Other portable valuables—such as carpets and stores of grain—were carried off as well.

Sarhadi *baluch* were warriors, fighters, raiders. They lived in a hard land and grew up tough. They were taught that they would have to fight and they learned how to fight. They told themselves that they were fearless and often acted fearlessly. When external raiding called for violence, they were ready (see chapter 10). When internal conflict required violence, they were ready. Being a man meant being ready to fight, always, however, within the constraints of tribal norms. Being a warrior was part of each Sarhadi Baluch's sense of himself.

Captives carried to the Sarhad were put to work cultivating, at the date groves and in the Sarhad, or traded south, although a few girls were married by tribesmen. One of the Dadolzai elders and a sometime member of the Halki Ja'far, Walli Mahmud, distinguished by a scar from one of General Dyer's bullets, had captured and married a Persian girl, who was, 40 years later, a camp matriarch. Once during the 1950s, this couple, the old Baluchi raider husband and the mature Persian captive wife, by then parents of grown children and grandparents, returned to her village of origin in Kerman Province, to meet and visit with remaining members of the family from which she had been wrenched as a young girl. How I would have liked to observe that event.

The energetic and repeated raiding by the Sarhadi Baluch enriched their economy through import, the terms of trade determined by the swiftness of the riding camels and the power of tribal arms. Livestock, grain, carpets, and captives flowed into the Sarhad as the raiding parties returned. To what use was all of this wealth put, and why were the Sarhadi *baluch* so insatiable? At least part of the answer is to be found in the ecology of the Sarhad, particularly in the dependence of the tribesmen upon scanty and erratic rainfall for local production, and their vulnerability in the face of frequent, recurrent, and serious droughts. As we have seen, the Sarhad was not the most generous of environments. Without rain, there was no pasture, and without pasture, there was no milk for young animals and for people. Without pasture and milk, animals went hungry and some died. Without rain, runoff cultivation failed. Without the fruits of livestock and cultivation, people went hungry and some of the weaker died. The Sarhad could not sustain pastoralism and runoff cultivation as anything but the riskiest of adaptations, unless there was a reliable inflow of resources. Raiding guaranteed that inflow.

Prior to the arrival of grain merchants in Khash after pacification and the expansion of irrigation in the Sarhad, the demand for grain outstripped the local supply. It was not uncommon for tribesmen, usually in large groups, to travel to agricultural areas outside of the Sarhad and exchange livestock, livestock products, and dates for grain. These trips took place about twice a year, usually to Saravan in the south, Sistan in the north, and Kerman to the northwest. Any shortfall of grain from local production and from raiding was thus made up by exchange.

Through the nineteenth century, the economy of the Sarhadi Baluch was based on multiple-resource exploitation, with local production supplemented by predatory extraction of external resources and limited external exchange. As we have seen, local production was largely subsistence oriented, most of the products being consumed by the producers. But, in this instance, subsistence production was not based upon isolation but was systematically linked with external, albeit predatory, engagement.

The inevitable concomitant to predatory importation was agonistic political and military engagement with the "outside" world beyond the Sarhad, as evidenced by repeated military expeditions sent against the Sarhadi tribesmen, from those of the Persian governor of Baluchistan, Abdel Fath Khan, in the 1880s to that of General Dyer in 1914–15. It was such a military engagement with external forces, the protracted campaign of 1928–35 ordered by Reza Shah, king of Iran, that "pacified" the Sarhad and suppressed raiding, depriving the Sarhadi Baluch of their imported riches, thus bringing about the depressed, poverty-struck Sarhad of the 1940s.

With the suppression of raiding, the Sarhadi Baluch were faced with a number of major problems, one of which is explored here. The fall in overall income from losing the spoils of raiding, and the removal of compensating income for the periodic failures of local production, left the Sarhadi Baluch with a major gap in their economy. How could this gap be filled? The military "pacification" by the forces of the Iranian state and the administrative "encapsulation" by agents of the state not only removed the possibility of predatory raiding, it also presented new options, opening the possibility of new kinds of economic engagement with the "outside." During the 1960s and 1970s, the Sarhadi Baluch, filling the gap left by the loss of prizes from raiding, increasingly pursued primarily two options for gaining income outside the Sarhad and bringing it home: selling their labor in Persian and foreign labor markets and importing and selling foreign goods in Persian urban markets.

## THE SUCCESSORS TO RAIDING

Military "pacification" and administrative encapsulation of the Sarhad and Baluchistan more generally by the Iranian state not only suppressed predation and depressed the local economy, it opened new opportunities for less hostile, if less profitable, forms of engagement with the "outside" world. The first opportunities in jobs paid with wages were in providing unskilled manual labor for constructing the provincial capital, Zahedan, and the district capitals, such as Khash, and building and maintaining roads, and related projects. Shortly after World War II, Ja'far worked as a laborer in the building of the railroad from Quetta (then in British India and now in Pakistan) to Zahedan. Exceptionally, a few Sarhadi Baluch entered agencies of the Iranian government and served in regular posts, such as Dur Mahmud (Yar Mahmudzai), a half-brother of the Yarahmadzai Sardar, who was an officer in the gendarmerie.

By the late 1960s, many Sarhadi Baluch engaged in wage labor. During the winter of 1967–68, when I was resident in the Halki Ja'far, most of the young men and many of the adult, family men were away working. Out of a total of 15 adult men, 9 were absent. In the brother camp, the Halki Halil, 6 out of 11 men were away during this period, and of the 5 remaining, 2, Walli Mahmud, who had fought General Dyer, and Dadol, were elderly. The pattern was if anything exaggerated during the winter of 1972–73. No tent was without an absentee, whether paterfamilias or unmarried son. Among the 17 male heads of household, 11 were away from camp working. In addition, 9 young men were absent working. In total, out of 17 tents, 20 men had left the camp and tribal territory to earn money.

Most of the Sarhadi Baluch were engaged in short-term, seasonal migrant labor. However, the seasonal determinant was not that of the work destination. Unlike agricultural laborers, for whom the availability of work is determined by seasonal agricultural tasks, Sarhadi migrant laborers, most of whom provided unskilled manual labor for construction, were not tied by the labor market to seasonal work. Rather, the Baluch were constrained by the seasonal requirements of their own multiple-resource, agropastoral production. For Sarhadi Baluch, the spring was a season of lively pastoral activity, during which camps commonly moved up to a dozen times, and it was also the time of date palm pollination, *iwar*. Summer and early fall was the period of the date harvest. The only relatively inactive time, when camps stayed put, animals were out only part of the day and date palms were left on their own, was winter. Less manpower was required in the winter than in the other seasons. So it was during the winter that men chose to go off to sell their labor in the market. But where did they go?

Sarhadi Baluch did not think of geography in terms of national entities with clear borders; they did not think of discrete, cohesive entities with names such as Iran and Pakistan. Rather, they thought of spatial, linguistic, religious, and even racial closeness and distance. For these Baluch, there was an ethnic and geographic continuity to the east, in Pakistani Baluchistan and even beyond in Sind, where the Baluchi language gradually merged with Urdu and Sunni Islam was the rule. And there was a geographic and racial continuity to the west, in Bandar Abbas and on the southern coast of Iran, a neighboring region where people did not look so different from the Baluch. There was a religious, racial, and geographic continuity across the Persian Gulf in Arabia, especially on the east coast of Arabia, in the Emirates and Oman. Specialists in ships of the desert though they were, Baluch have been crossing the Gulf and settling or working in Arabia for centuries (Thesiger 1959; Wilkinson 1977; Barth 1983).

Persian- and Turkish-speaking Iranians, all Shi'ite Muslims, living in great cities and peasant villages far to the north across the great central desert of Iran, were distant and alien to the Baluch. Upon my arrival in Pushti Kamal, I told people that I came from America. Halil, the headman of the other Dadolzai camp, at that time located next to the Halki Ja'far, asked if America was as far as Tehran. At first I took this to mean that Halil wondered if America might be as close as Tehran, but I later understood that what he meant was what he said: he wondered if America was *as far as* Tehran. For Halil and most other Sarhadi Baluch, Tehran was a vast distance in space and also in culture and ethnicity. So when Sarhadi Baluch thought of leaving the Sarhad to work for wages, they usually thought of Pakistan, the southern coast of Iran, and the Arabian emirates.

Of course, while "closeness" was desirable, so was good economic return, the raison d'être of the enterprise to begin with. Undoubtedly, among the many places generally deemed "close," those providing better economic opportunities, those paying more for less arduous work, would be for Sarhadi Baluch the chosen destinations. In the first decades after World War II, Sarhadi Baluchi worked in Khash and Zahedan, and if they ventured beyond, tended to go to Pakistan. For example, Karim Han, as well as working in Baluchistan, Kerman, and Bandar Abbas, worked in Dalbundi, Quetta, and Karachi, as did Ido, while Mahmud Karim worked in Karachi and Lahore. Neither Karim Han, Ido Mahmud, nor Mahmud Karim ventured to Arabia. In the 1960s and 1970s, responding to the growing Gulf oil economies, young men such as Dad Mahmud, Ghulam Mahmud, and Gam Dad chose to work in Bandar Abbas, with the more adventurous crossing to Dubai, Abu Dhabi, and Kuwait (see tables 6.1 and 6.2).

Those Sarhadi Baluch who ventured across the Persian/Arabian Gulf to the Emirates in many cases worked as manual laborers on construction sites for British construction companies. Earnings were between $50 and $70 a month, some of which was sent by mail to families back on the Sarhad. Illustrating this pattern were two instances in 1967–68 from the immediate family of Ja'far.

Ghulam Mahmud, who had grown up in Ja'far's tent after his father, Shah Mirad, Ja'far's brother, died young, and who was betrothed to Ja'far's daughter, Gol Peri, worked during the winter of 1967–68 for an English construction firm in Abu Dhabi (Baluchi pronunciation: Bozabi) on the Arabian side of the Gulf. He worked as an unskilled laborer on road and building construction, although other Baluch were drivers. He was there for five months, December through April, each month earning 400 to 450 toman (= $56 to $63), of which approximately one-quarter, around 100 toman, was spent on food and incidentals. There was no lodging to pay, for he was put up, without charge, in a company hostel. Thus each month he was able to save 300 or 350 toman. During this period he sent 300 toman to Ja'far. When he left Abu Dhabi, he took the 1,700 toman he had saved and bought cloth in Dubai, transported it to Kerman, which was on the route back to Baluchistan, where he sold it for a 200 toman profit, increasing his savings to 1,900 toman. In Kerman, he bought clothes

**Table 6.1.** Migrant Labor Destinations (to 1968)

| Older / Younger Men | Baluchistan | Iran | Pakistan | Arabia |
|---|---|---|---|---|
| *Older*[a] | | | | |
| Dust Mahmud | Saravan | | | |
| Dur Mahmud | Khash, Zahedan | | | |
| Ja'far | Khash, Zahedan | | | |
| Mulla Rustam | | Bandar Abbas | | |
| Lashkar Han | Khash, Zahedan | | | |
| Karim Han | Khash, Zahedan, Saravan, Iranshahr | Kerman, Bandar Abbas | Dalbundi, Quetta, Karachi | |
| Ido | Khash, Zahedan | Bandar Abbas | Quetta, Karachi | |
| Mahmud Karim | | | Karachi, Lahore | |
| | | | | |
| *Younger*[b] | | | | |
| Shams A'din | | Kerman, Bandar Abbas, Tehran | | |
| Mahmud Rahim | | Bandar Abbas | | Abu Zhabi |
| Id Mahmud | | Bandar Abbas | | Abu Zhabi |
| Mustafa | Saravan, Rask | Bandar Abbas | | |
| Mandust | Khash | Kerman, Bandar Abbas | | Dubai, Abu Zhabi |
| Gam Dad (Jan Mahmud) | Zahedan | Kerman, Bandar Abbas | | Dubai, Abu Zhabi |
| Ghulam Mahmud | Khash | Bandar Abbas | | Dubai, Abu Zhabi |
| Dad Mahmud | Iranshahr | Isfahan Chahbahar | Karachi | Kuwait, Dubai |

[a]"Older men" were those with adolescent or adult children.

[b]"Younger men" were unmarried, or recently married without children or with young children only.

**Table 6.2.** Migrant Labor, Members of the Halki Ja'far (Winter 1972–73)

| Tent | Away | Where | Activity |
|------|------|-------|----------|
| Dust Mahmud | Bahador (son) | Kerman, Bandar Abbas, Zahedan | Trading |
| Ja'far | Bahadin (son) | Bandar Abbas, Arabia | Wage labor |
| Reis | Shiruk (son) | Bandar Abbas, Arabia | Wage labor |
| Id Mahmud | Id Mahmud | Kerman | Trading |
| Shams A'din | Shams A'din | Kerman, Zahedan | Trading |
| Mahmud Karim | Mahmud Karim | Kerman, Zahedan | Trading |
| | Alluk (nephew) | | Wage labor |
| Jan Mahmud | Jan Mahmud | Quetta, Kerman | Trading |
| Baluch | Baluch | Kerman, Zahedan | Trading |
| Ido | Brahim (son) | Zahedan | Wage labor |
| Barkat | Barkat | Kerman, Zahedan | Trading |
| Abas | Abas | Bandar Abbas, Arabia | Wage labor |
| Abdul | Abdul | Bandar Abbas, Arabia | Wage labor |
| Gemi | Sharif (son) | Bandar Abbas, Arabia | Wage labor |
| | Sahib Dad (son) | Bandar Abbas, Arabia | Wage labor |
| | Baharam (son) | Kerman, Zahedan | Trading |
| Isa | Isa | Bandar Abbas, Arabia | Wage labor |
| Sahib Dad | Sahib Dad | Kerman | Trading |
| Komeron | Mahmud (son) | Bandar Abbas, Arabia | Wage labor |
| Ghulam Mahmud | Ghulam Mahmud | Kerman, Bandar Abbas, Zahedan | Trading |

and presents. On his return to the Sarhad, he gave 200 toman to Ja'far. The remainder of his savings were divided between paying off bridewealth and investing in his household, including 420 toman for 14 *man* (70 kilos, or 154 pounds) of goat hair toward the weaving of the tent that would become his new and independent home. Also working in Abu Dhabi, alongside Ghulam Mahmud, was Id Mahmud, in his early 20s, married to Ja'far's elder daughter Bibi Nur. While working, he sent money to his mother and sisters, and sent Ja'far 450 toman for the support of his wife while he was away.

As we can see following Ghulam Mahmud's external quest for income during the winter of 1967–68, he took a "multiple-resource" approach to his environment, engaging in two quite distinct, money-making activities: manual labor for wages and the importing and sale of goods. In fact, as in the traditional, Sarhadi multi-resource economy, the different sectors and activities supported one another. Ghulam Mahmud was able to purchase goods in Kuwait and bring them into Iran only because he had capital available for the purchase of the goods. This capital, as we have seen, came from his wages. So he effectively combined the wages and itinerary of wage labor to provide capital and a market for importing and trading goods.

The trading of goods, *sodayi,* was the other new, external economic venture of the Sarhadi Baluch. We have seen in the example of Ghulam Mahmud, that while conceptually distinct from wage labor, and requiring other resources, such as financial capital, the trading of goods was strategically interwoven with it. Many of those who seasonally left the Sarhad had in mind both wage labor and trading goods and often pursued opportunities where and when they found them.

Trading was attractive for Sarhadi Baluch not only because it could be combined easily with traveling on a regular route for seasonal labor migration. It was also consistent with Baluchi cultural patterns and personality, and thus individual personal experience as a result of the nomadic, multi-resource economy, in the need for calculation, and for choice between many options, and for independent action, and more specifically in the familiarity and comfort with mobility, including both packing and moving, resulting from nomadic migration. Similarly, the risks in the import trade, not least from the substantial overlap between trade and smuggling, were not so very different from the risks of pastoralism and opportunistic cultivation in a marginal environment, especially when we take into account rustling and conflicts over pasture, and even more when we include predatory raiding.

If the risks were higher in the import trade than in wage labor, the potential economic rewards were greater, quite aside from the preferability of light rather than heavy physical effort and of being one's boss rather than being on the lowest rung of an elaborate hierarchy of workers and supervisors, this latter particularly irritating for tribesmen used to being responsible and independent. In December 1972 and early January 1973, Shams A'din (son of) Gulap, of the Halki Ja'far, cobbled together a thousand toman of capital—200 from savings, 500 from wages from me, 100 from a loan from his brother, and 200 from a loan from Rahmat, then a campmate—and embarked on a trading venture. He joined in partnership with another man, Karam Dad Mahmud, of the Miradzai lineage, who was also at that time resident in the camp of Ja'far, who traveled with Shams A'din, supplying his own 1,300 toman capital, and with whom Shams A'din agreed to split the profits.

Planning to buy goods cheap in Zahedan and sell for a modest markup in Kerman, the men made six round-trips between the provincial capital, Zahedan, and the large, Persian city of Kerman to the northwest across the great central desert. Shams A'din and Karam carried bulk tea (*chi shakair* and *chi kalam,* two good varieties), used jackets and coats, balaclava hats, tablecloths, and bedspreads bought in Zahedan, all having previously been brought to Zahedan from Pakistan, the tea originating in India and the coats in Europe. Most of the goods had been smuggled into Iran. They bought almost all of their goods in the "Baluchi bazaar" on Khayaban (Avenue) Charah—a dozen stores and several open lots—in Zahedan. Many of the goods that came across the border turned up there. This bazaar was frequented mainly by Baluch, rarely by Persians. Shams A'din purchased from anyone who had what he needed and sold for a good price; he had no special contacts or relatives. Only the tea was purchased in the "regular" Persian bazaar.

The cost of the goods that they bought in Zahedan and the price for which they were able to sell it in Kerman are shown in table 6.3. The goods carried during the six trips are shown in table 6.4.

On the basis of the prices given, the investment per trip would be, respectively, 2,970, 2,195, 2,720, 2,552, 2,420, and 2,170 toman. Given the initial capital available and the other costs, around 85 toman per trip, they would have had to rely upon credit for part of the purchases on the initial trip. Other costs were as follows:

| *Cost* | *Toman* |
| --- | --- |
| Fare Zahedan-Kerman | 20 |
| Fare Kerman-Zahedan | 20 |
| Freight charge Zahedan-Kerman | 15 |
| Bribe for gendarmes | 20 |
| Food | 10 |
|  | — |
| *Total cost per round-trip* | 85 |

Once in Kerman, Shams A'din and Karam did not go from shop to shop trying to find buyers for their goods. Rather, they sold them to Baluchi "receivers" of goods who were staying in Kerman and who sold them to Persian traders who would carry them to the north to other Persian cities and to Persian shopkeepers in Kerman. Shams A'din and Karam sold all of their goods to a campmate from the Halki Ja'far. Id Mahmud, the son-in-law, *zamas,* of Ja'far, the very Id Mahmud who five years before, during the

**Table 6.3.** Trading Prices: Purchase and Sale
(in toman)

| Type | Cost in Zahedan | Sale Price Kerman |
|---|---|---|
| Bulk tea | | |
| (shakair and kalam) | 18 (kilo) | 20–21 |
| Suit or sport coats | | |
| (cheapest quality)[a] | 300 (50 units) | 400 |
| Balaclava hats | 75 (dozen) | 85 |
| Tablecloths | | |
| (embroidered *holah*) | 85 (each) | 100 |
| Bedspread | | |
| (*chadur*) | 35 (each) | 40 |

[a]Higher-quality lots of coats were available at 400, 450, and 500 toman. Overcoats were 25 toman each.

**Table 6.4.** Traded Goods: Types and Quantities

| Trip | Tea (kilos) | Coats | Hats | Tablecloths | Bedspreads |
|---|---|---|---|---|---|
| 1 | 30 | 200 | 120 | 4 | 4 |
| 2 | 60 | 100 | 60 | 0 | 4 |
| 3 | 60 | 150 | 96 | 0 | 4 |
| 4 | 54 | 150 | 48 | 2 | 6 |
| 5 | 60 | 200 | 0 | 0 | 4 |
| 6 | 40 | 150 | 0 | 4 | 6 |

winter of 1967–68, worked along with Ghulam Mahmud as a manual laborer on construction sites in Abu Dhabi, was staying in Kerman for the winter, and along with his two partners, his brother-in-law Lal Han (Kamil Hanzai) and Lal Han's brother, Malik Mahmud, was acting as middleman between Baluch bringing goods from Zahedan and Persian middlemen and shopkeepers in Kerman. Depending upon their Baluchi "receivers," Shams A'din and Karam therefore were able to trade without much knowledge of the Persian trade networks of Kerman and without having to cultivate linguistic and cultural skills to interact with Persians. While Shams A'din spoke some Persian, it was rudimentary. And although he was a fine and decent man, one of "nature's gentlemen," he was educated only in Baluchi culture and without knowledge of the different refinements of Persian culture. Of course, depending upon other middlemen had a cost; it meant that their own profit was smaller than it would have been had they been able to sell to Persian merchants directly.

During their time in Zahidan and Kerman, the men usually spent nights with friends; Jan Bibi, Shams A'dins father's brother's daughter, *naku zad,* was living in Zahedan and received Shams A'din as a guest, providing food and shelter, as she did for other kinsmen from the Halki Ja'far, such as Jan Mahmud, Sahib Dad (Gemi), Rahmat, and Mahmud Karim, when they came through. Shams A'din also occasionally stayed with Id Mahmud in Kerman. Usually, Shams A'din and Karam slept on the overnight bus to Kerman, spent the day selling their goods, sleeping on the night bus back to Zahedan. The men usually ate in cafés in Kerman, Zahedan, and on the road. Sometimes Shams A'din ate at Jan Bibi's, compensating her with a few toman or a tin of vegetable oil.

By staying with friends and sleeping on the bus at night, they were able to limit their expenses, other than the cost of the goods, to bus fare, freight charges, food, and the standard bribe for the gendarmes. After their first three round-trips of buying and selling, taking a couple of weeks, our two Sarhadi traders succeeded in making 1,000 toman net profit on their investment of 2,300 toman. The men then made a number of personal purchases, leaving them 1,600 toman for the next three trips, which brought in 1,000 toman. For the six trips, Shams A'din ended up with 2,000 toman, doubling his capital, a net profit of 1,000 toman, which was—taking inflation into account—perhaps twice as much as the 300 to 350 toman that Ghulam Mahmud, five years before, saved per month of manual labor. Shams A'din said that Karam taught him a great deal about what goods to purchase and how to sell them. Shams A'din felt that if he had been without Karam's help, he would not have been nearly as successful as he was. He was quite grateful to Karam for his help, and thought highly of him for giving it.

Of course, there was a substantial risk in the trading of imported or smuggled goods. On one of his trips from Zahedan to Kerman, carrying a load of goods of his own, Shams A'din saw the gendarmes confiscate all the goods on a bus ahead of him, with his campmate Barkat losing 2,000 toman worth of goods and being thrown in jail for a month for good measure. So each trader had to balance the desire for efficiency in carrying a large load, on the one hand, with the risk that any given load might be confiscated, making it safer to limit the size of each load. Trading, then, required savvy and nerve as well as capital. Youths without money or experience away from home thus tended to gravitate to wage labor, as we can see in the work destinations of the men from Halki Ja'far in 1972–73 (see table 6.2). Those who could trade successfully were not only their own bosses but could arrange their schedule and itinerary so as to keep in close touch with their families and to spend time back in their Sarhadi camps. Trading also provided opportunities for the most ambitious, daring, and capable, especially where it shaded over into smuggling. In 1976, one prominent Yarahmadzai shot and killed a gendarme during a chase involving a truckload of Pakistani tangerines, while another prominent Yarahmadzai tribesmen was himself shot dead in a firefight as he tried to smuggle in a shipment of opium.

**Table 6.5.** Proceeds of Trading: Goods and Food Purchased, Cash Disbursed (in toman)

| Household Goods | Amount | Clothes | Amount |
| --- | --- | --- | --- |
| Carpet | 330 | Shirt and pants for self | 60 |
| Mattress | 80 | Overcoat (trade-in) | 6 |
| Quilt | 38 | Sportcoat | 10 |
| Tea kettle | 10 | Sweater | 8 |
| Pot | 13 | Coat for son | 10 |
| | | Cloth for son's outfit | 10 |
| Total | 471 | Chadur for wife | 30 |
| | | Scarf for wife | 8 |
| | | Total | 142 |

| Food Supplies | Amount | Repayments, Loans, and Gifts | Amount |
| --- | --- | --- | --- |
| Flour | 90 | Repayment to Jan Mahmud | 20 |
| Vegetable oil | 12 | Loan to Ido | 30 |
| Dried milk solids | 14 | Loan to Reis | 70 |
| Dried tomatoes | 10 | Gift to Walli Mahmud | 15 |
| Sugar | 20 | Gift to Gaila | 10 |
| Tea | 40 | | |
| Rice (one meal) | 9 | Total | 145 |
| Total | 195 | | |

For those who succeeded in returning to the Sarhad with income, to what ends was this income directed? As we have already seen, Id Mahmud provided funds for his mother and sisters, as well as for the support of his wife while he was away. Ghulam Mahmud used his wages and profit to aid Ja'far, to pay off some bridewealth, and to buy household materials, particularly goat hair for a tent. What did Shams A'din do with his 1,000 toman capital and 1,000 toman profit? Repayment of loans of 300 toman for the original capital reduced the total to 1,700. Then there were the household goods and clothes, for a total of 613 toman, that he had purchased in Zahedan. In addition, Shams A'din purchased food supplies in the amount of 195 toman (see table 6.5).

Deducting the household goods, clothes, and food supplies purchased, a total of 808 toman, from the 1,700 toman remaining, left Shams A'din with 892 toman. From this, he repaid a small loan, gave two small loans, and gave two small gifts (see table 6.5). This left Shams A'din with 747 toman and 100 toman out in loans, just 147 toman, plus the 20 toman loan paid off, more than he had begun with. But he had learned a lot about trading, *sodayi*, which was intellectual capital that he could draw on in the future. And he had used his profits to provide substantial supplies as well as renew some of the material conditions of daily life for himself and his family in the Sarhad.

Other Sarhadi Baluch returning from economic migrations, especially longer ones, were able to invest in capital resources, both older types such as livestock and irrigation time, and newer types such as mechanized transport. From 1970, when a very rough, dirt road was cleared through the Morpish Mountains, the great annual migration to and from the Mashkil date groves took place not only by camel caravan but also by heavy-duty Mercedes-Benz dump truck, filled to the brim with ailing men, frail old women, little children, and everybody's baggage, and, on the return, hefty *gwal* crammed with dates. Such trucks were also used for smuggling large loads of goods, such as fruit, across the border. And for travel and transport around the tribal territories, a few light trucks carried people and goods for a fare. Individual travel until the 1970s was by foot, camel, and, in a few adventurous but ineffectual cases, bicycle, never really a great option on sand. But by 1976, appropriately sturdy and unrefined Russian motorcycles with large two-cycle engines, provided a taxi service over the stony plains and sand dunes, an efficient and inexpensive mode of travel for ordinary tribesmen going about their business. A not uncommon sight was four bearded and turbaned tribesmen in their flowing shirts and trousers lined up on a motorcycle sporting plastic flowers on its handlebars and carrying a goat tied on the back, bouncing over the sand dunes. Investment in a truck or motorcycle was a business opportunity for tribal entrepreneurs with a bit of capital—a bit more than Shams A'din had, admittedly—ready for an unconventional but promising enterprise.

This trading excursion of Shams A'din, and similar ones by other Sarhadi Baluch, represented significant changes at several levels. At the personal level, for Shams A'din himself and others like him, this initiation into trading was a new kind of economic engagement with the outside world, one involving neither wage labor nor direct subordination. At the economic level, trading represented the peaceful entry of Baluch into the wider, bazaar system of Iran and the channels of trade across international boundaries. Shams A'din and Karam participated in one link, the Zahedan-Kerman link, in a chain running in one direction through Pakistan to India and Europe, and in the other direction to Yazd, Tehran, and perhaps even beyond. The links between Pakistan and Kerman were dominated by a network of Baluch, most of whom were part-time traders with strong commitments to the countryside and their black tent homes, and to the other productive arrows in their multi-resource quivers.

At the geographical level, this excursion presumed a Zahedan much different from the one I had seen five years before, in the fall of 1967, when I had resided there for a couple of months. At that time, Zahedan was a raw, newly built, monochromatic, Persian administrative town, occupied by Persian bureaucrats, technicians, and military. No Baluchi garb of baggy *shalwar,* long *jamag,* and turban were to be seen. Any Baluch present were well shaven and well disguised in military uniforms or the Western-style suits and ties favored by Persian bureaucrats under the regime of Mohammed Reza Shah. Tidy shops in a designated bazaar area were uniformly manned by Persians. I became quite excited (ethnographically) when I saw my first Baluch in Baluchi garb, a man wielding a shovel in a deep trench that he was digging in the road.

By 1972, and even more so in 1976 when I was last there, Zahedan had been transformed by an influx of Baluch into—what seemed to me—a vibrant, crowded, multicolored town enriched by streams of bearded, tribal pedestrians, their *shalwar* and *jamag* rippling in the wind, their burdens carried over the shoulder in colorful cloths, their words and laughs filling the air, making Zahedan seem more like tribal Peshawar than the arid, Persian administrative town I had seen earlier. All of the Baluch were not traveling through; some, predominantly from the surrounding region, had moved in and set up house and shop. By 1972, for every tidy regular Persian shop, there was a ramshackle Baluchi shop, and more Baluch were occupying otherwise empty lots with their piles of goods and materials. It looked as if the Baluch were taking over the town. A bit later, just after the Islamic Revolution, when there was something of a political vacuum in Baluchistan, Persian Sistanis and Baluch fought over control of Zahedan. The Baluch chased the Sistanis out, but their victory was short-lived once the authorities of the Islamic Republic were able to turn their attention, and their troops, back to Baluchistan. Baluchi tribal leaders, including those of the Yarahmadzai, decided to take a "vacation" for a few years in Quetta, Pakistan.

At the cultural level, there was a great shift for Sarhadi Baluch between 1935 and 1975. From brave, relentless raiders they became diligent laborers and shrewd traders. They continued to venture forth outside of the Sarhad intent on bringing back income to provide the margin necessary for a secure life. Labor and trade provided a replacement for the lost income from the suppressed predation. Now the terms of exchange were determined by the market rather than Baluchi military prowess. And the social and cultural terms of exchange were different, determined by the others rather than the Baluch, who now had a weaker hand. It was the Baluch who had to learn foreign languages and foreign skills, not, as in the past, their erstwhile captives. It was the Baluch who had to take orders from strangers and find ways of providing satisfaction to strangers. From being independent and conquering, the Sarhadi Baluch became subordinate, politically, economically, and culturally. It is true that at an individual level, a Baluch could be more independent by engaging in trade or local entrepreneurship and avoid the direct subordination of selling his labor on the market. But the cultural dominance of foreigners and their languages, customs, and economies inevitably remained.

The cultural challenge to the Baluch, the invidious comparisons inherent in contact with more powerful superordinates, the continued pressure and potential erosion of *baluchi* identity, did not pass without taking a toll. I want to present just one example here. Ghulam Mahmud, the adopted brother's son of Ja'far and then his son-in-law, was in the Halki Ja'far a highly regarded young man. I did not get to know him very well; he was away most of the time and when present in camp seemed rather aloof in comparison with his agemate and friend, Id Mahmud, with whom I was on easy and cordial terms. Ghulam Mahmud was, however, kind enough to give me in 1972 a studio photograph of himself. Although I appreciated the gesture, I really did not like the photograph and put it away with a sense of distaste. In this photo, Ghulam Mahmud looks directly at the camera, his unsmiling but mild expression punctuated by heavy moustache and eyebrows. But it was not his face that made me uncomfortable. Rather, it was his clothes: he was wearing a three-button, houndstooth sport jacket, buttoned up to the third button over a white, spread-collar shirt, decorated with a tie of lively design. His hair was of medium length, with moderate 1970s sideburns, and his head topped with a fleecy astrakhan hat of the kind popular in Russia and northern Iran. In short, this was a photo that presented Ghulam as a man of the world, the generalized, Iranian world that had drawn heavily upon Western styles. There were no visible signs of Baluchi affiliation or identity; characteristic Baluchi clothes, headdress, and haircut were absent. I had come a long way, in several senses, to be in Baluchistan, and I was busy appreciating Baluchi culture and life. To see, in this photo of Ghulam Mahmud, an apparent suppression of Baluchi identity and culture, made me uncomfortable (see figure 6.1).

Of course, I had met other Baluch who to one degree or another had Persianized, some of whom had harsh judgments about Baluchi life and customs. The only Sarhadi Baluch I ever met who could speak English was a school teacher from Washt/ Khash. Soon after I met him, he left for Tehran and then for a stint at the University of Edinburgh, before pursuing his teaching career in Tehran. This man had learned well a rather dated discourse on modernity and progress and used this discourse to criticize the "backward," tent-dwelling tribesmen of the surrounding desert, who lived, he felt, dirty, unhygienic lives, and who needed to be enlightened and to settle down in tidy houses like civilized people. I do not want to be patronizing here, for I believe that this man was truly concerned about his fellow Baluch and meant his criticism kindly, even though, as we have heard, the small lineages of Washt sometimes suffered under the arrogant power of the surrounding desert tribes. My impression was that he honestly wanted to improve their situation through disabusing them of their "ignorance." At the time, I questioned some of his ideas, rather to his surprise, I think. But then, I had an interest, at several levels, in tent-dwelling nomads and did not feel great enthusiasm for any vision of their disappearance, whatever improvements—asserted but not demonstrated, and perhaps not forthcoming—might come from settling down and adopting more Persian-like customs. On the other hand, as an alleged agent of higher education, I could not ignore his plea in favor of schooling, never easy for the children of nomads.

In the Halki Ja'far, in Ja'far's own tent, Ghulam Mahmud was loved like an elder son. He was engaged to Ja'far's second daughter, Gol Peri, "Flower Fairy," a pretty,

Figure 6.1. Ghulam Mahmud, 1972. Studio photo presented to author.

spirited girl of 10 or so when we first met her in 1967–68. Her whole life she had looked up to Ghulam Mahmud, virtually worshipping him, so for her the engagement was both natural and ideal. They married in 1971, when she was a prepubescent 13 and he was in his early 20s. She passed through pubescence in 1972–73, virtually under our eyes. At 15, her grace was matched only by her beauty; she bore a startling resemblance to the girl in Vermeer's *Girl with a Pearl Earring.* I rather ashamedly was a bit sweet on Gol Peri, much to the annoyance of Joan, but I felt a bit better when the other young men in the camp admitted to being all a little bit in love with her. One day close to our departure for Canada in 1973, I happened to run into Gol Peri walking across the camp. While strictly speaking I should not have been conversing with her in the absence of others, I took the opportunity to put to her a slightly improper suggestion. "I am going back to America soon. Why don't you come along and live with me?" She looked directly at me and, eyes flashing, said, "I am ready." This exchange was, to my mind, a small compliment that we gave one another.

When I returned to the Sarhad in 1976, I had expected to find Gol Peri and Ghulam Mahmud living in their newly established household, and Gol Peri with child. What I found was Ghulam Mahmud gone, having definitively abandoned the Sarhad, and Gol Peri brokenhearted. Ja'far and Monaz hardly seemed in better spirits. Ghu-lam Mahmud had decided he could no longer live the *baluchi* life. He divorced Gol Peri and married a Persian nurse; they settled in Kerman. When earlier, in 1972–73, I had seen Ghulam Mahmud with Ja'far and the rest of his family, it was evident that there was friction, friction that brought mild-mannered and self-controlled Ja'far to the point of anger. The conflicts seemed small, but they represented something larger. Ghulam Mahmud wanted to play his radio a lot; he wanted to listen to music and other programs. For the increasingly religious consciousness of the members of the Halki Ja'far, this was a bit out of line. And when Ghulam Mahmud was invited to join the men in prayer, he declined. This did not go over well. These conflicts were one indication of a gap in expectations and desires between Ghulam Mahmud, on the one hand, and his Sarhadi family and community, on the other. But of course this is an old story: country boy goes to the glittering city and cannot make himself re-turn to the countryside. To adapt the song, "How are you going to keep them down on the Sarhad, once they've seen Kuwait?" Ghulam Mahmud had ventured forth from the Sarhad, had braved Persian and Gulf cities to work and make money, to win re-sources to support his Sarhadi life. But was he aware that he himself might change? For Ghulam Mahmud had become accustomed to "modern" life, to sedentary Gulf and Persian culture; he liked drinking beer and listening to the radio. He got along with worldly people and appreciated their company. He became comfortable in "Western" clothes. In the end, he had changed so much that he could not make him-self return to the Sarhad, could not return to living in a tent, could not make himself conform to Sarhadi expectations.

It was not that Ghulam Mahmud did not care for Gol Peri, but rather that Gol Peri was part of the Sarhad and knew nothing else. He could not leave without breaking with Gol Peri, so he did. And he almost broke Gol Peri. Of course, offers for her hand immediately flooded in, from men young and old, rich and poor. She refused to marry anyone. But her parents decided otherwise, and she was married to Shir Mah-mud, son of Reis, alias Shiruk, a close, patrilateral cousin, an attractive young man of the same age as Gol Peri. I thought her parents did the right thing and hoped that Gol Peri would come to care for her husband and find happiness in her new family. And I hoped that Ghulam Mahmud, having cut himself off from his kin and his origins, was able to find a satisfactory place for himself, and that he was not undone by the Islamic Revolution.

For Sarhadi Baluch, external engagement as laborers and traders had its risks, different from those of raiding and reprisal in the old days. Sarhadi Baluch, in their travels and their engagements, risked alienation from the lives and families they meant to support.

# 7.
# MIGRATING

Most Sarhadi Baluch were nomadic. By this I mean that they periodically, as part of their normal yearly round of activities, moved their family residences from one place to another. In this sense the term "nomadism" does not refer to the trips that individual members of households made, whether daily, as in shepherds taking out the flocks, or for weeks, as in the trip to Mashkil for *iwar,* or for longer periods, as in travel away from the Sarhad for migrant labor. Rather, "nomadism" refers to the migrations that families made as they changed the location of their households. When Sarhadi families took down their black tents and set them up in another location, that was nomadism.

Among the Sarhadi Baluch, displacement of the family residence, the household, was achieved in coordination with the displacement of other households. That is, a household moved as part of a migration of its residential community, the camp, *halk,* consisting of a number of nomadic families and their residences. The tent, *gedom*—a term that stood not only for the physical tent but the family that was using it as a residence—was, as we have seen, part of the cultural technology of the Sarhadi Baluch that oriented toward spatial mobility. As well, the entire technological complex of baggage animals and baggage existed primarily to support nomadic migration.

Nomadism was customary among the Sarhadi Baluch in several senses. First, it was an integral part of the way of life lived by the ancestors of the Sarhadi Baluch that I knew in the 1960s and 1970s. Second, the physical and intellectual technology of nomadism, including the equipment and the ways of making it and using it, had been handed down to the generation of Sarhadi Baluch that I knew from previous generations. Third, the ways that Sarhadi *baluch* made their livings—the multi-resource economy, including raising livestock, growing date palms, doing agriculture, and so on—depended upon nomadism. Fourth, migrations took place according to an established, seasonal round of activities. Fifth, nomadic displacement of households usually was within a fixed range, a specific known territory. And sixth, social arrangements, such as the constitution of camps, and political processes, such as decision-making in camps, were organized in a way concordant with nomadism.

To say that nomadism was customary for the Sarhadi *baluch* is not, however, to say that the *baluch* were nomadic because nomadism was customary. There was little ritualistic about nomadism in the Sarhad. Rather, nomadism was for the *baluch* a purposeful activity carried out to achieve various ends. Thus it was less of a custom than it was a technique available for a variety of practical ends. At the same time, the fact that nomadism was purposefully used for practical ends did not preclude nomadism from having meaning and significance for the *baluch* or from being part of the way they thought of themselves. The meaning of nomadism for the Sarhadi Baluch was overdetermined, multiply influenced by customary usage, by practical efficacy, and by contrast with non-nomadic populations. In presenting nomadism on the Sarhad, I would like to begin with a particular case, the migrations of the Halki Ja'far during 1968.

## MIGRATION DIARY 1967–68

### South-Central Pushti Kamal
*January 1–20, 1968*
In November 1967, the Halki Ja'far and Halki Halil settled for the winter in the south-central section of their customary winter camping grounds on the Pushti Kamal plain, about 50 kilometers to the east of Khash and 15 kilometers from the Morpish Mountains farther to the east. Some 50 kilometers to the north, visually dominating the plains, was the smoking volcano, Kuhi Daptan. The camps were set up in a sandy rather than rocky part of the plain, about a half mile south of the well said to be dug by Dadol, the apical ancestor of the Dadolzai lineage, members of which were well represented in the two camps. The camp of Ja'far was lightly populated, for many of the men were away, selling their labor outside of the Sarhad, leaving behind their families and animals in camp.

The pastoral activities were primarily devoted to keeping the animals alive and well, rather than extracting any produce from them. A significant investment of time, labor, and resources was devoted to providing the animals with food and shelter, especially the new lambs and kids dropped in December and January. (Much mirth resulted when, while I was playing with one of the cute newborn kids, it urinated on me.) While the adult animals were taken out by the *shwaneg* during the day, the pasture was minimal in Pushti Kamal as elsewhere. There was no thought of relocating to find better pasture, for there was no pasture anywhere at this time of the year.

*January 20–22*

The men of the camp began to talk about rain, which was expected to begin about this time. Ja'far, Isa, and Pati Mahmud agreed that if it rained, the *halk* would move to a new site several kilometers away. They agreed that the present area was over-grazed and even with rain would not be very promising for pasture. On the other hand, if it did not rain, there would be no pasturage and no point in moving. Decisions about migration were always contingent upon conditions; in this case, one primary contingency was rain. Peppering such discussions was the phrase, *malum abi,* "it will become evident," that is, it will become evident in the course of time what conditions would hold and thus upon what conditions we would have to base our decision. In this sense, there was nothing fixed and routine about migration on the Sarhad.

*January 23–February 8*

Several inches of rain fell, and it became clear that there would be good reason to relocate in the near future. Ja'far, the headman of the camp, had, after consultation, agreed to move several kilometers to the west, to the eastern section of the plain of Nilagu.

*February 9–12*

Ja'far was having second thoughts about migrating to the west. A number of camps had moved past Pushti Kamal westward, from the base of the Morpish Mountains in the east, to the plain of Nilagu. He felt that Nilagu would be overcrowded and that there would be much *sholug,* disorder and confusion, and consequently the possibility of conflict. Furthermore, Shams A'din had heard that some of the sheep and camels in the camps at Nilagu were sick and felt that disease was a danger to be avoided if possible.

However, Pati Mahmud, Isa, and Mahmud Karim still maintained that west was best. Pati Mahmud was quite explicit that the *halk* would move to Nilagu.

*February 13–16*

The debate continued. I too, in a small way, got drawn in. On the 13th, Ja'far called me into his tent. Pati Mahmud and Shams A'din were present also. Pati Mahmud said that he and Ja'far disagreed about where the *halk* should move, and they wanted to know what my opinion was. Certainly they were not concerned about my prediction as to where pasture would be found or which areas were too crowded. What I discovered later was that Pati Mahmud had told Ja'far that I would not stay with the camp if it moved to the northeast, but would migrate with the camp if it moved to Nilagu in the west. As my presence as a foreign guest was prestigious to the *halk* and also a potential source of material support of various kinds—not least being access to my Land Rover, the only motor vehicle in the camp—and so far I had shown my-

Figure 7.1. Breaking camp, 1968. (Photograph by author)

self to be harmless, Ja'far was concerned that I might leave. Pati Mahmud had, un-
beknownst to myself, recruited me as support to strengthen his case. My response
was that I would go with the *halk* wherever it migrated, and that I had no preference.
On this point I was accepted on my word and the question never again arose.

A couple of days later, there was a meeting in Ja'far's tent, attended not only by
the adult men of the Halki Ja'far, but by Dadol and Ido, elders of the brother Halki
Halil. These latter men spoke in favor of migrating to the northeast of Pushti Kamal.
Mahmud Karim, however, had scouted out the alternative locations and reported that
the pasturage was better in the west. He argued that the camps should move to the
west, and Ja'far supported him. The final agreement was that the two camps would
migrate together to the west and remain there until the pasturage improved in the
northeast, and then migrate to the northeast.

Three factors were being considered in this decision: a pull, an anchor, and a repulsion. The pull was toward good pasturage for the animals. The anchor was the irrigated wheat that some of the men had growing, or were working, to the east of
Pushti Kamal at Shagbond, and that needed regular attention. These men would have
to make fairly frequent trips to the fields and thus were in favor of camping at a distance that would inconvenience them the least while still providing adequate support
for their animals. It is noteworthy here that Mahmud Karim's arguments in favor of
moving to the west carried weight, because he too had to make trips to Shagbond,

Figure 7.2. Loading camels prior to migration, 1968. (Photograph by author)

and thus had similar interests with the men who wanted to move to the northeast. In contrast, Pati Mahmud had no concern with Shagbond, and his interests were not concordant with those who had. This, together with the fact that Mahmud Karim was Dadolzai and Pati Mahmud was not, resulted in more weight being given to the testimony of the former than the latter. The repulsion emanated from the crowded conditions resulting from a (relatively) high density of human and animal population, that is, any area where a number of camps were already located. It was this about which Ja'far was particularly concerned in the proposed move to the west.

*February 17–19*

Several factors militated against migration. Primarily, the tent cloth was sodden from the relatively continuous rain and would have been a burden too heavy for the camels. And migration in the rain, in which everything and everyone would get soaked, was to be avoided if possible. In addition, Ja'far had lent camels to another *halk* for their migration and these had not been returned, and Isa had not returned from a trip to Khash.

## Migration I: To Western Pushti Kamal

*February 20*

After several days of postponement because of rain, the *halk* migrated to the west of Pushti Kamal, a distance of around a kilometer (⅗ of a mile or so) from the winter camping site. This location was a compromise. For Ja'far, it was not to the more crowded Nilagu Plain. For the men with work at Shagbond, it was not too distant. For everyone, it was a clean camping location away from the winter site fouled by animal leavings and the refuse of the months of occupation. For the women, it was within a reasonable distance of the Dadolzai well. For the animals, it was an area not overgrazed and one that promised an early cover of young grass and shoots. Ja'far explicitly stated, however, that if trips to Shagbond were not necessary, the search for pasturage could be weighed more heavily and the camps would likely have moved farther than they in fact did.

*February 21–March 10*

This new location proved to be disappointing as far as pasturage was concerned, for grass did not spring up as expected. But Halk members were occupied with a wedding and the celebration of the religious festival, *aidi buzorg,* and migration was put off until these were over.

## Migration II: To Eastern Beadak

*March 11*

The Halki Ja'far migrated 5 kilometers (around 3 miles) to the northeast and set up camp in the eastern part of Beadak, a small plain to the north of Pushti Kamal, surrounded by rocky ridges. The Halki Halil followed the next day. *Beadak* means "without dryness" and alludes to the availability of water. In fact, there had been some disagreement about whether to camp in eastern Beadak, where pasturage for both grazing and browsing were relatively abundant, but where water had to be drawn from undependable holes dug in a runoff channel in the hills or from a small stream some distance from camp, or whether to camp in western Beadak, which had a more reliable and better-located stream but not such abundant pasturage. Shams A'din suggested western Beadak, but Ja'far, supported by Dur Mahmud and Pati Mahmud, thought that the water available at the eastern site would last as long as they would stay.

*March 12–19*

On March 17, most of the adult men, including Ja'far, left the camp for a three-week trip to Mashkil for *iwar*, pollination of the date palms. Only Shams A'din and Karim Han remained with the camp, leaving it with a minimum of labor power. Nonetheless, pressure began to mount for a migration. One problem was that the water sources were not holding out as well as had been hoped, and the women wanted to move where water would be more readily available. Another, even more important problem was that eight *pas* had sickened, four of Ja'far's, and had died or had to be slaughtered. In Ja'far's absence, his wife Monaz, representing their family and patrimony, took the position that "the ground here is bad" and was causing the illness of the animals, and for that reason the Halk should migrate elsewhere.

Exactly where the Halk might move was a problem. Some sentiment was expressed for moving back to the well at Pushti Kamal, but there were several difficulties with this possibility. One was that the well had not been used recently and had not had its regular maintenance cleaning. And since a number of men were necessary for this maintenance operation, it was impossible to carry out until the men returned from Mashkil. Another problem was that an area of untended wheat had been sown in a runoff area near the proposed site, and some in the camp feared that the animals would eat it. Shams A'din argued these points, and they were accepted by most people. But Monas was vehement about leaving Beadak, and if the best alternative was to western Beadak, that would have to do.

## Migration III: To Maraj

*March 20*

While many of the women complained about the water situation, when it came down to migrating without the men, their decisions, and their labor, the women hesitated. Those who had not lost animals were not so fearful about continued residence at Beadak.

Monas said that she was migrating, and that the others could come or not, as they chose. Shams A'din stayed neutral, and Karim Han indicated that he would have to stay because his daughter was sick. Monas began packing and taking down her tent, and the others of the Halki Ja'far, with varying degrees of reluctance, followed her example. The Halk migrated 3 kilometers (something less than 2 miles) to the southwest of Beadak, to Maraj.

*March 21–25*

There was a good supply of stream water at Maraj near the campsite, but the pasturage was quite scanty, and it was clear that prolonged occupation of this site would be to the detriment of the animals. This problem was discussed with the Halki Halil, which had remained at Beadak and was under pressure because of the water problem.

Dad Mahmud, the now adult son of Walli Mahmud and his captured Persian wife, recommended a move to Garonchin, rather far to the south, where there was a great deal of pasturage. Dad Mahmud had his own reasons for wanting to move to Garonchin; his wife was staying with her parents there and he wanted his camp to be close by so that she would not have to be separated from him in order to be with her own family. The Halki Halil was not overly enthusiastic about making this relatively long migration during a time when labor was very short, to an area customarily used by other groups. Furthermore, for those who had to return to Shagbond to tend the grain, the trip would be very far. While these arguments were just as relevant to the Halki Ja'far, the importance of good pasturage, especially the varieties favored by the camels, which were singularly absent at Maraj and not especially evident anywhere in the neighborhood, outweighed these considerations. And resistance was limited by the fact that current work at Shagbond only entailed tending the irrigation canals once every eight days.

## Migration IV: To Northern Garonchin
*March 26–28*

After five days at Maraj, the Halki Ja'far migrated south toward Garonchin. Delayed by a long initial packing period, which had been stretched out owing to the lack of labor, and then slowed down by the flock, from which camp members did not want to be separated during this period of milk production, the Halk covered a distance of 24 kilometers (15 miles) and set up a temporary camp for that night and the following day and night. Then they migrated again, continuing 15 kilometers (almost 10 miles) south to Garonchin.

*March 29–April 11*

There had been no definite site picked out ahead of time. Rather, there was a contemporaneous scouting of the area as the Halk passed through during the course of the migration. The desired conditions included a location in an unoccupied area of rich pasturage, which was distant enough from any cultivation to avoid damage from the group's animals, particularly the camels, which were allowed to browse without full-time supervision. These conditions were fairly well met by the section of northern Garonchin just to the west of the trail, although there was pump irrigation cultivation to the southwest and the camels would have to be watched carefully so that they did not get into the grain.

The Halki Halil had meanwhile migrated on March 27, and in spite of the location of the Halki Ja'far, the determination of Dad Mahmud to move to Garonchin, and the desire of Karim Han to rejoin Ja'far's camp, they decided that it was too much trouble to move as far as Garonchin. The pasturage at Pushti Kamal seemed to be adequate, and the wheat in the runoff area could be avoided by locating north of the ancestral Dadol's well. When they set up camp there, Dad Mahmud and Karim Han continued on to the camp site of the Halki Ja'far. Some were annoyed that the Halki Halil had stayed behind, but the pasturage, especially for camels, was abundant and the members of the Halki Ja'far were pleased with the results of their decision to migrate to Garonchin.

Before long, however, the Halki Halil decided that pasturage at Pushti Kamal was inadequate, and after a number of individual tents migrated to Garonchin, on April 5 the remainder of the Halki Halil moved to a site a quarter of a mile from the Halki Ja'far. At this time, Ido, instead of continuing with the Halki Halil, split off and joined his affines in the Halki Jahangi, also in northern Garonchin, because they had an adult *shwaneg,* shepherd. The animals of the Halki Halil were not being taken out at night for grazing by their young *shwaneg,* and Ido felt that his animals were suffering from the reduction of grazing due to this lost opportunity.

From April 6, Dad Mahmud began pushing for a move deeper into Garonchin. He said that the pasturage around the present site had been grazed over and that the pasturage in southern Garonchin was virtually untouched. But it was well known in camp that Dad Mahmud's wife, now residing with him, was anxious to be closer to her family, which was presently camped in southern Garonchin. And while Dad Mahmud's views were not disregarded on this account, it was recognized that other members of the Halk had interests divergent from his. It was clear, for example, that Dad Mahmud's arguments for migrating to the south on April 9 were unlikely to succeed because, first, the men had not yet returned from *iwar,* and no one wanted to move without them, and, second, the men were due any day, and the members of the Halk who were present, especially Monas, who had quietly been making many decisions, did not want to continue taking responsibility in this "lame-duck" period just before the men arrived, when she could wait and let them decide upon their arrival.

The men arrived on April 10, after their four-day trip from Mashkil, and were immediately presented with the problem of a migration. Their first reaction was that they were willing to migrate if the pasturage was really better to the south, but they wanted a day of rest first. But in two days Yelli Han had to be off to Shagbond to irrigate his fields, and so if he was to help with the migration, which his family certainly preferred, the Halk would have to migrate the very next day. The point was reluctantly accepted and the migration planned for the next day: *banda lardi konan, insha allah,* "Tomorrow we will migrate, with the will of God."

Now this was the common form when Sarhadi Baluch said that they were planning to do something; they would always add, *insha allah,* "with the will of God." This phrasing acknowledged the ultimate power of God and the dependence of people upon God's will in matters large and small. No Baluch would say that they were going to do something without adding this qualification. And, after I had lived in Baluchistan for a few months, I could not say that I would do something without adding *insha allah.* Of course, at first I was just imitating local linguistic practice and trying to avoid offending anyone. But quickly it became second nature. I would feel nervous, if I left off this qualifying phrase, as if I had offended powers greater than myself and would suffer from their displeasure. Even when I returned to North America, I felt uncomfortable saying that I would do something without uttering the proper qualification.

Promises and commitments qualified by *insha allah* allowed individuals to express intentions, or to purport intentions, but did not bind them absolutely to specific courses of action. Various unpredictable developments could arise that would make it impossible to carry out the promise or follow up on the previously expressed intention, and it was understood that the individual could not be held accountable. When intentions expressed with *insha allah,* with the will of god, were later thwarted, owing to *dasti huda,* the hand of god, responsibility for the results, or lack of results, was recognized to rest beyond the control of the individual.

The phrase *insha allah,* asserting that control of the future does not rest in the hands of men and women, expressed an uncertainty that reflected fairly frankly the everyday experience of Sarhadi life. The forces of nature and the demands of broad social networks, and the unexpected conjunctions of the two, made Sarhadi life uncontrollable and unpredictable. Who knew when livestock would sicken and die? How could one predict when water would run out? When would the folks who borrowed camels return them? There were no ironclad schedules, firm itineraries, or absolute commitments. Rather, there were general principles of obligation and a variety of strategies of adaptation and response. Active flexibility was the order of the day.

As for the projected migration of April 11, it never took place. Quite unexpectedly, Dur Mahmud had not returned from Shagbond, and his help was needed by his family. Given the desire of the men who had just returned from Mashkil to rest up, and the choice of doing without Dur Mahmud one day and Yelli Han the next, the men opted for the day's rest and put off the migration even though Yelli Han would be absent. In any case, it was argued, Yelli Han's son-in-law, Mandust, could do the heavy work.

There was some discontent in the Halki Ja'far, especially among a few of the older women, about all of the moving and the trouble that it entailed, but in general the camp members were primarily concerned about the animals, especially the camels, and went along willingly. Complaint was directed not so much toward the decision to migrate, which was seen as not unjustified, but the work that was necessarily involved.

## Migration V: To Southern Garonchin
*April 12*
The Halki Ja'far migrated 6 kilometers (not quite 4 miles) to the south and set up camp to the east of the trail and ⅓ kilometer from the Halk of Dad Mahmud's affines, who were located close to their well.

*April 13–25*
Shams A'din, for one, was not impressed with the pasturage in the vicinity of the new camp. Pasturage, he thought, was much better to the northwest, across the trail, although there was admittedly no water source there. But the best pasturage was farther to the north near the pump. He said, "Dad Mahmud had said that the pasturage in southern Garonchin was very good, and the Halk took his word, but clearly what was good for him here was the location of the Halk of his wife's people."

Ja'far, however, thought that the camel pasturage in the new area was better than that of northern Garonchin, which had been mostly browsed over. And while the pasturage near the pump was very good indeed, the chances would have been greater that the camels would have gotten into the grain and this would have been costly. The present area was all uncultivated countryside, and the camels could wander and cause no damage.

On April 22, Ja'far was saying that the Halk would stay at Garonchin for 8 to 12 days more. But by April 24, he had decided that the Halk should migrate back to Pushti Kamal. There were several reasons for this.

First, Dur Mahmud, who had passed through Pushti Kamal on the way from Shagbond to Khash, and who Ja'far had seen in Khash, had reported that the pasturage was coming out very nicely. Ja'far had told me this while we were standing on the main street of Khash, where we had gone for supplies. I was rather surprised and began discussing this unexpected decision with Ja'far in normal tones, questioning especially about the condition of the pasturage at Pushti Kamal. Ja'far quickly hushed me, indicating that there were many men from other camps nearby and that he did not want to publicize the fact that pasture conditions were good at Pushti Kamal, lest this information stimulate a rush there by other camps. But, I asked, were not other Yarahmadzai camping groups free to go to Pushti Kamal if they so chose? Of course they were, Ja'far said, but he had no obligation to inform them that the pasturage was good.

Second, the men who were tending grain at Shagbond were very tired of making the 50-kilometer trip, 100-kilometer round-trip, often by foot, every week. By moving to Pushti Kamal, they would be closer to Shagbond.

Third, the water level in the well of Dad Mahmud's affines had lowered considerably, not surprisingly, as water was being drawn not only for the household needs of two camps but for the camels as well. The other Halk, which owned the well, would not be pleased if their water source was depleted. Ja'far had planned to migrate on

April 25, but one of Pati Mahmud's camels was lost, and so the migration had to be put off.

## Migration VI: To Kwuhashkan
*April 26–27*

On the first day, the Halk migrated 20 kilometers (more than 12 miles) to the north and set up camp for the night at the same spot at which they had stopped on the way south to Garonchin during migration IV. On the second day, they traveled 22 kilometers (almost 14 miles) more, to a spot 2 kilometers (more than a mile) to the west-northwest of Gwanich, a small village consisting of a few mud-brick buildings, in the area to the south of Pushti Kamal.

In deciding where to camp, the Halk took into account the problems of pasturage and shepherds. The area around the well at Pushti Kamal, where the Halki Halil had migrated 10 days before, was rich in pasturage for sheep and goats, but only fair in pasturage for camels, whereas the area to the west of Gwanich was the converse. As there was equal concern for both the *pas* and the camels, this difference did not weigh in favor of Gwanich or Pushti Kamal.

The deciding factor was the availability of an adult *shwaneg* in the Ghulamzai Halki Abdul Samad, which was camped in the area to the west of Gwanich at Kwuhashkan. The importance of this factor grew out of the limitations of the herding personnel of the Halki Ja'far. The *shwaneg*, Abdulluk, a boy of 13 years, was afraid to stay out during the night with the *galagi pas*. The strategy of keeping the animals out all night so that they could graze in the relatively cool temperature was a way of maximizing their food intake during the only season of good pasturage. Not much time remained before *zard o bahar*, the drying of the pasturage, signaled the end of spring and the arrival of the extreme hot temperatures and aridity of summer, to be followed by the freezing temperatures of winter and poor pasturage until, it was hoped, the new pasture of the next spring. In short, spring was the best opportunity to extract from the animals the maximum amount of dairy products and to fatten and strengthen them in the face of the coming hardship seasons. The youthful *shwaneg* of the Halki Ja'far had difficulty staying awake through the night, and he was afraid of wolves, which had previously threatened the *pas* but been driven off by the guard dog. In the location chosen by the Halk, Abdulluk was able to take the *pas* out with the adult *shwaneg* of the other camp, which satisfied both his and the animal's needs.

This site also solved the problem of water, as the irrigation channels of Shagbond, 3 kilometers (less than 2 miles) to the northeast, were available for watering the animals, and the irrigation channels at Gwanich could provide household water. The pasturage more or less held its freshness, as the relative lateness of the winter rains in this area contributed to the late *zard o bahar*.

The length of stay at the Kwuhashkan site was conditioned by the maturation of the grain at Shagbond, and secondarily the growth of the grain in the runoff areas in

Pushti Kamal. While only a few of the *halk* members owned a share of the grain at Shagbond, all were planning to work in the fields during the harvest for a share in kind.

## Migration VII: To Shabond
*May 21*
The Halki Ja'far migrated 3 kilometers (less than 2 miles) to the east, on the northernmost land of the now abandoned village of Nugju and just to the south of Shagbond, and was there joined by the Halki Halil from central Pushti Kamal. Pati Mahmud, at this time, migrated to Gwanich, to help his brother harvest.

*May 22–June 11*
The harvest was the major object of attention during this period. The animals had to be moved away from the areas of cultivation to keep them from invading the fields of grain while at the same time providing them with access to natural pasturage.

As the harvest was completed from field to field, the animals were brought onto the land to feed on the stubble. At the end of the harvest, with the entire area cleared of grain, the owners of the plots, Yelli Han and Dur Mahmud, requested that the Halk relocate directly onto the fields, so that the animals would leave their droppings on the cultivation area and fertilize the soil.

## Migration VIII: Onto the Fields
*June 12*
The Halki Ja'far and Halki Halil broke camp and migrated the ⅖ kilometer (¼ mile) onto the fields. Here they did not maintain their usual tight pattern but spread across the fields so that, as the animals were kept by each owner's tent, the droppings would be distributed more equally over the entire area.

The locations near Shagbond were particularly advantageous for the animals because of the available water supply, an element of increasing importance for the animals as the temperature climbed toward its summer apex. As well, the stubble from the grain added to the natural pasturage as a source of nourishment.

From this time, there were no further migrations on the high plateau of the Sarhad. The attentions of the tribesmen were directed toward the date groves at Mashkil. The *pas*, supervised by the *shwaneg*, and the rest of the Halk, would move in different directions, the tribesmen focusing their attentions on their date palms.

## Migration IX: To Mashkil
*Late July*
*Hamin*, the time of the date harvest—August, September, October—begins with *ruro*, migration from the Sarhad high plateau to the Hamuni Mashkil. The tents were stored, the animals were left in the charge of a crew of professional and short-term

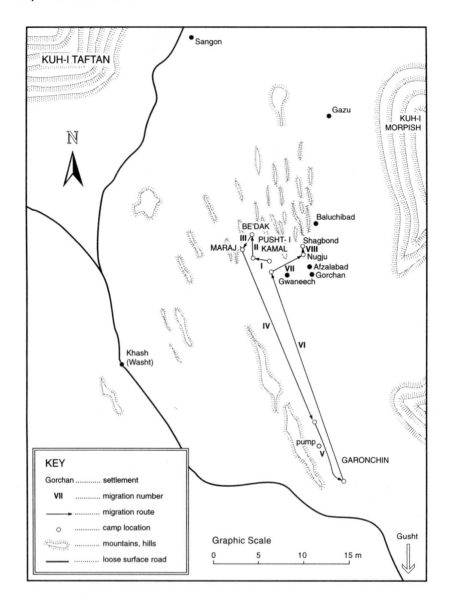

Figure 7.3. Pastoral migrations of the Ja'far-i Halk, January–July 1968.

shepherds, and the larger part of each *halk* moved down off the plateau to the low-land date groves. The members of the Halki Ja'far made the eight-day, 200-kilometer (124-mile) migration by camel, past Gazu and around the northern end of the Mor-pish mountain range, through the bed of the Rudi Mad Shadi, then southeast to Mashkil, most to Gorani, some to other grove areas. Members of the Gamshadzai tribe, whose territory bordered the Yarahmadzai south of Garonchin, took a more southerly route around the other end of the Morpish Range, and then turned northeast, passing Jalk, to arrive at their grove areas. Stores of flour and *rogani pas,* clarified butter, were carried on the camels, as well as the minimum of household necessities.

## Migration X: To the Sarhad
*Late September*

There were not enough camels to carry at the same time the produce of the date groves, the heavy bags of dates and date pits, and the families and their impedimenta. Thus prior to migration of the families back to the Sarhad was *shawarkashk,* the trip to the Sarhad of the camel caravan carrying the dates and date pits, while families and family equipment remained at Mashkil. Only after the men had returned to Mashkil with the camels could the migration of the families back to the Sarhad take place.

## PURPOSES AND PATTERNS OF NOMADISM ON THE SARHAD

What observations can we draw from the migrations of the Halki Ja'far during 1968 about the characteristic purposes and patterns of nomadism on the Sarhad?

### Purpose and Choice in Sarhadi Nomadism

Nomadism everywhere is a strategy for maximizing certain benefits and minimizing various difficulties in production, social relations, and daily life. This is clearly true in the Sarhadi case we have reviewed. We saw Ja'far, Monas, Shams A'din, Pati Mahmud, Dad Mahmud, and other camp residents thinking about, discussing, and advocating various alternative plans for migrating. There were always at least several apparently viable possibilities, often quite distinct as to timing, direction, distance, and alleged benefits. I think, on the basis of these observations, we may conclude that patterns of migration on the Sarhad were not very routinized, not cut-and-dried patterns that people followed in a repeated, mechanical way. Nor could migration be considered random wandering for its own sake. Rather, we have seen that nomadic migration took place as part of an ongoing decisionmaking process in which many variables were considered and many objectives weighed, within the particular environmental, economic, and social conditions of the Sarhad.

In many parts of Iran, most notably in the Zagros mountain range (Barth 1961; Beck 1986), and far beyond Iran (Campbell 1964; Ravis-Giordani 1983), nomadism was oriented toward macroenvironmental variations. For example, one pattern of "mountain nomadism" sometimes called "transhumance" responded to gross differences in season and altitude by moving livestock between winter lowlands and summer highlands, in order to avoid extremes of heat and cold and to provide the animals with the best pasturage available. These seasonal and altitudinal variations are quite dependable and predictable, and consequently patterns of migration, with only minor disparities, were regularly repeated annually. The migration pattern of the Basseri of south Persia, famously described in Barth's brilliant account (1961), was so reliable that it was conceptuatlized as the Basseri's *il rah*, tribal road. While it would be an exaggeration to imagine, especially in the Middle Eastern political context, that Basseri or any other mountain nomadism proceeded automatically and without potential disruption (Beck 1991), or that mountain environments never presented any surprises (Bakhtiari Migration [film]), gross, macroenvironmental variations did provide the possibility for relatively regularized nomadic exploitation.

In the Sarhad, however, the contingent nature of nomadic migration was determined by regional environmental and climatic circumstances. We have already considered the great annual variations in precipitation and consequently in pasturage on the Sarhad. Beyond this, we have seen, in one particular year, the members of the Halki Ja'far and Halki Halil looking here and looking there for pasturage and water, talking about moving one place or another, and then moving here and moving there. Spring migrations in the Sarhad were not for the most part responses to macroenvironmental variations; rather, these migrations were oriented to exploiting microenvironment variations, specifically the presence of pasture and water in particular places and times, presences that were not dependable or predictable. Nomadism as an adaptation to such microenvironmental variations is always opportunistic, exploiting unpredictable resources when and where they are discovered. Sarhadi nomadism was relatively regular and predictable only where it relied upon macroenvironmental variations: one such variation was seasonal, the increased nomadic activity during spring, when new pasturage, *bahar*, grew. The other was altitudinal, migration between the high plateau and the lowland date groves of Mashkil. Overall, Sarhadi nomadism was more opportunistic than regularized, in response to irregular and unpredictable microenvironmental variations.

## Nomadism and the Multi-resource Economy

When Mahmud Karim and Ja'far and the others were discussing migration and new sites, they considered not only the needs of their animals, but also various aspects of other productive sectors, such as grain agriculture, date arboriculture, and migrant labor. For example, the location of grain cultivation—how near or far fields were from camp sites, how easy or difficult it would be to keep animals from eating the grain—was a factor in decisions about where to migrate, where to stay, and how long to stay. Their involvement in date arboriculture—removing men from the camp for *iwar*—reduced the labor available and increased the difficulty of migrating, inclining the remaining camp members against migration, even for good pastoral reasons. Because the Sarhadi Baluch had a diversified, multi-resource economy and were engaged in a variety of different and spatially distinct productive sectors, they were constantly being pulled in several different directions, not least when they were considering changing the location of their residences.

It would thus be an oversimplification to call the Sarhadi Baluch "pastoral nomads," not only because they were seriously and extensively engaged in nonpastoral sectors, but because their nomadism was spatial movement that had to balance the needs of all of the different sectors of production. Ideally, there would be a conjunction, for example, between the needs of the animals and those of grain cultivation, such as the period of camping on the fields that provided stubble for the animals and fertilizer for the grain. But more often this happy conjunction was not to be. Nothing demonstrated the multisectoral nature of Sarhadi nomadism better than the clear disjunction between the *galagi pas* and the longest migration of the year to the date groves as Mashkil. This was a migration between productive sectors, between the *pas* pastoralism of the high plateau, where the flocks were left during *hamin,* and the date cultivation of the lowland drainage basin.

## Individual Interests and Nomadism

Different tents, different households, had different demographic profiles; some had lots of capable hands and legs to do many jobs, while others had only one or two active individuals upon whom to depend. For example, in 1968 Ja'far had several grown children and sons-in-law as well, while Shams A'din had no children yet. Similarly, different tents had different economic profiles of capital resources such as livestock, date palms, and irrigated land; some had a good number of livestock while others had only a few or none, just as some were involved in growing grain, while others were not.

These differences among households were reflected in the different priorities that different camp members had and expressed in their preferences for timing and destination of migration. For example, Pati Mahmud had no ties to Shagbond and the irrigation cultivation there and pressed for migrations that suited his livestock and his ties to Gwanich without regard for distance from Shagbond. For the men who were working the land at Shagbond, a distant site such as Garonchin, no matter how good the pasturage, added onerous travel to their regular labor.

Thus, provision of "information" and consultation among camp members was not only assessing the state of the natural and social environments in order to act effectively on given and known priorities. As well, this process of decisionmaking was doing more; it was forming a compromise that balanced the divergent individual and household interests, as these were implicitly or explicitly expressed and asserted by their members in the camp. At the same time, there was a weighing of political credit among members of the camp; long-term camp members and those belonging to the dominant lineage in the camp had more weight and their interests were given more consideration.

## Nomadism and Military Mobility

The Halki Ja'far responded on short notice to perceived threats, such as livestock disease, by moving camp. Sarhadi nomadism included movement of the human population, their housing, equipment and supplies, and the livestock, one of their main capital resources. This nomadism had also been used to avoid conflict or to escape hostile military action. A mild example was Ja'far's desire to avoid the crowded Nilagu Plain and the possibility of conflict with others over competition for scarce resources. But we have already heard about earlier military reprisals for Sarhadi raiding, and there have also been major conflicts between tribes and blood feuds within tribes. The technology and social organization of nomadism also provided Sarhadi Baluch with the capability of minimizing damage to themselves and their economy through avoidance of contact with hostile forces and escape from attack.

At the same time, looking back at the Sarhad before the Iranian conquest in 1935, Baluchi skills of nomadism, the habit of mobility, and the technology of riding camels were all facilitators in Sarhadi predatory raiding. While nomadism was only one cultural complex that contributed to predatory raiding, it provided ready-made, as it were, the necessary capability for rapid travel and transport in raiding, as well as the capacity for defense through escape. Not all nomads have been predatory raiders, but among raiders many have been nomads. General Dyer, not without reason, called his book about his campaign against the Sarhadi Baluch, *Raiders of the Sarhad*.

## MIGRATION DIARY 1972–73

The migrations of the Halki Ja'far in 1968 were typical of a fairly good year, and also rather uneventful. By contrast, the goings of the Halki Ja'far in 1972–73 were rather more lively. Let us begin with the migration to Mashkil and fill in some of the details about this longest migration of the year.

### Migration I: Planning for Mashkil
*July 10–17*
In the Sarhad many *halk* were clustered near or on agricultural sites. The Halki Ja'far was situated to the south of Shagbond and its fields. The Halk did not move onto the fields this year. People said that they did not have land there to fertilize, so why make the effort to move. Also, the animals would be closer to other gardens and would get into them and cause damage.

The grain harvest was over and much labor was being put into cleaning the grain and carrying it over to Gwanich to the mill, *assiob,* which is run off the motor that runs the irrigation pump. The heavy, woolen *gwal* of wheat were loaded onto camels and donkeys and carried to the mill, where those bringing the grain had themselves to pour the grain and collect the flour, *art.*

Much thought was being given to the coming migration to the date groves at Mashkil. People were considering who would go and who would not, when those that were going would go, and how those that were going would go.

Who would go? This question seemed to have increased in importance during the 1970s. Those people not going to Mashkil were mainly those involved in productive labor elsewhere. This included those people with increasing investments on the Sarhad in fruit, especially watermelon, but also figs, grapes, and other fruit that ripened in the summer. From the Dadolzai, Halil and Mulla Rustam fell into this category. Some of these people might come to Mashkil after the fruit harvest on the Sarhad. In addition, some people preferred to use this period to leave the Sarhad to sell their labor or to trade—for example, Isa was going to Bandar Abbas for labor— although most men wanted to avoid physical labor during the sizzling summer.

Those who did not themselves go to Mashkil either had to arrange for others to tend their palms or they had to make a long-term decision to abandon their investment in the date groves. Some individuals decided not to invest further in Mashkil, not to plant new date palms, but instead to expand investment in the Sarhad. But the difficulties of this strategy were what they had always been: expansion of investment in date palms at Mashkil was a matter of labor, whereas on the Sarhad, because of the paucity of water and the need to irrigate, investment was a matter of capital. Those who already had irrigation water rights were in a stronger position than others to make a commitment to economic investment in the Sarhad rather than at Mashkil.

There were social as well as economic reasons to go to Mashkil. As long as most people went to Mashkil, those who stayed behind or went elsewhere were away from their kin and friends. And those kin and friends put pressure on them to join the community at Mashkil. As well, the months of *hamin* at Mashkil were the established, "summer vacation" for the Sarhadi Baluch. It was a change from the usual landscape and the tent living of the Sarhad, to the—to Sarhadi eyes—luxuriant date groves and commodious brick housing. And there was holiday eating; fresh dates were available in large quantities, and, at Gorani at least, sweet water easily available. There was also the opportunity to reside with relatives who lived elsewhere on the Sarhad but had their date groves in the same location. There was somewhat less work at Mashkil than usual, with the flocks away on the Sarhad, most men back in their household to share the work, no grain or fruit cultivation to be tended, and water nearby, close to the surface, and easy to collect. Work activities were different, a change from the Sarhad. Men worked on the palms, women pitted dates and baked in cylindrical mud-brick ovens, *tandur,* and both wove *pish,* palm leaves. The men, women, and children of the Halki Ja'far looked forward to going to Mashkil, in spite of the arduous journey. The girls spoke excitedly about Mashkil. "We are going to eat dates" they said, their eyes flashing while they bounced slightly on the balls of their feet. People felt that Mashkil, or Gorani at least, was a very good place. Many said that they liked it better than the Sarhad.

When to go? The period for residence at Mashkil was delineated by established cultivation cycles. On the Sarhad, the grain had to be harvested and dealt with, a portion at least through the stage of milling into flour. This was the defining criterion for the earliest period at which it was possible to go to Mashkil. The defining factor for the latest period was the maturation of the dates. To avoid mature dates falling or being blown off their stems and onto the ground where they would be damaged or eaten, they had, as we have seen, to be bagged, *sund kort*. Thus the trip to Mashkil had to take place in time to bag the dates before they began falling.

On July 14, the Halki Ja'far planned to migrate in a week or 10 days. As the milling of grain was still in progress on the 13th, this timing would allow a bit of a rest before the extensive packing, hauling, and traveling. But on the 14th, Nezar Mahmud, brother of the Sardar, arrived from Mashkil bearing news that some dates were already ripe and that the time for *moksund*, the bagging of the dates, had arrived. Upon hearing this, after consultation, the schedule was changed, setting the migration for 2 or 3 days. The collection of supplies—tea, sugar, medicine—was initiated, as was the packing and storage of unneeded supplies and equipment.

## Migration I (Continued): To Mashkil
### July 17–26

How to migrate? Until 1970, the Sarhadi Baluch migrated to Mashkil by camel caravan, the Yarahmadzai tribe via Gazu and through the narrow gorge of the Rudi Mad Shadi to the north of the Morpish mountain range and then southeast, and the Gamshazai tribe around the southern end of the Morpish range and north through Jalq and then northeast to Mashkil. From 1970, when with government funds the northern track had been crudely cleared of obstacles, trucks began to use this route for the first time. Overland vehicles, such as Jeeps and Land Rovers, and heavy trucks started to make regular trips. At the time of this migration to Mashkil, heavy Mercedes-Benz dump trucks, open in the back, were available, for a price, to carry loads of Sarhadi Baluch and their belongings from the Sarhad to Mashkil, and later on the return trip as well. Charges varied but were of the magnitude of 10 toman per person. Charges for baggage—including clothing, personal effects, bedding, bicycles, lambs and kids, chickens, supplies of flour, kerosene, and the like—were assessed, not always without debate, according to weight and size.

While prior to the opening of the dirt track, everyone and everything went to Mashkil by camel caravan, in 1972, finances allowing, some people and some things were able to go to Mashkil by truck. So what had to be decided was, who and what would go by camel caravan and who and what would go by truck. One consideration was cost. Migration by truck required an immediate outlay of cash, which may or may not have been available at that moment. After all, cash had to be laid out for supplies, such as flour, sugar, tea, vegetable oil, medicine, and so on. It was not uncommon at that time of the year for people to sell livestock or borrow money.

A second consideration was the household capacity for camel migration. During the previous drought years, many camels died. Shams A'din had lost some and had only one camel remaining; Mahmud Karim had also lost camels. The paucity of camels for transport limited what could be taken by camel caravan. A third consideration was human labor. Who would make the arduous, six-day journey with the camels? Partly this was a question of skill and responsibility: who could take a caravan without injuring or losing any camels? Partly it was a question of willingness: who was prepared to make the effort and face the difficulties of the migration? The general rule enunciated was that the young women, the children, and the older people migrated by truck, while the young and mature men migrated with the camels. But this general rule was modified in particular cases by various factors, including those already mentioned, such as men staying behind to tend to agriculture on the Sarhad, and the unavailability of camels. The rule was also modified when one man, as part of a de facto labor partnership with other families, undertook the camel migration with the camels and loads of several families. So some cases of men traveling by truck reflected interfamilial collaboration rather than the workload being borne by youngsters or women.

Among members of the Halki Ja'far, the migration began for some on the 17th and for some on the 18th. Others, from Gwanich, for example, migrated a day earlier, on the 16th. Still others, such as those from Shagbond, migrated throughout the next week. The migration to Mashkil was not a migration of the herding camp. As residential communities, but not as collective herding enterprises, the *halk* were suspended until the return from Mashkil. So the migration was not that of a suprafamilial collective entity pursued in a compact formation. Rather, households, some going and some staying, some going to Gorani and some going to Musain-Nahala or Gazeh, made their own arrangements, usually traveling with close kin.

The combined members of Ja'far's and his daughter's tent, like those of many others, split between camel caravan and truck. One reason was that there was not enough money to send everyone by truck, nor enough camels to carry everyone who could not walk. Bibi Nur had two little children and was pregnant so would have to ride one way or another. Amir at 8 years and Mariumuk at 5 years were too small to walk, and even Gol Peri at 15 was deemed too young and without sufficient stamina both to walk and cook. Ja'far was seriously ill with ulcers and could not walk. So it was decided that Monas, 40, the female head of the family and Ja'far's wife, would attend the camel caravan and cook. She would be accompanied by Id Mahmud, her son-in-law and Bibi Nur's husband, and her sons Bahador, 13, and Rasul, 10. The others would go by truck (see table 7.1).

**Table 7.1.** Migration of Two Collaborating
Tents to Mashkil

| By Camel Caravan | By Truck | Fare in Toman |
|---|---|---|
| 3 adult camels | | |
| 2 young camels | | |
| 1 lamb carried in sling | | |
| *Tent A* | | |
| Id Mahmud | Bibi Nur | 10 |
| | Child Nasi | Free |
| | Child Hassan | Free |
| *Tent B* | | |
| Monas | Mariumuk | Free |
| Bahador | Amir | 5 |
| Rasul | Gol Peri | 10 |
| | Ja'far | 12 |

In contrast, another family migrated together—Yelli Han, husband and father; Zar Malek, wife and mother; younger children Abdul Ghapur, Nas Peri, and Shah Peri; with four camels and four lambs—with the exception of the eldest son, Shahuk, who got a motorcycle ride. The daughter Lal Malek and her husband Man Dust came by truck, bringing the equivalent of one camel load of flour, *yek bari art,* which was two large, woolen bags, *gwal,* of flour, by truck.

## Migration II: Back to the Sarhad
*Mid-September*

The return to the Sarhad, prior to the use of trucks in 1970, had always been a two-stage process. There were never sufficient camels to carry people and their baggage as well as the large load of dates and date pits up the mountain back to the Sarhad. Thus, prior to the migration back to the Sarhad, there was a trip, called *shawarkash,* undertaken by adult men to carry the dates and date pits to the Sarhad. The trip up the mountains with loaded camels usually took seven or eight days. Once on the Sarhad, the dates were quickly stored and the men rushed back to Mashkil, taking three or four days for the return.

In 1972–73, from Gorani only Yelli Han made the *shawar,* for he did not have the funds to send either his family or the dates by truck. He returned to Mashkil so that he could migrate, *lardi,* with his family back to the Sarhad. Everyone else from Gorani divided their households and baggage, most of the people doing the *lardi* by truck and taking whatever baggage could not go by camel, the camels returning with one male and as much baggage, dates included, as possible (see table 7.2).

**Table 7.2.** Camel Caravans Back to the Sarhad, September 1972

| Name of Drover | Camel Owners | Number of Camels | Returned by Truck |
|---|---|---|---|
| Mahmud Karim | Mahmud Karim | 2 | Family of M. Karim |
| | Shams A'din | 1 | S. A. and family |
| | Abdulla | 1 | A. and family |
| | Jan Mahmud | 1 | J. M. and family |
| | Musa | 1 | Musa and family |
| Id Mahmud | Id Mahmud | 2 | Family of Id M. |
| Bahador (son) | Ja'far | 3 | Ja'far and family |
| Sharif (br. Id. M.) | Sharif | 1 | Family of Sharif |
| Shiruk (son) | Reis | 2 | Reis and family |
| Dust Mahmud | Dust Mahmud | 2 | Family of Dust M. |
| Abas | Abas | 1 | Family of Abas |
| Suliman (son) | Dadol | 3 | Dadol and family |

*September 24*

Unlike the many days needed for the return by camel caravan, the truck trip from Gorani took only a half day, the passengers (not a few carsick) and their baggage arriving back on the Sarhad at Shagbond, the location from which they had set out and where their tents and the household equipment not taken to Mashkil were stored. At Shagbond, once again, the Halki Ja'far consolidated, the members putting up their tents, the flock continuing under the care of Ido. It was agreed that they should move fairly quickly to a new and fresher area.

## Migration III: To Beadak

*October 1–9*

Beadak turned out to be disappointing on a number of counts. First of all, the pasturage for the camels was not as good as that for the *pas*. Second, there was very little water for household use and it was very dirty. Of course it was well known that the area was rocky and that the sharpness of the rocks was hard on the sheep and the camels. So there was considerable dissatisfaction with the site.

Furthermore, Komeron, a relatively well-to-do *wasildar,* but not a close kinsman or lineage, *brasrend,* mate of the Dadolzai members of the camp, refused to join the Halk at Beadak, which he characterized as *kuhistan,* mountainous and rocky. Komeron said that he always resided in the winter around Jiandi Sah, a small mountain of black stone arising from the surrounding plain, some 10 kilometers (a bit more than 6 miles) west of Beadak. At that moment he was located to the east of Jiandi Sah, at Kamil Han Chah. Komeron's threat not to join the Halk posed a serious problem, especially for Ido, the *shwaneg,* who had already put in nine months labor on Komeron's animals and was afraid that he would not be able to collect his *hort,* his share of the newborn, if Komeron broke from the Halk and took his animals elsewhere. For this reason, Ido urged the others to leave Beadak and join Komeron at Jiandi Sah. Without the demands of Komeron, the Halk would probably have moved to another site within a few kilometers, probably the habitual winter camping area of the Halki Ja-far on the plain of Pushti Kamal. But under the circumstances, and the urging of Ido, the *wasildar* agreed to migrate to Jiandi Sah (also known as Jiandi Sahi) and join Komeron there. But there was not a lot of pleasure among the camp members from Komeron's ultimatum.

## Migration IV: To Jiandi Sah
*October 9–19*
The new site had its benefits. There was a great deal of dried grass, *kah,* for the animals. And the well, only a half kilometer away, would provide good water. The ground, in contrast to the sharp, rocky surface of Beadak, was soft and sandy.

However, after two weeks, one disadvantage of the current site out in the middle of the plain became apparent. There was no protection from the cold, northern wind as the weather inexorably cooled and fall transformed into winter. So people started talking about moving to another site, nearby, not too far from the well, but sheltered from the wind. A new location just to the south of a large hill would have served the purpose nicely. New sites were scouted by Ja'far, Reis, and Id Mahmud. Ja'far favored a site to the northwest about a kilometer (more than half a mile), but Reis, always supersensitive to the needs of his animals, objected that a *ramag* of sick animals had been located there the previous year and that it thus might be dangerous for the livestock. He favored a site nestled between the hills of Jiandi Sah. Idu, the *shwaneg,* thought that the camp was fine where it was.

## Migration V: To Jiandi Sah II
*November 19–February 16*
The Halk migrated, about half a kilometer (less than a third of a mile), to a new site at the base of Jiandi Sah, somewhat protected from the wind because of its location between two spurs of the small mountain. This new site was meant to be the winter site, occupied for the next two or more months. Consequently, tents were expanded to their full size—for example, tents with a third tent strip, *gedom,* used in warm weather as siding and raised during the day, were set up with all three tent strips as roofing—in order to accommodate the *pas* at night. Cave holes, *kudh,* and small huts, *dramshuik,* were constructed in the tents to house the newborn *pas* during the freezing, winter nights. The *gwash,* the section of the tent for the *pas,* was roped off. Tents and wall mats were patched and the tents made as secure as possible from the cold. Piles of brush were heaped around the sides and backs of tents for added protection from the wind.

It had not been a great burden to move to this new site. The tents had to be taken down and set up for winter in any case, so the change of site had not been much more trouble. Everyone was concerned about protecting the animals from the cold, for the young *pas* were especially vulnerable and it was easy to lose them if conditions were poor. While the ground was rockier at the new site, it was said to be less cold than the sandy soil, and so would be better for the young *pas*. There was more brush at the new site for piling around the tents. The main shortcoming of the new site was the increased distance from the well, now a full kilometer away.

*Wasildar* were caring for their *pas*, from which they had been separated during *hamin*, trying to prepare them for the coming winter. Many were supplementing the poor fall pasture by feeding fodder and foodstuffs to their weak animals. Shams A'din was feeding dates and crushed date pit gruel to two *plat*, one *gitaj*, four *gwareg*, and one *shaneg*. The three adult animals were weak and thin after having given birth, and the five newborn were weak. Shams A'din argued that unless he fed these animals, they would be too weak to survive the freezing winter weather.

Concerns about the winter were well justified, for there was an extraordinary snowfall in early January that blanketed the ground with over a foot of snow, keeping the people and the *pas* trapped in the tents and the camels trapped at their tethers for some 10 days. Animals were fed with whatever food was available, including dates, grain, flour, and bread, in their owners' tents. Some people who were foolhardy enough to venture forth got frostbite on their feet.

### Early to Mid-February

The Halk remained at the campsite protected by Jiandi Sah for all of the winter, almost three months. At the beginning of February, with the weather warmer and the *bahar* starting to come up, there was a shift to the spring, *bahargah*, regime. *Pas* were taken out earlier and went out again after late afternoon milking. The young *pas* were no longer kept in their caves or huts, but tied up inside the tent. Feeding of the *pas* dropped off as they nourished themselves on the pasturage, so the morning clunk-clunk of the date pits being broken was rarer. There was more milk for people to drink, and so the morning slush-slush of the butter being churned in skin bags became more common. By the middle of February the *pas* were kept out until 10 P.M.

The herding contract for the past year between *wasildar* and *shwaneg* was coming to an end. Making a new contract required a willing shepherd and willing *pas* owners. But who would be willing and who would agree was part of what was unclear. For some weeks, Ido the shepherd had been saying that he did not want to be *shwaneg* for the next year. It was well known in the camp that relations between some of the *wasildar* and Ido had not always been smooth during the previous year. Two of the large owners, Dust Mahmud (son of) Mulla and Komaron, were generally recognized in the camp to be very demanding, and they and Ido had had frequent arguments, some highly raucous. And the work was very strenuous for a man in late middle age, and some family members said that he was finding it a bit difficult. Ido himself said that he found it rather lonely to remain on the plateau for months while everyone else was at Mashkil. Furthermore, his date palms needed tending and he wanted to plant new palms. There was no shortage of genuine reasons for Ido to want not to continue. Also, of course, this hard-to-get attitude put him in a good bargaining position. Ido was perhaps less well placed than some others to find outside income elsewhere. He was not young enough to be ideal for manual labor. And when he had tried trading prior to his last shepherding contract, he ended up in jail. So shepherding was perhaps more attractive than the alternatives.

*February 8*
Ja'far, Reis, Dust Mahmud, Mahmud Karim, and others had been looking for and considering other possible *shwaneg* for the following year but had not found any good candidates. At this point, Ido agreed to take on the job of *shwaneg* for the next year, if the *wasildar* would accept different terms—not for payment, which would remain the same as the previous year. Rather, the changes would be in labor pattern: one major difference would be that the *ramag/galagi pas* would be taken out during the day not by Ido himself, but by his 13-year-old son Brahuk, with Ido stepping in to take the animals out at night. The other major difference would be that, instead of Ido remaining on the plateau with the *galagi pas* during *hamin,* his son Brahuk and Dust Mahmud (son of) Dad Huda would remain with the flock, while Ido joined the others at Mashkil. When this proposal was not received with enthusiasm from the *wasildar,* Ido promptly withdrew it. He then said that there had not been enough rain so far, and that next year looked like a bad year. Perhaps if it rained more, he would reconsider.

## Migration VI: To Sorikombori
*February 16*
The Halki Ja'far migrated a mile to the northwest, near the hill Sorikombori, so called because of its brownish, red stone. There had been some disagreement about the site, Ja'far having preferred a site about a kilometer and a half (a mile or so) south, but he deferred to arguments by Ido and others that the pasturage for camels was better at Sorikombori. But pasture was not the main reason for the move.

One major reason for the move was to leave the old, dirty site at Jiandi Sah, which had been occupied continuously for almost three months, with the animals in the tents. A new site, any new site, meant a clean ground and a sigh a relief.

The second reason for the move was to clarify the *karar,* herding contract, for the coming year. The contract year was over, but the old arrangements were still in force. Last year's *wasildar* flock and last year's residential group were still intact, even though a new contract had not been confirmed. Migration to a new site would make clear, *maluma bi,* what future arrangements would be, for it would require herd owners to decide whether they would migrate to the new site with the others and thus continue to be members of the group, participating in the new herding contract, or whether they would not join for the coming year. So migrating was like wiping the contractual slate clean, and setting up camp at a new site was sketching out the participants in and thus the presumed terms of the new contract.

Some expected and some unexpected things "became evident." As was expected and hoped, Komeron and his kinsmen would not participate in the new contract; he had asked Ido to include his animals in the new flock, but Ido refused to agree to a new contract and this in effect left Komeron out in the cold. He and his kinsmen stayed behind when the Halk migrated.

Much more remarkably, Ja'far and his close kinsmen Reis, Dust Mahmud Mulla and associated tents set up their camp at a distance from the others, symbolizing spatially that they were a separate group. This was rather a surprise for the others. The reason, it seemed, was that Reis and Dust Mahmud were not happy at the prospect of a combined flock and wanted two separate flocks, which meant two separate camps. Ja'far, as he presented his views to Shams A'din and other members from the other camp, seemed to be fairly neutral about the issue of one or two flocks. Reis, however, was adamant that there be two *ramag*. First, he did not think that Ido had done a very good job of grazing the *pas*. He said that Ido did not have a lot of animals himself and so did not care a lot about the animals. Furthermore, Ido's proposal that his son Brahuk take over during the days was not attractive. Reis could have his own young son graze his own animals, at no charge! So rather than agree to include their animals in a herd under the arrangement proposed by Ido, they decided to maintain their own separate *ramag*.

## Beginning of March

This split between the camps had not been taken lightly by the two groups, and after considerable lobbying, with no little invoking of their common brotherhood as members of the Dadolzai *brasrend,* an agreement was reached for a *karar* in which Ido would be the shepherd of a single, unified flock. The two camps were then reunified as the Halki Ja'far. Most camp members expressed pleasure that this unnecessary split had been healed. But had it been healed, or only patched over?

## Second Week of March

A new migration was being anticipated and discussed. The *bahar,* pasturage, for the camels was poor in the present location, and since a number of camels had now "dropped" their young—in reality the camel owners had with great effort pulled the baby camels out—good grazing would be required if the camels were to produce the milk necessary for their offspring. And while the *bahar* for the *pas* was fair, better was desirable.

First it was thought that Kamil Han Chah, the plain on the other side of Jiandi Sah, would fit the requirements. Ja'far was in favor of moving there. But Reis thought that better pasturage might be found farther afield. He had looked around in the north a bit, but the pasturage there was not good. Then he talked about a trip to Garonchin, some 50 kilometers to the south, to see if pasturage was better there. But on the evening of the 10th, a Dorahzai man called Ido, of the Sasumi Halk, stopped at the tent of Baluch, also Dorahzai, on the way home from Garonchin, and said that the pasturage was indeed good there. This decided Reis that the camp should migrate to Garonchin and seemed to swing opinion in that direction.

## March 11

Most people packed up for storage everything that would not be needed for warm weather and for the smaller, warm-weather configuration of their tents—all of their quilts, blankets, extra *gwerpat*—and whatever pots and equipment or supplies they did not want to carry during spring migrations. Each family took their stores to whatever location—Nilagu, Shagbond, Afzalabad—was available to them, especially where they themselves or their kin had brick dwellings in which they could lock their things. This sloughing off of impedimenta readied the tent dwellers for migration.

## Migration VII: To Garonchin or Kamil Han Chah
### March 12

On migration days, people often began early to pack up and take down their tents. But on this day, like the day in 1968 when Monas set off the migration out of Beadak, things got off to a slow start. First of all, Ja'far was in pain from his ulcer and was not sure he was in any shape to migrate. Second, some of the camp members were having second thoughts about the long move, which would take two or three days at least, because there were not enough camels to transport all of the tents at once. Somehow, some tents would have to stay behind and have camels sent back to bring them. This seemed a difficult and messy operation with the long distance involved. These doubts were compounded when Shadi Han, a Zabedzai man from the Halki Azam, arrived and reported that there was no *bahar* at Garonchin to speak of, and that it was certainly not worthwhile to migrate there.

In spite of the new, discouraging report, and the resistance of other camp members, Reis insisted on going to Garonchin, and Ja'far agreed to go with him. Id Mahmud, *zamas* of Ja'far, confirmed that Reis was the prime mover in this migration, and that no one else was really enthusiastic about going. Reis, as we know, was a hyperactivist when it came to his livestock. But other members of the camp continued to complain about the lack of camels and the difficulties of going to Garonchin and the questionable rewards for going there. No resolution to this disagreement was quick in coming. In spite of this, camp members did go about striking their tents and packing their camels.

Reis and Ja'far and associates were packed up first, and they went ahead a bit and then stopped to wait for the others. The others were then faced with a moment in which decisions could no longer be put off. Mahmud Karim and Shams A'din, two of the key men in the group of dissidents, decided that they were not going to Garonchin, but would go to Kamil Han Chah instead. So when the remaining group, or as many of them could be accommodated by the camels available, were loaded and ready to go, they moved off but did not join the first group waiting to go to Garonchin. Rather, they headed off toward Kamil Han Chah. At the same time, they sent someone to split the flock, so that they could bring their animals along with them. Then the first group of Reis, Ja'far and the others, moved on to its first leg of the Garonchin migration, while the group of Mahmud Karim, Shams A'din and the others, continued on to Kamil Han Chah. The Halki Ja'far had not only fissioned into two groups, but had physically split under my eyes as the two groups moved off in different directions.

What led to this unexpected, undesired, and dramatic split? There were a number of factors, economic, structural, and political, both ongoing and temporary.

One of the sources of disagreement within the camp that led to the split was the degree of motivation in regard to the *pas*. The four tents of the Reis-Ja'far faction owned about 110 *pas*, whereas the other 10 tents together owned around 90 *pas*. The amount of concern and willingness to take trouble for the animals seemed greater in the Reis-Ja'far faction, which was not too surprising given their greater economic interest in the flock. Reis and Ja'far both had relatively large household flocks, and both depended economically on their flocks rather than upon agriculture or trading.

Another source of the present disagreement was the disparity in camel ownership. The Reis-Ja'far group had enough camels to carry all their load, but the other group was short, which meant for them a doubling of travel for any migration.

These sources of conflict were aggravated by the feeling among the others that the Reis-Ja'far group were so concerned with their own economic interests that they did not honor the need for group solidarity, *topak*. There was thus a sense that an important value had been ignored and a basic norm violated.

With these disagreements and conflicting concerns having provided the substantive causes of the split, the organizational cause was the lack of ongoing consultation by the headman, *master*. The headman, through extensive discussion, could usually elicit a compromise if not a consensus. Had Ja'far been able to sound out the others adequately, he would have realized how dissatisfied they were with the plan to go to Garonchin, and that more definite plans for sending camels and for resolving other concerns were required if the plan was to be carried out. Unfortunately, Ja'far had been quite ill, suffering from severe pain from his ulcer, and was able to do little more than lie quietly in his tent during the planning of this migration. So he was not able to do the job of the headman, which was to hear everyone out and shape a compromise. A headman could only lead if the others wished to follow. When a headman did not perform to the satisfaction of the others, they could assert themselves by leaving, as they did in this case. Ja'far later complained that the others had split off without giving due notice of intent, that he had expected them to follow and instead they headed off elsewhere. He was unhappy about this and felt abandoned.

Ido, the *shwaneg,* was left with a flock of 90 *pas,* far too few animals to provide him with a living. He was angry with the Reis-Ja'far faction for breaking off, something that had happened previously in the not too distant past, and in this case only two weeks after a herding contract had been agreed. He did not know whether to blame Ja'far or Mahmud Karim, now the *master* of the other faction with which Ido was allied, for the split, or whether both were to blame. But he felt badly used and left in a difficult position.

Ido at this time was approached by a Rahmatzai *halk* to be their shepherd by combining their flock with the small remaining flock of the Mahmud Karimi Halk. They said that they would relocate close to the Mahmud Karimi Halk so that they could conveniently have a common *ramag.* The Rahmatzai had 200 *pas,* which together with those of Mahmud Karimi Halk, now up to 110 due to some added tents, would have made a good-sized flock, providing him with a handsome pay, *hak.* But Ido turned the offer down, on the grounds that the relatively poor pasture of a dry year such as this one could not support such a large *ramag.* The animals would go hungry, and wander, and would be difficult to handle. In a good year, with rich pasturage, such a flock would be fine, but not this year. And it was unlikely that Ido expected an enthusiastic welcome to such an offer from the *wasildar* of the Mahmud Karimi Halk, who had been having a difficult time agreeing about migration with a few of their fellow lineage mates, and who under the proposed arrangement would have found themselves the minority partners, in terms of both lineage affiliation and livestock numbers, in a Halk dominated by others.

In general, there was a tendency to blame Reis for the split. It was he who initially, at the time of the last migration, caused the camp to split—Ja'far had said that Reis asked him to join with them and thus directed the blame away from himself—and refused to participate in the herding contract for a unified herd and a common shepherd, preferring to keep his animals and Ja'far's separate, although he later relented. This time he had pushed and pushed for migration to Garonchin.

## Migration VIII (Ja'fari Halk): To Kamil Han Chah
*March 21*

While Mahmud Karimi Halk remained at Kamil Han Chah, the Halki Ja'far left south Qanati Sarhang, where they had stopped short of Garonchin because of Ja'far's illness, and probably also because of the split with the others, and made the migration back to Kamil Han Chah, ostensibly in search of pasture, and camped next to Mahmud Karimi Halk. But the two Halk remained separate.

*March 22*

In spite of the arrival of Ja'fari Halk, Mahmud Karim was saying that the Halk would migrate the next day. This was alleged to be a reaction to an event of the previous day. Some of the camels of the Halk had gotten into agricultural fields some 6 kilometers (over 3½ miles) to the south, eaten from the fields, and 15 toman in damages had to be paid. It was also said that pasturage was better at Beadak, which was the intended new site.

But the next day there was no move, for Musa's wife was very ill after a difficult delivery the previous night and in no state to move. She remained ill and was still immobile on March 25.

*March 25*

There were other factors militating against the move. One was the low and decreasing level of labor power, for several of the men had left camp and others were planning for an immediate *iwar* trip to Mashkil. The second factor was the chronic shortage of camels, which discouraged any migration. The third factor was that the intended site, Beadak, had in the meanwhile become occupied with the arrival of two other halk, Shah Miradzai and Gamshadzai, and the planned migration there of the Mahmud Karimi Halk would have crowded the pasture and put heavy demand on the limited water supply.

So between the internal and external problems, the Mahmud Karimi Halk decided it was better off staying where it was, which was finally decided on March 25. Mahmud Karim, in making the decision, cited all of the various reasons, and then invoked the testimony of Ido, the *shwaneg,* that pasturage was quite adequate at the present site, to support his position. So after days of agitation about a migration, the decision was to remain at the present site.

## Migration IX (Ja'fari Halk): To Beadak
*March 26*

However, the Ja'fari Halk did migrate, and it migrated to Beadak in search of pasturage.

## Migration X (Ja'fari Halk): To Nilagu
*April 12*

The Ja'fari Halk migrated from Beadak to Nilagu.

## Migration VII (Mahmud Karimi Halk): To Nilagu
*April 19*

The Mahmud Karimi Halk finally left Kamil Han Chah and migrated to Nilagu, where, after ongoing discussions behind the scenes, the Mahmud Karimi Halk and Ja'fari Halk reunited.

*Early May*

Members of the reunited Halk considered their current location. The great virtue of Nilagu was the convenient availability of water for the livestock from a *jube,* channel, of a nearby *kan.* Access to water was particularly important from this time of the year on, as the weather got hotter and the animals needed to be watered more frequently. The advantage of a *jube* was that the animals could go right up to it and drink the water. In contrast, well-water would have had to be drawn by hand for the entire flock of *pas* and the camels, which was more than the shepherd alone could do. So the easy availability of water was no small thing. However, at the same time, while the water situation was good, the pasture in the immediate area was poor, and the animals needed as much nourishment as possible before the summer sun burned it all and the animals had to get through the winter largely on what they had stored in their bodies. Other considerations were crowding caused by the presence of other *halk* in potential future locations, and also closeness to agricultural areas especially during this preharvest period.

Shagbond was considered, for it had been customary for a number of years to camp there in the pre- and postharvest periods, along with fellow Dadolzai lineage mates who had cultivation there. But it was felt that Shagbond was quite crowded enough with its own inhabitants, that access to pasture was poor from that location, and that access to crops on the part of the livestock was all too easy.

It was agreed that the most attractive site was on the other side of Gorchan, the winter seat of the Yarahmadzai Sardar, between the village and the Morpish Mountains. On the one hand, the open plain of pasture between Gorchan and the mountains was easily accessible. On the other hand, the animals could be watered at the *kan* of Gorchan.

*May 15*

The Ja'fari Halk made a *shawar,* trip, to the projected site, to carry enough of the camp's equipment to allow the *lardi,* migration, planned for the next day to take place in one move, all of the camp members together, in spite of the small number of camels in the several *bak* of the Halk. But by the afternoon camp members had heard that, that very day, some sick animals had been brought from the mountains to a camp near Gorchan. The inhabitants of Gorchan were incensed and threatened to make a formal complaint, *shekayat kon,* to the government court.

For the Ja'fari Halk, the danger of illness added a new factor to consider. Reis, who had been keeping a low profile because of his part in the earlier split in the camp and the subsequent bad feelings of the others—for he had been made something of a scapegoat—brought this news to the camp, informing Ido the shepherd. This new development threw into doubt the desirability of the projected site. While Reis did not insist on any particular course of action and was careful to say that he would go along with the rest, this did not stop the others from taking it out on him. At one of the apparently casual gatherings of the men in the afternoon, after Reis brought the news, Shams A'din, partly in response to Mahmud Karim's outburst a few minutes before, accused Reis of stirring up trouble and never being satisfied. Reis responded by saying that all along he had agreed to go wherever the camp went, that he had not pushed for any particular location, and that it was hardly his fault if sick animals had been brought to the proposed camp area the day of the *shawar.*

Later, in the evening, when Ja'far was sitting in front of his tent, Ido came over to discuss the situation. They were joined by Baluch and Dust Mahmud. Ja'far, speaking for himself, Reis, and associated tents, were prepared to go wherever he, Ido, and Mahmud Karim and his associates, decided. Surely, he argued, he and Reis could not be blamed for the bad news about the sick animals. He said that Reis had all along said that he was going to follow along and not try to influence, *kari nadasht,* the decision. Ja'far and Reis and their associates were not going to start their camels moving until the others were already on the road and taking the lead; they intended to follow along and did not want a repetition of the earlier incident. Ja'far sent over for Shams A'din and Mahmud Karim and repeated his position. Ido said that he was not trying to dictate, and that he did not want to take responsibility for what should be a collective decision and the responsibility of all herd owners.

While everyone took pains to show that they were not forcing the change, it was agreed that Gorchan was no longer a desirable site. And it was agreed that Pushti Kamal was the best alternative. Shams A'din agreed to take Karim's place in retrieving the tents and other household impedimenta sent to Gorchan with the previous day's *shawar.* Everyone was saying that they did not want to press the issue, and that they simply wanted an agreement satisfactory to everyone else. The gathering then broke up, with everyone feeling that a satisfactory agreement had been reached. During this meeting, Reis had pointedly stayed in his tent and not joined the discussants. But from his tent, located next to Ja'far's, he listened to the course of the conversation.

## Migration XI/VIII: To Pushi Kamal
*May 16*

The specific location of the new site became a matter of debate during the course of the migration when Ido and Mahmud Karim argued about whether to go to the well at Pushti Kamal or the *kan* of Shagbond farther to the south. Karim argued that it was better to be far from Gwanich and its fields, which were close to the *kan,* and won out.

While the others set up camp at Pushti Kamal, three of the poorer tents, with few if any animals resources—Gemi, Dust Mahmud (son of) Dad Huda, and Husein—continued on to Shagbond, where there was agricultural work during this preharvest and the following harvest periods.

## PURPOSES AND PATTERNS OF NOMADISM
## ON THE SARHAD, PART 2

The purposes and patterns discussed in relation to the migrations of the Halki Ja'far in 1968 can be equally observed in the migrations of the Halk during 1972–73. But other notable elements are also present.

### Means of Transport

Until around 1970, the ordinary tribesmen traveled and transported on the Sarhad and between the Sarhad and Mashkil primarily by foot and by camel. At that point, motor vehicles became available, usually on a pay-per-trip basis, for travel and transport both around the Sarhad and between the Sarhad and Mashkil. From 1970, large dump trucks could be hired for long trips with large loads. Then, increasingly, heavy motorcycles became available as desert taxis.

   In the multi-resource economy of the Sarhadi Baluch, the means of travel and transport were basic elements of the technology and economy. So much nomadic movement of households and so many short-term and longer-term trips were required that travel and transport were integral considerations in the calculus of time, energy, and money. The new, motorized means of travel and transport were expensive for ordinary tribesmen and so were used sparingly and according to the financial position of the individuals involved. Sarhadi *baluch* continued to travel by foot and to transport with camel as the cheapest means available to them. But when they were able, and the benefits seemed to justify it, they paid for rides on motorcycles, or sent their weaker relatives and heavy loads by truck.

   In pastoral regions elsewhere, but most notably where specialized pastoral production is strongly market oriented, trucks have come into extensive use in livestock raising (Chatty 1986, 1996). For the Sarhadi Baluch, whose diversified economy was oriented largely toward subsistence production, the regular use of motor vehicles remained far beyond their economic means. Nonetheless, the occasional use of motorcycles and especially trucks had become important, and the camel as a mainstay of travel and transport was beginning to decline during the 1970s.

### Nomadism and Social Ties

As we have seen, the nomadic mobility of the Sarhadi Baluch made possible spatial movement as a strategy for organizing production and, when necessary, defense. In addition, nomadic mobility allowed spatial movement to be used to organize social relations. The spatial arrangements of Sarhadi tent dwellers were not permanent; nomadic mobility made it possible for people to move closer to or farther from one another. Sarhadi tent dwellers were not tied spatially into a particular community; they were capable of physically leaving one community and joining another or establishing their own.

During the 1972–73 migrations of the Halki Ja'far, one set of members of the community, Komeron and his associates, were excluded from the new herding contract and thus effectively thrown out of the community. He had offended community members with arrogant and uncooperative behavior, especially in relation to the shepherd, and was no longer welcome. The other members were not forced to continue living with Komeron, the way they would have had to if they had been sedentary village agriculturalists. Once the community decided not to include Komeron in the new herding contract, the Halk's next migration literally left Komeron behind and out of the community.

Also during the 1972–73 migrations, differences in herding and migration priorities and policy between two factions of the Halk led twice to splits into two separate *halk*. Where differences in policy proved irreconcilable and members of a *halk* were not able to find a compromise, this could lead, as it did in the Halki Ja'far, not to the imposition of one policy on everyone and the continued cohabitation of winners and losers, but rather to fission into two separate groups. The largely unexpected and undesired fission of Ja'fari Halk, so dramatically manifested when the camel caravan of one faction, refusing to follow the caravan of the other faction, turned away and headed off independently in a different direction, redefined, at least temporarily, group membership, community boundaries, and leadership, as well as herding arrangements. The ultimate reuniting of the factions into a unified *halk*, resulted from the continual negotiation that was a characteristic of Sarhadi Baluchi life, and reflected the broader obligations and values of the lineage-based political system that tied together members of the two factions.

Every migration of a *halk* provided the opportunity for a reshuffling of the social deck. Even beyond migrations during which everyone packed up and moved, each tent dweller had the capability of packing up his or her tent at any time and moving to another community. To this extent, community membership and social ties were not set or fixed but were voluntary and endlessly malleable. Community membership was the result of an ongoing process of collaboration and negotiation, with nomadic mobility providing the spatial flexibility that allowed the results of this process to be manifested in changing residential group membership and community relationships.

The freedom of choice presented to the Sarhadi tent dwellers by nomadic mobility and selective sociality was interwoven with the Sarhadi character. Unlike sedentaries and peasants, Baluchi tent dwellers did not hold back their feelings, avoid overt conflict, feel anxiety and hatred, dislike authority, engage in indirect gossip, vandalism, and ritual action against enemies, and explode into aggression impulsively (Edgerton 1971). Rather, like pastoralists elsewhere (Edgerton 1971), they stressed independence, bravery, and self-control, felt affection for kinsmen and clansmen, and respect for authority, and engaged in direct aggression. In social relations, Baluchi tent dwellers did not have to put up with other people, swallow their feelings, and repress their reactions. They could, and did, speak up, fight back, and, if they felt it best, move away. While compromises were sought for broader ends, ends defined by the many overlapping ties that bound Baluch with one another, they were not stuck, they did not have to "eat dust," as they put it, kicked at them by others. These Baluch stood up for themselves, and, if desirable, refashioned their own community fabric. Destiny rested *dar dasti huda,* in the hand of God, but community and society were deemed to be the work of each and all.

# 8.
# WORKING AND LABORING

Some basic facts about Sarhadi life should by now be evident. First, to make a living, Sarhadi Baluch engaged in a number of different kinds, or sectors, of production, including pastoralism, grain cultivation, date arboriculture, and some form of external extraction of income. Second, the loci of productive activity in different sectors were dispersed spatially, each locus of work often being spatially distant from each other locus of work, the distances being negotiated in some cases by trips and in others by camp migrations. Third, the various kinds of work involved, as well as the movement between the loci of work, were labor-intensive, that is, required much time, attention, muscle power, and energy on the part of the Baluch, who had available to assist them very limited nonhuman energy sources, until the 1960s only animal power. This was true not only of primary production, such as herding livestock and planting grain, but also of processing raw material into usable products, such as grinding grain into flour, curing bags for water and milk, churning butter, and weaving tents, rugs, rope, mats, and bags.

If the intensive labor required of the Baluch to make a living was difficult, laboring on several tasks at once was even more difficult, and working at two different sites at the same time was impossible. Sarhadi Baluch constantly faced the dilemma of having to do several things at the same time and often having to do them in several places. It would not be an exaggeration to say that the Baluch were under pressure to accomplish these various tasks, for after all their living depended upon getting this work done. These labor exigencies led the Baluch to coordinate with one another in order to increase efficiency and decrease each individual's workload. This coordination is manifested in three groupings of different scale: the household, the work team, and the herding group.

## THE HOUSEHOLD

The household provided shelter and food for its members. Ideally and in general, the household was centered on and corresponded to a nuclear family, which was responsible for bioreproduction. The male and female family heads held property—the tent and its equipment, livestock, date palms, and the like—on behalf of the family, so there was substantial correspondence between the household and the property-owning family. The household operated as a locus of ownership and consumption.

Among Sarhadi Baluch, the link between property and consumption was subsistence production. That is, people used their property to produce the things that they needed to eat and use. This process of production required labor, including technological knowledge, physical skills and energy, and application. The simplest arrangement was for the members of the household, drawing on household property, to apply their labor to producing the consumables that they needed. In other words, people would devote their labor, using their property, to produce what they themselves would consume. And indeed, household self-sufficiency was an ideal held by Baluch, a goal toward which to strive, a circumstance in which to take pride and satisfaction. This ideal was one of the considerations underlying the desire, universal among the Baluch, for a large number of offspring.

The coordination of labor could be seen in the division of labor, an established pattern of some people doing some things while others did other things. Within the household, labor was divided according to both age and sex. In general, older people supervised and directed, and did delicate work requiring developed skills. Younger people did the more monotonous and arduous work requiring strength and endurance. Males engaged in primary production and females processed the products into consumables. The guidelines were clear, but application was flexible, much guided by feasibility in the face of demographic constraints, circumstantial pressures, and logistical requirements. Males and females, old and young, often worked together, especially but not exclusively on tasks that were on the margins of their defined spheres. For example, men and women often milked animals in concert, but only in unusual circumstances would women herd livestock or men cook.

The extent of household labor sufficiency depended upon the number and age profile of individuals in the household. The major source of labor was children. Many children, well spaced in age, provided much labor power. While the mother cooked, spun, wove, and provided general direction, young daughters collected wood, ran errands, and helped with the lambs, kids, and chickens. Older daughters fetched water, washed clothes, and helped with cooking and weaving. Given that daughters married between 12 and 16 years of age and then began a process, especially after the birth of their first children, of establishing separate households and gradually shifting their labor from their parents' household to their own, their effective contribution to labor in their parents' household spanned not much more than 10 years. Thus a continual supply of female assistance over a 30-year period would have required at least six daughters, well spaced.

The pattern was similar for males. While the father consulted with other male household heads on camp strategy and tactics, made husbandry decisions, did livestock and cultivation chores such as milking the *pas,* assisting camel copulations and births, shearing wool, weaving palm leaf twine, sowing grain, and pollinating date palms, sons were allocated to a variety of supplementary tasks and complementary spheres. Small boys were put in charge of the kids and lambs. Boys of 10 or 12 years were camelherds, with responsibility for taking and bringing back the camels, for ensuring that they were well grazed and watered, and for seeing that they did not graze in cultivated fields or otherwise cause trouble. Sons in their teens could herd for their fathers, assist a father who was *shwaneg* of the camp flock, or themselves be hired by the *wasildar* of the camp to be *shwaneg,* in charge of the flock of sheep and goats, with responsibility for herding, watering, protection, and assisting in births; and they could assist in assessments of pasturage and decisions about migration. Agricultural activities, especially in the recently expanded irrigation sector, benefited from the labor of strong young men. As well, sons in their later teens and early 20s were capable of working outside the Sarhad, in the past engaging in predatory raiding, in recent times for migrant labor, petty importing, and smuggling. Until they married in their early or middle 20s, sons could be expected to contribute heavily to their parents' household, and even taking into account new commitments to parents-in-law, their contribution to their parents' household tailed off only gradually. Even with the longer span of sons' contributions as household members, for perhaps 20 years, the variety of sectors and tasks to be covered, and the ongoing demand for external income, required the assistance of at least four sons between the ages of 4 and 24. With older sons leaving to form their own households, a total of six sons would have been just about adequate, and eight sons spread over 30 years would not have been an oversupply.

The ideal household, from the point of view of labor supply, would thus have consisted of parents and 14 children, 6 daughters and 8 sons, born over a 25- or 30-year period. Notwithstanding this ideal held by the Baluch, the reality was quite different. In the Halki Ja'far, at a moment when there were 15 tents, the average number of children was just over 3. The average number of children in that subcategory of families of more than 10 years' duration was 4.6. When we leave aside the children younger than 6, this average of 3 is well short of the several daughters and several sons needed for household sufficiency of labor at a given time.

In good part, the small number of children was the result of high miscarriage and infant and child mortality rates. Most women reported that they had had several or many miscarriages. Of 83 pregnancies brought to term, including several stillborns, 31 percent of the children had died by the age of 5, and a total of 36 percent had died by the age of 16.

It is obvious that these miscarriage and infant and child mortality figures represented a human reality and a significance for individual women and men that extended far beyond the fulfilling of labor requirements. Among the Sarhadi Baluch, children were greatly beloved, the blessing most hoped for, and the reward most appreciated. Children were a value in themselves. People were not shy about telling us this, or of asking when we were going to have children. These attitudes toward children were clearly demonstrated on a daily basis by the gentle and loving approaches that men and women took in relating to their children. Children up to 5 went virtually undisciplined, and corporal punishment was not used. Fathers and mothers were often found sitting in their tents cuddling their little children and conversing with older ones. Siblings were very close not only in childhood but also later in adulthood. Children were expected to contribute to the family not because they were a labor force but because they were loved members of the family.

For Baluchi women and men, to have children was to become adult. Neither women nor men were regarded as full adults or as fulfilled individuals until they had children. But Sarhadi Baluch knew from observation and experience that many pregnancies would end unsuccessfully and that some children, especially young children, would not survive. They did not expect any particular pregnancy to succeed or any particular infant to survive. Infants were not named, and in this sense not socially recognized, until the formal ceremony at six months of age. When a miscarriage ended a pregnancy, or a pregnancy ended with a stillborn, or an infant or child died, there was a stock explanation and justification: *dasti huda,* it was "the hand of God" that took the baby, and as it was God's will and action, it had to be accepted and not questioned. In the face of such events, people said *dasti huda* to others and to themselves. It was a stock phrase for stock comfort, but not only that: for many people it expressed their understanding of the world and of existence. Even principals, above all the would-be mothers and fathers themselves, but also their parents and siblings, almost-principals, held on to this explanation.

Not long after Joan and I for the first time joined Ja'far's camp, his eldest daughter, Bibi Nur, had a stillbirth. We felt bad for her and a bit nervous for ourselves, lest we be blamed for this result. We were childless ourselves, and we wondered if someone might think that our envious evil eye had brought about this stillbirth. Ja'far took a very definite line, saying that the stillbirth was *dasti huda,* and that was the last we ever heard about it. At least, if anyone entertained an alternative hypothesis, we never knew it. And our relations with the family, including Bibi Nur and her husband, Id Mahmud, remained positive and grew in warmth.

But it would be foolish to imagine that a theological justification, no matter how truly believed and sincerely accepted, could entirely heal the wounds of those most affected. For parents trying to start a family, such a loss was a real disappointment. For mothers there was a personal loss that went beyond knowledge and understanding, although for many the loss was muted somewhat by the mother's own realistic expectations and the social pressure to accept the loss and move ahead. But for some individuals, the loss was too much. One woman who lost her 14-year-old son after an inexplicable, rapid, wasting illness was inconsolable, crying and wailing for six months, even refusing to do household work. She suffered terribly and could not accept comfort. She received great sympathy for a while, but after months community opinion shifted somewhat, many, including her husband, feeling that her reaction was exaggerated and that she had to honor her responsibilities to the remaining members of the family and to the community.

The high miscarriage and infant and child mortality rates had three cultural aspects that should be noted here. First, the reactions of Sarhadi Baluch to real adversity, the loss of so many pregnancies and children, were conditioned by their expectations and by their cultural explanations. Sarhadi Baluch expected a high rate of loss, were able to justify it in religious terms, and did not count new additions as fully present and fully human until they had been around long enough to show their staying power. Second, for all of the cultural conditioning and social expectations, individuals among the Sarhadi Baluch, as individuals elsewhere, differed from one another and responded differently to similar situations. Some people were able to accept the losses and recover fairly quickly, while others suffered greatly and refused to accept the losses, withdrawing from social life and obligations. Third, as important as the labor of children was to Sarhadi households and the Sarhadi economy, and while this may provide at least part of a sociological explanation of the established social norm of large families, the meaning of children in the life of Baluch was personally and socially much more profound.

The reality for most Sarhadi *baluchi* households, even those long established, was that they could not count on the labor of more than four or five children, and the majority had to make do with the labor of even fewer children for much of the household's span of existence. After a young couple married, they had to manage without labor assistance by children for the first 10 years. It was usually a few years before young wives were able to give birth to live, healthy babies. Then some 8 years had to pass before any substantial assistance could be expected. Up to 6 or 8 more years had to pass before the most responsible or arduous types of work could be undertaken by sons. But in due course, some households could boast a good complement of labor from sons and daughters. An example was the household of Ja'far—about which we have already heard quite a bit—enlivened by four sons and three daughters, interspersed and well distributed in age, and supplemented by Ghulam Mahmud, an older son of a deceased brother, and latterly by Id Mahmud, a son-in-law married to the eldest daughter, Bibi Nur. As discussed earlier, Ghulam Mahmud and Id Mahmud, both in their early 20s, worked away from the Sarhad during the winter and returned to assist during the increased pastoral activity of late spring and the summer date harvest season. Two sons, in their early and middle teens, tended the camel herd and the flock, respectively. Thus Ja'far's major labor needs were met by members of his household, and he was freed for planning, coordination, and consultation, and for any additional serious task that needed attention, which was one of the reasons he was headman of the camping group. Similarly, with two teenage daughters fetching water, gathering brush for firewood, and assisting with cooking and weaving, Ja'far's wife, Monas, was able to organize and supervise a mostly self-contained household labor pool.

The substantial labor sufficiency of households such as Ja'far's provided a degree of flexibility and independence unavailable to households without or with few grown children to assist the parents. For example, during the drought of 1971–72, when smaller stockholders adapted to the difficult conditions by minimizing herding activities, Ja'far was able to initiate a more active herding policy by moving off on his own. This was possible because his sons, his brother's son, and his son-in-law provided the labor necessary for independent livestock management, and because his wife and daughters were able to manage the household on their own.

The flexibility made possible by household labor sufficiency was particularly important in dealing with unusual circumstances. When Ja'far was incapacitated with an ulcer and traveled with his brother's son to Quetta for an operation, three capable males remained in the household to carry out the necessary economic activities.

Neither the independence nor the flexibility of labor self-sufficiency was available to most Sarhadi Baluchi households, as the average of three children and the absence of child labor during the early stages of the family cycle indicate. In 1976, Mahmud Karim, only a few years junior to Ja'far, had one daughter, Zmorid, from his first union residing with him, and one child under five years of age from his second and continuing marriage. In basic productive activities, Mahmud Karim had no male assistance from his immediate family and could depend only on the help that his wife, Pati Hartun, and his older daughter could occasionally provide. During the same period, Shams A'din, Mahmud Karim's younger brother, had three children under five years of age and so was, at least temporarily, without male assistance; nor could Shams A'din expect his wife, Sazien, to manage more than the many tasks that were already her responsibility.

Faced with the discrepancy between labor needs and demographic realities, the *baluch* found a variety of alternative ways other than biological reproduction to provide labor. One was to transfer children from families who did not need them, did not want them, or could not support them to families who did need and want them and were able to support them. This process of transfer of labor supply could be seen in the households of Mahmud Karim and Shams A'din, who were recipients of children from other households (see table 8.1). For example, Dust Mahmud's 12-year-old daughter, Marium, was living with Mahmud Karim and Pati Hartun, while his 10-year-old son, Mahmuduk, was living with Shams A'din. As well, Shams Hartun's sons, 10-year-old Tutonuk and 6-year-old Azimuk, were living with their recently married brother, Abdul. Shams Hartun's 8-year-old daughter, Zaruk, was living with Shams

**Table 8.1.** Some Examples of Children Living with Related Families

| Work | Child's Name and Age | Own Parents | Living with |
|---|---|---|---|
| Household | Marium, 12 | Dust Mahmud D. H. | Mahmud Karim |
| Shepherd | Alluk, 15 | Shams Hartun | Mahmud Karim |
| Camelherd | Mahmuduk, 10 | Dust Mahmud D. H. | Shams A'din |
| Household | Zaruk, 8 | Shams Hartun | Zarbonu |
| Household | Tutonuk, 10 | Shams Hartun | Abdulla |
| Household | Azimuk, 6 | Shams Hartun | Abdulla |
| None | Nesa, 3 | Malik Hartun | Zarbonu |

Hartun's mother, Zarbonu. Thus the lack in some households of offspring of an age to provide labor assistance was ameliorated somewhat by the transfer of children from other households to those without children.

Most of these children were able to contribute much-needed labor to the households in which they were living. Alluk was working as a shepherd for another *halk* and was sending part of his earnings to the male household head, Mahmud Karim. On one occasion, he sent 200 toman, 100 for Mahmud Karim and 100 as part of an engagement process. Mahmuduk was working as camelherd for Shams A'din, Mahmud Karim, Abdulla, Jan Mahmud, Isa, Abas, and Ido. As this was not a full-time job, he was also available for other labor assistance. Marium and Zaruk were able to help with chores such as gathering firewood, watching the lambs and kids, and washing dishes. In return, the children were fed, housed, and provided with clothes and other necessities, and the arrangements for their future, including work and marriage, were looked after.

I do not want to give the impression that children were simply shifted about to provide a more efficient work force, one household "downsizing" while another was expanding. Children were rarely turned over to other households only because those households needed labor, although this was not uncommonly done to provide help for an elderly parent or infirm relative. There were various other reasons why it was sometimes deemed better if the children did not remain at home with their biological parents or parent. One was that the natal family had broken up because of death or divorce and the remaining parent could not take care of all of the children, or the remaining parent had remarried and the children from the previous union were felt not to be entirely welcome. A further factor was poverty and the natal family's inability to support the children or to find useful work for them. Most commonly, the sending of children to another household was overdetermined; that is, several distinct but converging factors encouraged this shift. Furthermore, the transfer was sometimes a temporary expedient, and the children would later return to their original household.

We must also recognize that, although children were sent away from their natal household to another household, they were moving from one part of their family to another part within a small and tightly woven community (table 8.2). Shams Hartun, whose first and second husbands had died and who remarried and moved to Zahedan, sent her sons Tutonuk and Azimuk to live with her eldest son and their older brother, Abdul, and his new wife. She sent Alluk to her brother and his uncle, Mahmud Karim, while she sent Zaruk, her daughter, to her mother, Zarbonu.

Dust Mahmud Da Huda, who had also remarried, was patrilateral parallel cousin of Mahmud Karim and Shams Adin; that is, their fathers were brothers and were members of the Dust Mahmudzai microlineage. As Shams Hartun's deceased husband was his brother, Rehim Dad, Dust Mahmud was also brother-in-law to Mahmud Karim and Shams A'din. His daughter Marium was sent to Mahmud Karim, but this was only temporary, for she was engaged to Alluk, also living with Mahmud Karim, and they would marry in a year or two, thereafter establishing their separate household. Dust Mahmud's Mahmuduk was living with Shams A'din.

Malik Hartun left her small daughter, Nesa, with her mother Zarbonu, to alleviate her own workload and brighten the days of her mother. How long this arrangement continued I do not know.

In general, however, and notwithstanding the transferring of children from one family to another, the basic principles of Sarhadi household organization—the residence principle that each nuclear family should have its own tent and form a separate household, and the corresponding inheritance principle that at marriage each son, except the youngest, should take a share of his natal family's productive wealth in anticipatory inheritance, combined with the high rates of miscarriage and infant and child mortality—virtually guaranteed that few Sarhadi households would be labor sufficient, despite the advantages and desirability of being so. It was almost inevitable that households fell short of this ideal, an ideal nonetheless upheld in theory and reinforced by the occasional successful example.

But even successful examples were successful only temporarily. Ja'far's household was labor sufficient only for a time before, as part of the usual Sarhadi family cycle, it split into smaller, less labor sufficient households. Ja'far's cooperation in 1971–72 with his brother's son, Ghulam Mahmud, who married Ja'far's middle daughter in 1971, and with Id Mahmud, married to Ja'far's eldest daughter in 1966, could be viewed by 1971–72 as cooperation not with members of a large family including affines, but rather as cooperation of three affinally allied but in principle independent households. The existence in this case of three independent households was obscured by the tendency for recently married daughters to reside close to or in their natal households and to be apparently reabsorbed into their natal households when their husbands were away from the Sarhad. When their husbands were away, recently married daughters commonly did not maintain a separate, household tent of their own, but folded their tents and moved back with their parents, particularly before they had chil-

**Table 8.2.** Kinship Ties among Households Shifting Children

|  | [Dust Mahmud]<br>V |  |  |  |  |
|---|---|---|---|---|---|
| [Da Huda]<br>V |  |  | [Gulap]<br>V |  | Zarbonu |
| Dust Mahmud<br>V | Mahmud K. | S. A'din | S. Hartun<br>V | | M. Hartun<br>V |
| Marium |  |  | Abdul | | Nesa |
| Mahmuduk |  |  | Alluk | |  |
|  |  |  | Tutonuk | |  |
|  |  |  | Zaruk | |  |
|  |  |  | Azimuk | |  |

dren. Strictly speaking, however, with these marriages and the formal if notional establishment of separate households, Ja'far's household lost an adult male, Ghulam Mahmud, and two adult females, Bibi Nur and Gul Peri. What resulted was not, to the Sarhadi way of thinking, an expanded or extended family, but rather an association of three independent households, connected by filial, kinship, and affinal ties, and unified by customary obligations and commitments as well as by sentiments favoring continued association and mutual support.

## THE WORK TEAM

The alliance of independent households, into which Ja'far's large household evolved in the normal course of its developmental cycle, was a strategy for the coordination of labor beyond the household, in order to increase efficiency in the demanding, diversified Sarhadi multi-resource economy upon which everyone depended for a living. The attraction of this strategy was particularly great for more typical households with young or few children, for they had few, very limited, internal labor resources upon which to draw. Coordinating labor with other households was at least a partial solution to their problems of having to do too many things and having to do them in different places. Not uncommonly, labor would be coordinated among a set of households already allied by kinship ties and common sentiment. Such households would often be associated over time. I choose to call these informal and somewhat amorphous associations for labor cooperation, "work teams."

The work team was informal in that there was no constitution, either in a contract specifying membership and duties or in a customary conceptualization identifying the group and its activity. Rather, work teams were an emergent social form resulting from de facto association and the coordination of labor over time by a number of individuals whose continuous participation defined their membership. The operation of a work team was evident in a series of coordinated tasks undertaken by a particular set of individuals. But there was no clear-cut membership boundary, and some individuals were more marginal than others and might be associated with more than one group. The work team as a group was based primarily upon generalized reciprocity, people helping out others with the implicit understanding that they would at a later time be helped out by those whom they had helped.

Certain kinds of tasks were characteristic of those undertaken by work teams. Camel searches, weaving, and hut construction were carried out by a number of individuals on behalf of an individual, which was one form of coordination. Transporting and milling of grain, pollinating date palms, bagging and harvesting date palms, and migrating with camels to the date groves were often done by one individual on behalf of a number of others, which was another form of coordination. For convenience of reference, let us call the former "joint labor" and the latter "divided labor."

"Joint labor" involved a number of people working together at one place and one time to accomplish a task on behalf of one individual that could be done more efficiently by several people in concert. "Divided Labor" involved different individuals doing different tasks, perhaps at different times or in different places, on behalf of others as well as themselves. Particularly in regard to tasks suitable for divided labor, task allocation included the rotation of various tasks among individuals as well as among individuals over time. These informal work teams often corresponded to the more formalized camelherding groups.

Let us examine one of the work teams in detail. In the Halki Ja'far during 1972–73, six male household heads—Mahmud Karim, Shams A'din, Jan Mahmud, Isa, Abdulla, and Abas—frequently participated with one another in coordinated labor. For convenience, I will call this set of households the Gulap Work Team, for a number of the team members were children or grandchildren, or their affines, of the deceased Gulap. Most of these men were in their 20s or 30s, and most of their children were only a few years old, so there was virtually no labor power in their households beyond that of husband and wife. None of these households began to approach labor sufficiency, so they compensated by coordinating labor among households (see table 8.3).

Sometimes one or two worked for the others. Shams A'din and Isa transported bags of grain from the households of Mahmud Karim, Ido Mahmud, the elder Walli Mahmud, and Jan Mahmud, as well as their own, to the motor-driven mill at Gwanich. They assisted in the milling and brought the flour back to camp.

Sometimes all worked for one. On an occasion when one of Mahmud Karim's camels was missing, joining the search along with the owner were Shams A'din, Abdulla, Abbas, Jan Mahmud, and Isa Rasul. When a few days later, while Isa was away from camp, one of Isa's camels disappeared, a search party was formed by Mahmud Karim, Shams A'din, Abdulla, Abbas, and Jan Mahmud.

**Table 8.3.** A Sample of Coordinated Activities of the Gulap
Work Team, 1972–73

| Activity | Workers | Work Done for | Notes |
|---|---|---|---|
| Transporting and milling grain (postharvest, 1972) | Shams A'din, with some help from Isa | Shams A'din, Isa, Mahmud Karim, Jan Mahmud, Wali Mahmud, Ido, Ghulam Mahmud | |
| Camel search (July 1972) | Mahmud Karim, Shams A'din, Abdulla, Abas, Jan Mahmud, Isa Rassul | Mahmud Karim | Isa out of Sarhad |
| Camel search (July 1972) | Mahmud Karim, Shams A'din, Abdulla, Abas, Jan Mahmud | Isa | Isa out of Sarhad |
| Work on date palms, including *iwar*, pollination, *sund*, bagging, and *bur*, harvest (spring and summer, 1972) | Shams A'din | Shams A'din, Mahmud Karim (K), Abdulla (K), Jan Mahmud (C), Isa (C), Abas (C), Wali Mahmud (C), Pir Dad (C), Ghulam Mahmud (C) | |
| Work on date palms (1973) | Mahmud Karim | Mahmud Karim, Shams A'din (K), Abdulla (K), Abas (C), Pir Dad (C), Wali Mahmud (C) | |
| | Jan Mahmud | Jan Mahmud, Ido (K?) | |
| Trip to Mashkil, with camels (1972) | Mahmud Karim | Mahmud Karim, Shams A'din (T), Abdulla (T), Jan Mahmud (T), Isa | |
| Camel herding at Mashkil (1972) | Mahmuduk Gemi[1] Mahmuduk Dust Mahmud[2] | Mahmud Karim, Shams A'din, Abdulla, Isa, Abas, Jan Mahmud | 1 resided with Shams A'din, 2 with Mahmud Karim |
| Camel herding on Sarhad (winter, 1972–73) | Mahmuduk Dust Mahmud | Mahmud Karim, Shams A'din, Abdulla, Isa, Jan Mahmud, Abas, Ido | Mahmuduk Gemi herding camels for Gemi, Barkat, Dadol |

*(continued)*

**Table 8.3** *(continued)*

| Activity | Workers | Work Done for | Notes |
|---|---|---|---|
| Transporting palm trunk for roof construction, Mashkil (1972) | Shams A'din, Mahmud Karim, Abdulla, Abas, Brother of Isa, 11 others | Shams A'din | Isa away |
| Hut repair, Mashkil (1972) | Shams A'din, Mahmud Karim, Abdulla and 5 others on first day, 8 others on second day | Shams A'din | Isa and Jan Mahmud away; Abas working on his hut |
| Hut construction, Mashkil (1972) | Mahmud Karim, Shams A'din, Abdulla and 10 others | Mahmud Karim | Isa and Jan Mahmud away |
| Hut construction, Mashkil (1972) | Abas, Mahmud Karim, Shams A'din, Abdulla, Jan Mahmud and 12 others | Abas | Isa away |

*Note:* K = *kumaki*, free, without payment or return; C = *charki*, for one-quarter of the produce; T = traveled by truck.

Three tasks in the yearly round required extensive and difficult travel and a great deal of work. These were *iwar,* the pollination of the date palms at Mashkil, the migration to and from Mashkil during and after the date harvest, and *shawarkashk,* the trip carrying the dates from Mashkil to the Sarhad followed by the return trip to Mashkil. In the spring of 1972, Shams A'din made the *iwar* trip and pollinated his palms and those of Mahmud Karim, Abdulla, Jan Mahmud, Isa, Abas, Walli Mahmud, and two others. In the summer of 1972, Mahmud Karim made the migration to Mashkil with his camels and those of Shams A'din, Abdulla, Jan Mahmud, and Isa, these others making the trip by truck. In the spring of 1973, Mahmud Karim made the *iwar* trip and pollinated his palms as well as those of Shams A'din, Abdulla, Abas, Walli Mahmud, and one other; Jan Mahmud also went, pollinating his palms and those of Ido Mahmud.

Each of these examples of coordination of labor either helped an individual to do a task he could not do very well himself, cases of "joint labor," or freed a number of individuals from doing a task so that they could engage in other productive activities, cases of "divided labor."

What drew together individuals from independent households to coordinate their work? Was the work team based upon a totally instrumental arrangement involving an otherwise random set of individuals? Not at all. While kinship and affinal ties did not automatically generate work teams, such relationships tended to underpin work team membership, as they tended to underpin long-term coresidence, and, given the difficulty of travel and communication, labor coordination virtually required coresidence. Consider once again the Gulap work team.

- Mahmud Karim and Shams A'din, sons of Gulap, were brothers.
- Abdulla was the son of one of Gulap's daughters, and thus the sister's son of both Mahmud Karim and Shams A'din.
- Jan Mahmud was Mahmud Karim's wife's brother and was married to Shams A'din's wife's sister.
- Isa was married to Mahmud Karim's daughter and was thus *zamas* to Mahmud Karim and to Shams A'din.
- Abas was Shams A'din's wife's mother's brother.
- One sometime participant was Ido, Shams A'din's and Jan Mahmud's father-in-law and also Shams A'din's and Mahmud Karim's mother's brother.
- Another sometime participant was Isa Rasul, who was Mahmud Karim's and Shams Adin's brother-in-law.

There were many additional and overlapping matrilateral and affinal ties, a result of Sarhadi preferential, bilateral endogamy, in which marriages with close kin was encouraged. In addition, the six core members of the Gulap work team and their wives, and most of the others involved, were patrikin, descended from a common male ancestor, in this case Dadol, which made them members of the Dadolzai lineage, which was vested with important collective political and welfare responsibilities.

I have begun this account of the Gulap labor team by describing labor coordination among the men, partly because I followed the men more closely than the women—and might have been in trouble had I followed the women any more closely than I did—and partly because on a day-to-day basis the men's activities were more visible and overt than the quiet cooperation of the women. But the coordination of work and of mutual assistance among the men was paralleled if not outstripped by that of the women. The borrowing and lending of supplies and equipment were virtually continuous—so much so that it was sometimes difficult for a woman to hang on to the supplies needed for her own tent—and daily visiting brought together hands for sharing work as a matter of course. Tasks such as cleaning wool or hair, spinning, and weaving called for and received joint labor, as did drawing water from a well, or a trip to any water sources for collecting water or washing clothes. Sazien, Nur Bibi, Pati Hartun (wife of Mahmud Karim), Pati Hartun (wife of Abas), and Zmorid visited, shared, and coordinated work together as the other half of the Gulap work team. These women were also closely tied by kin and affinal ties:

- Sazien and Nur Bibi were sisters.
- Sazien and Nur Bibi were both sisters-in-law of Pati Hartun (wife of Mahmud Karim).
- Pati Hartun (wife of Mahmud Karim) was the stepmother of Zmorid.
- All of these women were also related by other overlapping kin and affinal ties, such as Sazien and Nur Bibi being Pati Hartun's father's brother's daughters, and all three being father's mother's brother's daughters of Zmorid.
- As well, all of these women were members of the Dadolzai lineage.

These kin ties and the collaboration in labor coordination influenced the layout of tents in the camp, as I described earlier, and the propinquity of these women's tents facilitated their labor coordination.

The Gulap work team illustrated labor coordination among independent house-holds, each with quite limited labor power available from household members. An-other common pattern was illustrated, as described above, by the association in the 1970s of Ja'far's household with those of his young married daughters and their hus-bands: the alliance of a strong household, having considerable labor power, with oth-ers of limited labor. In this case, the association was between Ja'far's household and those of his two daughters, Gul Peri and Bibi Nur, and sons-in-law, Ghulam Mahmud and Id Mahmud. Ja'far coordinated labor with his sons and sons-in-law, while Monas coordinated labor with her daughters. The same pattern was seen in cases where a father's household coordinated with his sons' households.

## TERMS OF EXCHANGE

The "work team" was based primarily upon generalized reciprocity. Tasks were com-monly undertaken on this basis, and done *kumaki*, "as help," without immediate or specified compensation. To represent this arrangement, I use the term "coopera-tion." A "cooperative relationship" involved coordinated labor without explicit com-pensation specified and tended to be open-ended and symmetrical in the long run. Generalized reciprocity, an expectation that exchange of labor would balance over time, was the basis.

In other cases, however, work was undertaken with compensation specified, such as harvesting dates *charki*, literally "a quarter," for one-quarter share of the dates, or women weaving a tent for specified pay in cash. To represent this arrangement, I use the term "contract." A "contractual relationship" involved an explicit agreement about task and compensation and was usually delimited in scope and therefore often asymmetrical, with one individual doing a task for another. Specific reciprocity, that is, an immediate balance of exchange, was required.

In general, coordination of labor based upon "cooperation" was more common among those with close kin ties, such as father and son, father and son-in-law, and brothers; whereas "contract" was more common among more distant kin. Among core members of work teams, people who coordinated their labor regularly and who rotated tasks among themselves, cooperation was the common modus operandi.

However, certain kinds of tasks, directly productive tasks of considerable, extended application, such as harvesting dates, were more likely to be compensated on a contractual basis. Reviewing the activities of the Gulap work team in 1972–73, we find that activities such as transporting grain, searching for camels, migrating with camels, and brick-dwelling construction were done *kumaki,* as cooperation. And while working on date palms was done for some people *kumaki,* for others it was done *charki,* for a share, based on a specified contract. In 1972, when Shams A'din was working on date palms, he did those of his brother Mahmud Karim and his sister's son Abdul *kumaki,* as cooperation; his work on other palms, those of his cousin, Jan Mahmud, his distant cousin and brother's daughter's husband Isa, his wife's mother's brother Abas, Walli Mahmud, Pir Dad, and Ghulam Mahmud, was done for a share, *charki.* In 1973, Mahmud Karim worked the palms of Shams A'din and Abdulla *kumaki,* and those of Abas, Pir Dad, and Walli Mahmud *charki.* Several of the individuals for whom work was done *charki* were not in a position to reciprocate: Walli Mahmud and Pir Dad were elderly men, and Abas was not very well. Others—such as Ghulam Mahmud—were not close kin or work team members. One—Jan Mahmud—was a work team member, a brother-in-law and second cousin, but from a different microlineage. While paying Shams A'din to work his date palms in 1972, Jan Mahmud worked his own date palms and those of his father's brother, Ido Mahmud, in 1973. Contractual coordination was thus most likely for lengthy and intensive work when there was no established pattern of task rotation in that particular sphere.

Specific reciprocity, as in contractual agreements, was prominent in camelherding arrangements. A number of camel owners coordinated their camelherding by pooling their camels into a unified herd, *bak,* and hired a boy to be camelherd, *bakjat* (table 8.4). Because camels were mainly used for transport and riding rather than primary production and were relatively few in number, arrangements for camelherding were secondary to those for herding *pas,* sheep and goats. Camelherding was organized within the given parameters of the camping group, defined by the prior and primary *pas* herding contract. Camelherds were compensated according to set and agreed upon terms. Very often the camel herds corresponded to the collected camels of work teams.

The coordination of labor tasks involving contractual arrangements specifying compensation—such as harvesting dates for a quarter share, or herding camels for payment per herd—was specific reciprocity, because the service was immediately

**Table 8.4.** Camel-Herding Groups in the Halki Ja'far,
1972–73

| Camel Owners | Microlineage Affiliation | Camelherd (*bakjat*) |
|---|---|---|
| Herd 1 | | Rassuluk Ja'far |
| Ja'far | Shirdelzai | |
| Dust Mahmud | Shirdelzai | |
| Reis | Shirdelzai | |
| Id Mahmud | Shirdelzai | |
| Herd 2 | | Mahmuduk Gemi |
| Gemi | Komeronzai | |
| Barkat | Komeronzai | |
| Dadol | Shadi Hanzai | |
| Herd 3 | | Mahmuduk Dust Mahmud |
| Mahmud Karim | Dust Mahmudzai | |
| Shams A'din | Dust Mahmudzai | |
| Abdulla | Dust Mahmudzai | |
| Jan Mahmud | Shadi Hanzai | |
| Isa | Shadi Hanzai | |
| Abas | Shadi Hanzai | |
| Ido Mahmud | Shadi Hanzai | |
| Herd 4 | | Waluk Komeron |
| Komeron | Mirgolzai | |
| Sahib Dad | Yar Mahmudzai | |
| Isa | Jehan Shahzai | |
| Karam | Miradzai | |

paid for and the exchange was formally closed. But these contracts were in reality part of a wider set of understandings and commitments within the work team. Members of teams expected to give and receive help from other team members over the long run. Those for whom a team member worked on contract were expected to work on that team member's behalf, on the same terms, at a later time. And the same individuals who had some contractual dealings were also repeatedly and continually involved, while helping each other with a variety of other tasks, in free cooperation on the basis of generalized reciprocity. In this sense, even contractual coordination of labor for payment took place within a framework of mutuality and generalized reciprocity among team members.

To sum up, work teams were informal associations of independent households coordinating joint and divided labor by means of generalized reciprocity and specific contract. The increased efficiency of joint and divided labor in comparison with labor by individuals enabled households with insufficient labor capacity to engage effectively in the wide range of productive activities characteristic of the diversified

Sarhadi Baluchi multi-resource economy. These informal work team associations were built upon a complex of kinship and affinal ties within a context of coresidence and residential propinquity. The common interests of lineage affiliation and the commitments of kinship and affinal ties provided an ongoing basis for unity and generalized reciprocity.


## THE CAMP AND ITS SHEPHERD

Local groups among the Sarhadi *baluch* were constituted as herding groups and manifested residentially as herding camps of black tents. *Wasildar,* owners of sheep and goats, *pas,* contracted, *karar kort,* to form a unified flock, *ramag* or *galag,* and to hire a shepherd, *shwaneg,* and in so doing, formed with their households a residential group, a herding camp, *halk.* Each herding group and camp had one and only one flock-herding contract and one and only one associated flock. Labor provision for the flock, a major capital resource, required coordination among livestock owners because household flocks were rather small, the flocks needed regular supervision and care, and the tribesmen faced many conflicting labor requirements from other sectors.

First, flocks had to be an appropriate size, usually between 200 and 300 adult *pas,* depending upon the condition of the pasturage. There were several reasons for this. If the flock was too large or too small, the animals would not stay together but would stray, and, feeling insecure without the flock around them, would not graze well. Also, the pasturage of the Sarhad, even in a good year, could not support a larger flock. At the same time, the flock had to be large enough to provide adequate compensation for the shepherd. Therefore, the household flocks had to add up to an appropriate number of animals for a unified camp flock of the right size. If there were too many *pas,* some households had to leave; if there were too few *pas,* some new households had to be enticed to join, or else a substandard shepherd had to be accepted.

Second, small stock, *pas,* sheep and goats, but especially the sheep, were vulnerable and needed close care. Being mobile, delicate, and none too astute, they required protection from human and animal predators, direction in finding pasturage and water, and assistance in illness and birth. The austerity of the Sarhadi environment required round-the-clock pasturing in spring and summer. Lactating animals had to be milked regularly and the young had to be separated to avoid uncontrolled suckling but had to be provided adequate access, whether or not owners were available for these tasks. In some seasons, notably *hamin,* the date harvest, owners' households had to leave their flocks, and full-time care for all of the *pas* fell to the shepherd.

Third, the demands of other economic sectors precluded livestock owners from devoting all their time to the needs of their household flocks. Responsibility for care of the flock thus had to be delegated to an agent who was capable of making a more or less full-time commitment, who could be relied upon to carry out the complex and arduous tasks involved in flock supervision, and who was knowledgeable and shrewd enough to make astute judgments where the welfare of the flock and thus the welfare of their owners' households was at stake.

For these reasons, the livestock owners contracted with a shepherd to take charge of their combined household small stock and to manage them as a camp flock. It was by no means easy to find a shepherd knowledgeable enough, hardy enough, and responsible enough to satisfy fully the exacting standards of experienced and demanding livestock owners. The call for good shepherds was high, the compensation modest, the expectations of the owners great, and the opportunities in other sectors attractive. The low density of animals supportable on the limited pasturage in many dry years, and thus the typically small flock size, stunted the aggregate per animal compensation, which was paid in cash and in a percentage of new offspring. At least during the 1960s and 1970s, there was a sellers' market for the labor of shepherds. Livestock owners had to either pay more for more capable shepherds or accept less in labor from the less capable. The annual pay, *hak* or *mor,* for the *shwaneg* customarily included regular payments of bread, cash per head of livestock, goat hair, clothes, a portion of the newborn livestock, and milk (table 8.5).

What were some of the considerations in selecting a *shwaneg*? If the individual involved was a minor living with his parents, brothers, or other close kin, he frequently had no choice and had to be *shwaneg* if his elders demanded it. This was usually the case in small camps, especially in a one-household camp. This arrangement, whereby a young *shwaneg* was obliged to take the job, was most workable with a smaller herd, in relatively undemanding conditions, for a boy could not move the animals such great distances, keep them out through the night, protect them from the predators, or assist in the reproductive processes as effectively as an experienced adult. With larger herds, it was preferable to have an experienced adult as a *shwaneg,* but no adult was obliged to take the job. Many factors had to be weighed before one decided whether or not to take on such a post.

One consideration was the kind of *wasildar,* herd owners, one would be working for. Would they be unreasonably demanding, or would they be unwilling to do their share of the herding, or would they try to avoid paying their fair share?

A second was the terms being offered. While there was a set of customary payments, the values in certain categories were flexible and sensitive to market conditions, reflecting both the local labor market for *shwaneg* and the extralocal labor market. The size of the herd was an important consideration, too, for a large part of the recompense was a portion of the return, in offspring, wool, hair, and milk.

A third was the kind of year that it was likely to be. No one wanted to be *shwaneg sardokal,* during a drought, for the work would be more onerous, the *pas* in decline, the return small, and the *wasildar* miserable and thus difficult to work with.

A fourth consideration was the alternatives to working as *shwaneg.* Was one pre-

**Table 8.5.** The Annual Pay, *Hak* or *Mor*, for the *Shwaneg*

| Type of Payment | Terms of Payment |
| --- | --- |
| *nan*, bread | |
| 1. *nan* | For the first three months of the year, one *man* (5 kilos) of flour for each 15 animals, per month. |
| 2. *nani* | For the remaining period, 1 *man* grain or flour for each 3 animals; paid in two installments, one-half at *duro*, grain harvest, and one-half upon return from Mashkil in the autumn. |
| *Pish kareh* | For each animal, a sum of money to be paid at the beginning of the contract period, or as soon as possible. |
| | In 1968, the amount paid by the Halki Ja'far was 5 rials. In 1973, the amount paid by the Halki Ja'far was 20 rials. (This difference reflected partly the difference between the value of the inexperienced boy who was shepherd in 1968 in comparison with the experienced man who was shepherd in 1973, and partly the general inflation in pay for shepherds, owing to scarcity in the local labor market resulting from competition with the extralocal labor market.) |
| *Mudi*, hair | For each 10 animals, the wool or hair of 1. |
| *Chawart* | One pair of good sandals, *chawart*, one heavy overcoat, and one heavy cloth, *chadur*, to be used as cloak or bag, bought collectively by the *wasildar*. |
| *Hort*, newborn *pas* | One of 10 born during the year of the contract. |
| *Shir*, milk | All milk during *hamin*, when the *wasildar* were away at the date groves. |

pared to leave the local area to work in town or on the roads, or to leave the region for a job in a Persian city or in one of the Arabian Emirates, or to engage in small-scale smuggling across the Iran-Pakistan border?

## Three Shepherds

Abdulluk (Little Abdul) Dadolzai, son of Shams Hartun, sister's son of Shams A'din and Mahmud Karim, was *shwaneg* for the Ja'fari Halk in 1967–68. He did not have much choice in taking the job, which was more or less thrust upon him; his mother was twice widowed, and thus his household was in need, and his uncles pressured him to do it. In 1972–73, Abdulla, as he was then called, recently married and a young adult, would not consider taking the job. He preferred carrying trading goods between Zahedan and Kerman. The work was less and the pay better than in shepherding, and most important, one did not have *wasildar* on one's back all the time.

Abdulla's younger brother, Alluk, was prepared to be a *shwaneg*, but not for his adult kinsmen in the Ja'fari Halk. He felt that they would take advantage of him, treating him as a young kinsman who owed them services, rather than as a contracted worker to be duly recompensed. Indeed, his brother had felt that he had not been fairly paid during his time as *shwaneg* for his kinsmen. If one did work for another halk, however, one's kinsmen would back one up and see that one got a square deal. And so it was, for before Alluk became *shwaneg* for Kasumi Halk, his uncles shopped around among several *halk,* acting as intermediaries to see that he received a good initial offer, and thereafter acted as monitors to see that he was being treated well and being paid according to the agreement.

Ido Dadolzai was reluctant to continue as *shwaneg* for the Ja'fari Halk in 1973–74. The first problem was that he was unwilling to continue having Komeron Mirgolzai as *wasildar,* for this man was very demanding and stubborn, and there were no mitigating kin ties. Second, there had not been much rain, even by local standards, and pasturage in the coming year would probably not be very good. Third, Ido had date palms at the Mashkel Basin, and as *shwaneg* he would have to remain on the Sarhad with the herds when the others migrated to the palm groves. Not only would he not be able to tend his palms, but he would have to suffer a solitary life during this period. Fourth, the physical demands of this exacting job were beginning to weigh heavily on him, as he was no longer a young man. During the time that Ido was considering these factors, he was asked by a Rahmatzai camp to be their *shwaneg.* Leaving aside social factors, he was concerned that the good size of the herd of that *halk,* while it would provide a substantial return in a good year, would be a problem in a bad year, which the next year seemed likely to be. Thus, on the one hand, and this was a fifth problem, he was unhappy with the relatively small Dadolzai herd, because his share would be small, but, on the other hand, he was unhappy with the prospect of the large Rahmatzai herd, for in the coming bad year it could not be tended adequately. Ido finally arranged to share the job of *shwaneg* for the Dadolzai Halk with his son Brahuk.


## INEQUALITY AND THE EXPLOITATION OF LABOR

As we have seen, the annual round of work tasks of each Baluchi household reflected the diversified multi-resource economy of the Sarhad. This economy depended heavily upon human labor, for most work was done by human muscle power. The labor used in carrying out the multiple tasks of the economy was organized partly upon a division of labor of age and gender, and partly in terms of reciprocal coordination of labor.

But we must remember that what we are considering is not only a formal system of actors filling parts. We are also considering how people made a living, and how well or how badly they lived depended upon how successful or unsuccessful they were at producing the things they needed. Furthermore, although we have been giving considerable weight to human interactions with the natural environment and with the nonhuman, domesticated and nondomesticated, species and other resources in their environment, the way people interacted in the course of making a living could have a substantial and even determining effect on the outcome. This is obvious in the rather extreme example of the predatory raiding by the Sarhadi Baluch and the consequent punitive raids against them.

Were there winners and losers in the Sarhadi Baluch economy? Were there people who did better and people who did worse, and did some people do better at the expense of others? Was labor exploited for economic profit, and were some categories of people victimized for the benefit of others?

The general model of pastoral tribes prevalent in anthropology during the three decades after Evans-Pritchard's (1940) seminal account of the segmentary political organization of the Nuer was of an egalitarian society, in which individuals and families were independent and had equal access to the resources—pasture and agricultural land, water, fishing sites, targets of predatory raiding, and livestock—necessary for making a living. Nuer, according to Evans-Pritchard, did not accumulate capital resources or products, but rather—through distribution, assistance, and sharing—invested in fellow tribesmen, thus maintaining solidarity through support and equality.

This model of the segmentary, egalitarian tribe came to be challenged, beginning in the 1960s, and was superseded in the 1970s by a Marxist model of tribes characterized by inequality, differentiation of power, dependence, class organization, and exploitation of labor (Asad 1970; Bradburd 1980, 1990; Black-Michaud 1986; Bonte 1990). On the whole, this Marxist model predominates in current anthropological thought (Fratkin, Roth, and Galvin 1994: *passim*; Young 1996:58–61, 66–67; cf. Salzman 1999a).

In part, the two models differ in emphasis; the earlier "orthodox" model stresses certain aspects of social and economic life that can be construed as "egalitarian," while the later "revisionist" model stresses certain aspects that can be construed as "inegalitarian." But exactly what should count as "equality" or "inequality" is not always obvious. For example, all Sarhadi tribesmen had equal access to the natural resources—water, pasture, vegetation, wood, and minerals from natural sources—in their tribal territories. At the same time, some ended up with more livestock than others, and some ended up reasonably well off and others not very well off. Did the equality of access make the Sarhadi tent dwellers egalitarian or did the differential ownership of livestock make them inegalitarian? Were shepherds and livestock owners equal partners in a reciprocal, contractual exchange, or were *shwaneg* inferior to the superior *wasildar,* or was it the other way around? Consider, too, the differences in activities. Were men, raising livestock and growing crops, and women, processing the livestock and cultivation products into equipment and food, doing different but equally important tasks, or was the work of one more important than the work of the other?

In the analysis of any specific ethnographic case, identification of equalities or inequalities may be correct, just as either may be exaggerated and oversimplified. But there is more to it than that. Neither the "orthodox" nor the "revisionist" model is adequate because both are ideal-typical models, exaggerating certain aspects of society at the expense of others and identifying a universal essence of "pastoral" or "tribal" societies. For this reason, neither is capable of adequately representing the real differences between different communities, societies, and cultures. What, to my mind, is needed is a more balanced and precise approach that recognizes the different aspects and degrees of equality and inequality, independence and dependence, and sharing and exploitation that exist in different places. Thus, an approach that focuses on a number of dimensions of variation, rather than general characterizations of "equality" or "inequality," is likely to be truer to individual ethnographic cases and to the variations between ethnographic cases, and thus more fruitful for understanding and explanation.

While a comparative model based upon dimensions of variation cannot be elaborated here, the assumption that I would make, that there is great variation from one pastoral tribe to another, is relevant to our Sarhadi case. This position makes the conditions of any particular tribe at a particular historical moment an empirical matter, to be assessed by investigations about the tribe, rather than deduced from an ideal-typical model. It thus is a matter of investigation in what ways and to what extent the Sarhadi Baluch are equal or unequal, independent or dependent, benefiting from sharing or suffering from exploitation. In the following discussion, taking up one of these questions, I focus on the presence, absence, or degree of economic exploitation.

### Children's Labor

Let us begin within the household. The success and expansion of the household economy depended heavily upon child labor and the labor of children. Children did arduous and boring work and were not paid for it. Now the term "child labor" has for us a nasty connotation of stealing a child's childhood and of depriving a child of her or his future for the benefit of others. Could child labor in the Sarhad be considered an example of the exploitation and abuse of children?

One consideration in assessing the role of children in contributing labor is that they were benefiting members of the household for which they worked. The fulfillment of the children's needs as individuals depended on the income of the household. To say that they were not paid for their work may be strictly correct, but they were not employees; rather they were joint owners of the household economy, even though they were not directors. This became clear later in their life cycles, when they received a share of the household patrimony as anticipatory or regular inheritance.

A second consideration was the "loss of childhood" through application to work. However, we should not forget that our notion of "childhood" as a time of play separate from work is a cultural concept that has developed out of our history and way of life, especially the relatively recent separation of the workplace from the household. For *baluchi* children, childhood meant being part of the family household and participating in its activities. Even so, *baluchi* children ran free for five or so years and then only gradually were given occasional serious tasks, such as following the *hort*, baby lambs and kids, for a while. They undertook serious responsibilities, such as collecting firewood or minding the camels, only when they approached the age of 10 and real tasks were interspersed with carefree activities. From that time, girls began to prepare for marriage, which usually took place by their fifteenth year, and for the establishment of their own independent households. Boys at 15 entered the first stage of manhood and took up serious work. While the rapid arrival of adulthood reduced the length of childhood somewhat, it would be difficult to argue that Sarhadi children's lives were distorted by the labor that they gradually contributed to their households.

A third consideration was the sacrifice of children's developmental activities, such as schooling, for productive labor. On the Sarhad, however, just as work and household were not separated, education and household activities had never been separated. Children were educated by parental and community instruction, by watching and imitating, and by learning through doing, through participation in the activities of work and life in their tents and camps. Education and work were not in opposition; working was one of the activities through which children learned. Furthermore, learning through working was learning what one needed to know to make a living in the Sarhad.

By the 1960s and 1970s, formal education at the lower levels was available in the Sarhad, in Khash and in country schoolhouses manned by drafted members of the Iranian Education Corps, *Sepahi Danesh*. Classes were conducted in Persian, *zaban-i farsi*, not the native Baluchi, *baluchi labs*, of the children. Their school learning, based on a national Iranian syllabus, was not very relevant to anything the Baluchi children knew. And formal schooling for most Baluchi children meant living away from their families. But some children, mainly boys, were sent and lived with settled relatives; those who learned Persian and succeeded at their schoolwork, even going to Zahedan for high school, gained an entrée into Persian society. At the same time, some children were also being sent to a Sunni religious school, *madraseh*, sponsored by the Yarahmadzai Sardar and located at his winter residence, Gorchan, and run by a learned religious leader and teacher, *maulawi*. But in all, the number of boys from black tents receiving any formal education did not exceed 10 percent, and the number of girls was probably closer to 2 percent.

We got to know some unusual school teachers on the Sarhad. During our various trips to the Sarhad, we received kindness, hospitality, and friendship from the American Peace Corps members who were stationed in Khash. They were teaching mostly English in the Khash school. Their poor impressions of the Baluch came from the children in their classes, who appeared to them morose and dense. When these volunteers came to visit us in our herding camp residences, they were astonished by the vitality, energy, and exuberance of the children of the camp, including some they knew from classes. Of course, the children must have felt more secure in their own communities. But the difference went beyond this. For Baluchi children, most of whom were struggling to learn Persian, which at least they could hear in the streets of Khash, the prospect of tackling English must have been catatonia inducing. They were very far from their own milieu, being presented with material that had no apparent connection with their lives and futures as they could understand them. My Baluchi friend who had gone on to study in Scotland and eventually teach English, quite a leap from the Sarhad, had grown up in Khash and seen commerce and literate activities his whole life. For the children of the black tents, even sedentary life in Khash was a big jump.

I do not want to enter the debate about the virtues of local versus national cultures and local-oriented versus national-oriented educations. This is something Sarhadi Baluch were debating and will debate for themselves, just as they, individually and collectively, will choose their children's educations from the options available as they see fit. The conflict between formal schooling and household labor was just beginning in the 1970s and inevitably must eventually become a serious dilemma, even if it had been postponed owing to the disruptions of the postrevolutionary period and the potential conflicts between Shi'a and Sunni versions of education. Important though such questions are, for our immediate inquiry, it would be difficult to say that during the 1960s and 1970s Baluchi children were deprived of education by having to contribute their labor, when working taught them what they needed to know in order to live and make a living in Sarhadi society.

I conclude from these considerations that the children of the black tents were not economically exploited, were not abused by being pressed into laboring for their households, and were not victimized by being put to work. There are undoubtedly many places in the world where children are exploited terribly and child labor may legitimately be considered a crime against humanity, but this may not be said about the black tents of the Sarhad.

## The Gender Division of Labor

Let us now turn to the gender division of labor. In broad outline, men attended to the primary production of livestock, grain, and dates; hunted; left the Sarhad for migrant raiding/trading/labor to gain income; and saw to the transport of household goods. Women collected wild species of plants, firewood, and water; processed primary products into consumable form, as in baking bread, churning butter, and weaving hair tents and wool rugs and bags; and maintained household items, as in washing clothes.

The boundary of this broad delineation was rather hazy, and there was a great deal of crossover as circumstances demanded. Men, for example, processed date palm frond leaves, a raw material, into usable products, particularly rope of various sizes and for various uses, while women wove the leaves into flat mats used for tent sides and flooring. Now there is a certain logic for this, too; much of the rope was used for animals, primary production, and transport, while the mats were used for the tents, which were woven, owned, set up, and looked after by the women. But even here, the categories are not quite so tidy, for without rope to support the tent, the tent could not stand. There was in delineating the division of labor considerable convention and convenience that overlay tidy categories.

Recent developments contributed to this overlay. For example, milling grain into flour had been women's work, done in the camp with a *hash*, a handmill for grain, made of two, circular, flat stones. The top stone had a hole in the center, into which the grain would be poured, and a hole close to the edge of the top stone, into which a stick would be inserted to act as a handle. The top stone would be turned, the grain would be ground between the two stones, and the ground grain, or flour, would come out at the outside seam between the two stones. This was a stage in processing the grain from primary production, supplied by the men, into consumable bread. Handmilling flour was a long and tedious job, and with bread being the primary staple, a daily one. However, when motor-driven mills were established in Khash and in a few countryside settlements, women were relieved of handmilling, and men undertook the task of transporting grain to the mill, assisting in the milling, and transporting the flour back to the camp, as well as paying for the milling. Here is one recent case, driven by new technology, in which an ongoing, tedious task done by women was transformed into intermittent, heavy work done by men.

In addition to the weight of men's labor, men had the responsibility for defense and had to sustain the risks involved in this sphere. Raiding, warfare, and vengeance feuding were more prominent features of tribal life prior to 1935, but they continued, in a sporadic fashion, to call upon Sarhadi men through the 1970s and since.

Overall, did men or women carry a heavier load of labor? On the basis of the spheres of work and activities undertaken, we may answer this question in terms of the amount of time, skill, effort, stress, and danger involved in their respective labor obligations. My assessment is that men and women invested equal time in the labor and were equal in skill needed, but that men's work required substantially greater physical effort, engendered much greater stress, and exposed men to considerably more danger. Men worked harder than women and paid the price in terms of work-related injuries, ailments, and deaths. Furthermore, technological advances, such as motor-driven wells and mills, motor vehicles, and sewing machines had in almost every case reduced women's labor and increased men's labor.

Can we say, then, that Sarhadi men were exploited and women had an easy life, benefiting from men's labor while not contributing an equal share? I do not believe so, for two reasons. The minor reason is that women did put in as much time and needed as high a level of skill as men, even though their work was less demanding in other respects. Women's work was no less necessary for supporting the household than that of the men. The household could not function without the work that women did, and men could not have done both their work and the work that women did. The Baluch said that there could not be a household without a woman; men could not live on their own.

The second and major reason is that we cannot justly weigh men's labor against women's unless we take into account other spheres beyond production, as we have for men in noting their role in defense, notably the role of women in reproduction. To assess realistically their contributions to the household, women's reproductive labor in carrying and giving birth to children must be included with their other work. Whatever effort, stress, and danger were lacking in women's household labor was more than made up for by the effort, stress, and danger of pregnancy and birth in the desert. Women were attended by older women, experienced in birth, but modern medical facilities and formally trained personnel were not available. As I mentioned earlier, many pregnancies ended in miscarriage or stillbirth, and many infants were lost. Even worse, women were lost.

An event of this nature in which I personally was involved in a minor fashion occurred in 1973, when a new tent joined the Halki Ja'far. The young family was not close in descent or kinship to most camp members. I did not know the family well. The young husband quickly went off to work or trade, leaving his pregnant wife, a lovely woman of around 20 years of age. He was still away when she gave birth and came down with puerperal fever. After a couple of days, the baby died and the young woman showed no improvement. In response to expressions of concern by camp members, I suggested that she be taken to the doctor in Khash. Well, yes, that was a good idea, everyone agreed, except no one in the camp had the right to act on her husband's and family's behalf. They had sent word, but the husband's whereabouts were unknown, and her family lived in Gazu, so it would take about two days for anyone to arrive. As I was the only one with a car, I felt that some responsibility fell on me to transport this woman to the doctor. I therefore offered to drive, if a woman and others of the camp would accompany me. But no one was enthusiastic about following this plan of action. This was because, I was instructed by my campmates, if I took her to the doctor, and she died, I could be held responsible jurally for her death, according to tribal norms. This could mean, I thought, a large blood wealth payment or even an attack on myself or my wife. What could we do then, for we could not just leave her to weaken and die? We must wait, I was told, for her kinsmen to come and take her. And that is what we did. A couple of days later her kin from Gazu arrived and took her to the doctor in Khash. He said it was far too late to do anything for the young woman, and she soon died. My campmates regretted this result and turned their judgment to the person responsible, in their view: the neglectful husband who was not with his wife when he was needed. I kept thinking with sadness about this young woman, feeling a little sick about her death. I tell this story to drive home that Sarhadi women in reproduction—particular individuals, campmates of ours, women that we knew—were in great danger for their lives, and many were lost.

In the black tents of the Sarhad, both women and men make full contributions to their families and households. There does not appear to be any basis for suggesting an imbalance of labor that benefited one gender at the expense of the other. Whether or not this may be the case elsewhere (Bradburd 1990), gendered economic exploitation was not present among the Sarhadi Baluch.

## Shepherds

Do labor relations outside of the household show any signs of exploitation? A clear and obvious case of exploitation—however, for the Sarhad a historical case—was that of slaves captured by the Baluch or born of captives, who were put to agricultural work. And while they undoubtedly misled General R. E. F. Dyer when they told him that they were fed only dung-rolling beetles, they may well have been supported at a fairly low level, permitted to consume considerably less than they were producing. And it is not likely that they were allowed to inherit from the families for whom they were working. On the other hand, as we know from other cases (e.g., the Nuer [Evans-Pritchard 1940]), captives were integrated into some tribal societies and incorporated into families, living much like family members. I have already reported one case of a captive who was married by her captor and fully assimilated into Baluchi society as if she had been a Baluch. The question really is how exploited the slaves were, and on this there is little information. But that there was exploitation of slave labor seems highly likely. Of course, there were no slaves in the Sarhad when I was there, and the descendants of slaves, the Ghulamzai, lived independently and worked for themselves. As the reader will recall, the Halki Ja'far in the spring of 1968 migrated to Kwuhashkan so their young shepherd could collaborate with the shepherd of an independent Ghulamzai camp.

A prominent form of employer-employee relations in the economy of the Sarhad was that of *wasildar* and *shwaneg*. The shepherd worked for other livestock owners, looking after their animals and producing pastoral wealth for them. The question is whether the shepherd was being paid fairly or was being exploited.

One approach to this question takes a Marxist position, drawing on the labor theory of value. The labor theory of value reasons that if some people work for others, whatever the others get really comes from the work of the employee, and except for the "theft" inherent in capital, in the ownership of livestock or land or factories, all of the fruits would go to the workers. In this view, every employee is exploited. Its adherents ignore the fact that the capital, in the case of livestock as in many others, is the accumulation of previous labor, often by the owner himself. Furthermore, the risk of loss remains largely with the owner, so if disease strikes the livestock dead, all previous investment by the owner in the livestock—or date palms, or irrigation system, or whatever the capital resources at work—is lost. Since the Marxist approach slips the answer—yes, all employees are everywhere exploited—in with the assumptions, it does not really illuminate the situation of the Sarhadi shepherd.

According to the market theory of value, if employers are free to hire at the lowest price for which they can find employees, and employees are free to seek the highest price they can get from employers, then the true value of labor will be determined by the free market. This approach is useful in that it identifies a variable, the extent to which the market is free rather than restricted and predetermined, that can be used as a criterion for judging fairness of pay. At the same time, though it does not prejudge positions in the economic system, for example, employer and employee, the way the Marxist approach does, it takes for granted rather than questions the economic system, positions of the participants, and the distribution of wealth. But it does give us a place to start in understanding Sarhadi practices.

Beginning with the market approach, can we say that the market for shepherds in the Sarhad was free? Adults who sought jobs as shepherds were not tied to particular groups of herd owners and in theory could have applied to any herd owners trying to hire a shepherd. This was true within the boundaries of each Sarhadi tribe. But there were practical considerations that inhibited choice.

First, moving away from one's kin and friends, one's established "work team," one's lineage mates, removed a shepherd from his main source of labor coordination, and from political and emotional support and sustenance. This was equally so for the female household head and for the children as it was for the man taking the job as shepherd. Hence moving, even for an economically attractive offer, was not taken lightly. It was, however, a choice made and a decision taken by the principals themselves rather than by someone else.

Second, the age of the shepherd was an important consideration. If a boy was in his early or middle teens—such as Abdulluk, who was *shwaneg* in the Halki Ja'far during 1967–68, was not the head of his own household, and was to a degree under the control of his parents and senior kinsmen—he was not a totally independent actor. If he was wanted as a shepherd by his family and his senior kinsmen, he did not really have the freedom of movement an adult had, or the same bargaining power. His dependence on his family restricted his market possibilities and influenced the terms of his labor. However, Abdulluk's younger brother, Alluk, learned from Abdulluk's experience and refused to work for his uncles, taking a shepherding position with another group instead, and drawing upon his uncles for political support. So even a young teenage boy could, if he insisted, decide for himself.

Third, a tribal labor market could on occasion be restricted by politics, as when a blood feud between lineages or sections required avoidance between members of the conflicting groups and restricted economic collaboration between them. A shepherd from one group would have been at great risk among the adversaries of his group.

The second issue raised by the market approach is what alternative labor possibilities existed for people seeking a job. Sarhadi Baluch were not restricted to the pastoral sector in seeking work. Their multi-resource economy provided multiple opportunities to invest their labor independently—in grain cultivation, date arbori-culture, and external raiding/trading—and also to hire out their labor in other sectors, internally in grain cultivation and externally in manual labor. The extent of accessible labor opportunities and their levels of compensation influenced the internal market for shepherds. The historical evidence indicates that there were three periods in the twentieth century with markedly different market conditions for the Sarhadi Baluch.

For the first third of the century, the Sarhadi Baluch were actively engaged in large-scale raiding outside the Sarhad. Men gained wealth through raiding, which was an alternative to engaging in primary production for oneself or working as a shepherd. This would have reduced the number of those seeking work as a shepherd. Further-more, the inflow of livestock would have increased the demand of herd owners for shepherds. Both of these conditions would have made it a "sellers' market" with good terms for those working as shepherds. Most likely, with the larger household herds derived partly from raiding, herding groups would have consisted of fewer tents, and elder sons would have carried much of the responsibility for herding. Thus the pat-tern would have been more similar to the mountain camps of the Morpish, discussed in chapter 2, or to Ja'far's strategy during the *dokal* of 1970–71.

During the second third of the century, beginning with the conquest of the Sarhad by Reza Shah and the suppression of raiding, and continuing through World War II and the postwar period, the economy of the Sarhadi Baluch declined and labor op-portunities were nugatory in the Sarhad, in Baluchistan, and not very accessible else-where. Some Sarhadi Baluch migrated far, for example, to the Sind, to find work as agricultural laborers, started families, and became indebted, effectively trapped in ex-ile. With the declining wealth in the Sarhad and the dearth of alternative opportuni-ties, there were many Baluch seeking work and a much reduced larder from which to pay them. This was a "buyers' market" and shepherds were not paid well.

By the beginning of the final third of the century, Sarhadi Baluch in large numbers were taking advantage of labor opportunities beyond the Sarhad, notably manual la-bor in the Gulf Emirates and the trading of goods imported from the Gulf or Paki-stan in the wider Iranian goods markets. The Baluch who worked outside of the Sarhad were aware of the growing wealth of Iran and the increased opportunities. In fact, by the mid-1970s Baluch who usually strongly identified themselves with their lineage and tribe, and their locality and region, and who otherwise did not have a lot good to say about Iran, were beginning to talk about "*our* oil wells," which no Baluch I met had ever seen, as the wells were far away, on the other side of Iran. Once again, with Baluch flowing out of the Sarhad and wealth flowing in, the local labor market for shepherds returned to being a "sellers' market." Payment per animal, said in the 1960s to be customarily 5 rials per head, had inflated to 20 rials in the 1970s. This was at least in part a reflection of labor market conditions.

By the late 1970s, the Sarhadi Baluch were so satisfied with their increased standard of living and their economic prospects that they even began calling back long-term exiles. In 1976, a major project among several members of the Halki Ja'far was the rescue of Sab Han (son of) Jan Mahmud Dadolzai from his exile in the Sind. As a young man, more than two decades previously, Sab Han had migrated to the Sind to escape the poverty and bleak prospects of the Sarhad, had founded a family, and had inexorably fallen deeper and deeper into debt, surviving day by day and week by week as an agricultural worker on the land of others. But with the conditions on the Sarhad having improved and the Dadolzai having become more prosperous, Sab Han and his family had to be rescued and brought back to the Sarhad, so his brother Ido and his sister's son Mahmud Karim argued vigorously. To prove and advance their case, Ido and Mahmud Karim took steps to satisfy Sab Han's debt and costs of transport, contributing and collecting from close and distant kinsmen well over 10,000 toman, and they made available a tent and household equipment, contributed and collected livestock for a small herd, and arranged marriages for Sab Han's marriageable children. Sab Han and his family, somewhat bemused by the radical changes in their lives, arrived and took up residence in the Ja'fari Halk during the spring of 1976, an event that I was present to observe.

The Islamic Revolution in Iran took place shortly after Sab Han was repatriated, and the Gulf War followed more than a decade later. Any increased restriction on international travel across the Gulf would have limited or closed the Gulf market previously important to Sarhadi Baluch. There was military disruption in Baluchistan for a period after the Revolution, and jobs from public works, such as road construction and maintenance, would have been suspended. New opportunities did arise for some Baluch, as Baluchistan became a major escape point for urban Iranians, many wealthy or well-to-do, on their way via Pakistan to the West. Negotiating the deserts and mountains of Iranian and Pakistani Baluchistan was a serious matter, and Baluch demanded a high price and were paid well to lead and escort the anxious emigrants. But at least for a time restrictions on travel and a declining national economy must have reduced the opportunities in the external labor market. This downturn would have increased the number of Sarhadi job seekers, leading in turn to greater competition for jobs as shepherds and a decrease in remuneration.

Overall, we may conclude, the labor market for shepherds was both fairly free and fairly open, although susceptible to variations in response to both internal and external circumstances. Compensation for shepherds was accordingly fairly good, although better in a sparsely occupied labor market and less generous in a crowded one. But can we assess whether remuneration for shepherds was fair? This is as much a value judgment as an empirical calculation, so a definitive conclusion is impossible. But various criteria could be considered.

An obvious one is how the standard of living of shepherds compared with that of *wasildar*. How different were the tents, furnishings, clothes, and diet of shepherds from those of their *wasildar?* If the *wasildar* lived much better than the shepherds, then one might ask whether the shepherds were being fairly treated. But if the shepherds lived as well or better than their *wasildar,* then there would be a prima facie case for the fair treatment of shepherds. My assessment for hired shepherds of the Sarhad is that their standard of living was equivalent to that of *wasildar* of the middle rank, somewhat less than that of the wealthiest *wasildar,* and somewhat better than that of the poorest *wasildar.* On this basis, we can say that shepherds were not economically exploited.

Another criterion, one that has been referred to by other authors (e.g., Bradburd 1990; Irons 1994), is whether a shepherd's income was sufficient to allow him to accumulate a herd of his own, so that he too could become an independent pastoralist and live off his flock. During the period 1960–70, shepherds on the Sarhad received—in addition to subsistence supplies, 10 percent of the wool and hair, a per head payment, and the entire flock's milk for three months, milk that could be turned into salable clarified butter—1 newborn in 10 from the flock. In a good year, the number of young *pas* produced was, at each of the six-month gestation periods, about half the size of the total herd, so that in one year, the young should number about the same as the adult herd. If the herd amounted to 200, the young would be something below 200. Of these, the shepherd would receive 15 if there had been 150 newborn, including both male and female. In a poor year, the numbers decreased substantially. During extreme droughts, many or most young *pas* died, a disaster for *wasildar* as well as shepherd. But considering that the average household herd in the Halki Ja'far in 1968 was 6.5 adult *pas* and in 1972 was 13.5 *pas,* a shepherd receiving 15 mixed-sex *pas* or even 10 *pas* would seem to be in a good position to build his own herd. In mid-February 1973, from a flock of 170, Ido was due 13½ *hort* (table 8.6).

Of the total 13½ *hort* that Ido was to receive, at least 5 were females, with the possibility of 7 being females. While the males could be sold, the females would provide more reproductive stock for Ido's own household herd. In terms of shepherd's pay allowing the shepherd's household to build a flock, we would have to conclude that Sarhadi shepherds were treated fairly in that the shepherd was provided the means for independent production and therefore was not dependent on selling his labor in future years. Thus the shepherd among the Sarhadi *baluch* could not be said to be economically exploited.

Why were shepherds well compensated in the Sarhad when elsewhere (Bradburd 1990) they appeared to have been exploited economically? There are two underlying reasons.

The first is the Sarhadi personality. Sarhadi tribal men were raised as warriors, taught to be courageous, to face down difficulties, to take chances. They took pride in penetrating the world beyond the Sarhad and in returning with the rewards of conquest. They were as ready to cross boundaries of danger and the unknown as to cross those of geography, language, and culture. Innovation was for the Sarhadi Baluch ad-

**Table 8.6.** *Hort* Payment for *Shwaneg* Aido, 1972–73

| Paid | Name | Number *Pas* | Number Due[a] | Type Due[b] |
|---|---|---|---|---|
| x | Ja'far | 30 | 2 | 1 male shaneg<br>1 female shaneg |
| x | Dust Mahmud | 20 | 2 | 1 female shaneg<br>1 male gwarag |
| x | Reis | 30 | 2 | 1 female shaneg<br>1 male gwarag |
| x | Komeron | 15 | 1 | 1 male shaneg |
| x | Sahib Dad | 14 | 1 | 1 male gwarag |
| x | Yakbar | 8 | 1 | 1 female gwarag |
| x | Jangi Han | 11 | 1 | 1 female gwarag |
| —[c] | Shams A'din<br>and Zarbonu | 10 | 1 | 1 female shaneg<br>or 1 male gwarag[d] |
| —[c] | Jan Mahmud | 15 | 1 | 1 male shaneg |
| —[c] | Mahmud Karim | 10 | 1 | 1 female shaneg<br>or 1 male gwarag |
| —[c] | Abdulla | 7 | ½ | 1 male shaneg |
| | Total | 170 | 13½ | |

[a]The number of *hort* was based upon the number of newborn and not the number of adult animals in the flock. So there was no direct correspondence between the numbers in the two columns.

[b]Both number and type of *hort* to be paid were to a degree a matter of interpretation and negotiation. In some cases discussion was lengthy and the final result not entirely satisfactory to one or both parties.

[c]Ido collected first from more distant kin, with whom he might or might not be living after the new herding contract, leaving until later his close kin, with whom he had much closer ties and in whom he had much more confidence.

[d]A rough equivalence in value was given to female kids, *shaneg*, and male lambs, *gwarag*. Sheep are given a premium over goats on the market.

venture; new opportunities to win wealth were new fields to conquer. Sarhadi men were ready and able. Sarhadi personality was one of the main reasons that the market for labor was open, that it included opportunities well outside the confines of the Sarhad. Sarhadi personality guaranteed that the men of the black tents would not be a captive labor force in the Sarhad. Sarhadi personality, in consequence, guaranteed a decent return for laboring in the Sarhad.

Shepherds were well compensated also because exchange relations among the Baluch of the black tents did not exist in a social vacuum. The saying "business is business," which implies that exchange follows a strictly economic, market logic, could not apply to the social milieu of the Sarhadi desert. Not only did Sarhadi *baluch* form communities of multiple, overlapping relations—kin, descent, affinal, residential, congregational, and cooperative—but some of these relations, notably descent relations, were vested with the basic welfare tasks of nurturing and support and the basic political tasks of social control and defense. Sarhadi tent dwellers depended upon their fellows, not only for labor cooperation and sociality, but also for economic and political security. Consequently, short-term economic gains earned by driving a hard bargain could lead to hard feelings in those upon whom one depended in the long run for welfare and political support. The saying applicable in the kind of society found in the Sarhadi desert was "What goes around, comes around," and Baluch tended to keep this understanding in mind in their dealings with their fellows. The common and collective welfare and security interests shared by the Baluch led each to see his economic interests as at least partly interrelated with the economic interests of others, rather than opposed to the economic interests of others.

Among tribal, warrior pastoralists like those of the Sarhad and elsewhere (Irons 1972, 1994), exchange relations were never strictly economic relations but always included considerations of political solidarity (Salzman 1992:54–64). Similarly, tribal warriors were never a likely captive labor force, as they were always ready to push outward in search of a happier destiny (Salzman 1999a, 2000). In contrast, peasant pastoralists (Salzman 1996), peaceful shepherds under the control of state authorities, tended to be on the defensive and to have more defensive personalities. They were oriented toward avoiding difficulties by holding to the known and hoping for the benign, and for this reason were captive to their niche. At the same time, security for peasant pastoralists lay not in collective ties with their fellows, but in vertical ties with powerful patrons. So solidarity among peasant pastoralists tended to be more apparent than substantial, and unalloyed economic considerations could be given greater reign.

## Sharecropping

Sharecropping in grain cultivation increased in the Sarhad as irrigation agriculture expanded. As we saw earlier, agricultural laborers—responsible not only for plowing, sowing, weeding, and harvesting, but also for watering and maintaining *jube*, the minor water channels—received 30 percent of the crop, the provider of water and seed 60 percent, and the provider of the plow animal 10 percent. Other harvesters got 4 percent each, presumably "off the top" before the principals received their shares. In addition, the sharecropping laborer received the use of a small plot and water to cultivate his own grain.

The provider of the water was responsible for the maintenance of the capital-intensive *kan* irrigation tunnel or the pump motor and well. This was a considerable investment for the provider of water. Inadequate maintenance could lead to a complete breakdown of the irrigation system and the end of cultivation, as happened at Nugju.

Were the sharecroppers selling their agricultural labor exploited economically? Or did they get a fair return for their labor? Much that has been said about shepherding applies equally to sharecropping labor. The market was free in that one could choose whom to work for and could search for better terms, or, alternatively, one could choose not to engage in this work at all. Income could be supplemented in a range of alternative ways. Likewise, *sharik,* sharecroppers, often worked land owned by lineage mates, with whom they had long-term relations of mutual interdependence: for example, in 1968 Shams A'din and Mahmud Karim worked the Shagbond land of Halil, all three being members of the Dadolzai *brasrend.*

In southern Baluchistan, *shahri* agriculturalists in oases such as Kuhak and Isfandak (Salzman 1978b) who had no water of their own sharecropped for 25 percent of the produce. In rural Kerman, the Persian province adjacent to Baluchistan, theory has it that the five factors of land, water, seed, plow animals, and labor each received 20 percent; sharecroppers providing only labor would thus have received 20 percent of the crop (English 1966:88). But in practice, contracts varied.

> At lower elevations in stable alluvial fan villages the peasant receives 30% of ground crops and 20% of tree crops in return for his labor. In the mountain valleys the peasant's share of ground crops is still 30%, but his share in the tree crops increases from 20% to 30%. In high mountain hamlets sharecroppers receive 50% of the total harvest. In all areas the peasant supplies the same element, labor, and the landlord supplies all other factors in the production of the crop. These differences in the terms of crop-sharing agreements appear to vary according to the needs of the peasant household relative to crop yields. Because yields are lower in the mountain valleys and high mountain hamlets, the peasant's share is correspondingly higher. (English 1966:89)

In Iran in general, sharecropping in irrigation was based upon five factors—land, water, seed, draft animals, and labor—which allocated 20 percent of the crop to the laborers (Lambton 1953:306). But the practice varied greatly from place to place and crop to crop (Lambton 1953:chap. 17).

Sarhadi agricultural laborers, receiving 30 percent of the crop plus the total crop from an additional small plot, appear to have enjoyed somewhat better terms than many sharecropping laborers in irrigation agriculture elsewhere in Baluchistan and Iran. Though the fairness of the terms is a matter of judgment, it seems to me—in view of the open market, alternative possibilities, and share received—that no obvious case can be made that Sarhadi agricultural laborers were exploited economically.

## Standard of Living

Let us consider economic exploitation of Sarhadi Baluch in their relations with the external society. Does the apparently modest standard of living in the Sarhad reflect exploitation by the larger society?

Until the 1930s, the Sarhadi Baluch were effectively independent of outside control. As predatory raiders and slavers, they were the exploiters. The military "pacification" and political "encapsulation" of the Sarhad by Reza Shah and then by Mohammed Reza Shah put an end to raiding and extended control of the government of Iran to the Sarhad. This altered relations between Sarhadi Baluch and the surrounding regions of Iran, ending exploitation of Persian peasants and commercial caravans, but it did not reverse the equation in any obvious way.

In fact, the flow of resources into the Sarhad continued under government aegis. It included supplies, such as famine relief during recurrent droughts, and capital investment, such as the diesel irrigation pump at Garonchin and the road through the valley of the Rudi Mad Shadi between the Sarhad and Hamuni Mashkil. As well, a certain amount of government-funded employment was opened in Baluchistan, such as manual labor on construction and the maintenance of roads and buildings, and positions in local administration, the military, and education. At the commercial level, Sarhadi Baluch were devoting their labors to importing and smuggling foreign goods into Iran for their own pleasure and profit. And while the government and its Persian constituents may have looked to the Sarhad for future profit in mineral extraction or irrigation agriculture, except for a few small Persian peasant villages slowly being infiltrated by Baluch, nothing very substantial had come to fruition up to the Islamic Revolution.

However much economic exploitation was characteristic of stratified agrarian Iran—with its absentee landowners and peasant villagers, its craftpersons, craftchildren, and trading bazaar merchants, and its royal and military elites—remote tribal areas such as the Sarhad of Baluchistan often operated largely beyond the reach of the state and its dependents and operated according to tribal rules. Under latter-day state encapsulation, the Sarhad had changed a great deal, but Sarhadi labor and resources experienced no discernible exploitation by the wider society.

# PART THREE

*Living in Order
and Conflict*

# 9.
# TIES THAT BIND

The Sarhadi Baluch spoke in several ways about the ties that bind people. We have already heard about the formal agreements, *karar*, used to organize herding units and the resulting residence groups, and also about ongoing collaboration in the coordination of labor. Later on I will discuss tribal unity under the chief and the congregational ties of religion. Here we shall explore another prominent "symbolic idiom" used for relating people one to another: that is, the symbolic idiom of biological reproduction, or kinship. The ties established using this idiom were central to the Sarhadi *baluch* as they organized their social life.

The Sarhadi *baluch* identified closeness in biological reproduction with social closeness, and distance in biological reproduction with social distance. But biological closeness was not always calculated the same way. For different purposes, what counted as biological closeness differed. In relationships between individuals, kin ties reckoned bilaterally were deemed most important. But in relations between groups, and between individuals as members of groups, descent through the male line was the criterion used to determine closeness or distance.

## BILATERAL KIN

Filiation, links traced through parents, was a symbolic idiom often used among the Sarhadi Baluch for expressing closeness and distance in diadic relationships between individuals.

### Kinship Terminology

Closeness extended beyond one's own tent, to aunts and uncles and cousins, and farther. This was clearest in the terminology of address, where relatives distinguished

**225**

**Table 9.1.** "Consanguinal" Kinship Reference
Terminology of the Yarahmadzai Baluch

| Generation | Term | Relation |
|---|---|---|
| 3 | Bum piruk | Male great-grandparent or sibling |
| | Bum baluk | Female great-grandparent or sibling |
| 2 | Piruk | Male grandparent or sibling |
| | Baluk | Female grandparent or sibling |
| 1 | Pes | Father |
| | Mas | Mother |
| | Naku | Father's or mother's brother |
| | Tru | Father's or mother's sister |
| | Piruk zad | Grandparent's male sibling's children |
| | Baluk zad | Grandparent's female sibling's children |
| 0 | Bras | Brother |
| | Gohar | Sister |
| | Naku zad | Parent's male sibling's children |
| | Tru zad | Parent's female sibling's children |
| +1 | Zag | Son |
| | Dotag | Daughter |
| | Brazad | Brother's children |
| | Gohar zad | Sister's children |
| | Rend | Children of naku zad |
| | Baluk zad | Children of tru zad |

as closer and less close in the referential kinship terminology—for example, brothers, *bras,* and cousins, *naku zad* and *tru zad* (table 9.1)—were addressed with the same words. For example, male siblings and first cousins were all addressed with the term *laleh,* and female siblings and first cousins were all addressed with the term *dadeh,* and by extension more distant cousins could also be addressed by these terms (table 9.2). Similarly, mother, *mas,* and aunts, *tru,* were both addressed as *mukay.* Even the referential terms were often extended to more distant relatives, for example, in referring to a grandparent's sibling's child, precisely a *baluk zad* or *piruk zad,* as a *tru* or *naku.* But especially the referential terms for brother, *bras,* and sister, *gohar,* were extended to cousins and beyond.

Using these terms of address, a child addressed mother and aunts with the same word, addressed brothers and male cousins with the same word, and addressed sisters and female cousins with the same word. This terminological equivalence implied social equivalence, in effect specifying the equal closeness of mother and aunts, of brothers and male cousins, and sisters and female cousins. The same was true in the use of the referential terms *bras,* brother, and *gohar,* sister, for cousins. The conventions of terms of address and, to a degree, terms of reference expressed and rein-

**Table 9.2.** Terms of Address

| Relation | Term |
| --- | --- |
| Father and children (reciprocal) | *Babeh* |
| Mother, aunts, and children (reciprocal) | *Mukay* |
| Uncle and nieces, nephews (reciprocal) | *Kakeh* |
| Brothers and male cousins | *Laleh* |
| Sisters and female cousins | *Dadeh* |

forced the categorical equivalence of a range of kinsmen and thus their equivalent closeness. In effect, these terms and usages asserted that kin of two degrees, ego's mother's sister, was as close as one of one degree, mother. Or that kin of three degrees, mother's sister's child, was as close as one of two degrees, ego's mother's other child, that is, one's sibling. This meant that aunts and cousins, and to a lesser extent uncles and other kin, were conceptually drawn into the circle of maximal kin closeness. The psychological and social consequences were that Sarhadi Baluch felt and expressed this closeness in their interactions and relationships with kinsmen outside of their immediate nuclear families.

### *Kom, Peskom,* and *Maskom*

Relatives traced through father and mother—one additional link to grandparents, aunts and uncles, and siblings; two additional links to great-grandparents, first cousins, and children of siblings; and so on—identified one's kin, *kom,* from the point of view of the individual, the "ego" at the center of a network of kin ties. As such, the *kom* did not have definite boundaries; but, in principle if not always in practice, the higher number of links needed to reach someone, the weaker was the kinship connection. Nor, of course, did the *kom* form a discrete unit, for the *kom* of "ego" overlapped partly with those of his or her cousins on each side.

Sarhadi Baluch referred to relatives through the mother as *maskom* and those through the father as *peskom.* But there was not a strong emphasis on one or the other. The important consideration for most purposes of individual relationships was how close, irrespective of on which side, the individuals were. For example, Ido Mahmud was Shams A'din's father's father's brother's son's son, a second cousin in the male line, but he was also Shams A'din's mother's brother, and this was how Shams A'din usually referred to him, as *naku;* and for his part, Ido referred to Shams A'din as his *gohar zad,* sister's son.

The equivalence of matrilateral and patrilateral kin, the *maskom* and *peskom,* was expressed in several ways:

First, Baluch stated explicitly that *maskom* and *peskom* were *yeki,* that is, one and the same, and equivalent in value.

Second, this assertion was consistent with referential kinship terminology (see table 9.1), in which the same terms were used for patrilateral and matrilateral kin. For example, father's brother and mother's brother were both *naku;* father's sister and mother's sister were both *tru;* father's father and mother's father were both *piruk;* first cousins on both sides were aunt's children, *tru zad,* or uncle's children, *naku zad.* No difference between *maskom* and *peskom* was expressed in terms of reference.

Third, terms of address followed this equivalence between *mascom* and *pescom.* For example, all male siblings and cousins on both sides were addressed as *laleh* and all female siblings and cousins on both sides were addressed as *dadeh.* Mother and aunts on both sides were addressed as *mukay.* Uncles on both sides were addressed as *kakeh.* No difference between *maskom* and *peskom* was expressed in terms of address.

Fourth, the marriage preference was for close kin, *maskom* and *peskom,* both serving well. For example, of the five marriages of the children of Gulap and Zarbonu, there was an even distribution between *maskom* and *peskom:* two were to father's brother's children, two were to mother's brother's children, and the fifth was more distant. Likewise with the marriages of Ja'far's two daughters, one each to *maskom* and *peskom:* one was with a father's brother's son, the other with a father's mother's sister's daughter's son.

In spite of the often-stated equivalence of *maskom* and *peskom,* however, there was an uncertainty and sometimes a slightly uncomfortable acknowledgment that *peskom* was a bit more important. The reason for this was not hard to find. The formation of kinship groups, lineages, which were invested with important political and welfare responsibilities, was based upon unilineal descent through males. The presence and major role of patrilineages gave to the paternal side an additional weight. This additional weight was conceptualized symbolically in terms of biological inheritance. Sarhadi Baluch used the term *pusht,* back, to represent the father's side. From *pusht,* they said, comes *huien,* blood, and bone. The term *lap,* abdomen or gut, was used to represent the mother's side. From *lap,* they say, comes only *pust,* skin. This formulation, which gave more weight to the *pusht* of the *peskom* and less weight to the *lap* of the *maskom,* provided a symbolic basis for groups defined in terms of the patriline.

Strictly speaking, any greater weight given to patrikin in relation to matrikin should have been contingent upon the sphere of action, that is, whether it was a matter of interpersonal relations, in which case *kom* of equivalent distance were equal irrespective of line, or whether it was a matter of group, political action, in which case the patriline was the basis of association. But, as we have seen in other spheres where specific interactions were skewed by the multiple overlapping relations of the individuals involved, the lineage system threw a shadow of influence over the bilateral kinship, weighting slightly more the patrikin.

But it would not be precise to say that there was general or conscious favoring of the patrikin. My impression is that people preferred to keep the two spheres—bilateral kinship and unilineal descent—separate and not to think about any possible contradiction. When I raised the issue, no one was keen to talk about it, and when they did, they tended to say contradictory things. But even when there was an acknowledgment of some greater weight having to be attached to patrikin, this was in many actual cases moot, more a conceptual than practical matter. The reason for this is that many marriages were with relatively close patrikin, so that matrikin were in fact also patrikin. Shams A'din's and Mahmud Karim's matrikin, relatives linked to them through their mother Zarbonu, were also patrikin of two generations' greater distance. The pattern was even tighter when fathers' brothers' children married, for then the matrikin of the children were patrikin only one generation more distant.

The ties of the *kom* were diadic ties of one or more links. The links connected through women as well as men, irrespective of the crossing of descent group boundaries. For example, Ja'far was Id Mahmud's mother's, mother's sister's son, and referred to himself as Id Mahmud's *naku*, uncle.

Each individual, then, had a network of relatives, *kom*, centering on her- or himself. These relatives were obliged, in a general way, to give aid and support, the degree of obligation being roughly related to distance. Such generalized support would consist of access to resources, financial aid, political assistance, residential place, and supervision of women, children, livestock, and property. The *kom* was looked to for a spouse. But it would be incorrect to see the *kom* as a network with cut-and-dried rights and duties. Rather, the obligation vested in these ties was a recognition of the legitimacy of claims for assistance. But previous interaction and exchange between the parties, and the particularities of the individuals concerned and the circumstances, all affected the outcome of the requests.

Furthermore, the concept of *kom* was stretched, when convenient and desirable, to characterize relationships of some distance. In other words, the kinship idiom was used to justify and sanctify relationships entered into by reason of expediency or need.

For example, Malik Hartun was said to be *naku zad*, uncle's child, to Isa, indicating that they were fairly close *kom* before marriage. The actual tie, however, was that Malik Hartun was Isa's father's mother's brother's son's son's daughter, and Isa was Malik Hartun's father's father's father's sister's son's son, which even by Baluchi reckoning is not close kin. But it suited everyone that Malik Hartun and Isa be *kom*, and so she was deemed his *naku zad*.

But even the concept of *kom* could stretch only so far. When Karim Han, after searching nearby, ultimately took a wife from the unrelated Gonguzai at Gazu, he had to say that he had married outside his *kom*.

Likewise, it would not have been possible to go to a distant member of the tribe and attempt to gain access to his well on the grounds that they were *kom*. Such a use of the idiom would have had no credibility and carried no weight. Where there were links that could credibly justify the use of the *kom* idiom, the significance of those links were overcommunicated by those wishing to agree to some assistance or to some common project, and undercommunicated by those not agreeing.

Similarly, the kinship idiom was used in some situations to deny and ignore any distinction between *maskom* and *peskom,* while in other situations the distinction was invoked and emphasized. Haji Komeron's wife, Nur Bi, was referred to as Dadolzai, although only her *lap* was Dadolzai, her *pusht* being Mir Alizai. Rahmat's wife was said to be Rahmatzai, but that was her *lap,* her *pusht* being Nusherwani and not related to the Yarahmadzai tribe at all. Musa, in the context of his plan to join the Ja'fari Halk, asserted that he was Dadolzai. Mahmud Karim independently referred to Musa as Dadolzai. Musa's *pusht* was Dust Mahmudzai, but his father's mother was Dadolzai. Gul Sim, being referred to by someone who did not like her, said that she was Hoseinzai, and she heard and piped up to say that her *pusht* was Dust Mahmudzai Miradoli, which showed that she was from the Soherabzai tribal section just like the Dadolzai, and thus closer than the Hoseinzai tribal section. Jangi Han justified his presence at the *bonendi* Dadolzai, the Dadolzai settlement at the Gorani date groves, by saying that he was Dadolzai, and other Dadolzai agreed. That Jangi Han's *maskom* was Dadolzai and his *peskom* Hoseinzai did not matter, made no difference, according to the other Dadolzai. However, when it was thought that Jangi Han had stolen some property, the members of the Dadolzai were quick to disassociate themselves from him, saying that he was Hoseinzai and not Dadolzai.

Sometimes, the Sarhadi Baluch stretched kin labels and ignored kin distinctions such as *maskom* and *peskom* to associate people, to stress their common identity. At other times, they made stricter use of kin labels and carefully applied kin distinctions such as *maskom* and *peskom* to identify differences among people and to disassociate some from others, distancing them from one another. The difference in usage was usually situational and conditional, according to the demands being made and the normative costs involved, but also had a temperamental dimension, according to the individuals involved and their personal relationships.

## THE PATRILINEAGE

The other important social idiom based upon natural procreation focused not upon filiation from ego, but more selectively upon descent through the male line. Sarhadi tent dwellers, using this idiom, formed discrete, nonoverlapping groups, lineages.

### Lineage Theory in Baluchistan and in Anthropology

For the most part, my Baluchi friends and acquaintances were interested in me in immediate and specific ways rather than in a more general fashion. That is, they were initially interested in whether I was, like other Westerners of whom they had heard, going to try to convert them to Christianity, whether I was going to report their activities to agents of the Iranian government, or whether I would drive them places in my Land Rover. Although I was always ready to discourse on the differences between North American society and culture and Baluchi culture and society, the Baluch expressed very little interest—and this they shared with some of my students back in North America—in hearing my lengthy and perhaps turgid sociological accounts.

I was asked how Joan and I were related before we were married, and it certainly did get our Baluchi friends' attention when I told them that Joan and I were not related at all, and that our marriage was not in fact arranged, that we had met on our own and decided to marry on our own without any need to consult our parents. At this our friends were astonished and pleasantly scandalized. But they did not show great curiosity about where I came from or what my life was there in general. However, two things were commonly asked. One was how much money I made, a question that is standard in Persian society and that they must have picked up outside the Sarhad where they and others sometimes worked for wages and salaries. The other was how large my lineage was. When I answered that where I came from we did not have lineages, there was a kind of stunned silence. The standard follow-up was, "What do you do if you get into trouble; who do you go to?" My reply that we go to the police to get help always generated great mirth and raucous laughter, a reaction similar to what we would hear in less advantaged parts of our own society. This question about my lineage put to me by the Baluch was, however inappropriate to my life, strongly indicative of the Sarhadi frame of reference and the organization of the lives of Sarhadi tent dwellers.

Lineages—corporate groups defined by unilineal descent—played a large part in the social thinking of the Sarhadi Baluch, and the Baluch believed that lineages played an important part in the way they lived. Through descent, everyone belonged to a series of more and less inclusive lineages, which defined to a degree individual identity and established certain rights and responsibilities. Lineages were vested with specified obligations and in certain situations became groups in order to act on behalf of their memberships. What, then, was the part played by lineages in the life of Sarhadi Baluch?

We do not come to this subject with a blank slate. On the contrary, the nature and significance of lineages has been the subject of intense discussion among anthropologists for at least 50 years (Kuper 1988:chap. 10). This is not the place to review the literature in detail, an exercise that itself would take at least an entire book. But it may be useful for me to make clear my position and to situate my discussion of the Sarhadi Baluch within this ongoing discourse.

The apical ancestor of lineage studies is E. E. Evans-Pritchard, whose account (1940) of the segmentary lineage system of the Nuer provided anthropology not only with a brilliant account of an acephalous tribal political system of "ordered anarchy," thus challenging Hobbesian social philosophical assumptions of chaos in the absence of a hierarchical sovereign, but also a general model of fission and fusion and balanced oppositions that could be applied to other acephalous societies (e.g., Evans-

Pritchard 1949). Whether Evans-Pritchard intended to provide a general model is doubtful, but taken up the lineage model was, and with a vengeance. For at least two decades it was dignified as a theory, and anthropologists at ethnographic sites around the world tried to apply it.

By the 1960s "lineage theory" had been overstretched, and a backlash was generated by a new generation of anthropologists anxious, as always, to make their own contribution. Whereas a few short years before, "lineage theory" had been deemed widely applicable, it quickly became rejected as a model *non grata,* inapplicable most everywhere and not even reflecting any reality among those peoples who held it as a "folk model," as part of their cultural framework of social organization (e.g., Peters 1967; cf. Salzman 1978c). We were even treated to the amazing insight that lineage theory, derived as it was from acephalous pastoralists living in vast rural terrains, did not describe with accuracy social relations in cities and towns governed by a state apparatus (Geertz 1979; Rosen 1984). Even today, there remains some small, deconstructionist cachet in "lineage theory" bashing, although it is more a stirring up of the dust of a long destroyed icon than anything else (e.g., Munson 1993, 1995; reply by Gellner 1995). There are even those who, apparently desperate to score points, purport to discover corrupting lineage theory in the works of those who intend, and to most readers appear, to take a quite different approach (e.g., Street 1990, 1992; Wright 1992, 1994; cf. Barth 1992; Salzman 1995a).

Many theoretical approaches and analytical models in anthropology have had similar fates to lineage theory, enjoying a period of enthusiastic endorsement as a brilliant new insight that transformed our understanding and buried earlier, outmoded approaches, then suffering a rejection as the approach itself became the target of new and alternative theories and models. Evolutionism and stages of development, diffusionism and borrowing across cultures, configurationalism and cultural themes, personality and culture and typical personality, functionalism and the interconnection of institutions, transactionalism and individual decisions, structuralism and deep structure, political economy and class, symbolic analysis and meaning, right up to today's postmodernism and subjective moralism—all these approaches have had their advocates and ascendancy as a dominant theory, followed rapidly by their critics and collapse. Now a cynic might say that anthropological thought at any given moment is driven more by the intellectual imperatives of career advancement to invent a new paradigm, theory, or model and become the initiator of a new "school," or by ideological enthusiasms to support a favored ethnicity, class, or gender, than by a disinterested desire for a real increase in understanding of our purported subject matter. Even a sympathetic observer might comment that our radically individualistic research strategy makes it very difficult for any anthropologist to examine more than one aspect of society and culture, which encourages futile and self-defeating theoretical debates about which aspect is most important.

Whatever the reasons, the ethnographer who takes the view, as I do, that there is a reality "out there," and that he or she is obliged to provide as accurate as possible an account of the social and cultural reality of the people under study, is left in a quandary by this repeated round of theoretical fads and fashions. What happens if what is going on among the people being studied is not, at the moment of research or publication, theoretically "correct"? As a structuralist in search of deep structure, must one ignore economic classes, exploitation, and class conflict? Does a political economist have to downplay individual calculations, decisions, and initiatives? As a symbolic analyst looking for meaning, does one assume that personality structures are unimportant? Although some anthropologists, mostly those of the postmodern persuasion, having enthusiastically emersed themselves in the swamps of epistemology, have declared that everything is subjective and that there is no reality to be known, I prefer to follow the lead of people who are actually living lives and who welcome a "reality check." So I would say that the ultimate referent for anthropological knowledge is social life and culture "out there," beyond the lives and thoughts of anthropologists. Without this empirical referent, anthropology is no more than a precious conceit, even if an entertaining one.

The question then becomes not what is the hot issue or model in anthropology at the moment, but what is important in the lives of the people about whom we are purporting to report. If we are looking at landless agricultural workers, questions of class and economic exploitation might be highly relevant. If the people we are considering face major changes and new opportunities, questions of personality and choice are likely to be relevant. In the case of the Sarhadi Baluch, tent-dwelling nomads living on the margins of state control, lineage "theory" might prove to be relevant. It is the ethnographic case that should determine what is relevant and important, not the anthropologist. In other words, in ethnographic research, the existence and importance of economic class and exploitation, or entrepreneurship, or lineages is an empirical question rather than a theoretical one. The answer should be determined by the lives of the people being studied, not by the current theoretical discourse in anthropology.

When I initiated research among the Sarhadi Baluch, I knew perfectly well that different peoples organized themselves in many different ways, and that nomadic tribes varied one from another in their principles of organization (Salzman 1967). Barth's (1961) account of the Basseri, which documents a nomadic tribe politically organized primarily in terms of a hierarchical chiefship and economically organized primarily in terms of individual decisions at the household level, and in which there was no segmentary lineage system, was well known to me when I set out for the field. I certainly did not set out for the Sarhad in search of lineage organization or even with expectations that I would find lineage organization. While necessary to assert, because of the current, subjectivist, antiempirical mode in anthropology, it is nonetheless astonishing to have actually to declare that I went to the Sarhad to learn what Sarhadi Baluch were doing, to discover the ways that they set about organizing themselves and pursuing their lives, rather than to impose on the Sarhad some model of organization that I imported with me. Now this does not mean that my account is correct, or accurate, or complete. There are vast territories between hope and achievement, between intention and result. But to this extent, some confidence is justified: what is said about lineages among Sarhadi Baluch has been largely derived inductively from my observations on the basis of what Baluch said and did, rather than having been imposed by myself, deductively from "lineage theory." If the Sarhadi Baluch—or the Somali (Helander 1998), or the Berbers (Kraus 1998)—clung unfashionably to a theoretically passé form of social organization, the fault was theirs, not mine.

## Constructing Lineages

In the Sarhad, the concept of descent from a common ancestor through the male line was recognized and used as a basis for organizing groups. People, both men and women, were deemed to belong to the same descent group, or lineage, if they were descended from a particular common ancestor, whereas if they were descended from different ancestors of the same generation, they belonged to different lineages. Because descent through one line provided each individual with one and only one ancestor at each generational level, lineages were exclusive groups; each person was a member of one and only one lineage at each level of generational depth. At the same time, the farther one went back in the genealogy of ancestors, the more people were included as members of the descent group, or lineage. Similarly, the closer one came in the genealogy of ancestors, the fewer people were included as members of the descent group.

The Sarhadi term for patrilineage was *rend*. This term also had more general meanings, including "line" and "track," of which the notion of descent can be seen to be a particular case. Another term for descent was *zat,* which was used in exactly the same fashion as *rend* in its restricted sense. Its more general meaning was to give birth and was related to *-zai,* the suffix used with a name, for example, Abdulzai, to indicate the descendants of the person named, Abdul.

Depth of the patrilineage, from living members to the founding ancestor, was not indicated by the term *rend. Rend* could be used to refer to an entire tribe, such as the Yarahmadzai or Gamshadzai; the members of the Yarahmadzai tribe were the "descendants of Yarahmad," and the members of the Gamshadzai tribe were "descendants of Gamshad." *Rend* also was used for tribal sections, such as the Soherabzai of the Yarahmadzai, for maximal lineages, such as the Nur Mahmudzai of the Soherabzai, for minimal lineages, such as the Dadolzai of the Nur Mahmudzai, and for microlineages, such as the Dust Mahmudzai of the Dadolzai. The term *rend* was used for both the line of patrilineal descent and the descent groups defined by reference to a particular apical ancestor.

**Table 9.3.** Some Genealogical Ties among Selected Members
of the Halki Ja'far

|  | | | |
|---|---|---|---|
|  | | *The Shirdelzai* | |
| gen 3 | | (Shirdel) | |
| | | V | |
| gen 2 | (Shakar) | (Mulla) | (Isa) |
| | V | V | V |
| gen 1 | {Karim Han} | Reis & Dust Mahmud | Ja'far |

|  | | |
|---|---|---|
| | *The Dust Mahmudzai* | |
| gen 3 | (Dust Mahmud) | |
| | V | |
| gen 2 | {Gulap} | (Dad Huda) |
| | V | V |
| gen 1 | Shams A'din, M. Karim, Shams Hartun | Dust Mahmud |
| | V | |
| gen 1A | Abdulla | |

*Note:* (deceased); {deceased during fieldwork}.

Let us illustrate by looking at the lineage membership of selected individuals in the Halki Ja'far (table 9.3). Ja'far's father's father was Shirdel, who was also father's father of Karim Han, Reis, and Dust Mahmud (son of) Mulla. Together they formed the Shirdelzai microlineage. Shams A'din, Mahmud Karim, and Dust Mahmud (son of) Dad Huda had a common father's father, Dust Mahmud. Together they formed the Dust Mahmudzai microlineage.

At this level of genealogical depth (three generations counting up from mature adults), the Shirdelzai and the Dust Mahmudzai formed two separate lineages. However, Shirdel and Dust Mahmud were brothers, and so at the next level up, their father, Dadol, was the common ancestor of all of their descendants (table 9.4). At this level, the Shirdelzai and the Dust Mahmudzai disappeared into the Dadolzai. The Dadolzai was part of more encompassing lineages, up to the tribal level (table 9.5).

## Using Lineages

The significance of these genealogical connections was that the Sarhadi Baluch used them in organizing social and political relations. Several principles defined the use of genealogy.

First, at a formal level, all the members of a common ancestor were deemed to be members of an exclusive group. The size of the group generally depended upon the depth of the genealogy; the farther back the ancestor was, the larger the number of living individuals in the group.

**Table 9.4.** The Dadolzai and Its Subsections

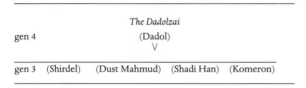

| | The Dadolzai | | | |
|---|---|---|---|---|
| gen 4 | (Dadol) V | | | |
| gen 3 | (Shirdel) | (Dust Mahmud) | (Shadi Han) | (Komeron) |

**Table 9.5.** The Yarahmadzai Tribe and Its Major Divisions and Some Subdivisions

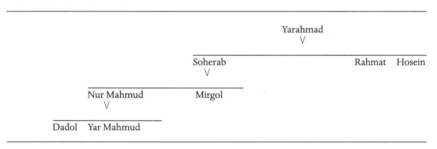

Yarahmad V

Soherab V — Rahmat Hosein

Nur Mahmud V — Mirgol

Dadol Yar Mahmud

However, whether individuals at any given moment thought of themselves and took action in terms of descent group membership, and if they did, which descent group defined by which common ancestor at what genealogical depth, depended upon the circumstances. That is, each Baluch could think of himself or herself and act on a number of different bases: as a member of a tent; as a party to a contractual tie, such as *wasildar* and *shwaneg*; as part of a web of bilateral kinship, *kom*; as a member of an informal work term; as a member of a residential community, *halk*; as a participant in a religious congregation; and as a member of a number of more or less inclusive patrilineages. In certain situations, particularly those of conflict, Sarhadi Baluch usually thought of themselves and others as members of patrilineages.

The second principle defining the use of genealogy was what has come to be called by anthropologists "complementary opposition." This was the rule that determined which, among the larger or smaller lineages to which each individual belonged, was relevant in any given situation. The criterion was the genealogical distance of the other individuals involved in the dispute or conflict. The closer the individuals were to one another, the more recent the genealogical referents and the smaller the opposed lineages; the more distant the individuals were, the farther back in the genealogy were the appropriate referents, and the larger the lineage groups involved.

For example, Ja'far in opposition to Mahmud Karim was Shirdelzai while Mahmud Karim was Dust Mahmudzai; but in relation to a member of the Yar Mahmudzai, both Ja'far and Mahmud Karim were Dadolzai. In confrontation with someone from the Husainzai section of the tribe, Ja'far, Mahmud Karim, and men and women from the Yar Mahmudzai would consider themselves Soherabzai, as in fact happened in events to be recounted later.

One corollary of complementary opposition was that each individual saw lineages opposed to his or hers from the outside as unitary entities, even though they, too, were made up of numerous smaller lineages. Consequently, although people knew well the subdivisions within their own line, most did not know most of the sublineages in collateral and occasionally oppositional lineages.

For example, the Dadolzai and Yar Mahmudzai were both Nur Mahmudzai, and were distinguished from the collateral line Mirgolzai, although both Nur Mahmudzai and Mirgolzai were Soherabzai. Members of the Nur Mahmudzai referred to all members of the constituent lineages of the Mirgolzai as Mirgolzai, not distinguishing between members of the Mirgolzai minimal lineages: Balachzai, Nasra Dinzai, Subazai, Dad Mahmudzai, Kaderzai, Shah Golzai, Mah Betzai, Mir Hanzai, and Mirakzai. Similarly, Mirgolzai tended to refer to members of the Nur Mahmudzai as Nur Mahmudzai, without reference to such subdivisions as Dadolzai and Yar Mahmudzai.

Members of the Soherabzai tribal section did know that the Hoseinzai tribal section had three important divisions, although they did not always agree on what they were. Nezar Mahmud, the brother of the tribal Sardar, identified the major divisions of the Hoseinzai section as the Huseinzai, Rushanzai, and Shiruzai, as did Ja'far. Walli Mahmud, the elder who had fought General R. E. F. Dyer and who later took a Persian peasant captive as wife, said the divisions were Rushanzai, Shiruzai, and Surizai. The elder Lashkar Han did not know subdivisions, while Sayid Mahmud said that Husein was a son of Soherab. A Rushanzai informant was, of course, able to give a detailed account, indicating that Hosein had two sons, Saidi and Mir Bik, and that Rushan and Shiru were Saidi's sons and Husein was Mir Bik's son. Returning to the point of view of the Soherabzai, what they found important were the three strong subdivisions of the Hoseinzai section, not their exact genealogical connection.

The place of the Surizai was also a matter of disagreement. Suri was said by Nezar Mahmud, Lashkar Han, and Sayid Mahmud to be a son of Yarahmad and brother of Soherab, Hosein, and Rahmat. Walli Mahmud said that he was a son of Hosein. Ja'far said that Suri was the brother-in-law of Yarahmad, which would mean that the Surizai were not members of the Yarahmadzai tribe. At various points, some people said to me that the Surizai were Yarahmadzai and others said that they were not. This uncertainty suggests that the Surizai were politically marginal to other Yarahmadzai, perhaps because of small size and distant location.

Similarly, Yelli was identified by three of the informants as a son of Yarahmad and brother of Soherab, Hosein, and Rahmat, while two, including Nezar Mahmud, the brother of the Sarhad, did not mention Yelli at all. This indicates that the Yellizai was a small and politically unimportant section. In fact, I never heard a reference, outside of these genealogical recountings, of the Yellizai.

The third principle defining the use of genealogy was the well-established and valorized central tenet of Sarhadi tribal social and political philosophy that genealogical closeness was equivalent to social and political closeness, and that this closeness had to be manifested in solidarity among individuals. This principle was expressed through the concept of *topak,* solidarity. From the point of view of Sarhadi tent dwellers, individuals descended from a common ancestor should show solidarity toward one another. A descent group, those individuals descended from a common ancestor, could be *patopak,* acting with social and political solidarity, or *beatopak,* acting without social and political solidarity. For Sarhadi *baluch,* to say that a group was *patopak* was always an approbation, while to say that a group was *beatopak* was always a disapprobation.

The principle of genealogically based solidarity consisted of two precepts. One was that the individual was obliged to side with and support those genealogically closer in preference or in any opposition to those genealogically more distant. The other aspect was that one was obliged to provide support, sustenance, and care for fellow descendants of common ancestors, the more so the closer the ancestor and thus the closer one's fellow descendants were.

However, certain levels of the descent group were specially marked. One was the tribal level. The Sarhadi tribes—Yarahmadzai, Gamshadzai, Ismailzai—were descent groups that functioned as the largest unit of permanent political solidarity, beyond which relations were thought of as foreign relations. The other marked descent group was the only one with a special name; the "minimal lineage," as I have called it, was in local terminology the *brasrend,* "lineage of brothers." This was the largest lineage, usually between 50 and 150 adults, within which there was considerable coresidence and frequent, sustained, and deliberate face-to-face interaction. It was within the *brasrend* that collective responsibility was clearest and the demands of assistance most binding. It was the *brasrend* that was most salient in the minds of the Baluch, most relevant for self-identification—although the principle of cognitive complementary opposition operated, so that Sarhadi identity was to a degree contextually defined. For most Baluch, it was with the members of one's *brasrend* that one had most day-to-day business, most ongoing ties, most demanding responsibilities.

While the concept of *topak* was meant to apply at all levels of descent group, it was to the *brasrend* that the notion of *topak* was most especially applied. A *brasrend* that would come to one's aid—militarily in conflict, politically for conflict resolution and influence, economically in labor and contribution, socially in emotional support—a lineage that will *jama kon,* come together, for collective action on behalf of its members, was regarded as *patopak.* It was most commonly to *brasrend* mates that one turned in time of need, and it was they who more than others were obliged to provide support and assistance. Security was to be found, if anywhere, in one's *brasrend,* and it was upon one's *brasrend* that one ultimately depended. Mother's relatives, *maskom,* and affines of other lineages might assist as individuals, but *brasrend* were obliged to assist; *maskom* might be close and dependable, but members of one's *brasrend* had an obligation to be *patopak.*

To illustrate, let us return briefly to the migrations of the Ja'fari Halk and to the fission, or splitting, of the Halk in the spring of 1973. At the most overt level, the split was between two factions of *wasildar*, one of larger herd owners who insisted on an aggressive migration policy and intensive care from the shepherd, the other of smaller herd owners who had a variety of interests, who wanted to pursue extensive migration only when absolutely necessary, and who were satisfied with the work of the shepherd. At the time of the split, the headman was ineffectual owing to illness and was not capable of reconciling the two factions. In principle, this is all as it should have been, for the *halk* was a herding group based upon an annual shepherding contract between *wasildar* and *shwaneg* and was designed to allow differences of interest to be manifested and to allow splitting and reorganization of the *halk*.

The matter was complicated, however, because Sarhadi *halk* members were not only partners in a herding contract but had many other relationships that overlapped those contractual relationships. One such relationship was lineage ties, which, with their associated obligations of solidarity and support, could influence and thus distort other relationships, such as the ostensibly, interest-based, contractual herding relationships.

In reviewing the events of the split in the Halk, we can see the influence of lineage ties as they pulled and tugged at the frankly economic herding interests of the parties. One puzzle was why Ja'far twice agreed to split off with two other camp members, thus separating from the bulk of the Halk. Reis and Dust Mahmud had argued that in the interests of their livestock they had to separate from the others. Further, they argued that Ja'far had to join them because he and they were *bras*, brothers. What this meant was that they—Ja'far, Reis, and Dust Mahmud Mulla—were closer in descent than the other camp members, because they were Shirdelzai Dadolzai, fathers' brothers' children. The others, who were Komeronzai, Dust Mahmudzai, and Shadi Hanzai Dadolzai, were more distant fathers' fathers' brothers' children. In other words, Reis and Dust Mahmud called upon Ja'far to honor microlineage solidarity and support, even though herding camp arrangements were not, strictly speaking, lineage business.

Ja'far stated that he agreed to separate with Reis and Dust Mahmud because they had few tents and few animals. And he publicly denied that lineage affiliation was a consideration in his mind; he was, he asserted, equally close to both groups. Ja'far refused to use lineage idiom to justify his choice, but his statement that he was equally close to both sides, that all were fathers' brothers' sons, was in fact a distortion. Whether or not Ja'far was swayed to join the other Shirdelzai in their separation from the other Dadolzai by reasons of agnatic affiliation, the split was indeed along cleavage lines between descent groups.

The split was thought of as lineage based by many of the others, members of the Dust Mahmudzai, Shadi Hanzai, and Komeronzai, such as Ido and Mahmud Karim, who during the course of this separation referred at least occasionally to the other halk as the Shirdelzai. Ja'far, in his denials of preference for the Shirdelzai over the other, in referring to all Dadolzai as fathers' brothers' sons, and in his refusal to use a lineage idiom, was undercommunicating differences within the Dadolzai, a common rhetorical technique of an experienced leader, and an overt expression of *topak* with the Dadolzai as a whole. He also took care to indicate that he was asked by Reis, and that he did not initiate the split, thus shifting elsewhere as much responsibility as possible. Reis, who always insisted on following an aggressive migration policy, was called *beatopak*, lacking in proper solidarity, by some Dadolzai of the other faction, for his unwillingness to compromise so that they all could reside together.

Although the herding contract and *halk* formation were not lineage matters, both factions invoked lineage *topak* to advance their cases. One faction invoked microlineage *topak* to split the camp, while the other invoked *brasrend topak* to unite all factions in one camp. Ja'far, in the end, undercommunicated microlineage affiliation in order to assert *brasrend* unity. The repeated resort to the rhetoric of lineage solidarity, particularly in regard to matters for which it was not strictly relevant, suggests the symbolic power among the Sarhadi tent dwellers of lineage organization and its associated norms of solidarity and support.

The importance of the *brasrend* and the necessity for *topak* was nowhere clearer than in political conflict and violent confrontation, for the *brasrend* was the entity that had collective responsibility for blood vengeance. This subject is taken up in chapter 10.

## AFFINITY

Marriage among the Sarhadi Baluch established a relationship not only between a woman and a man, but also between their kin (see table 9.6). Marriage did not establish a diadic tie, but a complex one both among many individuals and between patrilineages as well.

### Marriage: Choosing a Spouse

Marriage was a family affair in several senses. First, marriage was the start of a new family of procreation and eventually, usually sooner than later, a separate household. Second, marriage was preferably between close kin, the closer the better beyond the limits of forbidden, incestuous ties with parents, parents' siblings, siblings, and siblings' children. Third, marriage established yet new ties, affinal ties, among people in many cases already related through lineal descent and lateral kinship, if not earlier affinal bonds. Fourth, marriages, and the various payments and promises relating to them, were usually arranged by elder relatives, particularly mothers and fathers if they were alive, of the bride and groom.

In the selection of mates for their children, parents looked closely at a number of

**Table 9.6.** Affinal Kinship Reference Terminology of the Yarahmadzai Baluch

| Term | Relation |
|------|----------|
| *Zamas* | Male married to female of one's lineage |
| *Neshar* | Female married to male of one's lineage |
| *Halk* or *jan* | Wife |
| *Shu* | Husband |
| *Waserk* | Spouse's close male relatives, including father, uncle, and brother |
| *Dozkech* | Spouse's sister |
| *Wasu* | Spouse's mother and female siblings of parents |
| *Piruk* | Spouse's male grandparents (and siblings) |
| *Baluk* | Spouse's female grandparents (and siblings) |
| *Hamjurad* | Wives of two brothers |
| *Bonjan* | Senior wife in a polygamous union |
| *Sarjan* | Junior wife in a polygamous union |
| *Pizasag* | Children of husband's other wife; spouse's children by his/her previous spouse |
| *Jedmadar* | Children of father's other wife |

factors: degree of kinship closeness, character of the individual and of parents and siblings, work capability and productivity, physical perfection and beauty, and cost of marriage exchanges. There were general categories of people who were proscribed as ineligible spouses for Sarhadi *baluch:* Ghulamzai, the descendants of slaves; and Luri, the small groups of itinerant blacksmiths. Nor, in general, were *shahri,* sedentary, agriculturalists, regarded as desirable spouses. The case of *shahri* was slightly complicated: *shahri* was a social category, contrasted with *baluch.* The contrast between *shahri* and *baluch* can be likened to that between "sedentary" and "nomad." So while a *shahri* from Khash/Washt might have been deemed ineligible, a Yarahmadzai tribesmen living in Khash, having the same occupation as the Khashi, but notionally still a *baluch,* would have been deemed eligible. *Baluch* could live in a *shahr,* settlement, without becoming *shahri* (Salzman 1978b). Shams A'din said that he would not let his daughter marry a *shahri,* for example, a Khashi, although he would let his daughter marry a Yarahmadzai tribesmen who happened to live in a *shahr.*

The general prescriptive rule was that it was best to marry close, in one's *kom.* Sarhadi *baluch* said, "Marry your kin and you know what you are getting." This was, of course, literally true, for people grew up knowing most of their kinsmen and had spent considerable time observing and interacting with them. This applied to potential spouses and affines alike.

If one's *maskom* was of a different *brasrend* than one's *peskom,* it was considered better to marry *peskom.* The reason for this is clear: strong and specific obligations of blood responsibility tied members of the *brasrend* together. If you married within your patrilineal *brasrend,* your affines would also be your allies in blood responsibility;

thus you would have many common interests with your affines, and they would be less likely to cause difficulties over issues pertaining to marriage. It was desirable to marry, in order of preference, one's *naku zad* and *tru zad,* uncles' and aunts' children; a member of one's *brasrend* (e.g., the Dadolzai); a member of one's intermediate section (e.g., the Nur Mahmudzai); a member of one's maximal tribal section (e.g., the Soherabzai); a member of one's tribe (e.g., the Yarahmadzai); a member of a neighboring allied tribe (e.g., the Gamshadzai); a member of a more distant Baluchi tribe.

These rules and rationales provided a general normative and social framework within which decisions about spouse choice were made, but they were mostly preferential rather than obligatory. Various other practical considerations come into actual choices:

- *Availability.* The demographic factor was how distant did one have to go to find an unpromised individual of the appropriate age. The economic factor was whether the individuals considered suitable partners could be had at an affordable price.
- *Desirability.* The qualitative considerations were whether the individuals were judged to be desirable as partners, hard working and of good character, physically attractive and unflawed, and whether the kin were desirable as affines, of good character, peaceful and cooperative.

These factors were important influences, but the general rules were never denied. Specific deviations from the norm were said to be *kesmat,* fate, or God's will, *dasti huda,* rather than a contradiction to the normative principles.

Who actually selected spouses, decided who was to marry, varied somewhat from case to case. But there was usually a strong element of parental determination in marriages; that is, most marriages were, to one degree or another, arranged by parents or guardians rather than by the spouses. Some engagements were arranged by parents when the spouses-to-be were small children. Engagements were said to be a matter for the father to decide, but fathers in their power and wisdom often deferred to the advice of their wives, the mothers of their children, who were commonly keen observers of junior relatives and their adult kin.

Shams A'din's marriage was arranged by his mother, Zarbonu. His father Gulap did not entirely approve, for he thought the *geshtar/deshtar* (female fiancée) too young, but grudgingly gave his consent. The *geshtar,* Sazien, was Zarbonu's brother's daughter. At the time, Shamuk, as Shams A'din was then called, was seven years old when he became Sazien's *wastar* (male fiancé), and Sazien was three or four. Following the successful request, *wahudi ko,* by Zarbonu, cloth for a dress and for a chadur was given, and each year in the summer some cloth, or dress, or pants were given to seal the engagement.

If no childhood engagement had been arranged, the potential spouses were differentially placed as regards decisionmaking, according to gender. Girls were usually given in marriage around the onset of puberty at 15 years, but preferably before. As females were believed to have strong sexual desires, this timing was seen as avoiding problems with premarital sex. Girls in their early teens were not encouraged to participate in the choice of their spouse. This choice was usually monopolized by the girl's parents. However, brides were asked by the mulla, as part of the marriage ceremony, if they consented to the marriage.

Males, on the other hand, were usually in their early 20s at the time of marriage. Their agreement to the engagement and marriage was necessary for the establishment of the union. Notwithstanding the arrangements between his mother and his uncle, and the annual engagement gifts that had been exchanged, Shams A'din said that he himself decided to marry Sazien. As he put it, "If a man does not want a particular bride, he will refuse. This is not a matter that can be decided by force."

Sometimes, the prospective grooms were the active directors of the process. Id Mahmud did not have his marriage arranged for him. His father had died when he was young, and his mother did not initiate any arrangement. According to Id Mahmud's account, his father's brothers told him, when he was still young, that they would not give a daughter to him. Later, when he had grown up, they changed their minds, but he turned them down. He had decided that he wanted to be *zamas*, son-in-law, to Ja'far, his *naku*. In fact, Ja'far was rather more distant, Id Mahmud's mother's father's brother's daughter's son. Also, Id Mahmud liked Ja'far and thought that the Dadolzai were peaceful and agreeable people. He thought that Ja'far would be a better *waserk*, father-in-law, than his father's brothers, who fought too much. He also liked what he saw of Ja'far's daughter Bibi Nur. He asked Ja'far to give him his daughter, and Ja'far agreed. Bibi Nur, aged 12 years, became his *geshtar*, and he, aged 20 years, became her *wastar*. Two years later they married.

Some years later, when Bibi Nur was in her 20s and a mother in her own right, I asked her what she thought about marrying someone chosen for her, and whether girls should not have a say in the matter themselves. Bibi Nur was not, even then, too old to giggle in an embarrassed way, but she answered with definite certainty: "How would young girls know who would make a good husband? Their fathers know who is good and must choose for them."

Other things being equal, the older a *geshtar* and *wastar* were at the time of engagement, the more influence they had on the choice. Even the ability to choose oneself does not guarantee acceptance. Abas, looking for someone to fill the place left by his first wife, married a girl from a different lineage who was not considered one of his *kom*. He said that it would have been better to have married a girl from his *peskom* or *maskom*, but there were none available at the time, so he married a girl who he said was "close," by which he meant that she was a member of the same intermediate section, the Nur Mahmudzai. He had tried to find a girl closer, but there were few older girls; most were very young. Abas had, before Bibi Nur's engagement to Id

Mahmud, asked Ja'far for Bibi Nur, but was refused. Ja'far and Monas told me that Abas had been too old for their young daughter and that Abas was not an especially hard worker and would not help them or provide for her as well as a more energetic man would. Thus Abas went to Pir Dad, outside of his own lineage, and asked for his daughter. Pati Hartun, although attractive, was not well fitted out with nice clothes and had not attracted requests. At this point in her late teens and without many requests, she was given to Abas as a replacement wife, about which she was not initially entirely happy.

If we look at the overall pattern of marriage bonds, we find—on the basis of a non-systematic sample of 117 Yarahmadzai marriages from the Sahib Dadzai, Dorahzai, Yar Mahmudzai, Zabedzai, Dadolzai, and Mirgolzai *brasrend*—that 31 percent of marriage unions were with members of the same minimal lineage, *brasrend*, while 69 percent of unions were outside the minimal lineage, of which as many as 23 percent were outside of the Yarahmadzai tribe. However, from the point of view of any specific *brasrend*, because an internal union requires two members of the lineage, on average 47 percent of its members were married to lineage mates from the same *brasrend*, while 53 percent of its members were married to outsiders. Of those unions in which both partners were from the same *brasrend*, many were fathers' brothers' children; among the Dadolzai, of 13 internal unions recorded, 9 (or 69 percent) were fathers' brothers' children. A few unions were conceptualized in terms of *maskom*, such as mother's brother's son/daughter, although at the same time they were also more distant patrilateral marriages, that of father's father's brother's son's children. Of the external marriages with individuals outside of ego's own *brasrend*, many were with close *kom*, such as mothers' brothers' or mothers' sisters' children, when the mothers were from other *brasrend*, or with fathers' sisters' children, when the sisters had married outside of the *brasrend*.

## Replacement Husbands

Because children were regarded as part of their father's line and the lineages based upon that line, children were deemed the responsibility of father and his *peskom*. If a husband and wife divorced, the children were allocated to the custody of the father, although they were often left with their mother, with upkeep provided by their father, until they reached six years of age, after which they usually came to live with their father.

Mahmud Karim's daughter Zmorid, from his union with his first and divorced wife, lived with him and his second wife. Similarly, after Yelli Han and his first wife divorced, the children remained with him and his second wife.

If a husband died, his *peskom* assumed responsibility for supporting his children and often tried to supply a replacement husband for the widow. A brother of the deceased husband was seen as an appropriate replacement. The rationale was that the children would then be *bras zad* to the stepfather, and he would know them and care about them.

Shams Hartun of the Dust Mahmudzai Dadolzai married Rehim Dad, her father's brother's son, and from this union came Abdulla. When Rehim Dad died, his brother Nezar Mahmud married Shams Hartun. Unfortunately, he too soon died, and, when Shams Hartun married more distantly and moved to Zahedan, Abdulla remained with his *peskom* in Halki Ja'far.

## Exchanges

A marriage—beginning with the engagement, through the wedding, and beyond—was a relationship celebrated by the exchange of material goods or promises of material goods. These exchanges involved not only the bride and groom but their families as well. The amount of goods to be exchanged or promised was established by formal negotiation. One offering was *lahb,* a presentation of goods from the groom and his family to the father of the bride. Another was *mahr,* obligatory for Muslims, which was a promise of compensation from the groom to the bride should the marriage end in divorce. The father of the bride presented to the new household the *behr,* which had to be at least one major item, camel, palm, or *pas.*

In 1968, the idiom for discussing *lahb* was camels, and the general guideline at that time was 15 camels for *lahb.* Terms of equivalence were one camel equaled 5 sheep or goats, or 10 date palms, or 100 toman cash.

Shams A'din, the son of Gulap, reported that when he married Sazien three years earlier, he gave Ido 2 camels, 5 sheep, 20 palms, and 500 toman. As well, he promised 500 toman *mahr.* The *lahb* given by Shams A'din appears to be of the same magnitude given by his father 40 years before. Gulap reported that when he married Zarbonu 40 years earlier, he gave as *lahb* 3 camels, 12 sheep, 10 palms, 300 toman, and one tent.

On February 11, 1968, an exchange negotiation, called *sang bandi* or *mal o maldai,* was convened to establish the amounts to be exchanged on the marriage of Gam Dad (later known by his adult name, Jan Mahmud) and Nur Bibi. A delegation of five male elders accompanied by Gam Dad was hosted by Nur Bibi's father, Ido, accompanied by two male elders and his son-in-law. No women were present. The prospective groom, Gam Dad, sat at the lowest status location by the door. The host and his son-in-law busied themselves bringing and serving tea. The discussion, which lasted two hours, eventually followed by a lunch of *morgi hatuk,* was quite animated; sometimes several people were speaking or shouting at once. But the debate was carried on with a festive spirit of cordial competition, and discussion of the exchanges was interspersed with jokes and laughter. The argument focused on two factors. One was how close or distant the couple was. In this case, they were father's brother's children, so could not have been any closer. The other was how much other people had given and thus what was a reasonable standard. At the end, it had been agreed that the *lahb* would be 12 camels, with the following equivalences:

For 2 camels    4 palms would be given
For 2 camels    2 tent strips would be given
For 1 camel     1 carpet would be given
For 2 camels    1 camel would be given
For 5 camels    460 toman would be given

The equivalences in this case were quite low, compared with those generally proposed. Rather than 10 palms per camel, here 2 palms were accepted. And 1 camel was accepted as payment for 2 camels! Similarly, the *mahr* was quite low, only 500 toman. And the story did not end there, for much of what was presented was to be returned by Ido to the new household: 2 tent strips, 1 carpet, ½ a camel, and 360 toman worth of household goods. Remaining with Ido would be ½ a camel, 4 palms, and 100 toman. The relatively low level of presentation by the groom and the high level of return by the prospective father-in-law was a concession to the kin closeness of the prospective son-in-law and father-in-law, the former being the *bras zad,* brother's child, of the latter.

How much of the *lahb* should be directed to a new household was a matter of public debate in Dadolzai camps during this period. Mulla Rustam, the religious leader who resided in the Dadolzai Halili Halk, had pronounced on this issue in one of his postprayer sermons. He argued that the bride's father should not "eat" the *lahb,* should not keep it and use it for his own purposes. Rather, it should go to the daughter for use in her new household. He went so far as to declare keeping the *lahb* forbidden, *haram,* and the passing of it to the daughter, sanctified, *hilal.* This view was not received with great enthusiasm by all future fathers-in-law. Dad Mahmud, for one, was prepared to complain to all willing to listen that Mulla Rustam's position was totally unfair. He said that raising a daughter was very expensive and required a large investment, not to mention a great deal of effort. When daughters married, their work and their children belonged to their new household, and they might go away to live with their husband's relatives. So why should there not be some recompense for the father? It was quite unreasonable, he felt, that everything should be given to the daughter's new household and nothing remain for the parents that brought her up.

The amount of *mahr* was also a matter of discussion at this time. Pati Mahmud was upset that the *mahr* agreed for his daughter in her marriage to Nur Mahmud was 1,000 toman. This seemed inadequate to Pati Mahmud, who argued that in the past the *mahr* had been 3,000 or 4,000 toman.

Five years later, in 1973, a noteworthy symbolic change had taken place in the idiom of marriage exchanges. The camel idiom previously used for discussions of exchange had disappeared, and *lahb* was set in terms of money, reflecting the increased monetization of the Sarhadi tribal economy.

In early February 1973, Mulla Sidik, son of Rahmat, came to his father's brother, *naku,* Dust Mahmud (son of) Mulla, and asked permission to marry his daughter, Zuruk, and a *sang bandi* was organized. He thus had chosen to make a request for Zuruk rather than Hajijat, the daughter of Reis, who was equally close, structurally equivalent in fact, as she was his father's other brother's daughter. It was generally felt that Reis and his wife were better people than Dust Mahmud and his wife, and would make better affines. Furthermore, Zuruk was *geshtar* of Suliman, Dadol's son, although it was alleged that he had not given much—only 2 dresses, 1 chadur, and 10 toman—and had made no definite arrangements about a *sang bandi*. But it was thought that breaking off would anger Suliman and his father Dadol. This breaking off in favor of Mulla Sidik was itself testimony to the dicey character of Dust Mahmud.

So why did Mulla Sidik ask for Zuruk rather than Hajijat? Hajijat was available and the right age. In fact, Dust Mahmud's son Bahadin had, until not long before Mulla Sidik's arrival, been *wastar* to Hajijat, this having been arranged by the fathers when the children were small. But Bahadin, now grown, had broken off the engagement. The reason he cited was that Hajijat had a deformed leg and limped badly. Hajijat was deemed imperfect, and although she could work, and pursued her chores energetically, was a poor prospect on that account. I have to confess that I felt bad for Hajijat, for as far as I could tell she was a pleasant, hard-working, and cheery girl, and I feared that she would not marry or not get the partner that she deserved. I do not know what Mulla Sidik thought or felt, but he decided to take the girl who was not lame and the in-laws who were.

Before the *sang bandi*, Zarbonu went to Dust Mahmud and his wife to say that it would be good to have a *mulla* in the camp and that they should accept Mulla Sidik. Mulla Sidik told Reis and Ja'far, who were representing him, that he would agree with whatever amount they arranged. Dust Mahmud began, undoubtedly for show, by asking for 12,000 toman, and Ja'far and Reis bargained for less. Finally, 3,000 toman was the amount agreed for the *lahb* and 2,000 toman for the *mahr.* The equivalences were as follows:

| | |
|---|---|
| For 1,000 toman | cash would be given |
| For 500 toman | two tent strips |
| For 500 toman | a large, flat woven rug |
| For 500 toman | one camel |
| For 500 toman | 5 *pas,* sheep and goats |

The breaking off of engagements was not infrequent, especially those arranged by parents when the parties were children. If the engagement was broken off by the girl's side, it was sometimes possible to be compensated for engagement gifts given. If the engagement was broken off by the boy's side, no stigma fell on the girl, and her prospects for a future marriage were not usually harmed.

## Weddings

The wedding of Mirad, son of Boinyad, and Zar Bibi, daughter of Dadol, took place on May 31 and June 1, 1968. On the first day, Dadol, the father of the bride, gave a dinner to assembled guests. There were around 60 guests, mostly the men of the two Dadolzai camps. The women of the camps were not guests; either they pitched in as cooks for the meal or else went about their families' tasks. Invitations had been sent to the seat of the Sardar at Gorchan, and Nezar Mahmud and Nur Mahmud and their wives attended. Two *pas* were killed to provide meat, and *gushti hatuk,* bread, and tea were served. At around 7 P.M., dinner was served to all of the guests at once, some sitting in tents but most sitting in a large circle in front of the tents. The women guests from Gorchan ate separately from the men, in a tent restricted to women. Mulla Isa, who, because of his extensive religious education and knowledge, had qualified for the title of *maulawi,* was also present for the meal and presided over evening prayers. After Mulla Isa left, the *suruz*—a small string instrument, held vertically and played with a bow—was brought out and there was music and singing for several hours into the night.

On the second day, Boinyad, the father of the groom, killed five *pas* to provide the *gusti hatuk* to be offered for lunch to the well over 100 guests. Food was prepared from early morning through early afternoon. Serving began at 9 A.M. and continued until 2 P.M. Guests ate in several tents, in shifts, until all had eaten. Luris from Gwanich helped to prepare and serve the food, as they always did at weddings, and were paid the customary fee: some flour, 10 toman cash, and the old clothes of the groom.

At about 5 P.M., the groom and a number of his relatives, both male and female, mostly young, went off to Shagbond for the prewedding bath and a change of clothes. Mirad stripped to the waist and was washed by a male Luri in a large *jube,* irrigation ditch, accompanied by *suruz* music, with the onlookers singing, clapping, and cheering him on. He had earlier, with greater privacy, shaved his facial and body hair. He changed into all new clothes: white *jamag* and *shalwar,* and a new jacket and shoes. He then mounted a horse—rarer, and thus more impressive than a camel—loaned to him by his uncle for the occasion, and was led back over a hill and across the plain to the camp, with guests in the camp providing an audience. Still on his mount, he was led to his soon-to-be father-in-law's tent, where he told Dadol that he would only dismount and, by implication, continue with the ceremony, if Dadol gave him a camel. Dadol, following custom, at first refused and then relented, promising the camel. Mirad then dismounted and entered Dadol's tent.

In the meantime, in the same tent, the tent of the bride's father, in the small private space between the *purr* and the closed end of the tent, the bride's female relatives were washing her and dressing her in new clothes and jewelry and making her up in cosmetics, such as *kohl* for her eyes. The bride remained there, in privacy, so that when her groom entered the tent, he knew she was there but could not see her.

The signing of the *mahr* document took place at about 8 P.M. in the tent of the father of the bride, Dadol's tent. The *maulawi* presided. He chanted from the Qoran. He wrote up the *mahr* document, in this case in the amount of 1,000 toman. He directed two men from the two families to ask the bride, who continued sitting hidden behind the *purr,* who she wanted for *wakil,* the man responsible for getting the *mahr* for her if the occasion arose. Zar Bibi named Ja'far as *wakil.* The groom and then Ja'far signed the *mahr* document and swore to uphold it.

After the signing, several men went out to set up a small tent some distance from the line of tents in the camp, in which the newly married couple would spend their first two nights. But then the bride refused to leave her father's tent unless her father-in-law, Boinyad, gave her something. He agreed to give her a date palm. Sometimes a *pas* was given in response to this standardized request. Zar Bibi then was led out of her father's tent to her honeymoon tent, where the groom had preceded her.

The newly married couple presumably had sexual relations, because the next morning female relatives of the groom went to examine the clothes of the bride to determine that she had been a virgin, which they duly declared. After two days, the new couple moved back into camp.

## Relations between Spouses

Sarhadi spouses entered into marriage not as the culmination of a fiery romantic liaison, as some versions of the Euro-American model prefers it, but rather as a conclusion to a collective, social process of selection. Spousal partners were selected because they were deemed good prospects by parents and other elders. Brides were usually very young and commonly went along with what they were advised; grooms had their say but in general said what they were advised.

A substantial majority of Sarhadi Baluch—and an even larger one if we consider only first marriages—married close patrilateral or matrilateral relatives, people whom they had known all of their lives. Many new spouses thus were building on an already established, life-long kinship relationship. If they were first or second cousins, they probably had called each other *laleh* and *dadeh,* terms that assimilated siblings and cousins into one category of very close, same-age kinsmen. Cousins who married had thus called each other by the same terms as they called their brothers and sisters! So while the spouses were strangers in the romantic sense, they were not at all strangers in the social sense.

Furthermore, most brides during the first years after marriage remained with their natal family. At the start of a marriage, the bride was not much more than a girl, often several years before puberty, while the groom was a young man in his early 20s.

The couple lived as husband and wife and engaged in conjugal relations. Initially, however, they resided at or by the tent of the bride's parents. So the bride did not experience an abrupt severing of ties with her natal household. She continued to meet with her natal family, and especially her mother and guide, on a daily basis. If the tent of the new spouses was not completed, the bride's parents and the bride and the groom divided her parents' tent into two parts. Or if the husband was away from the territory working for a significant period, the bride would be reabsorbed, temporarily, into her natal household.

Marriage was not seen as the melding of two persons into one, as in the romantic model, or even the melding of two families into one, but rather as a step toward the social maturity of two persons, who together were initiating a new and independent household and family. For the Sarhadi Baluch, adulthood came with and was defined by the establishment of an independent household and family. This meant providing an income, whether through primary production or other means, for supporting the household, and populating the household with a family, that is, children, which both continued the family and provided labor to assist in supporting the family.

What did all of these circumstances mean for the relationship between husband, *shu,* and wife, *jan?* One major consequence was that the relationship of spouses was part of a dense web of relationships, and their actions subject to the observation and comment of many close relatives. Their roles as husband and wife were considered not just in relation to each other, but also in relation to their kinsmen, affines, and immediate community, who were all present and interested. In short, they had to think not only of each other but of everyone else as well. So there was no isolation or involution in their relationship.

There was a convention that wives, at least young wives, not express warm feelings about their husbands. It was not because such expressions would be considered *bihaya,* immodest, because they would not, at least according to my informants. What these young wives did commonly say with some passion, when their fathers, brothers, uncles, and cousins were away from camp, was that they missed their fathers and their brothers, and so on. Lal Malik said to me that *delam mont,* "my heart waits" for the return of her half-brother from his migrant labor, but she volunteered no comment about her husband Man Dust. Similarly, Gol Peri expressed longing to see her brother, Bahadur, but no mention was made of her husband, Ghulam Mahmud, who was away more frequently for longer periods. When asked about this, the young wives denied that they missed their husbands and even that they liked their husbands. Their explanation was that husbands may come and go, but brothers are forever. Now I think that I have good reason to believe that some of these young wives were really quite sentimentally attached to their husbands. But the expression of sentiment about brothers and not about husbands was indicative of both the ongoing importance of natal family ties and the public expectation that marriage was about serious matters that went beyond personal emotion.

One male informant, Shams A'din, concurred, explaining young wives' expression of feeling for brothers and not husbands by saying that a woman can have a husband one day and he can leave her the next, but brothers are always there to depend upon, to defend and help her in relation to her husband, to provide her with food and other necessities when she is in need. Furthermore, he argued, if a woman was always talking about how much she likes her husband, it raised a question in the minds of others whether she was trying to cover up something by these exclamations. Finally, he argued, in maintaining the power balance between spouses, expression of affection by the wife might be used by the husband to lever a stronger position within the relationship.

However, this recommendation for spouses to keep their feeling to themselves did not stop this same informant, Shams A'din—in the company of his wife, father-in-law, and assorted children from other tents honoring my presence—from saying that he cared for his wife very much and was very *gamgine,* unhappy, when he was away working in Bandar Abbas.

A second major consequence of the conditions described above was that the relationship between husband and wife was very much a practical partnership upon which both parties depended. Husband and wife relied upon each other every day for the food that they ate and the water they drank, the fuel they cooked with, and the tent that sheltered them from the elements. Each needed the skills and labor of the other, and neither could maintain a separate household alone. The instrumental necessity of the partnership was a large part of the spousal relationship, and the mutual dependence contributed to a balance between the partners. Consultation between spouses on practical matters was a constant necessity.

One critical element of this partnership was the production of children. The Sarhadi *baluch*—well, Sarhadi women—told me that their children were the most important thing in their lives. To be a fully adult man or women, one had to have children. When a man became a father, he signaled this to the Baluchi world by the growing of a full beard. Children, among other things, were necessary additions to household labor power. Generally, women tried to have as many children as possible. There was for a married couple a strong impetus to produce children. Children were a joint project that benefited both parents as individuals and as family members. It should, however, be noted that birth control pills were in the 1970s recently available in Khash, and at least a few tribal women, already having had a number of children, were using them, although not necessarily with the knowledge or consent of their husbands.

One of the main reasons that men divorced their wives or took second wives was that their first wives had not had children. So there was a lot of pressure on wives from male and female affines alike, to conceive, carry to term, give birth to live babies, and ensure that the babies lived and grew. In the Sarhad, much more was riding on this than a simple personal desire for children.

As children were produced and grew, enlarging the family and household and increasing labor power and political support, the relationship of spouses was reinforced by their common commitment to and dependence upon their children, and their need to manage the children's daily activities. The spouses' stature grew as parents and heads of a substantial family.

In sum, spouses were part of and accountable to an ongoing, dense network of family members and kinsmen, within which they and their joint enterprise were situated. In this setting, spouses were first and foremost partners in the practical enterprise of making a living and making new lives. They were obliged to coordinate and cooperate to make possible production and reproduction. It fell to spouses as parents, kinsmen, and community members to enculturate and socialize their and other children. In marriage, sentiment did not lead, it followed.

## Polygamy, Divorce, and Infertility

Baluchi men, under the regulations of Islam, were permitted to marry up to four wives at one time, as well as remarry upon divorce. But most, at least 95 percent, of Sarhadi men and women, were in monogamous unions. The few polygamous unions involved in almost all cases a man and two wives, usually married more than a decade apart. Polygamous unions were more common in the chiefly lineage than elsewhere. In the chiefly lineage, political motives involving the use of marriages in establishing political alliances, encouraged and justified multiple unions.

In polygamous unions, each wife had to have a complete establishment of her own. Women were supposed to and usually did bring their own tents, household equipment, and personal effects to a marriage. Each woman, and thus each wife in a polygamous union, had to have control of an independent household of her own and be the mistress of her household. Husbands were normatively obliged to treat their wives equally, supplying or supporting them both with an equivalent amount of income, and visiting them and engaging in conjugal relations equitably on an alternating basis. Not infrequently in polygamous families, a man's wives resided in different camps or settlements.

Another motive for polygamous unions was infertility. If after some years of marriage, no offspring were forthcoming, a man was faced with the decision of continuing without offspring or taking a new wife. If the latter decision was taken, a man could divorce his first wife and marry again, in which case the new union would be monogamous. But if the man did not wish to divorce his first wife, he might marry a second, in the hopes that she would provide offspring, thus forming a polygamous union. Of course, in cases where the infertility resulted from the husband and not the wife, taking a new wife proved to be a futile strategy. There was one Yarahmadzai who had sequentially married three wives polygamously without ever succeeding in producing offspring. It was eventually obvious that the husband's infertility was to blame. He was a bit of a laughing stock among tribesmen for ending up appearing ridiculous, but perhaps we should not be surprised that tribesmen would sometimes laugh at disastrous situations that they themselves so feared and that, but for the grace of God, they might have suffered themselves.

A major constraint on the establishment of polygamous unions was economic. The husband was obliged to support his two (or more) wives, and few Sarhadi men had an income adequate to support more than one household and one wife. The men of the chiefly lineage, drawing partly on resources made available to them through the political process, were financially better off and more able to support multiple wives and households. Another constraint on the establishment of polygamous unions would have been opposition from a first wife, but the weight of this factor would have depended a great deal on the individuals involved and probably on the support that the first wife had from her natal family.

Even among those who did not avail themselves of polygamy, infertility would sometimes but not always lead to divorce. Sometimes the couple was so attached that they individually and together were willing to face the future without producing children. And some who were later to have children pondered this possibility: Shams A'din told me emphatically that he would not divorce Sazien even if she proved infertile. In the case of childless couples, their situation was somewhat ameliorated, as we have seen (chapter 8), by the long-term transfer of children from their birth families to related, childless families, who would then bring up these children. This was commonly done to alleviate pressure on the birth-family, to aid and assist the receiving family, whose difficult situation was appreciated, and often by both situations in conjunction.

Some couples divorced as a result of incompatibility. While I do not have systematic information, the instances with which I am familiar suggest that this was more common among couples who were distant relations or strangers. There are two reasons for this. One is that people who married close kin knew their spouses and in-laws quite well and were able to make an informed decision to marry. The second reason is that women living away from and without the support of their own kin were more likely to be criticized and to feel unappreciated. But these comments are tentative and must await more systematic information for confirmation (or refutation).

Men had the right to divorce, but women could leave and go back to their natal families. Usually they were given the support they wanted from their families. My impression is that women were not forced to remain in marriages that they wished to leave. But this is another point on which I do not have detailed information. Divorced women, along with widows, did usually remarry without difficulty. The avalanche of offers for the sadly divorced Gol Peri (see chapter 6) is a case in point.

## Relationships among Affines

The wife-taker was the *zamas*, son-in-law. The father of the wife was *waserk*, father-in-law and wife-giver, and so were all the members of her lineage. If the husband was not of the lineage of his wife, he was *zamas* of all members of her lineage, who were in the formal position of parents-in-law to him. For example, Isa Rasul and Azim Han were *zamas* of the Dadolzai. If a man married within his own *brasrend,* but into a different microlineage, as in the case of Isa of the Shadi Hanzai Dadolzai marrying the daughter of Mahmud Karim Dust Mahmudzai Dadolzai, he was *zamas* only to the other microlineage, in this instance the Dust Mahmudzai. In the case of marriage with a father's brother's daughter, the husband was *zamas* only to his wife's father.

Relations between *zamas* and *waserk* were somewhat formal, deferential on the part of the *zamas,* and respectful on the part of the *waserk.* The relationship was somewhat delicate, and participants could be rather touchy. Further, the *zamas* had a debt to the *waserk,* both the wife's father and the entire lineage of his wife, and an obligation to help and support him and its members. We have already seen sons-in-law sending money from work to their fathers-in-law, some to support their wives, but also some for the fathers-in-law. But relations did not always go smoothly, and parties on both sides sometimes showed considerable sensitivity to apparent slights, increasingly so with greater structural distance between lineages of the *zamas* and *waserk.* Relations between affinal kin from different lineages were sometimes greatly affected by circumstantial relations between their lineages, as could be seen in the following instance, which was colored by a serious dispute—see chapter 10—between the two tribal sections to which the affines belonged.

On December 6, 1972, Isa (son of) Rasul, Rahmatzai, husband of Malik Hartun (daughter of) Gulap, Dadolzai, returned to the Rahmatzai *halk,* located near Bilery, where his tent had been since their migration back to the Sarhad from Mashkil the previous fall. He had been away trading for a couple of months and had come home to visit before going back to work. But when he arrived, his wife and children were not there.

Isa's wife's brother, Shams A'din, had come the previous day, December 5, and taken Isa's wife Malik Hartun and their children back to the Ja'fari Halk camp to visit with her mother, Zarbonu. When the news of Isa's arrival in his camp was brought to Shams A'din's and Zarbonu's camp by a traveling companion of Isa who happened to live in the Dadolzai camp, Malik Hartun determined to return the next day, December 6. But having just made the trip, her brother Shams A'din was anxious to put off the return for another day. Malik Hartun, with her mother's agreement, insisted, but by that time the camels were gone to pasture for the day. Nor did they get going early the next day.

Then their departure became moot, because at midday on December 8, Isa arrived in camp. He knew the Ja'fari Halk well, because he had resided there for several years previously, when he and his young wife stayed close to her mother and family, as newlyweds often do, before he moved his tent to his own people. Upon his arrival in the Ja'fari Halk, however, he did not go to one of tents of his brothers-in-law, but to that of Baluch, a non-Dadolzai resident of the camp. He then sent for his wife.

This was taken by his brother-in-law Shams A'din as a grave insult. Isa, for his part, said that his wife had been taken from their home without his permission, which no one had a right to do. Shams A'din asked him how he dared to come into camp and go to another tent and send orders for his sister. It was not right at all—he should have come and made a proper greeting and drunk tea and eaten and talked properly. Ja'far, the Dadolzai *master,* headman, coming to support Shams A'din, said that if Isa was not prepared to behave properly, he could take his children and leave—his Dadolzai wife would remain with the Dadolzai. Malik Hartun, meanwhile—caught against her own desires between these conflicting men, and having visions of being abruptly separated from her children and her husband—was crying. Furthermore, Ja'far said, no Dadolzai would ever visit his tent again.

Isa, under this heavy barrage, and feeling that things were getting out of hand, re-lented, saying that he really had not understood, that he had made a mistake, and that he had not really meant to insult the Dadolzai and his brother-in-law. With this ca-pitulation, peace was restored, and Malik Hartun and the children went off with Isa. Ja'far and Shams A'din were fairly satisfied with the final outcome, but not with the original behavior of Isa. The next day they were still talking about it, and making dep-recating remarks about Isa and derogatory comments about the Rahmatzai.

Within the *kom,* and increasingly with those having close kin ties, sensitivities be-tween *zamas* and *waserk* were muted by solidarity and multiple overlapping ties. When in March 1968 the recently married Shams A'din and Sazien had an argument and Shams A'din slapped Sazien, she left his tent and returned to her parents' tent. Soon after, she returned to Shams A'din. Her father, Ido, had avoided a confrontation and directed Sazien to reconciliation. "What could I do?" he said to me, "I couldn't hit him. He is my *gohar zad,* sister's child."

The Dadolzai, and doubtless other Sarhadi tent dwellers, were always saying that unions with outsiders were fragile and less likely to last, while those with *kom* were much less fragile and more likely to last. Their explanation was that Dadolzai—or in the case of other lineages, they themselves—were better people and more likely to do the right thing. An alternative explanation that the observer might suggest is that Dadolzai were not so much better people than outsiders; rather, the difference was that they treated each other better than they treated outsiders. And what Dadolzai spouses did was more likely to be seen as the right or acceptable thing, whereas out-siders were more likely to be criticized and condemned. It would appear that Dadolzai spouses were given more latitude and more moral support than non-Dadolzai spouses. Endogamy has its privileges.

Well, we might be tempted to say, affinal ties were strained by too much testos-terone, too much male competition. But relations between female affines were sub-ject to strain as well.

One of the first "events" after my initial arrival in the Ja'fari Halk at the end of 1967 was the blowup between Dadol's wife Maka and her daughter-in-law—Suliman's wife Sangi—while Suliman was away working in Abu Dhabi. Sangi said that she could not live with her mother-in-law any more and left to return to her father's tent. This required quick diplomatic action, and Ja'far and Isa went off as *wasta,* intermediaries, to negotiate a return.

At the beginning of the next summer, when the Ja'fari Halk was moving to Shagbond, a problem arose for Nur Mahmud, the *zamas* of Pati Mahmud. Nur Mahmud and his wife Tili Hartun had been sharing a divided tent with her parents. Pati Mahmud had decided to leave the Ja'fari Halk and move to Gwanich to help his brother with the harvest. Nur Mahmud wanted to join his mother at Shagbond, but Pati Mahmud said that it was too far and that he wanted his daughter close by. Perhaps more critical was the fact that the tent of Nur Mahmud and Tili Hartun was being woven and not yet available for occupancy, which would have meant that they would have had to move in with Tili Hartun's mother-in-law. Tili Hartun put her foot down; she would not live in the tent of her mother-in-law. Everybody got rather hot under the collar, and it required several days of cooling tempers and *wasta* intervention to work out a solution. In the end, Tili Hartun stayed with her parents through *duro,* harvest, but then, for *hamin,* went to her husband's *bonend* at the date groves of Mashkil.

## Relations between Lineages

The segmentary lineage system based on descent through the male line had a complete logic of its own. But it did not operate in a social vacuum, any more than any other basis of relationship—bilateral kinship, contract, reciprocity—operated on its own in the Sarhad of Baluchistan. The multiplex relationships of multiple overlain and overlapping ties so characteristic of Sarhadi social life engulfed and distorted the clear and symmetrical logic of the lineage system.

Marriages between individuals of different lineages established affinal ties between those lineages. This affinal relationship between lineages was called *sharigdar.* If further marriages between the lineages followed—as sometimes happened, encouraged by the appeal of socially sanctioned marriages with close, matrilateral kin—a web of affinity came to bind the two lineages closer together.

This process of selective affinal binding of patrilineages could be seen clearly within the Dadolzai. The Dadolzai had four minilineage sections consisting of the descendants of four of Dadol's sons: the Komeronzai, the Shirdelzai, the Shadi Hanzai, and the Dust Mahmudzai. In the elder generation, there had been, in addition to marriages within the minilineages and outside of the Dadolzai, a scattering of marriages among the Dadolzai minilineages: for example, Gemi of the Komeronzai married Patima, sister of Abas and Gailah, of the Shadi Hanzai; Reis of the Shirdelzai married Medina of the Komeronzai; and Gulap of the Dust Mahmudzai married Zarbonu, sister of Ido, of the Shadi Hanzai. These were echoed in the younger generation primarily between the Dust Mahmudzai and the Shadi Hanzai, when the male children of Gulap and Zarbonu, Shams Adin and Mahmud Karim, themselves Dust Mahmudzai following their father, took wives from the Shadi Hanzai, their mother's lineage. The connection was further extended to the next generation, when Mahmud Karim gave his daughter to Isa of the Shadi Hanzai. The consequence was that the Dust Mahmudzai and the Shadi Hanzai, formally structurally equivalent in distance to each other and to the Komeronzai and the Shirdelzai, became repeatedly tied through affinal bonds and thus, in practice, intermingled and entangled, and so developed a higher level of mutual dependence and sympathy. The Dust Mahmudzai and Shadi Hanzai were, undeniably, closer to each other than either were to the Komeronzai or Shirdelzai. This was seen in the constitution of the "Gulapzai labor team." The relative fragility of the tie between the Shadi Hanzai and Dust Mahmudzai, on the one side, and the Shirdelzai, on the other, exacerbated by the structurally fortuitous differences in ownership of and emphasis on livestock, was seen in the dispute in the Ja'fari Halk and the resulting temporary fission of the Halk.

Another example came to light during the prolonged conflict of the mid-1970s between the Soherabzai and the Rahmadzai. There was a Rahmatzai *halk,* the Jome Hani Halk, near the Kanati Sarhang. From the Soherabzai point of view, the Rahmatzai were the enemy; there were unsettled blood debts between them. But the Dadolzai, active participants as Soherabzai, nonetheless verbally excluded the Rahmatzai of the Jome Hani Halk from the conflict. The Dadolzai said that this group was closer to the Soherabzai because they had married with the Soberabzai and thus were closer to the Soherabzai than other Rahmatzai groups and a little more distant from the Rahmatzai because of the marriage ties. Marriage ties with Soherabzai made these Rahmatzai—from the point of view of the Dadolzai—"our" Rahmatzai. This was thus a case of "the peace in the feud" (Gluckman 1959:chap. 1), in which cross-cutting affinal ties inhibited conflict between some members of opposed lineage vengeance groups, and the contradictory loyalties flowing from structurally overlapping descent and affinal bonds favored settlement rather than aggression.

Even at the level of major tribal sections, intermarriage drew lineage groups closer. The Surizai and Hoseinzai were said to be close, were said by some to be *yeki,* one, because they had intermarried. The Sardar, Haji Han Mahmud, said that Suri and Husein were both sons of Yarahmad, but their descendants had married together and thus become closer to each other than to the other sections. Lashkar Han Heibut, an elder, took this same view.

Although lineages as defined by genealogical lines were deemed to be structurally equidistant from all sibling lineages, lineages as actual political groups were influenced by affinal ties in their relative closeness. Those lineages that intermarried were politically and practically, if not formally, closer and were recognized to be such by members of other lineages.

## Marriages among Chiefs

While for the ordinary Sarhadi tent dweller, marriage among close kin and within the *brasrend* was attractive, marriage in the chiefly families was often directed outside the tribe, to the chiefly families of other tribes and the leading families of other populations. Marriages between tribes that were regarded as unrelated through descent crossed the divide by establishing affinal ties, which became for the children of those unions matrilateral ties.

Hubyar Han, the Sardar of the Yarahmadzai during 1935–58, father of Sardar Han Mahmud who succeeded him, had over his lifetime six wives. His second and third wives—Mirad Bibi, daughter of Pasons Shiruzai, Huseinzai; and Miradi, daughter of Gemi, Rushanzai, Huseinzai—were from the other major Yarahmadzai tribal section, as opposed to the Soherab section to which the Sardar and his lineage belonged. The other four wives were from other tribes or other smaller groups—Hubyar Han's first wife, Dur Bibi, was the daughter of Dorah, the leader of the Jamalzai of Khash; Zmored was the daughter Kasum Shah Dadzai of Kuhi Berg; Nur Hartun was the daughter of Mesri of the Mir Baluchzai Kord; and Jenet Harun was the daughter of Alehar Han of the Natuzai, Rigi tribe. In sum, two of Hubyar's marriages were with daughters of the largest opposing Yarahmadzai section, two marriages were with daughters of smaller but strategically located populations—the Jamalzai and Mir Baluchzai—and two marriages were with daughters of other major tribes, the Shah Dadzai and Rigi. So although around half of his followers—if the tribal marriage patterns were similar during Hubyar's to that of Han Mahmud's—married members of their own small *brasrend,* and many of them married a father's brother's child, Hubyar Han's marriages were much more strongly outward oriented, into a distant tribal section and into other tribes.

Hubyar Han had 17 children who lived to adulthood and who married 20 times, a few being polygamous marriages and second marriages. Of these 20 marriages, 4 unions were within their own Yar Mahmudzai *brasrend;* 2 were outside of the Yar Mahmudzai but within the Soherabzai section; 3 were in another major Yarahmadzai section; and 11—55 percent of the total, well above the 23 percent recorded for tribesmen of nonchiefly lineages—were outside of the Yarahmadzai, with members of the following lineages or tribes, in order of frequency:

| | |
|---|---|
| Mir Baluchzai Kord | 3 |
| Jamalzai, Khash | 2 |
| Gamshadzai tribe | 2 |
| Shah Dadzai tribe | 1 |
| Yadigarzai, Khash | 1 |
| Irandegan | 1 |
| Kord, Saravan | 1 |

We can see in these marriages a certain continuity between generations, for the affinal ties between Hubyar Han and the Mir Baluchzai, Jamalzai, and Shah Dadzai were repeated in the marriages of his children, as was the affinal tie with the Hoseinzai section of the Yarahmadzai.

Most Sarhadi marriages were to a degree strategic, in that they established ties of alliance between families. Most if not all marriages by Sardar were strategic, aiding either the binding together of the Sardar's own group or the political alliance with other, external groups. This was not a mystery or a secret; the tribesmen spoke of this openly.

For example, the Gamshadzai tribe, of the major Sarhadi tribes, was spatially closest to the Yarahmadzai. Over the generations there had been serious conflicts between the tribes, both over the control of resources and arising from blood injuries between members of the two tribes. Affinal ties between the chiefly lineages of the two tribes had not precluded conflict and confrontation, but they did provide personal relationships between the leadership of the tribes, a moral constraint on conflict, a preference for the peaceful settlement of conflicts, and channels of communication. Thus there was an ongoing effort to maintain affinal ties between the Yarahmadzai and Gamshadzai.

Nur Bibi—the daughter of Yarahmadzai Sardar Jiand Han who led the Yarahmadzai until exiled by the Persians—married Sardar Lashkar Han of the Gamshadzai, who had succeeded his father's brother, Sardar Halil Han, Jiand Han's ally against the British under General Dyer and later against the Persians (table 9.7). Sardar Lashkar Han was succeeded by his son, named Halil Han after his father's father's brother, the earlier, heroic Sardar. Gamshadzai Sardar Halil Han's mother was thus Nur Bibi, the daughter of the previous Yarahmadzai Sardar. With a Yarahmadzai Sardar's daughter the wife of one Gamshadzai Sardar and the mother of the next Gamshadzai Sardar, the affinal ties between the two tribal leaderships could not have been closer. Hubyar Han probably thought it was redundant for him to marry a Gamshadzai.

Yarahmadzai chiefly marriages with the Gamshadzai thus skipped a generation. But by the time Yarahmadzai Sardar Hubyar Han's children were grown, further marriages with the Gamshadzai were needed. Two of his sons, including Han Mahmud, who succeeded him, married into the Gamshadzai chiefly family. Their wives were the granddaughter and the great-granddaughter of Nur Bibi, Jiand Han's daughter. The affinal tie between the Yarahmadzai and the Gamshadzai was thereby reaffirmed (table 9.7).

Another, and, as we shall see, related example was the marriages with the Shah Dadzai, a tribe located in the Kuhi Berg on the other side of Gamshadzai territory. Hubyar Han, as we said, had married Zmored, a daughter of the Shah Dadzai. Now the Shah Dadzai, about whom we have not previously spoken in this narrative, did not loom large in the life of the Yarahmadzai. They were not close neighbors and had not participated, as far as I know from the sources, in the great dramas of warfare

**Table 9.7.** Marriages between Yarahmadzai and Gamshadzai Chiefly Families

```
          Yarahmadzai                          Gamshadzai
          [- - - - - - -]              [- - - - - - - - - - - - - - - - -]
           V       V                        V                    V
          Bijar   Jiand Han[a]            Palawan            Halil Han[a]
           V       V                        V                    V
      Shah Sawar  Nur Bibi            Lashkar Han[a]        Yar Mahmud
           V      [- - - - - - - - - - - - - - - - - - - - - -]        ]
           V                             V        V                    ]
      Hubyar Han[a]                 Halil Han[a]  Han Bibi             ]
      [- - - - - - - - - -]              [- - - - - - - - - - - - -]
       V        V                             V              V
      Kadra    Han                        Gran Bibi         Mirad
      Baksh    Mahmud[a]                       ]            Mahmud
      [        [- - - - - - - - - - - - - - - - - - - - - - - -]        V
      [                                                              Malik
      [                                                              Hartun
      [- - - - - - - - - - - - - - - - - - - - - - - - - - - - - - - -]
```

[a]Sardar.

with the British and the Persians. But the affinal alliance of Hubyar Han was renewed in the next generation when his son Shah Baksh married Meram Harun, daughter of Sab Han, Shah Dadzai.

Why were the Shah Dadzai of interest to the Yarahmadzai? The members of the Sardar's lineage were quite clear about the purpose of these marriages. The Shah Dadzai had intermarried with the Gamshadzai and were potential political supporters of the Gamshadzai. The marriages between the Yarahmadzai and the Shah Dadzai were meant to keep the Shah Dadzai neutral in case of a conflict between the Yarahmadzai and Gamshadzai. The objective was for the affinal ties to draw the Shah Dadzai close enough to the Yarahmadzai so that the Shah Dadzai would be reluctant to actively assist the Gamshadzai against the Yarahmadzai.

While affinal ties were in many cases established to prevent difficulties between tribes, in other cases a marriage was part of a settlement of a dispute or conflict. When there was a blood injury, the giving of a bride to the offended lineage as part of a settlement was deemed to wipe out the blood debt. The marriage between Hubyar Han's sister Han Bibi and Azim Han, the Kord Hakom of Saravan, was part of a settlement of the long-standing dispute between the expanding Yarahmadzai and the retreating Kords (table 9.8). The way this was put by the Yarahmadzai Sardar's lineage was that when Azim Han Kord became *zamas* to Shah Sawar, father of Han Bibi and Hubyar Han, he gave Shah Sawar the *kalat,* fort, in Khash. My reading of the situ-

**Table 9.8.** Marriage Ties between the Yarahmadzai Chiefly Family and the Hakomzat of the Daptan Kords

| *Yarahmadzai* | | *Kurd* |
|---|---|---|
| Shah Sawar | | |
| [------------------] | | |
| V | V | V |
| Hubyar Han[a] | Han Bibi | Azim Han[b] |
| V | [--------------------------] | |
| V | | V |
| Ambar Hartun | | Yakup |
| [----------------------------------------------] | | |

[a]Sardar.

[b]Hakom.

ation is that this marriage, following years of fighting between the Yarahmadzai and the previously dominant Kords, signaled the acceptance of a new balance of power, in which Yarahmadzai ascendancy on the plains south of Kuhi Daptan was recognized and accepted by the Kords. This affinal tie was renewed by the marriage of Hubyar Han's daughter Ambar Hartun to Yakup, the son of Azim Han and Han Bibi. Ambar Hartun Yarahmadzai was thus marrying her father's sister's son, while Yakup Kord was marrying his mother's brother's daughter. Established matrilateral and patrilateral ties thus eased the reproduction of such affinal alliances, making them at once marriages with close kin and alliances between leaders of distinct political entities.

# 10.
# LINEAGES AND LEADERS IN ACTION

Within the Sarhadi tribal system, *baluch* who found themselves threatened by losses of property or by bodily injury were able to call upon a standardized, culturally validated set of procedures for responding. These procedures were part of what I would call a segmentary model. They included balanced opposition of groups and mediation by structurally neutral parties and were based upon structural norms of collective responsibility, group solidarity, complementary opposition, and resolution requiring equivalence of injury or restitution. This segmentary model, as held by Sarhadi Baluch and by other tribal societies near and far, transformed threats and conflicts into an opposition between equals, usually between equal collective entities such as lineages, tribes, and tribal alliances.

The Sarhadi tribesmen that I observed between 1967 and 1976 were living in a tribal system encapsulated by the Iranian state. In the Sarhadi political field of that time, the tribal system was partly but significantly modified or distorted by the forces of centralized state power. In order to observe more precisely the operations of lineages and leaders in this context, let us review a number of incidents and explore in more detail the development of several conflicts.

## KARIM'S PALM TRUNKS

Mahmud Karim was furious. It was August 25, 1972, at the Dadolzai *bonend*, settlement, of the Gorani date groves, at the Mashkil drainage basin. Some palm trunks that Mahmud Karim had prepared—shortened, smoothed, and split—for the roof of his new *ban*, mud-brick dwelling, had been carried off by Nezar of the neighboring Kamil Hanzai *bonend*. It was true, he admitted, that the trunks were palms near the Kamil Hanzai *bonend*, but, he was at pains to point out, they were from

**Table 10.1.** Members of Dadolzai "War Party," August 25, 1972

| Name | Relation to Mahmud Karim | Lineage Affiliation (*brasrend*) |
|------|--------------------------|----------------------------------|
| Shams A'din | Brother of Mahmud Karim | Dadolzai |
| Abdulla | Sister's son of Mahmud Karim | Dadolzai |
| Jan Mahmud | Brother-in-law of Mahmud Karim | Dadolzai |
| Abas | MFBS of Mahmud Karim | Dadolzai |
| Sharif | Son of Gemi, other microlineage | Dadolzai |
| Shahuk | Son of Reis, other microlineage | Dadolzai |
| Ghulam Mahmud | Son-in-law of Ja'far, other microlineage | Dadolzai |
| Id Mahmud | Son-in-law of Ja'far | Mirgolzai |
| Abdulla | Son of Baluch | Dorahzai |
| Suliman | | Gamshadzai |
| Majid | | Gamshadzai |

palms belonging to the *kom* of Mahmud Karim's son-in-law Isa, and not to the Kamil Hanzai.

What Mahmud Karim wanted to do was to gather up a party of men to go with him and take back the trunks, and to fight for them if the Kamil Hanzai put up any resistance. A number of individuals from the *bonend* joined Mahmud Karim in this foray: seven Dadolzai and four non-Dadolzai (see table 10.1). These men, mostly young, carried various light weapons: *lart*, a stick; *tabar*, an ax; *sang*, a stone; *karch*, a knife; brass knuckles; a wand of flexible wire rods with a lead ball on the end; but no firearms.

This confrontation was spoken of by Karim and the others in terms of lineages, the Dadolzai versus the Kamil Hanzai. As they saw it, a man of one lineage had violated the property of a man from another lineage, and the offended man called upon his lineage mates to assist him. The two lineages were equivalent *brasrend*, both being Nur Mahmudzai. Usually these lineages were thought of as close. Not only were they neighbors, but there were some prominent affinal alliances between them. Ja'far's mother was Kamil Hanzai, so they were his matrikin. But this did not stop Ja'far from supporting Mahmud Karim and allowing his two sons-in-law to accompany Karim. After all, in this context—as my Baluchi informants rhetorically put it— it is the father's side that counts; one takes women from anywhere.

Among the Dadolzai party going on the retrieval foray, eight were Dadolzai and four were not. The first four on the list were immediate kin of Mahmud Karim, members of the same informal but ongoing "work team" and lineage mates in the Dadolzai *brasrend*. The next three were coresidents and members of the Dadolzai *brasrend*, but members of other microlineages, subdivisions of the Dadolzai. The final four were associated with the Dadolzai, one as son-in-law and coresident and the others as coresidents. Of these four, two were from the Gamshadzai tribe, one was from a lineage more distant than the two in conflict, and the other was from a lineage that was structurally equidistant.

Why was there this immediate movement to an armed band? Why was not someone sent to inquire, or to try to settle the matter first? In fact, the group was not really a "war party," for its purpose was not to fight. Rather, the group was gathered together to retrieve and transport the trunks, a task for which a dozen men were needed. They armed themselves and were prepared to fight in case the Kamil Hanzai put up a resistance. But the question remains: Why was the response the sending of an armed band?

The sentiments supporting this collective action by members of the Dadolzai and their allies were several. First, there was the desire for immediate action to redress a wrong. Property had been stolen and had to be retrieved. The palm trunks were needed. Second, people felt that they had to come to the aid of their lineage mates, in this case Mahmud Karim. He was in need of help, and it was their obligation to provide it. Not only was it right to do so, but Karim had helped them in the past and would do so in the future. Third, there was fear that lack of action by the Dadolzai would reflect badly on their reputation. If they would not stand up for their rights, they would be regarded as weak, without character, without *topak*, solidarity. Fourth, if they were regarded as weak, others would not be afraid of offending them. They would then be open to all kinds of infringements on their rights and property by others. Their willingness to fight to defend their interests had to be known, so that others would avoid trespassing on the Dadolzai. It was for this reason that the Dadolzai sent an armed party ready to fight, rather than an emissary to ask and request.

As it happened, Mahmud Karim and his group retrieved the trunks without incident and brought them back to the Dadolzai *bonend*. The trunks—two large trunk halves and two small—had been in a grove near but not within the Kamil Hanzai settlement proper, and the Kamil Hanzai did not come out to the location of the trunks. The group brought the two large trunk halves, needed for the roof, but left the two small ones, with Mahmud Karim's agreement. The group was not able to bring all of the trunk halves in one trip and thought better of returning a second time. Mahmud Karim and the others appeared satisfied with the result.

But the situation remained ambiguous and could not be left as it was. It was necessary, now that the trunks had been retrieved, to inquire about the original act of misappropriation and to find out whether a state of hostility existed or did not exist. A neutral intermediary, *mardi monjine* (= Persian: *mianji*), a man without membership in either of the conflicting lineages, had to be sent to the Kamil Hanzai to clarify the situation. Had a Dadolzai gone, and the discussion turned nasty, he would have been at the mercy of the Kamil Hanzai. Gemi, son of Pir Dad, of the Mir Alizai *brasrend* was chosen. It was said that he was a member of neither party and so was not in danger. It was not Gemi's job to make peace, but only to inquire and then to report the current state of the relationship. Had the report been of hostility, "the Dadolzai," according to some opinion, was prepared to go off the next morning in an armed group and fight it out with the Kamil Hanzai.

The report that Gemi brought back was one of reconciliation. Nezar said that he had made a mistake, that Musa—who Mahmud Karim had paid to cut the two palm trunks lengthwise—had told him he could take the trunks, and that he had not realized that they belonged to Mahmud Karim. He furthermore offered to replace the two halves of the small trunk that were left behind. This news was received with pleasure by the Dadolzai, who felt that they had successfully protected their interests. The Dadolzai said that they regarded the matter as closed.

Ja'far, answering my inquiries, said that he, in response to Karim's entreaties, granted permission for the group to go to collect the trunks. He said that they would not have gone without his sanction. But he had instructed them not to go to the Kamil Hanzai settlement itself, as he was not looking for a fight. He told them that they should fight only if they were stopped by force from taking the trunks. Ja'far felt sure that Mahmud Karim was in the right, for he had a report from Musa, who said that Nezar had taken the trunks by force. Even if Musa had said that Nezar could have the trunks, they still had to be retrieved. Furthermore, Ja'far knew that Mustafa, the *master* of the Kamil Hanzai and his *maskom*, would not be enthusiastic about a fight with Ja'far, and so Ja'far felt pretty safe sending his party out.

In this case, Ja'far went on, the Dadolzai had had to stand together against the Kamil Hanzai, for the Dadolzai were *brasrend*, and the Kamil Hanzai were only *maskom*. However, he elaborated, in other circumstances the Dadolzai would support the Kamil Hanzai. If, for example, the Kamil Hanzai were to be fighting with the Mirgolzai or any other more distant lineage, Ja'far and the Dadolzai would support the Kamil Hanzai and fight along with them.

The next morning, August 26, Mustafa, *master* of the Kamil Hanzai, came to see Ja'far, to make sure that good relations had been reestablished. He promised that Musa would bring along another split palm trunk to replace the one left behind. Ja'far assured him that all was as it should be.

## THE GREEDY CAMEL

One reason for the nonaggressive response of the Kamil Hanzai was their immediate involvement in another, more serious conflict. Only two days before the affair of the palm trunks, on August 23, 1972, a fight had broken out between a member of the Kamil Hanzai and the Rahmatzai. The cause of the conflict was a stray camel eating dates off some palms. When Mirad, the Rahmatzai owner of the camel, came in search of the animal, he found it tethered, in the possession of Rashid, the Kamil Hanzai date palm owner. Mirad asked that his camel be released, and Rashid said that he would do so just as soon as the dates the camel had consumed were paid for. The men argued, exchanged unpleasantries, and finally exchanged blows. It was said that Mirad, the Rahmatzai, got the worst of it. He returned to his settlement at Raja, where most of the Rahmatzai in northern Mashkil resided.

When the Dadolzai spoke of this conflict, they identified the parties as Kamil Hanzai, on the one hand, and Rahmatzai, on the other. But these labels referred to nonequivalent groups and levels of organization. The Kamil Hanzai were a *brasrend* of the Nur Mahmudzai maximal lineage, which was part of the Sohorabzai tribal section. The Rahmatzai were another tribal section, structurally equivalent with the Soherabzai, although much smaller in population. So the Dadolzai were seeing the Rahmatzai from the outside, and thinking of the Rahmatzai as an undifferentiated collectivity. Furthermore, as all members of lineages were deemed collectively responsible for the acts of their members, any and every lineage member was open to retaliation for injuries caused by one or several lineage mates. Thus, from the point of view of the Kamil Hanzai, all Rahmatzai were seen as being in a state of conflict with them and their Soherabzai allies, and each and any Kamil Hanzai and member of an allied lineage might be the target of attacks by Rahmatzai. For a Rahmatzai, all Soherabzai were potential attackers as well as legitimate objects of retaliation.

The next day, August 24, three prominent members of the Kamil Hanzai rode on a motorcycle to Rutuk, near Gorani, to check on their date palms there. The Rahmatzai who live at Rutuk, when they saw these Kamil Hanzai, formed a group and chased them away. This was followed, three days later, on August 27, by a violent encounter between a group of 12 Rahmatzai and 6 travelers—Abdul Karim and Shah Bik (both Kamil Hanzai), Mulla Mirza of the Ganguzai, Isa of the Hoseinzai, and two women—on their way back to Gorani from Gwalishtanab, Pakistan. According to the Kamil Hanzai, the young Shah Bik was beaten badly and the older men, including the respected Abdul Karim, and the women were pushed around. This incident, as reported and perhaps exaggerated, caused considerable agitation among the Kamil Hanzai and other members of the Soherabzai. They vigorously and repeatedly stated that it was quite wrong to act disrespectfully to distinguished elders. Furthermore, the Rahmatzai had, by interfering with the elders and women, gone beyond equal reciprocity for the original injury to Mirad the camel owner, which would have allowed roughing up the young man. This was deemed an unjustified escalation.

Earlier, on the night of August 24, after the confrontation at Rutuk, the Kamil Hanzai and other lineages of the Soherabzai collected together and talked about going to Raja to fight the Rahmatzai. It was late and dark, and the tribesmen ultimately decided not to go that night. But after the violent incident on August 27, the Kamil Hanzai and their allies were determined to act. Furthermore, some travelers coming through gave them reason to believe that the Rahmatzai were prepared to meet them in battle.

## The War Party

The next day, August 28, groups of Kamil Hanzai and their Soherabzai and other allies, accompanied of course by this ethnographer, set off across the desert for Patingaz, a clump of wild trees located between Gorani and Raja, in the expectation that the Rahmatzai would join them in battle. They came mostly on foot, carrying only their weapons. Some of the weapons, such as light sticks, appeared to be mainly symbolic; others—mainly clubs, axes, sickles, and brass knuckles—were more dangerous. No firearms were visible, and no defensive accoutrements. Young and adult men had come, but also youths and boys, and older men and a few quite old men. Along with 30 Kamil Hanzai, there were 20 Dadolzai, 25 Mirgolzai, 7 Mehimzai, 5 Yar Mahmudzai, 4 Dorahzai, and 12 Mogolzai, for a total war party of just over 100 fighters.

The tribesmen seemed quite willing to fight, but did not seem passionate. It was only the individuals who were most closely involved structurally in the original conflicts who appeared to have strong emotions about it. Nonetheless, said the allies, they were ready, they would fight! One had to support one's brothers. This was the *baluchi* way. People collected behind their *pusht* and fought with them, never mind affinal ties with the other group.

Although the Kamil Hanzai were the principals in this conflict, all of the other lineages of the Soherabzai were implicated. They were all closer to the Kamil Hanzai and had to support them. Three days before, the Dadolzai were ready to do battle with the Kamil Hanzai, and now they had come as allies to fight alongside the Kamil Hanzai. The reason stated was that they were *yeki,* one. Kamil Han and Dadol were brothers and were Soherabzai. The Rahmatzai were not Soberabzai. Brothers join together to fight their common enemies. Some of the other lineages—such as the Mirgolzai—that joined the Kamil Hanzai were not as close as the Dadolzai, were not in fact Nur Mahmudzai, but rather the descendants of Nur Mahmud's brothers; but they were all Soherabzai, standing together against the Rahmatzai.

The Soherabzai stood together, but the war party ended up standing around, for the Rahmatzai did not show up on that day. Along with some of the others, I—having found a post at the top of a sand dune, my camera at the ready—was both disappointed and relieved at the anticlimax. I had been excited at the prospect of seeing tribal conflict, and observing firsthand how it developed, and was disappointed when no confrontation took place. I was also relieved, because I am not enthusiastic about violence in general or about people—especially my friends, not to mention myself—getting hurt. But, really, I had already seen the most interesting part of the process: the lineage system at work, dividing people up into balanced segments, and unifying them in opposition.

## The Enemy Within

One of the coresidents of the Dadolzai was Isa, son of Rasul, Rahmatzai, who was married to Malik Hartun, sister of Mahmud Karim and Shams A'din. He had prior to the migration to Mashkel been living in the Ja'fari Halk on the Sarhad and was during this dispute living in the Dadolzai *bonend* at Gorani. That he was there was known by the Kamil Hanzai and others, and threats had been directed his way. The Dadolzai stood behind their Rahmatzai *zamas*, son-in-law, saying that he was under their protection, and, as a consequence, or so was the understanding in the minds of the Dadolzai, there were no attacks on him.

On August 29, as had been planned for reasons unrelated to the conflict, Isa left Mashkil for Khash. In Khash, he met Sab Han, one of the *master* of the Rahmatzai, who had come to gather up Rahmatzai to return to Mashkil so that they could support their fellow lineage mates. By August 31, he had succeeded in sending a dozen or so Rahmatzai to Mashkil. Sab Han recruited Isa to return to Mashkil and join the other Rahmatzai. He agreed and left the Dadolzai, switching his residence to his lineage mates. It was said among the Dadolzai that, if necessary, Isa would fight against his Dadolzai in-laws.

Although the Dadolzai stood up for Isa Rasul, "bracketing" him off from the Rahmatzai-Soherabzai conflict, and giving him their protection, this dispute colored the relationship between these affinal kin. The argument—discussed in chapter 9— which took place during early December 1972 between Isa and his brothers-in-law and the other Dadolzai, and the bad feelings that so quickly arose, must be understood in terms of the bitter atmosphere of the broader Rahmatzai-Soherabzai conflict. This was what explained the disdainful comments about the Rahmatzai by the Dadolzai. Such sentiments were to a great degree contingent on the contemporary dispute, for if this had been a long-term assessment, why had the Dadolzai accepted Isa Rasul as a *zamas* in the first place?

### The Sardar's First Moves

When the Yarahmadzai Sardar Haji Han Mahmud heard about this dispute in the last days of August, he returned quickly to Mashkil, to his *ban* in the Mirgolzai *bonend*. He immediately spoke with representatives of the Kamil Hanzai. On September 1 he went to Raja, to the Rahmatzai. His goal was to bring about a peaceful settlement of this dispute. The discussion was reported to me by several Soherabzai sources.

SARDAR: The Rahmatzai and Kamil Hanzai are all brothers, should not be fighting, and should settle the matter peacefully. You, the Rahmatzai did not call upon me to settle the matter, which was wrong of you. But if you would give the Hamil Hanzai 5,000 toman and two girls for marriage without bride-wealth payments, the matter would be settled. After all, you manhandled Abdul Karim, an old and important man of the Sohorabzai, and this puts the balance of blame on you.

MAHMUD SELIM, *speaking for the Rahmatzai:* No, we absolutely will not pay. We
are one *kom* and the Sohorabzai are one *kom* and the two are equal. The Rahmatzai is prepared to fight but not to pay.

SARDAR: The Rahmatzai should then give 3,000 toman, and I will see that it is settled.

MAHMUD SELIM: No, the Rahmatzai will not pay.

From this point my sources differed, one source close to the Sardar saying that the
Rahmatzai simply refused to pay. But other sources reported the following.

MAHMUD SELIM: The Rahmatzai will not pay. And furthermore, you, Han Mahmud, no longer have our *kabul,* consent, as our leader. We repudiate you as
our Sardar.

Perhaps because the Sardar himself was Yar Mahmudzai Soherabzai, they felt that he
was taking the Soherabzai side. Certainly from the point of view of segmentary politics, the Sardar was not structurally neutral, being in descent quite close to the Kamil
Hanzai, Kamil Han and Yar Mahmud having been brothers.

SARDAR: I have come to make peace, even though you did not send for me. If you
do not wish to make a peaceful settlement, you cannot expect me to help you
when you find yourselves in difficulty. I have the support of the *dolat,* the government of Iran, and they will use their force as I say. If anything happens to
any of the Rahmatzai, I will not do anything about it.

MAHMUD SELIM: We Rahmatzai are Pakistani not Irani, and are thus safe from
Iranian government interference. As far as the Sardar and the Soherabzai are
concerned, the Rahmatzai are a separate tribe.

Now I must confess that when I heard about the Rahmatzai claiming to be a separate tribe, I felt rather uncomfortable and slightly alarmed. Oh no, I thought, the
Yarahmadzai tribe is breaking up! But, of course, what the Rahmatzai were expressing was the principle of segmentary opposition, and this expression really should not
have been a surprise to anyone, not even the ethnographer still feeling his way around
tribal life.

The Sardar returned to the Kamil Hanzai *bonend* and reported the results of his
discussion. While he might not have been surprised at what he heard, he was never-
theless very irritated with the Rahmatzai. He authorized punitive actions by the
Kamil Hanzai and other Soherabzai. On September 5, a group of some 40 Sohorabzai
from various lineages, led by Mustafa, *master* of the Kamil Hanzai, and including
Mahmud Karim and some other Dadolzai, set off for Rahmatzai territory. Having
arrived, they spoiled four shallow camel wells by filling them with dirt and palm

branches. Mustafa alone had a rifle, of ancient vintage, and he brought it into play by shooting at a distant Rahmatzai, who sped off on his camel. Mustafa was later reported as saying that he did not wish to kill anyone but the leaders of the Rahmatzai, Sahib Han and Mahmud Salim. Whatever Mustafa's intent, there were no further contacts with Rahmatzai on that excursion.

Fear was growing among the tribesmen. At Gorani, in the Soherabzai settlements, there were frightening rumors. One was that Rahmatzai with rifles were sneaking in at night to kill some lone Soherabzai. This rumor lost some of its power when a particular rifle carrier was later identified as a Soherabzai.

Around 8 in the evening on September 6, a group of some 10 Soherabzai from a mix of lineages set off for Gazeh, with the goal of continuing to the household of Azat, a Rahmatzai, at Kalesagon, in order to beat him up. But the news had reached Azat, and he had left for Raja by foot after sundown prayer at 6. When the Soherabzai party arrived, only Azat's wife and children were there, and they were very afraid. But the Soherabzai left without taking any action.

There was no further activity on September 7 or 8, but the tribesmen anticipated that fighting would break out again and predicted that this time there would be shooting. According to some sources, the Sardar said that Mahmud Salim, Sahib Han, and Haji Abdul should be killed, and that he would take care of any problems that arose with the government. According to other sources, the Sardar had said that these men should be beaten, not that they should be killed, although he did say that if anyone died, he would intervene with the government to protect those responsible. In any case, the Sardar gave his *dastur,* order, for action against these Rahmatzai leaders. The tribesmen said that anyone who killed under the Sardar's orders and was taken by *dolat* would be released at the Sardar's request. But in spite of all of this threatening talk, no one undertook an attack on the leaders of the Rahmatzai. Perhaps the intent was to let news of the *dastur* sink in among the Rahmatzai and to see whether the threats would bring any movement toward settlement.

Meanwhile, in Khash, during the first week in September, Soherabzai and Rahmatzai were going about their business and interacting peacefully, with no sign of conflict. This was explained by the fact that there were no Kamil Hanzai present. Other Soherabzai would fight with the Kamil Hanzai against the Rahmatzai, but the fight itself was between the Kamil Hanzai and the Rahmatzai, and other lineages of the Soherabzai would not fight without provocation. Had Kamil Hanzai and Rahmatzai met in Khash, I was told, they would have fought.

On September 10, officers of the gendarmerie from Jalq and Saravan—in response to a request from the Sardar or from Ars Mahmud, father of the injured Shah Bik, according to the source—arrived at Gorani. They stayed overnight and the next day drove to the nearest Pakistani police station at Gwaleshtanap. The gendarmes were investigating the conflict, and asked the Pakistani police to do the same among the Rahmatzai. They intended to communicate the results of their investigation to the

Pakistanis and then they or the Pakistani police could act on the conclusions to punish the offenders. But these inquiries did not seem to lead to any decisive action or to bring about any resolution to the dispute.

At the end of October, after almost two months of cooling down, with perhaps some pressure by the police on both sides of the border, a party of Rahmatzai came to the Sardar wishing to settle the dispute. The Rahmatzai were represented by Mahmud Salim, his son Said Mahmud, Abdulla, and Azat Han; Sahib Han did not attend. The Kamil Hanzai were represented by Mustafa; and Abdul Karim and Ars Mahmud, the injured Shah Bik's father, were also there. The Rahmatzai agreed to the 5,000 toman demanded by the Sardar for the elderly notable Abdul Karim. The Sardar was pleased with this offer and said that the Rahmatzai would have to provide only 4,000 and that he would collect the other 1,000 from contributions by other lineages. However, Ars Mahmud demanded an additional 3,000 toman for himself and his son, and was supported by Mustafa. The Rahmatzai refused to pay the additional 3,000 toman, and the Sardar supported them. After considerable wrangling, the parties failed to agree. But now the Sardar was satisfied with the Rahmatzai offer and was annoyed at what he regarded as the excessive demands of the Kamil Hanzai. So the Sardar took the position that he would no longer support the demands of the Kamil Hanzai.

Though this meeting failed to bring about a formal peace, the Rahmatzai attempts to settle and the Sardar's repudiation of the further demands of the Kamil Hanzai took the edge off the dispute. Some prominent tribesmen, such as Ja'far, thought that the dispute was on the way to being settled, and that it would be resolved before spring, when the Rahmatzai customarily brought their herds to Garonchin. However, if the dispute was not settled by *hamin* and fighting broke out again at Mashkil, the Dadolzai would once again support the Kamil Hanzai. As a number of Dadolzai said, "They are our brothers and we must support them." Perhaps the Kamil Hanzai were asking too much and being unreasonable, and perhaps they should have accepted what was offered. But for the Dadolzai, fault or blame did not bear on the question of support; they would support the Kamil Hanzai. But, on the whole, the Dadolzai felt that the dispute was over even if it was not formally closed. The Sardar would pressure the Kamil Hanzai to accept resolution and would discourage further conflict.

Through the winter and spring the Sardar continued to think about ways to bring about an end to this dispute. He told me that he thought that Mustafa was not holding out for more money, but did not want to settle. He did not know why, but thought that Mustafa might *bakshist*, forgive, the debt and close the matter. But he, the Sardar, would not ask the Nur Mahmudzai or Soherabzai to *bejara kon*, to contribute to the blood money, as he often did as part of a final settlement. Rather, he would pay the 1,000 toman himself, not as a member of the Nur Mahmudzai or Soherabzai, but as Sardar, or he would accept donations from the Hoseinzai, the third tribal section. But he would not ask the Soherabzai relatives of the abused elder Abdul Karim to contribute. It was a great offense by the Rahmatzai to have abused a respected elder. In other cases, when young men were involved, yes, even fraternal lineages contributed to the blood money paid by distant lineages.

## Reprise

Between 1973, when I left Baluchistan, and 1976, when I returned, the dispute between the Rahmatzai and the Kamil Hanzai and other Soherabzai continued to smolder, breaking out in flames from time to time, increasing in intensity in the summer of 1975. Some people were referring to it as *jang,* war. The events were described to me by Soherabzai as follows.

Dissatisfied with what appeared to them an outstanding blood debt, three members of the Kamil Hanzai conspired with Sol Mahmud, a Mirgolzai, to kidnap Haji Nur Bik, a Rahmatzai then residing at Garonchin. Sol Mahmud, not a Kamil Hanzai and thus not a primary in the dispute, went to Nur Bik's tent as a guest and ate with Nur Bik. He told Nur Bik that Juda Han, the famous Mirgolzai smuggler, had buried some goods, and that he, Sol Mahmud, knew where they were buried. He proposed, because he could not do this himself, that he and Nur Bik go together and dig up Juda's smuggled goods. Nur Bik found this offer too good to pass up and went along with Sol Mahmud. But what waited hidden for him was not illicit wealth, but three Kamil Hanzai, intent on avenging the blood debt. When he arrived at the appointed spot, the Kamil Hanzai grabbed him, hit him twice with a stick, and hauled him off to the elder Abdul Karim, the injured Kamil Hanzai party. The captors of Nur Bik asked Abdul Karim what he wanted them to do with Nur Bik. Abdul Karim said that he wanted them to do nothing, and that he would *baksh* his injury. Nur Bik was then released.

Another incident, unrelated specifically to the previous one, but infused with the atmosphere arising from the general conflict, involved Isa Rasul. While at the Dadolzai camp, he fought with Ghulam Rasul, son of Harun, Mah Malikzai, Soherabzai, over a 50 rupee debt. Ja'far and others broke up the fight and Ghulam Rasul left. But later he returned, accompanied by Halil, son of Kasum, Dorahzai, and Nezar Mahmud Mogolzai. In spite of Dadolzai intervention, Halil managed to hit Isa Rasul on the wrist with a stick. Isa, accompanied by Rahim Taj Mahmud and Mahmud Hassan Rahmatzai, then went to the *pasgah,* the gendarmerie station, and made a complaint against Halil. Meanwhile, the Sardar had heard about this incident and came to the *pasgah,* accompanied by other Soherabzai of the Yar Mahmudzai, Zabedzai, Dorahzai, and Dadolzai lineages. Under the Sardar's direction, all of the tribesmen formed a *diwan* (=Persian: *divan,* royal court, tribunal of justice), a meeting for deliberation. This *diwan* quickly degenerated into charges and countercharges, then slaps; and then, much to the horror of the Sardar, the Soherabzai all fell on the Rahmatzai and beat them badly. The Sardar jumped in to stop this attack, cursing and even hitting the attackers, but could not stop the beating of the Rahmatzai.

Meanwhile, in response to the kidnapping of Haji Nur Bik on the Sarhad, four Rahmatzai from Raja made a complaint to the police in the provincial capital of Quetta, Pakistan, that Islam, son of Nezar, Kamil Hanzai, was not a Pakistani but an Iranian and had no right to be in Pakistan. This Islam Nezar customarily worked on both sides of the border; in the fall, winter, and spring he traded, using Mirjaveh in Pakistan as a base, while in summer he grew grain on his irrigated land at Gazu on the Sarhad, and then went to Gorani at Mashkel for dates. As a result of this complaint by the Rahmatzai, Islam Nezar was arrested and taken to the police station. But Islam had in fact seen to the formalities and had a Pakistani identity card, and so was released.

The news of this complaint and arrest was conveyed by some members of the Rigi tribe, who were in Quetta at the time, to Islam's father Nezar, who was on the Sarhad. Nezar then made a complaint in Khash naming Gol Jan, a *master* of the Rahmatzai, and three others, saying that they had had his son jailed in Quetta. All of these men were called to the *dadgah*, court, in Khash and told to make peace there and then. But the encounter in court degenerated quickly, and some dozen Soherabzai and Rahmatzai began to fight—at the court!—as a result of which six men were arrested, the others having run away and escaped arrest. Nezar, it was said, sustained an injury with at least some evident blood, a diacritic for Sarhadi Baluch of serious harm.

In response to the fight at the *dadgah* of Khash, and to avenge the blood debt from Nezar's injury, six Soherabzai—four Kamil Hanzai, one Dadolzai, and one Yar Mahmudzai—sought out Lah Han, brother of Mahmud Selim, Rahmatzai *master* at Raja, who was working at Karvandar on the Sarhad. Lah Han was beaten, and some of his blood was spilled.

The beating of Lah Han incensed the Rahmatzai, some of whom made up a war party of 16 men—a truck with 10 men and three motocycles with 2 men each—to find some Soherabzai and take revenge. Salu Han, returning north by motorcycle from Garonchin, had the misfortune to run into this war party. They chased him, and he sought refuge in a house, where he armed himself with a knife. Salu Han and the war party threw rocks back and forth until finally Salu Han was hit in the forehead and some blood was shed. The women of the house yelled at the war party, the members of which finally left, came to Khash, and announced with some exaggeration that they had killed Salu Han.

Not to be outdone, and to avenge the Rahmatzai outrages on Salu Han, the Soherabzai—mostly Kamal Hanzai and Dorahzai, but including some individuals from the Mirgolzai, Mah Malikzai, and two from the Dadolzai—formed an even larger war party of 30 men on 10 motorcycles. Their target was a Rahmatzai *halk*. But when they arrived, they found that all of the men had fled and hidden, as it turned out in Haji Abdulla's residence at Neelagu. Undeterred, the Soherabzai war party searched out a Rahmatzai *halk* in Garonchin, where they found 3 men, one hidden under a quilt, and beat two badly, drawing blood.

The Rahmatzai went to the gendarmerie in Khash and made a complaint against the Soherabzai. The Rais of the Pasgah brought a good-sized contingent of gendarmes to find the Kamil Hanzai at Burienbella, but when they arrived the men had already escaped to the hills. Id Mahmud told me that they were not afraid of the *dolat* or even of jail but wanted to avoid having their heads shaved! Better to be criticized for vanity, I suppose, than for cowardice or fear.

The gendarmerie called in the Sardar and told him that if he did not stop this fighting they were going to hold him personally responsible and he would see what trouble they would cause him. The Sardar, for his part, was just as irritated with this dispute as was the gendarmerie. To try, once again, to resolve it peacefully, the Sardar went to Burienbellah and announced a *diwan*. The *diwan* was held in Khash, with perhaps 100 men. The Sardar, I imagine, would have said the standard things: this behavior was shameful; these events were making a laughing stock of the tribe; the Yarahmadzai were all one, all brothers; were they not big enough to settle this matter. But this time the Sardar went farther; he said that he himself would not tolerate any further fighting, and that he himself would support the gendarmerie in suppressing the violence and punishing the culprits. To that end, he explained, he intended to arrange with the court that anyone fighting would be fined 5,000 toman. And this he did. In the end, the Sardar succeeded in bringing about a settlement. No money was exchanged. The Rahmatzai were acknowledged to be, at that point, the most injured, but they *baksh kort*, forgave the debt. The *jang* of the Rahmatzai versus Soberabzai was settled.

## United We Stand

The events of the Dadolzai–Kamil Hanzai and Rahmatzai-Soherabzai disputes—even in my undoubtedly incomplete accounts—are indicative of the part played by segmentary organization among the Sarhadi Baluch. Let us consider what we have heard.

The initial events in both cases were threats or apparent threats to the property of an individual: the loss of valuable palm trunks; and the loss of dates eaten by a camel, followed by a demand for compensation. In the first case, it was feared that an attempt to retrieve the palms would meet violent resistance. In the second case, the demands for immediate compensation prior to the release of the offending camel led to a violent fight. In both instances, many other individuals were quickly involved.

The reason that others were quickly and, as we have seen, often willingly involved, was the sense of collective responsibility among the tribesmen. For a tribesman, the presumption was that individuals were not isolates but members of groups, patrilineages, which they represented and which would support them morally, politically, and militarily. The Sarhadi view was that all lineage members were responsible for each lineage member, and that each lineage member was responsible for all of the others. This collective responsibility had two main aspects.

First, lineage members were obliged to protect and assist every other lineage member. In practice, this meant that one had to come to the aid of lineage mates in difficulty, whether from violent threat by outsiders or from economic need, illness, or social distress. There was a strong sense of generalized reciprocity among lineage mates, and an appreciation that those who relied upon you at one moment, you would have to call upon in the future. In cases of blood debt, each lineage member was obliged to contribute to the financial compensation, sometimes substantial, in any settlement.

Second, each lineage member was deemed by all outsiders to be responsible for the acts and actions of all other lineage members. In this sense, members of lineages were considered to be not unique individuals, but interchangeable equivalents. Thus retribution by outsiders for an injury could be directed at any lineage member. So, for this reason among others, individuals were far from indifferent about the acts of their lineage mates. Any individual might have been called upon to pay for what his or her lineage mates did. There was thus considerable social pressure within lineages to keep members from engaging in unjustified and foolish initiatives.

For Sarhadi tribesmen, the social order that allowed daily life to proceed without conflict, that provided security for the person and for property, and imposed social control over people's action, consisted primarily of the corporate lineage system. In the absence, illegitimacy, or ineffectuality of hierarchical power that characterized tribal life, order and security rested upon the collective unity of the lineages and upon a balance of power among the lineage segments. A balance of power among lineages provided peace and security by guaranteeing that unjust appropriation of property or injury to the person would result in retribution and equivalent loss.

The rights and obligations of individuals as members of lineages were spelled out normatively, of course, but were by no means solely normative. Mutual aid, generalized reciprocity, and solidarity among lineage mates were not only nice things to do. Tribesmen saw these also as being in their interest, for they believed that their individual destinies were dependent upon the character of their particular lineage and how it was perceived by members of other lineages. Everyone wanted their lineages to be seen as solidary, brave, and tough, so that others would avoid any hostile actions. Thus any act by an outsider that could be perceived as deleterious to the interests of the lineage had to be responded to in a decisive fashion, lest others see the lineage as weak and its members as easy targets. The tribesmen believed that each offense against its members that was not strongly answered would lead to other offenses, and these would lead to yet more. In tribal Baluchistan, the price of security was eternal vigilance.

## Who We Are Depends on Whom We Face

A balance of power may have maintained, in a rough way, the security of the tribesmen. But what maintained the balance of power? Here we address two technical problems: How can a balanced opposition be maintained as descent groups vary in size and population? How can balanced opposition be maintained in spite of the advantage that several groups would have in ganging up on one group?

The size of descent groups depended, among other things, upon accidents of health and fertility. What happened to balanced oppositions when some groups were large, with many people, and others were small, with only a few? This was a biological problem solved by social means. A variety of conceptual manipulations and social alliances were used to ensure that lineages were large enough to be viable and to play their parts in balanced opposition. In some segmentary systems, such as the Cyrenaican Bedouin (Peters 1960), manipulation of the genealogy justified contemporary lineages of the appropriate size. In other societies, such as the northern Somali (Lewis 1961), explicit forms of alliance were used to build viable groups. Among the Sarhadi *baluch,* some conceptual manipulation took place, as we have seen with the incorporation of the Surizai as a section, although it was also accepted that some lines grew strong while others petered out. Among the Hoseinzai, as we have seen, the grandsons of Hosein, apical ancestors of three strong lineages, became more important structurally than the Hosein's two sons. Another important measure that could be used to incorporate weak lines into unified lineages, and thus maintain a viable lineage and a balance among lineages, was affinal alliance. Among the Dadolzai, the multiple intermarriages of the Shadi Hanzai and Dust Mahmudzai enabled them to act politically in a unified fashion in relation to the other Dadolzai sublineages.

Even if all of the *brasrend* "on the ground" were a viable size, from 50 to 150 persons, what was to keep two or three *brasrend* from ganging up on one, if this happened to be politically expedient? This social problem was solved by biological—at least conceptually biological—means. In the segmentary lineage system, contingent political affiliation was predetermined by genealogical closeness or distance, which was normatively privileged as the basis of alliance. One was obliged to side with a brother against a cousin, with brothers and cousins against more distant kin, with other *brasrend* of one's maximal segment against another maximal segment, with other maximal segments of one's tribal section against another tribal section, and so on. Similarly, in a dispute between cousins, ego was structurally neutral and so was not supposed to take sides, although one could and perhaps should try to settle the dispute.

The genius of the segmentary lineage system was that, through this complementary opposition, a balance of power was maintained. The splitting or clumping of lineages according to the descent of the individuals in conflict ensured at least a rough equivalence of number among disputants, a critical parameter in a tribal setting where most adult males were potential warriors. Through this equivalence, a balance of power was maintained, and through the balance of power, a degree of peace and security.

What I have called "lineage complementary opposition," as part of a "segmentary model," was the way Sarhadi tribesmen viewed political alliances and action. This set of rules was believed and asserted by the Sarhadi tribesmen. The disputes of the Dadolzai versus the Kamil Hanzai and the Rahmatzai versus the Soherabzai were two examples of the way that this model played out in practice. In these disputes, the Dadolzai opposed the Kamil Hanzai and were ready to resort to violence, and then, as members of the Soherabzai tribal section, closed ranks with the Kamil Hanzai to support them in opposition to the Rahmatzai tribal section. While the principals in the dispute, particularly those injured, were primary points of reference, and the *bras-rend* of the injured parties, in this case the Kamil Hanzai among the Soherabzai, had the responsibility for taking vengeance, seeking redress, or accepting a settlement, other lineages of the tribal sections were expected to provide support and did participate actively in the conflict.

The position of Isa Rasul, a Rahmatzai married to and living among the Soherabzai, illustrated the power of lineage and sectional affiliation. Although under the protection of his affines, the Dadolzai, Isa remained under threat from other Soherabzai. But more important was his obligation to come to the aid of his patrikin, even to the extent of having to fight his own affines. It was this obligation that led him to change residence, to leave his affines and return to the Rahmatzai. The ongoing dispute between his Rahmatzai lineage mates and his Soherabzai affines soured relations between him and his affines, as we saw in his angry dispute with the Dadolzai. Let us now examine a case in which the norm of complementary opposition was violated.

## THE TRAITOR

Early in 1973, the Kamil Hanzai, who had occupied Nugju before the *kan*, irrigation tunnel (see chapter 5), broke down, came to an agreement with Juda, Mirgolzai, owner of the pump at Gwanich, that he would supply the funds for restoring the *kan* for a half-share of the water. Juda decided, instead, to restore an old *kan* running to the side of Nugju. As this *kan* was being restored, members of the Hoseinzai section of the tribe asserted that this *kan*, in functioning order or not, was theirs, for it had been constructed by their *piruk*, grandfather.

Juda said that he would not give up the *kan* to them. The Hoseinzai threatened to fight, and Juda said that they could do so and everyone would see whether the Hoseinzai or Sohorabzai were stronger. The Hoseinzai went to the local *pasgah*, gendarme post, and put their case to the Reis, a corporal. He said that he could not judge but would ask some *piri mard*, old men, for information about ownership. He questioned Sahib Han and Zame Han of the Zabehzai Soherabzai and Walli Mahmud of the Dadolzai Soherabzai, and they agreed that the *kan* was previously under the control of the Hoseinzai and that they themselves had on occasion helped the Hoseinzai with the harvest. The *reisi pasgah* wrote to the court that Juda had no right to the *kan* and was withholding it from the rightful owners by force.

An important supporter of the claims of the Hoseinzai was Halil, recognized *master* of the Dadolzai, and a respected figure among the Soherabzai. Halil was tied affinally to his Hoseinzai neighbors in the agricultural location of Shagbond. However, his support for the Hoseinzai against Juda was an alliance against a fraternal lineage—the Dadolzai were Nur Mahmudzai, and Nur Mahmud and Mirgol were brothers, and both were of the Soherabzai tribal section—in favor of a more distant tribal section, the opposing Hoseinzai.

Whatever the tribesmen thought about the legitimate rights of ownership of the disputed *kan*, Halil's support for the Hoseinzai against his own Soherabzai caused no end of consternation among members of the Soherabzai, including Ja'far, *master* of the Dadolzai second to Halil, and even the Sardar, himself Nur Mahmudzai Soherabzai, like the Dadolzai. Juda was furious at Halil for his treasonous support of the Hoseinzai and threatened to kill him.

Speculation among the Soherabzai about Halil's action focused on his Hoseinzai wife and her pressure to support her kin: as if Halil could avoid responsibility by saying "My Hoseinzai wife made me do it"! Blaming the non-Dadolzai wife appeared to me to be a rather lame excuse, aimed at shifting the blame away from Halil. Some also raised the question of material interests, whether Halil thought he would benefit from the new Hoseinzai *kan*. Furthermore, it was reported that the previous year Halil and Juda had had an argument about the upper section of the *kan*, Juda saying that it originally belonged to Nugju and Halil saying that it had always belonged to Shagbond. So Halil and Juda had already had a history of disputing about *kan* ownership. In any case, so the excuses continued, at the beginning of the dispute, the conflict was merely about property, with no threat of blood or injury involved.

Whatever the excuses and justifications, it was ringingly affirmed among the Soherabzai that supporting more distant lineages against closer ones—"one's own kin," situationally defined—was a terrible offense. Tribesmen went so far as to say that a lineage would suspend action against an opposing lineage to deal with renegades among its own constituent parts.

While a decision from the court was pending, an event took place that changed the course of the conflict. Juda announced that an unknown assailant had shot at him, three pistol shots that narrowly missed. Juda notified the gendarmerie, and consequently a team of investigators consisting of the Reis of the gendarmerie in Khash, the doctor, and the head of the court came out to Gwanich. The Hoseinzai was accused by Juda, although he could not identify any individual. The Hoseinzai said that the alleged shooting was a fraud cooked up by Juda, but bullets were found, and the doctor verified that there was a bullet hole in Juda's trousers.

Nezar Mahmud, the brother of the Sardar, said that Juda shot at himself. And he argued that if the dispute had really become a matter of blood, Halil would have supported Juda because of their common lineage affiliation. But these remarks were speculation only.

Just at that time, the Sardar returned from a trip to Teheran, and the gendarmerie requested that he try to settle the matter before Juda's complaint came to court. The Sardar called a *diwan* of all the relevant people. After hearing testimony, he said that the Hoseinzai should release their claim to the *kan* and give Juda three of their daughters, free of any brideprice, as *bimayari*, penalty, for the attempt on Juda's life. Haji Pez Mahmud and Haji Ahmad, both of the Hoseinzai were to give a daughter to Juda. And—most interesting for the anthropological observer—Halil, *master* of the Dadolzai, was also to give a daughter to Juda, for having sided with the Hoseinzai against his own kin. Juda, in return, was to cancel his complaint to the court and thus preclude legal action and perhaps jail sentences for the Hoseinzai. Both sides agreed, and there the matter ended, except that after a month Juda relinquished his claim on the three girls.

Halil, for whatever reason, had chosen to oppose a close kinsmen and support more distant kinsmen. He violated the segmentary norm that directed him to support close kin against distant kin. Halil's deviance, I would submit, did not demonstrate the weakness of the norm. The strength of the norm was reflected in the strength of the social reaction to his deviance. Even Halil's closest kin condemned his siding with the Hoseinzai against Juda. Public opinion, at least as expressed, was unanimous against Halil's act. This condemnation was manifested in the penalty—determined by the Sardar on behalf of the tribe as a whole—that Halil was obliged—and agreed—to pay: giving a daughter free of brideprice to the offended Juda.

## SEPARATED SONS AND DISTANT BROTHERS

It is understandable that those kinsmen who have lived together, intermarried, and worked together should feel an obligation to support one another against outside threat. But among the Sarhadi *baluch,* collective responsibility and lineage solidarity went beyond the sentiments built up through quotidian reciprocity. According to the Sarhadi tribal view, political support extended as a matter of principle along the lines of patrilineal descent and was limited to ties of patrilineal descent, ignoring relations based upon affinal ties and reciprocity.

In the case of Isa Rasul, the protection extended by the Dadolzai, although it showed the strength and solidarity of the lineage, deviated from the segmentary principle. But the subsequent move of Isa back to his home lineage and the cooling in relations between Isa and his affines were concordant with segmentary norms.

One of the residents of the Ja'fari Halk in 1972–73, named Baluch, was a Dorahzai. Although Baluch camped with the Dadolzai, he and others denied that he did not get along with his lineage mates, although everyone agreed that it is best to reside with one's lineage mates. However that may be, and whatever the exact reasons that Baluch preferred living with the Dadolzai to living with his own Dorahzai, there was no doubt in the minds of the Dadolzai that, in terms of any political conflict, Baluch's primary political loyalty lay with the Dorahzai. According to the Dadolzai, if a Dorahzai came to see one of the Dadolzai and got into a fight, Baluch would have to come to the aid of the Dorahzai. This assessment was not presented as a criticism of Baluch, but as a simple recognition of what he should do and would do.

This rigidity of the segmentary lineage system, providing a stable framework of political affiliation and security, was what allowed individual tribesmen, during periods of peace, to move from one camp to another and to associate with any other tribesmen in making a living and daily sociability. Wherever they lived, whoever they associated with on a daily basis, tribesmen knew that they could count on their lineage mates in cases of conflict. This belief was put to the test by another man named Baluch, son of Shakar, Shirdelzai Dadolzai, and his son, Mahmud, in the spring of 1976.

Baluch Shakar, brother of the deceased Karim Han who had resided as part of the Ja'fari Halk, had 25 or 30 years before married a Kordish women, Zar Malik, and had lived for decades in Kordish territory, north of the Yarahmadzai area, in the valleys of Daptan, near Sangu, the seat of the Kord Hakom. Baluch and his family had thus long been spatially distant from his Dadolzai *brasrend* and had not been involved in the daily life of his lineage mates.

Baluch began to rethink his situation when one of his older sons had a fight. Baluch's son Mahmud had gone to ask Sol Mahmud, son of Gemi, Kamil Hanzai, for a *shaneg* that was owed to his younger brother, who had served Sol Mahmud as *shwaneg*. There was a disagreement and unpleasantries were exchanged, followed by some pushing and a fall. Mahmud had grabbed Sol Mahmud's jacket and beard; Sol Mahmud had knocked Mahmud down. Mahmud said that Sol Mahmud had hit him with a rock and broken his tooth; Sol Mahmud said that Mahmud had fallen and hit his tooth on a rock. But no one denied that Mahmud had broken a tooth, which counted in Sarhadi reckoning as half of a blood injury. The next morning, so it was reported, Mahmud also bled from the ear.

After this fight, Baluch came to the Ja'fari Halk, walking much of the way from Daptan, to discuss with Ja'far moving his tent from Daptan and joining the Halk. He said that for many years he had lived "alone," that is, without other Dadolzai, in Daptan, but that after his son's fight, he did not want to live alone any more and wanted to join his Dadolzai lineage mates. Ja'far agreed to his joining the camp. Baluch had arranged to borrow camels and planned to migrate the next day. A party of Dadolzai, mostly young men—Isa Say Han, Abdulla Rehim Dad, Solar, Ghulam Mustafa Sab Han, and another of Baluch's sons, Abdulla, married to the daughter, Nuras, of the deceased Karim Han—went to Daptan to help Baluch migrate and to defend Baluch and his family against any attack from the Kamil Hanzai.

Mahmud, assisted by Azim Han, *master* of the Zabedzai, his brother-in-law, went to court in Khash and made a complaint against Sol Mahmud. Subsequently, the Reis of the gendarmerie in Khash called the disputants in and asked them to solve the matter among themselves. If this proved impossible, he would then send the case to court. The Sardar, intervening to promote settlement of this dispute, arranged a *diwan*. Attending the *diwan* were Azim Han and Dadolzai including Ja'far, Gemi, Haji Reis, Suliman Dadol, Hamal Dadol, Mahmud Karim, Ido, Shams A'din, Isa Say Han, Baluch's sons, Mahmud Selim and Allah Baksh, and the injured party, Mahmud, as well as Id Mahmud Mirgolzai, the *zamas* of Ja'far, Jan Mahmud, Hakim, and Dust Mahmud of the Dust Mahmudzai, Shandi, Dust Mahmud, and Mulla Nur Mahmud Gol Mahmudzai, Shir Mahmud, Mahmud, Halil, and Baluch Dorahzai, Nader Surizai, Abas and Ghulam Shah Hoseinzai, and Ghulam Mahmud Gamshadzai. The other principal, Sol Mahmud, was also present, supported by Gholam Mahmud and Pahlawan Kamil Hanzai. The Sardar could not himself attend, but instead sent a letter—the original is in my possession—which freely translated reads,

> Dear Agha Azim Khan and Agha Ja'far, Be healthy.
>
> Let me tell you what I have done: I have sent Sol Mohammed and Gholam Mohammed to you. I ask you to accept their willingness to reestablish peaceful relations. You [Azim Han] are the son of Sab Khan. Agree to their [Sol Mahmud's and Ghulam Mahmud's] desire to settle, because your father [a respected peacemaker] always supported people's willingness to settle and reestablish peaceful relations. There is nothing else to say.
>
> Sardar Khan Mohammed Shah Navazi
>
> [P.S.] If you do not accept their wish to settle the dispute and to reestablish peaceful relations, I will be unsympathetic to your position and unhappy with both of you.

In fact, the Dadolzai had not favored making a complaint to the Persian authorities, preferring to settle the matter themselves. Azim Han had taken it on himself to push the formal complaint, for, he said, if the dispute had not been settled, the Dadolzai would have had to fight the Kamel Hanzai.

There were some discrepancies between the stories of Mahmud and Sol Mahmud. One observer, Id Mahmud, whose Mirgolzai *peskom* was equidistant from the two opposed lineages, believed that Sol Mahmud was more credible, for he said that Sol Mahmud did not lie. And though most agreed that Mahmud had suffered an injury at the hands of Sol Mahmud, there had also been physical provocation by Mahmud, so he shared some of the blame for the incident. In the end, it was judged that a small amount of money, 1,000 toman, should be given to Mahmud. Id Mahmud said that this was *huieni pul*, the blood payment, and that it was a small amount because the injury was small. Ja'far reported that the *tap*, injury, was *bakshist*, forgiven, by Baluch after considerable pressure by his Dadolzai lineage mates. Otherwise, said Ja'far, the payment would have had to have been a substantial amount of money. According to Ja'far, the money collected was to cover various expenses of motorcycle travel and the like.

Contribution to the 1,000 toman came not just from the perpetrator of the injury, Sol Mahmud, and his Kamil Hanzai lineage mates, but rather from a variety of lin-

**Table 10.2.** Compensation Contributions

| Structural Position | Contributor | Compensation (toman) |
|---|---|---|
| Offending | Kamil Hanzai: | |
| | Sol Mahmud | 100 |
| | Pahlawan | 100 |
| Fraternal lineages structurally equidistant from both the Kamil Hanzai and Dadolzai | Zabedzai: Azim Han | 100 |
| Fraternal lineages of the Nur Mahmudzai, to which both the Dadolzai and Kamil Hanzai belonged, and thus structurally equidistant from the conflicting parties and their lineages | Gol Mahmudzai: | |
| | Dust Mahmud | 100 |
| | Mulla Nur Mahmud | 50 |
| | Dust Mahmudzai: | |
| | Hakim Jan Mahmud | 100 |
| | Dust Mahmud | |
| From other tribal sections, structurally both distant and equidistant from the conflicting parties | Surizai: | |
| | Nader, Sol Mahmud was his MZS | 100 |
| | Hoseinzai: | |
| | Abasa, *maskom* was Kamil Hanzai | 100 |
| From other tribes, also distant and equidistant | Gamshadzai: | |
| | Ghulam Mahmud, Sol M.'s affine | 100 |

eages, including those offending and those neutral (see table 10.2). The total donated was 850 toman rather than the 1,000 promised, and Baluch complained long and hard about it, but the Dadolzai and others asked him to *baksh* the remainder, and he finally did, closing the discussion and the dispute.

The contribution of the blood money, or costs, whichever it was, did not follow segmentary logic, in which the opponent responsible had to pay the recompense and structurally equidistant parties were neutral and paid nothing. In this case, 650 of the 850 toman was contributed by members of lineages, such as the Dust Mahmudzai, Gol Mahmudzai, Hoseinzai, Surizai, and even by members of another tribe, the Gamshadzai, who were not only structurally equidistant and neutral, such as the Zabedzai, but were farther from the opposed lineages than the opposed lineages were from each other (table 10.3)! How can we explain this peculiar, antisegmentary pattern of compensation contributions? As we shall see, this was the standard Yarahmadzai practice in collecting compensation for injured parties in the settling of disputes.

## BEJAR

Among the Yarahmadzai, contributing to compensation for injured parties in a dispute settlement was not based upon the genealogical position of the contributors.

**Table 10.3.** Structural Relations among Contributing Parties:
Settlement of the Dispute between Mahmud and Sol Mahmud

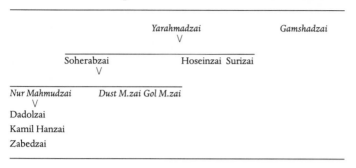

Other than the lineage of the injured party, which could not contribute because it would be paying itself, and in addition to the offending lineage, any and all other lineages, near or far, close or distant, were encouraged to contribute. We have seen this *bejar* in the settlement of Mahmud and Sol Mahmud, a minor dispute between close lineages, when contributions for settlement were made by members of distant and unaffected lineages, and even by members of a neighboring tribe. And we have also had a hint of *bejar* in the settlement of the Rahmatzai-Soherabzai dispute, when the Sardar said that he would pay 1,000 toman, 20 percent, of the penalty himself, or see that it was contributed by other lineages.

In another case from 1972 that was reported to me, Mahmad Gol Mahmudzai Soherabzai was badly beaten by Shah Nezar Rushanzai Hoseinzai and another lineage mate. Shah Nezar and Mahmad had been partners in smuggling, and Shah Nazar thought that Mahmad had cheated him and "eaten" his money. Mahmad was in the *behdari*, hospital, for 15 days. After he got out, he *shekayat kort*, made a formal complaint to the court. The court referred the matter to Sardar Han Mahmud for a settlement. The Sardar arranged a *diwan* and agreement was reached on a 3,000 toman compensation. The Sardar announced that various lineages should contribute, and Shah Nezar himself went around to different lineages collecting contributions. The distribution of contributions was as follows:

*Hoseinzai section*
Shah Nezar        1,000 toman
Others            1,000 toman

*Soherabzai section*
Gol Mahmudzai     recipients
Yar Mahmudzai     500 toman
Dadolzai          200 toman
Mirgolzai         200 toman

Kamil Hanzai          100 toman

*Rahmatzai section*    nil

Figures for the smaller amounts were estimates, because various individuals, such as Jan Mahmud and Mahmud Karim of the Dadolzai, gave in kind; the Dadolzai contributions were bags of grain. It was furthermore explained to me that in this case and in others like it, not all lineages would contribute because the total amount of compensation needed was small, and contributions from a few lineages satisfied the need.

From our point of view, the interesting thing is not primarily the number of lineages that contributed, but their structural positions. Once again the logic was not that of a segmentary lineage system. Rather, lineages—the other Soherabzai lineages, such as the Yar Mahmudzai, Dadolzai, Mirgolzai, and Kamil Hanzai—that were united with the Gol Mahmudzai in their dispute with the Hoseinzai section Rushanzai and would have fought alongside the Gol Mahmudzai against the Hoseinzai, contributed funds to their distant kin, the Rushanzai, so that the Rushanzai could compensate the Soherabzai lineages' closer kin, the Gol Mahmudzai.

If considerations of genealogical closeness and distance disappeared like a mirage when peacemaking required contributions to compensate the injured, and thus the logic of segmentation was not the norm and not a guide to action, what was the operating logic? The logic of conflict was segmentation; what was the logic of peacemaking? It appears to me that the logic of peacemaking was that of tribal unity, of the equity of all tribesmen as "brothers" and "sisters."

As we have seen, the Sardar stood symbolically and practically for the unity of the tribe. The Sardar's particular mandate internal to the tribe was peacemaking among the tribesmen. The idiom of peacemaking always included reference to the tribesmen, of however distant lineages, as being *yeki*, one, as being all brothers. The peacemaking process was one of reestablishing unity, of drawing the members of the tribe back together. As such, unity and equivalence were overcommunicated, while differences in genealogical distance among lineages were undercommunicated. In drawing compensation from lineages near and far, from those who had been adversaries, from those close to and far from the injured party and from those close to and far from the perpetrator of the injury, the equivalence and unity of the tribesmen were manifested.

In short, while conflict was conducted according to segmentary logic, peacemaking was conducted according to unitary logic. This is one reason why it was prestigious among the Yarahmadzai to *baksh* an injury. Not only did it show that a lineage was able to rise above the consideration of material compensation or retribution, but it demonstrated that the lineage was willing to sacrifice its narrow interests to benefit the greater whole.

The sequential processual alternation between the segmentary logic of conflict and the unitary logic of peace manifested and reenforced the structural duality of Sarhadi tribes: the remarkable fusion of the decentralized segmentary lineage system with the centralized chiefship. At the same time, the continuing operation of both of these systems during the 1960s and 1970s indicated the relatively loose encapsulation of the Sarhadi tribes in the state structure of Iran. The Sarhadi tribal system continued to operate, and the Iranian state military and judiciary apparatus, by following a policy of indirect rule giving responsibility to the Sarhadi tribal chiefs, contributed to the maintenance of the tribal system. What the tribal chiefs had lost as their role of war leaders was suppressed, they gained as the middlemen between their tribes and the government and between the government and their tribes.

## INTERTRIBAL CONFLICT

Intertribal conflict in the Sarhad and beyond almost always played out according to segmentary logic, just as international conflicts do between state societies. And just as, in the Sarhadi tribal system, there was no political authority higher than the tribal Sardar, the Sarhadi tribes also shared no common genealogical structure on which prescribed alliances might be based. Nor was there any fixed relationship between the tribes and the Kordish hakomate in Daptan, although the Kordish hakoms had tried, unsuccessfully, to make the tribes into *riyati*, political dependents. Thus intertribal conflict was the confrontation of independent polities without genealogical or unitary commonality as a buffer. Only the affinal and matrilateral bonds, mainly between the chiefly families, bridged the gaps between the tribes.

To illustrate the vagaries of intertribal conflict, I here repeat accounts as told to me about four such confrontations. I cannot vouch for the accuracy of these accounts, but, as Freud taught in *The Interpretation of Dreams,* the retelling itself points to a profound truth, no matter what the original stimulus was. As historical incidents become quasi-mythical in the retelling, they reflect a, if not every, cultural truth about the particular subject that the teller shares with his fellows. So I think we can consider these stories as reflecting at least part of the truth about intertribal conflict.

### The Gamshadzai versus the Yarahmadzai I

During the time when Hubyar Han was Sardar of the Yarahmadzai, a dispute broke out over date palms in a grove at Mashkil. The ensuing fight culminated in a member of the Gamshadzai tribe killing two Yarahmadzai, thus putting the Gamshadzai in blood debt to the Yarahmadzai and opening the Gamshadzai to vengeance attack, and even warfare, by the Yarahmadzai. One of the victims was Mehrab of the Dohrahzai and the other was Sapar of the Yar Mahmudzai, the lineage of the Yarahmadzai Sardar. To make matters worse, Sapar was Sardar Hubyar Han's mother's sister's son.

In a preemptive demonstration of repentance, Sardar Lashkar Han of the Gamshadzai—with a retinue including, among others, Mahmud Shah Sebasuron, Merab Han Buzurgzadeh of Jalq, Mir Mirad Barakzai of Shastun, Maulawi Hasrat Sahib of Ghosht—came to Sardar Hubyar Han and said that he was *mayare,* at the mercy of, Hubyar Han. Lashkar Han said that if Hubyar Han insisted on blood to pay for the life of Sapar, he could kill Lashkar Han's brother, who was also among the retinue. If Hubyar Han wanted blood payment, Lashkar Han had brought 50 camels, 20 rifles, 200 *pas,* 1 sword, and 1 cloth for a shroud, and he would also offer 100 *mach* at Mashkil. Or Hubyar Han could *bakshist.*

Hubyar Han said that he did not want any blood payment from the Gamshadzai and did not want blood in return for Sapar's blood. Rather, Hubar Han would *bakshist* Sapar's blood. Thus no blood debt was owed to the Yar Mahmudzai *brasrend* by the Gamshadzai.

Lashkar Han, accompanied by Hubyar Han, then went to the Dorahzai. The Dorahzai said that if Lashkar Han would give his daughter to Mehrab's brother, they would *bakshist* Mehrab's blood. Lashkar Han said that he would not do that, but would give some other kind of payment. The Dohrahzai refused, and said that they wanted nothing else, and if Lashkar Han would not give his daughter, he could leave, which he did.

Hubyar Han later told the Dohrahzai that he could do nothing himself, for he had given his word to *bakshist* Sapar's blood. But he encouraged the Dohrahzai to strike at the Gamshadzai by killing Lashkar Han's brother. The Dohrahzai sent a party of men to Lashkar Han's camp, where they seized and shot dead Lashkar Han's brother. One of the bullets ricocheted off of a rock and wounded a young girl, Lashkar Han's sister's daughter.

The killing of Lashkar Han's brother canceled the debt of Mehrab, but the injury of the girl had to be settled. Later, Hubyar Han paid a one-half blood payment for the injury to the girl, and the matter was closed. Peace was reestablished between the Yarahmadzai and Gamshadzai.

## The Gamshadzai versus the Yarahmadzai II

In the early 1960s, during *garmon,* just before *hamin,* a fight over pasture at Garonchin broke out between two shepherds, one a Gamshadzai and one a Yarahmadzai. The Yarahmadzai shepherd was beaten pretty badly. The members of his *halk,* which consisted of Dorahzai and Rushanzai, went to the Gamshadzai camp and beat up a number of people. And so the matter rested for a few weeks.

After everyone had migrated to Mashkil for *hamin,* a group of Rushanzai and Dohrahzai were fired upon, with a rifle, as they traveled from one *bonend* to another. One of the Rushanzai was shot through the head and killed.

Sardar Han Mahmud cautioned restraint, and said not to inform the gendarmerie.

He suggested that Yarahmadzai undertake no further action, but remain calm and await developments to see if the dispute could be settled.

About a month later, with no further developments having taken place, five Rushanzai, on their way from Mashkil to the Sarhad, came across a lone Gamshadzai in the Morpish Mountains. The Rushanzai, lacking firearms, fell on the Gamshadzai, stripped him of his clothes, beat him, and then cut his throat with a *harrag,* the serrated blade sickle used on date palms. They then dumped his body onto the mountain slope.

When Sardar Han Mahmud heard of this, he went to the Gamshadzai Sardar Halil Han and argued that, since one man of each tribe had been killed, they were quits and should consider the issue settled. Halil Han agreed, and the matter was regarded as closed.

## The Gamshadzai versus the Yarahmadzai III

Although in segmentary logic group support for a member is unconditional, among the encapsulated Sarhadi tribes of the 1960s and 1970s support was not always unconditional and thus not always forthcoming, as is illustrated by the following account which was reported to me.

In 1965, Musa of the Dorahzai, Yarahmadzai, undertook a rustling excursion in the Morpish Mountains, near the Dast Kord pass. In the course of stealing a flock of 30 *pas,* he killed a young Gamshadzai *shwaneg,* shepherd. Musa carried off the *ramag* and sold it to a Brahui residing near Esmailabad to the northwest of Khash. Musa then fled to Zahedan.

Meanwhile, the boy's father went to his Sardar, Halil Han, to ask for aid. A Gamshadzai search party was formed and the tracks of the *ramag* were followed to the Brahui purchaser. Having been found in the possession of the flock by the Gamshadzai posse, including the grieving relatives of the slain *shwaneg,* the Brahui prudently identified Musa and agreed to turn the animals back to their rightful owners.

Yarahmadzai Sardar Han Mahmud was informed of these developments by Gamshadzai Sardar Halil Han, who declared that unless the killer was found and dealt with by the Yarahmadzai Sardar, the Gamshadzai would take matters into their own hands and take revenge by killing a Yarahmadzai. Sardar Han Mahmud offered blood money, but the Gamshadzai would not accept. Halil Han also threatened to go to the *dolat,* government, if Han Mahmud would not act. Exactly how Halil Han reconciled the two contradictory strategies—threatening segmentary vengeance and at the same time requesting state intervention—was not reported to me.

Sardar Han Mahmud and a number of other Yarahmadzai formed a search party, went to Zahedan, and found Musa. They brought him back to Khash and turned him over to the police. He was sent to jail and shortly thereafter was executed. This ended the matter as far as the Gamshadzai were concerned.

But Musa's lineage mates, the Dorahzai, were not happy. They, showing their segmentary solidarity, had gone to the Sardar and asked him not to turn Musa in. But the Sardar replied that Musa had committed a crime and that no other Yarahmadzai—whoever happened to end up the target of Gamshadzai retaliation, and his family—should suffer for it.

So although the Sardar had been willing to support Musa to the extent of paying Yarahmadzai money to settle the blood debt, he was not willing to sacrifice any other Yarahmadzai's blood to save Musa. Here the Sardar had modified the segmentary logic by attaching conditions of behavior. Group members were to be supported as long as they had not, of their own volition, committed crimes, in which case they would have to take personal, individual responsibility for their acts. Furthermore, the Sardar was himself prepared to be proactive in bringing one of his own tribesmen "to justice."

## The Surizai versus the Kords (Kurds)

The territory to the east of Daptan was dominated by the Kordish Hakomzat, centered at Sangu. But some Baluchi groups, such as the Kerahzai and Surizai, have lived and pastured their livestock in this region for generations.

In the spring of 1970, the Halki Lashkar Han Surizai had stopped on the eastern slopes of Daptan and was grazing its flocks as usual. Nearby were several Kord camps. From one of them came Haji Halil, the brother of the Kord Hakom, Haji Amir Han. He went to Lashkar Han's tent and told him that he was trespassing and encroaching on Kord pasture, and that he would have to move.

Lashkar Han was furious, and threw a sandal—a particularly disrespectful act, for footware is considered ritually dirty—at Haji Halil and told him to get out. This was the area that Lashkar Han's father and grandfather had occupied and he was not about to leave it. Lashkar Han then called upon his Surizai and Hoseinzai kinsmen to come and support him. His pleas for segmentary solidarity did not fall upon deaf ears: some 60 or so of his lineage and section mates came to his camp, ready to give him support, moral and physical, if the Kords came to force him and his Halk out.

The Kerahzai, a smaller Baluchi group in the vicinity, itself not pleased at the show of arrogance by the Kords and afraid for their own access, also gave support to Lashkar Han. As well, they raised, once again, questions about the death of Lashkar Han's brother six years earlier: "First the Kords kill your brother, and now they want to drive you from your pasture." This was a sore point with Lashkar Han and did not help to cool things down.

What had happened six years before was that Lashkar's brother Hair Mahmud had a fatal fall from a cliff while on a hunting party with Haji Amir Han and some of his kinsmen. At that time, the Kords maintained that the party had split up to find game, and later when Hair Mahmud did not return they went in search of him, only to find him at the foot of a cliff. The Kords carried Hair Mahmud to the Surizai, but he died without regaining consciousness.

The Kords denied responsibility, Haji Amir Han saying that he had no possible motive to harm Hair Mahmud, an assertion that the Surizai had no reason to dispute. A *mulla* was called in, and the Kords swore on the Qoran that they had not been involved in the death. This was accepted by the Surizai and the matter dropped.

The recent, unpleasant encounter with Haji Halil had brought back old memories and raised old questions. These strengthened Lashkar Han's resolve not to give in to the Kords and his determination to fight, if necessary, to maintain his standing and his access to this territory.

However, Amir Han, the Kord Hakom, having heard about Haji Halil's confrontation with Lashkar Han, quickly sent a message of reconciliation to Lashkar Han, saying that no conflict was desired, and that Lashkar Han had every right to locate where he was and that if he wanted to bring two or four additional camps to that area he was most welcome. As a gesture of peace, Amir Han sent Lashkar Han 12 bags of grain. This was accepted by Lashkar Han, and the matter was deemed settled.

## Segmentary Security

In intertribal conflict, as in confrontations between fraternal lineages, security rested in the military support of one's lineage, defined situationally, according to complementary opposition, so that one's group was equivalent or relatively equivalent in strength to the one you faced, so that your group balanced the threat of the other group. Integral to this security was the commitment of group members, which was ensured by norms of collective responsibility that made each of them a target and called on each of them to contribute to settlement. Here, too, tribesmen were committed to their kinsmen not only out of a sense of moral obligation, although that was present and important, but also out of a strong sense of self-interest. Security for each individual rested in lineage unity and strength.

Security meant not only defense of the person, but access to resources, including livestock, pasture, water, cultivation, and commerce. Conflicts commonly began, as we have seen, with disputes over property matters such as camels that had eaten dates, the ownership of date palms or of palm trunks, and the use of pasture. Whereas within the Sarhadi tribes, "natural" resources such as pasture, streams, and rainwater were in principle and generally in practice open to all tribesmen, the territories of tribes were in principle closed to outsiders, although outsiders were often admitted with explicit permission. The Sarhadi tribes were conceived by their members as independent entities, and so relations between and among tribes followed most strictly segmentary logic.

Of course, disputes between individuals of different tribes were not only attempts to maintain the security of persons and property and to maintain the regional status quo ante, but often were manifestations of incremental or massive encroachment, whether through design or circumstance, by one tribe on another. For example, Gorchan, a small agricultural village that in the 1960s and 1970s was the winter seat of the Yarahmadzai Sardar, had earlier in the century been owned by a Kord. But after a conflict in which a Dorahzai Yarahmadzai was killed by a Kord, rights to settle and control of the then disused *kan* were accepted by the Dorahzai for the blood settlement. The political outcome of this process—a dispute, a fight, an injury or death, and a settlement—depended upon the terms of the settlement. If in a settlement a weaker party gave up nonrenewable capital resources, such as territory, the effect was that the receivers of the territory expanded at the expense of the givers. And if one party was constantly crowding or encroaching upon the resources of the other—water, pasture, agricultural land—disputes, fights, injuries, and deaths were inevitable. The stronger party was in a position to demand a lot in a settlement and de facto came out the winner in the conflict.

In other cases, conflicts led to fights and fights led to broader warfare. The area between Khash and the Morpish Mountains was occupied not only by the Kords, but also by tribal populations, such as the Sholibur. The Yarahmadzai competed with the Sholibur for pasture, which led to conflict, fights, and warfare. In this case, there was no formal settlement; the Sholibur just fled, to the Jaz Murian Basin, south of the Sarhad, beyond Saravan, and only later returned to the Sarhad, where they settled in the area to the west of Khash, leaving their old area to the Yarahmzadzai.

Thus the segmentary lineage structure was not only a security and social control system, but, as Marshall Sahlins (1961:203 in 1968 reprinting) pointed out long ago, an organization for predatory expansion.

> A segmentary lineage system develops in a tribe that intrudes into an already occupied habitat rather than a tribe that expands into an uncontested domain. . . . [G]rowth in the face of opposition selects for complementary opposition as a social means of predation. Thus the *first* tribe in an area is unlikely to develop a segmentary lineage system, but the *second* tribe in that area is more likely to.

Sahlins's description appears to fit the Yarahmadzai as it expanded out of the Morpish onto the broad highland plateau of the Sarhad. There is no way to know whether the Yarahmadzai were the first in the Sarhad to develop complementary opposition, as a means to consolidate strength for expansion against the Kordish Hakomate and against other tribal groupings. But we must remember that on the Sarhad other large tribes—such as the Ismailzai, the Gamshadzai (the traditional rivals of the Yarahmadzai), and the Rigi (traditional enemies of the Yaramadzai)—also had a similar system. Sahlins (1961:203 in 1968 reprinting) suggests that segmentary systems fade away after being successfully used.

That the segmentary lineage system occurs among intrusive tribal societies also suggests that, from a long-term view, it is likely to be ephemeral. Once a society has succeeded in driving competitors from its habitat, the selective force favoring fusion disappears and the fragmenting tendencies of the neolithic economy are free to express themselves. In other words, the segmentary lineage system is self-liquidating.

Yet the use of the segmentary lineage system by a number of competing Sarhadi tribes suggests that complementary opposition, like state formation (Cohen 1978: 154–57), can be "secondary," that is, in defensive or aggressive response to tribes that are already so organized. If the Yarahmadzai could *jama kon,* unite together to fight, then the Gamshadzai and Ismailzai and Rigi had better be able to do so, and the result would be the spread of the segmentary lineage system, rather than its "self-liquidation." Smaller groups—such as the Sholibur, Mir Baluchzai, Yadigarzai, Ganguzai—who did not manage to unite together, either had to surrender resources to the segmentary tribes or become their dependents. The Mir Baluchzai, Yadigarzai of Khash, and Ganguzai of Gazu formed affinal alliances with the Yarahmadzai and accepted its protection.

Aside from intertribal conflict and territorial expansion, the segmentary lineage system is important for providing security and social control within a segmentary, decentralized tribe, for providing a means to safeguard its members. And it accomplishes this without reference to spatial location; that is, the segmentary lineage system is a nonspatial framework of affiliation and is not disturbed by the spatial movement of lineage members This is particularly important where resources, such as pasturage and water, are unreliable and unpredictable, and where irregular spatial mobility is a major technique for primary production. Wherever people move in their tribal territory, and however mixed they become, they remain protected by their lineage affiliation. This provision of security in a nomadic milieu would, in my view, be sufficient in itself to recommend the segmentary lineage system to nomadic tribesmen. In short, there are good reasons other than territorial expansion for independent nomadic pastoralists to cleave to a segmentary lineage system.

As we have seen, the unifying processes of the Sarhadi tribes went beyond the segmentary lineage system to the establishment of permanent, centralizing leadership, the office of Sardar. The reason was the confrontation with the more highly organized hakomate of the Kords in Daptan. This, too, was expected by Sahlins (1961:203 in 1968 reprinting).

> The segmentary lineage system develops in a specifically *intertribal* environment, in competition between societies of the tribal level. . . . [A] segmentary lineage system would be ineffective in competition with chiefdoms and states. To oppose—let alone to prey upon—societies of this order requires large-scale organic integration of economic and political, especially military effort. Limited economic coordination, the relativity of

leadership and its absence of coercive sanction, the localized, egalitarian character of the polity, the ephemerality of large groupings, all of these could doom a segmentary lineage system if brought into conflict with chiefdoms or states.

While Sahlins may have been overly pessimistic about the capacity of segmentary tribes to challenge and even overcome state societies (Irons 1975; Gellner 1981:chap. 1), the development of chiefs for tribal societies probably arose through confrontation with other chiefdoms or states. The confrontation with the Kord Hakomate led to the development among the Yarahmadzai of the ingenious combination of the segmentary lineage system and the chiefship, a structure intermediate between the totally decentralized, segmentary tribe and the substantially centralized chiefdom.


## IDENTITY

Within tribes, "all men," as Gellner (1988:97) puts it, "tend to be both producers and warriors": "The need for perpetual collective self-protection endows these groups with considerable cohesion, and turns them into the most formidable fighting units in the land." This cohesion was expressed among the Sarhadi Baluch by the concept of *topak*, group solidarity, which was manifested in many actions of aid, help, support, assistance, collaboration, and cooperation. Cohesion manifested itself also in the psyches of Sarhadi tribesmen, both in their cognition about right and wrong, rights and obligations, gains and losses, and in their emotional identification with their lineages and lineage mates, tribe and tribal leadership. Most tribesmen, especially when faced with external challenges to their lineages, felt a sentiment of "all for one and one for all."

An individual's identification with lineage and tribe could be manifested in peculiar circumstances. Id Mahmud provided me with the following account. In 1966 Id Mahmud was on his way to the Arab Emirate of Abu Dhabi to work on a construction site. He and a dozen or so Sarhadi tribesmen were crossing from the Iranian to the Arabian side on a crowded launch. There was only room for some to stretch out and sleep, and this competition for space led to some confrontations. One of the Rigi tribesmen began abusing a Kerazai. He said that the Kerazai Sardar was a thief, and so was his father and mother. Now the Kerazai are a small group, and while they have a leader, he was not important enough to be called a Sardar. In any case, when asked to identify the object of his taunts, the Rigi said Han Mahmud, who was of course the Yarahmadzai Sardar.

Whether this was a mistake or a deliberate provocation was not clear, but the Yarahmadzai present were extremely displeased and prepared to defend the honor of their Sardar. Upon landing, the five Yarahmadzai and one Kerazai fought the eight Rigi in an alley. The fight was stopped when local people called the police. All of the tribesmen were taken to the police station. The police said, according to Id Mahmud—and the comment as reported is quite interesting whether it is a precise quote or Id Mahmud's misrepresentation—that they were right to defend their group against the slanders of outsiders, and that furthermore it would have been better if they had killed them!

Id Mahmud's explanation was that it was all right for Yarahmadzai themselves to criticize the Sardar, as Id Mahmud did regularly, but that outsiders, people from other tribes, could not be allowed such liberties. As Id Mahmud put it, in relation to people from other tribes, "the Sardar is my father."

Sarhadi tribesmen, both men and women, defined themselves as members of lineages, the relevant lineage—smaller or larger, more or less inclusive—being contingently defined, on the basis of complementary opposition, according to the particular circumstances. Especially in contexts of confrontation or conflict, need, or difficulty, people thought of themselves as members of lineages.

As part of this lineage identity, all men—young and old, strong and weak, healthy and infirm, with the exception of *mullas* exempted for religious reasons—conceived of themselves as warriors: ready to defend themselves, their families, their lineage mates, and their property, by force of physical violence. This was their commitment to themselves and to their lineage mates. They were the first line of defense, the primary guarantors of security. No Sarhadi tribesmen could afford to forget this, and none did forget it. They were all fighters and, when necessary, they fought.

# II.
# THE TRIBE AND THE CHIEF

Local communities of tent dwellers in the Sarhad did not live on their own. Rather, they were subsumed under a broader tribal organization, within which they operated. It would be erroneous to think of the herding camps as natural social units complete unto themselves, upon which another, tribal, level of organization was superimposed. Similarly, it would be a mistake to imagine that daily life in the tents and camps, and the productive activities that took up much of the time and energy of the tribesmen, was natural and basic, while the political acts of social control and leadership were additional and subsidiary.

In the Sarhad, local communities were formed and operated within the framework of the tribal structure, which provided internal order, access to natural resources, and protection from external threat. The security provided by the tribal structure made it possible for local groups to be flexible in membership and spatially mobile, and thus adaptable in the face of challenging and variable conditions of their desert homeland. Each tribal territory with its natural pasture and water resources was secured by tribal control, and for this reason was open to access by all members of the tribe, and to outsiders with permission. The more rigid, overarching structures of tribal organization provided the framework within which local groups were formed and daily life was pursued.

I began this account of the Sarhadi Baluch at the most concrete level, discussing tents and tent life, local groups and economic production, because these are easiest for a stranger to the Sarhad to grasp, not because they are ontologically primary or causally dominant. If anything, those institutions dealing with social order, social control, and access to productive resources are primary and dominant. On the Sarhad, this was the tribe.

## DEFINING THE TRIBE

Each and every Sarhadi *baluch* traced his or her descent through male ancestors and belonged to a set of corporate patrilineages, each based upon descent from a common ancestor (see chapter 9). Each *baluch* belonged to quite small patrilineages, defined by descent from her or his great-grandfather, or somewhat larger ones defined by descent from his or her great-great-grandfather. More distant ancestors defined more inclusive and thus larger patrilineal groups. This continued up to a level beyond which ancestors no longer were reference points for any group. On the Sarhad, the ultimate level, defined by the ancestor beyond which no more distant ancestors defined groups or social boundaries, the point of ultimate group identification, defined an operating political entity, which I call the tribe.

This correspondence found on the Sarhad of maximal descent groups with functioning polities, tribes, was not always found elsewhere. Among other tribal peoples with segmentary lineage systems—the Nuer (Evans-Pritchard 1940) of the southern Sudan, the Somali (Lewis 1961) of the northeastern Horn of Africa, and the Yomut Turkmen (Irons 1975) of northeastern Iran—distant ancestors defined large, ethnic populations, consisting of a number of smaller political entities, sometimes labeled tribes by anthropologists (e.g., Evans-Pritchard 1940; Irons 1975), defined by specific, political criteria. Making up the large Nuer population, estimated to be around 200,000 (Evans-Pritchard 1940:110), were some 15 tribal polities (Evans-Pritchard 1940:117), famously defined, we may wish to remind ourselves, as follows: "A tribe has been defined by (1) a common and distinct name; (2) a common sentiment; (3) a common and distinct territory; (4) a moral obligation to unite in war; and (5) a moral obligation to settle feuds and other disputes by arbitration" (Evans-Pritchard 1940:122). Similarly, the Yomut Turkmen (Irons 1975), a large population defined by descent from a common ancestor, was broken down into smaller polities:

> The next largest residence group above the level of the oba [a corporate group which shares a joint estate] is a group known as an il. The meaning of "il" in Turkmen cannot always be translated with the same English word. However, when it refers to a contiguous group of obas that have traditionally been on peaceful terms with one another, it is translated for purposes of this study as "tribe." . . . The word "il" is used in Turkmen both as an adjective and as a noun. As an adjective it means a state of peace between two individuals or groups. As a noun it refers to a group of obas that are on peaceful terms with one another and are united against hostile outsiders in mutual defense.
> (Irons 1975:49)

It was common on the Sarhad, as elsewhere, to refer to a patrilineage by the name of the apical, and sometimes epical, ancestor from whom all members were alleged to descend and who thus defined the membership of the group. The members of the

**Table 11.1.** Genealogy of the Yarahmadzai: Rahmatzai Version

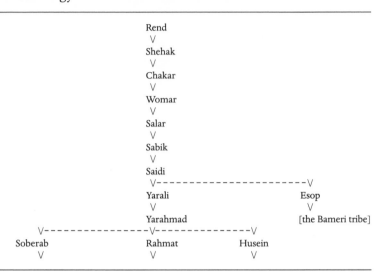

Yarahmadzai believed that they had descended, through the male line, from Yarahmad. They could—without always agreeing with one another on the details—also name the ancestors of Yarahmad, for example, as in the version given by a member of the Rahmatzai (see table 11.1).

While the Sarhadi Baluch who traced their descent to Yarahmad recognized and acknowledged their descent from Yarahmad's ancestors, from Yarali and Saidi and so on up the line, they did not think of themselves as members of groups defined by Yarali and Saidi and so on. By their way of thinking, there was no grouping that could call itself Yaralizai or Saidizai. They recognized a distant relationship with the Bameri tribe, descended from the *naku* of Yarahmad, but did not think of themselves as members of a more inclusive Saidizai of which the Bameri were also part. Rather, their group membership stopped with Yarahmad, who was the ultimate referent, in regard to descent group formation, in their genealogy. The largest group that they recognized, with which they identified, and for which they felt loyalty was the Yarahmadzai, the collectivity that I label the tribe.

Aside from descent group formation, there is another criterion that identifies the tribal level, as distinct from the line of more distant ascendent ancestors who were not referents for groups, and as distinct from the lineages that were major sections of the tribes, or notable subsections, or smaller, operating *brasrend*, or smaller microlineages. This criterion is office. The Sarhadi tribes, those groups that were the largest lineages to be recognized as such by their members, each had a *sardar*, political and military leader, which I gloss as "chief"; only the tribes, and no smaller tribal section or smaller lineage, had a *sardar*. The *sardar* was the "head" of the tribe and "represented" the tribe. But what exactly was involved with being "head" of the tribe, and in what sense, and how, did he—and it was always a "he"—"represent" it? These are questions to be addressed in this chapter.

It is obvious, by office and title alone, that the *sardar* had some kind of precedence in the tribe, and thus took a position in a tribal hierarchy. As a political leader and representative, he was a central focus of the tribe, and this indicates some degree of centralization.

It should be noted at the outset that these vertically oriented principles of hierarchy and centralization—the nature and degree of which remain to be established—were divergent from those of the tribal segmentary lineage system discussed above. The segmentary lineage system, which in political terms was horizontally oriented, grouped individuals into lineages and specified for political purposes the closeness and distance of other lineages; it treated all individuals equally, dispersed power throughout, and privileged a balance of power. The segmentary lineage system advanced equality, democracy, and decentralization. Thus a key question in understanding Sarhadi politics is the nature of the conjunction between the egalitarian and decentralized segmentary lineage system and the hierarchical and centralized chiefship.

Impressionistically, Yarahmadzai political structure might be characterized as a segmentary lineage system with a chief on top. Now both of these institutions—segmentary lineage systems and chiefs—were familiar presences in the Middle Eastern tribal scene. Yet this conjunction presents something of a puzzle. The awkwardness of the Yarahmadzai political system for the anthropological observer lies not so much in the separate parts of the system, but rather in their juxtaposition, their combination as parts of a system. Chiefs and segmentary lineage systems do not, should not, fit together very well, as evidenced by classic examples of tribal peoples. The segmentary Nuer (Evans-Pritchard 1940) and Somali (Lewis 1961) had no chiefs, and the Basseri (Barth 1961; Salzman 1995a) and Qashqai (Beck 1986, 1991) had chiefs but no segmentary lineage system.

So there is something not quite right about saying that the Yarahmadzai political structure was "a segmentary lineage system with a chief on top." After all, the egalitarian, decentralized segmentary lineage systems had no tops, and thus there was no top for a chief to be on. So where was the chief, or, to put it another way, how could there have been a chief in a system with no top? For we mean by "chief" the office of highest political authority in the group, and so there must be a hierarchy of authority at the top of which the chief may reside. But the "segmentary lineage system" was a set of equal lineages allied relatively and contingently for political action, decisions being made by assemblies and councils, with no offices and no hierarchy of authority, and thus no top.

Chiefs and segmentary lineage systems would thus seem to be incompatible, both logically and practically; a chiefdom is hierarchical, centralized, and based upon

Figure 11.1. Nezar Mahmud
Yarmahmudzai, son of Yarahmadzai Sardar Hubyar Han,
sometime aspirant to the office of *sardar,* brother of Sardar Han Mahmud, man of action, man of romance, great
storyteller in the traditional
fashion, fine conversationalist,
curious observer of life, con-
siderate and gracious host,
1968. (Photograph by author)

stable relations among its constituent groups, whereas a segmentary lineage system
is egalitarian, decentralized, and based upon variable and contingent relations among
its constituent groups. Given, then, that the Yarahmadzai political system may be
seen as being made up of structurally contrary and apparently incompatible elements, how did it work? Before pursuing this question further, let us examine a little
more closely the basis of the chiefship among the Yarahmadzai.

## POLITICAL SENIORITY

In considering the chiefship, we note that, while in some respects it was a unique
office in the Sarhadi tribes, it also was a manifestation of a general principle, that of
political seniority, *master.* The term *master,* used as both an adjective and a noun, implied a comparative, relative value. One was *master,* senior or a senior only in relation
to junior or a junior. An eldest brother was *master* to a middle brother, who was in
turn *master* to a youngest brother. Various degrees of deference and obedience, depending upon the roles involved, were directed toward the *master.* The association be-

tween relative age and active respect, captured in the concept *master,* was general throughout the role structure.

Such a concept of political seniority is found in other segmentary tribes. Lancaster (1981:77) describes this notion among the Rwala Bedouin:

> *Al-Tsebir* simply means "the big man" and is used to refer to the most influential man in an encampment, if his name is not known. It is neither a title nor a form of address: the leader of a large goum can be referred to as *al-tsebir,* but so can the elder of two brothers who camp side by side alone.

Beyond age alone, there was another criterion, perhaps implied in Lancaster's description of *al-tsebir,* that was in certain contexts incorporated into the notion of *master.* This criterion encompassed personal authority, leadership status, social stature, and can be summed up in the phrase "political seniority." In this sense, men were frequently *master* to those older than they. This sense of *master* was very important in the Sarhad for political leadership at all levels.

We have already seen it in *halk* organization and in collective decisionmaking in the *halk.* There was always one male household head acknowledged to be the *master,* the camp headman. Who that person was depended upon who the members of the halk were. The *master* of a halk was always of the dominant lineage. But no one was *master* in a absolute sense; political seniority depended upon who else was present. When the Dadolzai formed one halk, Ja'far was recognized as *master* to the others and thus as the *master* of the camp. When there were two Dadolzai camps, Mahmud Karim was recognized as *master* to the other members and as the *master* of the second halk. When the camps recombined, Ja'far was once again recognized as *master* of all members.

There were many men older than Ja'far in the camp. Walli Mahmud had been Dadolzai *master* for a long period years before but was now old and inactive. Others were as old or older than Ja'far, but they were not successes economically, did not speak well, were not skilled at handling others. Ja'far had sired a large family, maintained a large herd and prosperous household, spoke well and in general was deemed to speak in the interests of the collectivity, and assiduously exemplified both tribal norms and tribal notions of Islamic norms. He was welcoming, enjoyed the role of *nandeh,* breadgiver, a generous host, and was soft-spoken and noncombative but firm.

And, of crucial importance, Ja'far was sensitive to public opinion and skilled at eliciting compromise. As Ja'far's Dadolzai followers put it when they described Ja'far and the role of *master,*

> The *master* of a halk had final say in decisions about operations of the halk, such as who to admit and who to deny, where and when to migrate, and how to deal with conflict. And the camp members had to accept the final decision of the master. They

recognized his authority, deferred to his position, and follow his directives. He was the leader, and they the followers; he was the senior and they were junior.

These pious sentiments were expressed by the tribesmen, but they did not, as we have already seen in detail, reflect the reality of *halk* decisionmaking. They did reflect a part of the procedure, in that the *master* gave a directive that was acted upon. But the reality was that the master was able to lead because he "decided" to go where his campmates wished to go. His final decisions, "which must be obeyed," were based upon extended consultation with the other household heads, especially the most *master* of them. If no consensus was forthcoming, the wise headman put off the decision. If no consensus was forthcoming but a decision could not be put off, the skilled headman would squeeze out a solid majority opinion. He really could do nothing else, for if he tried to lead the *halk* in a direction that it did not wish to go, he found himself abandoned, a general without an army.

For the *halki master* had little in the way of sanctions to apply in order to enforce his will. Certainly no corporal sanctions were possible. And when one was dealing with independent household heads, each with his and her own resources, and no substantial economic advantage in the hands of the *master,* what economic sanctions were available? Finally, and crucially, each household in the camp was mobile and could move under its own power in a matter of hours. Furthermore, as part of a large tribal system, and with extended networks of kin ties, no household was without alternative residence groups to join. The authority of the *halki master* thus rested most heavily upon the fact that he represented, in a very concrete and case-by-case fashion, the collective opinion of the camp. When this was not so, the response and reaction were often definite and clear. As we have seen, when Ja'far was not able to draw effectively on camp opinion and struck out on a course not favored by others, the majority of his camp members broke away and his *halk* fissioned, in effect vetoing his decision and revoking, at least temporarily, his leadership position.

Political seniority was also operative at the level of the *brasrend*. Among the Dadolzai, Halil, son of Walli Mahmud, was during the 1960s and 1970s recognized as *master*. In Halil's absence, Ja'far was recognized as *master* of the Dadolzai. Above the *brasrend,* up to the tribal level, there were no specified authority roles and leadership was somewhat vague and situational. I never heard anyone referred to as the leader of the Nur Mahmudzai subsection or of the Soherabzai major tribal section. When tribesmen mobilized as members of the Nur Mahmudzai or Soherabzai, prominent *master* members stepped forward and operated as an informal council. At the tribal level alone, the political seniority expressed in the concept of *master* was made permanent rather than contingent by the office of *sardar*.

The identification of the chiefship as being rooted in the more general principle of political seniority does not remove the puzzle about the nature of the tribe, centering on compatibility of its elements, the fit between the chiefship and the segmentary lineage system. Rather, as it recognizes the hierarchical and centralized political authority system throughout the tribe, it extends the question of compatibility. How did permanence and contingency, egalitarianism and hierarchy, authority and democracy, and centralization and decentralization fit together?

## THE INTERPLAY OF LINEAGE AND CHIEFSHIP

The tribal polity, based upon contrasting structural principles of the lineage system and the chiefship, fit its parts together through two basic processes: public opinion and mediation, *wasta*. The position of the chief among the tribal sections, subsections, and *brasrend* was in a structural sense not so different from that of the *halki master* among the microlineages of his camp, in that he did not have great power and had to deal with lineage segments that naturally fell into opposition in times of disagreement.

### Public Opinion

The chief led most effectively when he followed public opinion. The sounding, teasing out, and shaping of public opinion was one of the *sardar*'s most important tasks. The *sardar* used his *ru*, influence, to shape opinion, and, once successful, was in a position to act, for he would then have the support of his tribesmen. He could not use force, *zur*, on his followers. Lancaster (1981:96) says much the same about the sheikhs among the segmentary Rwala Bedouin: "Any attempt at enforcing a decision would simply result in the fading of influence for it would imply a lack of equality and consensus. Decision by consensus and public opinion are the only 'rule' that free Bedu will tolerate."

The Sardar was a leader, not a ruler. The tribesmen were supporters, not subjects. The principles of hierarchy and centralization represented by the Sardarship were in practice highly qualified and restricted, as we shall see. It was by acting on behalf of public opinion that the Sardar was able to lead effectively.

### Mediation

In a segmentary system based upon balanced opposition, the political lubricant that made possible movement toward settlement of conflicts and social reconciliation was mediation, *wasta*. Between the opposed segments, structurally neutral parties could stand for the larger, encompassing unity and stroke the conflicting parties toward resolution. *Master* at all levels of the tribe engaged in such mediation between parties to whom they were structurally equidistant or to whom they convincingly represented the larger, encompassing lineage or tribe. The Sardar intervened and played the role of the *wasta* in major conflicts within the tribe and also in more minor conflicts, at the request of the participants. He was able to use his *ru*, influence, to bring about a settlement. Successful mediation added to the *hezat*, prestige and honor, of the mediator.

The importance of mediation in segmentary systems is well established. Some Berber tribes (Gellner 1969) had special nonviolent, religious sections that provided professional mediation. The Bedouin of Cyrenaica (Evans-Pritchard 1949) established close relations with the Sanusiya religious order, which placed lodges on the boundaries between tribes and tribal sections and mediated conflicts. Settlements sometimes served as formally neutral locales for the meetings of opposed tribes (Bujra 1971). In other tribal settings, such as that of the Rwala Bedouin, tribal leaders were those who succeeded at mediation (Lancaster 1981:87): "The sheikh's prime task is mediation and negotiation."

## Related Processes

Two other processes were at work, complementing public opinion and mediation. One was an allocation of spheres, a division of activities between the two contradictory political frameworks, such that one kind of circumstance elicited response in terms of one framework, that is, the segmentary lineage system, and another kind of circumstance elicited response in terms of another framework, that is, the chiefship. The second process consisted of the trespassing of one system upon the other, thus making the operation of each system skewed, as it were, by the influence of the other. Here the contrast of the two organizational frameworks sometimes manifested itself in contestation, in claims and counterclaims, interactions reflecting the cross-purposes of the actors, resulting in a certain amount of inefficiency, confusion, and conflict.

## THE YARAHMADZAI POLITICAL STRUCTURE, 1850–1935

Let us now approach the Yarahmadzai political structure through a more detailed examination of the chiefship, situated in specific historical conditions. In general, the role of Sardar among the Yarahmadzai was more or less typical for the effectively independent tribes of Iranian Baluchistan, such as the Ismailzai / Shah Bakhsh and the Gamshadzai of the Sarhad, and the Bameri of the Jaz Murian. The authority of the Sardar was quite limited and his power severely constrained; he was, as we have said, much more a leader than a ruler, his tribesmen much more followers than subjects.

That *kabul*, consent, of the tribesmen was the basis of the tribal polity was evident from the process for recruitment of a new Sardar to office. According to tribal norms, succession was supposed to honor descent through the patriline, while taking into account pragmatic consideration of age, seniority and status of mother, and ability. Brothers, sons, and sons of brothers of the previous Sardar, and even sons-in-law were possibilities from which candidates had to assert themselves or be chosen. Commonly, several claimants would try to seize the office by acting out the role, and over time the consensus of opinion among the tribesmen would become evident—by who was referred to as Sardar, by who was approached and asked for assistance—and the issue would be resolved in favor of one candidate.

The complex of factors entering into a successful succession could not be reduced to a set of simple qualities, for the weights of the different factors and the relative weights of the factors changed from succession to succession with the new candidates and the new circumstances in which they were evaluated and in which they would have had to operate should they become Sardar. It seems clear, however, that succession to the Sardarship depended heavily upon the support and consent of the tribesmen, which to some extent were a result of consensus through discussion. Lineage and seniority provided the range of candidates, but an evaluation of willingness to act and effectiveness in representing tribal interests, especially in relation to the external forces, decided between the candidates.

Let us turn now to six specific aspects of the tribal polity—scale, contingency, centralization, specialized offices, scope of authority, and enforcement—with special attention to the role of the Sardar.

## Scale

According to the account of the tribesmen themselves, in the approximately 200 years of its development, the Yarahmadzai tribe grew from a handful of emigrating individuals to a population of several thousand souls, or, as they themselves said, *musil-men*. Estimates vary, but perhaps the safest figure for the period of the late 1960s and early 1970s was around 5,000; this is certainly the correct order of magnitude: many more than hundreds, and considerably less than 10,000. If the development of the tribe is at all accurately reflected in the genealogy—and I am aware of no contrary evidence—in earlier decades the population would have been substantially smaller, and the farther back, the smaller the tribal population was. Now the purpose of this elementary and imprecise exercise in demography is to establish the size of the polity and the numerical constituency of the Yarahmadzai chief. The tribe in the 1970s was relatively small compared with others in Iran and at the turn of the century was at best half its present size. So Jiand Han, who fought General R. E. F. Dyer during the Great War (Dyer 1921), and the other Yarahmadzai Sardars who followed, led a small tribe: the warriors numbered in the hundreds, and the tribal economy was that of households numbering in the hundreds. From the demographic perspective, the tribe was small and thus not especially powerful, and the Sardar had a relatively modest following.

## Contingency

The Yarahmadzai tribe was an ongoing maximal political entity, a permanent focus of ultimate political loyalty, a framework of ties and obligations that remained relevant, even if occasionally contested, whatever the political issue and the level of subgroups involved. This permanence was both manifested in and advanced by the office of Sardar, which stood for the tribe as a whole. The tribal level of political organization did not lie inactive until being brought into life by certain political events and structural configurations; on the contrary, the tribe was an ongoing entity at all times, and tribal membership was a relevant fact for all tribesmen at all times.

However, this is not to say that the tribe as a polity came even close to monopolizing political status within the tribe. Lower-level units maintained substantial political rights, duties, and responsibilities. The most important of these was protection of life and property, manifested in self-help and collective responsibility, which was organized, as we have said, in terms of patrilineages of structural equivalence that were activated contingently. Control of certain resources, such as wells, also resided with minor lineage groups. Thus, within the ongoing tribal framework, subunits of various levels were contingently activated and deactivated and reactivated in response to conflicts over life, injury, and property. The individual tribesman found himself not infrequently acting as a member of a lineage of greater or lesser depth, depending on the structural distance of the adversary, in regard to matters of the gravest importance, matters that were clearly political, in a fashion that was clearly political. The degree of contingency within the tribe, among the subsections of the tribe, must therefore be considered significant.

The coexistence of the noncontingent tribe with a series of contingent political subgroups can be seen not only as a limitation on the efficacy of the tribal units but also as a potential threat to the unity of the tribe—as in the assertion of political independence by Mahmud Selim Rahmatzai during the Soherabzai-Rahmatzai feud—and thus to its existence as an ongoing entity. To a degree, a balance was maintained, and the tribal unit reinforced, by a division of spheres between the tribe and its subgroups. While the lineages had the right and obligation to defend members and property through self-help, to take revenge and demand compensation according to the laws of blood feud, the tribe as a whole, represented by the Sardar, had the right and obligation to press for peace, to encourage settlement, and to compensate the injured. This division of rights was seen most dramatically in the formation of adversary groups according to the roles of structural equivalence, and the contrary structuring of compensation after peacemaking, in which minimal lineages of the tribe other than the offended one, whether close to the offending or offended minimal lineages, contributed to the compensation of the latter. That is to say, in the settlement compensation, minimal lineages acted as members of the tribe as a whole in redressing the grievance of the offended lineage. Thus, in spite of the contingent subgroups and the heavy political content of their rights and responsibilities, the tribe as a whole maintained its presence and influence, never disappearing, hovering always in the background, asserting its presence in ongoing and decisive ways.

In sum, the tribe as a unit, although far from monopolizing the political rights and responsibilities of tribal life, was able to maintain a continuing influential presence. Tribal affiliation and tribal claims continued to be in the minds of the tribesmen, even when they were acting as members of subgroups, even when the claims of subgroups took first priority. That this was the case was largely the result of the office of chief, for the Sardar was the living symbol of the tribe as a whole and was the active advocate of tribal claims: reminding, encouraging, threatening, pleading, manipulating, and agitating on behalf of the tribe in the name of the tribe as a whole. The Sardar's mantra was "We are all brothers. We are one." Certainly, the tribe as a political unit was greatly constrained by the contingent political subgroups within it, for these groups carried rights and responsibilities that were outside the control of the Sardar, and the subgroups therefore presented a continual threat to the unity of the tribe. Limited in power, competing for loyalty with its constituent subgroups, threatened by schism and disunity, the tribe as a political unit nonetheless existed continually, and continually influenced the course of events.

## Centralization

The Yarahmadzai tribe was highly decentralized. As already indicated, defence and vengeance rested with the lineages that made up the larger tribal entity. And while the tribe had peacemaking as a legitimate area of application, such processes were far from limited to the tribal level; bilateral peacemaking between lineages was built into the roles of blood feud and was available at any level, subject only to the will of the parties involved.

Access to pasture and natural water sources within tribal territory was a birthright and not subject to any central allocation or control. Livestock and cultivation were owned, controlled, and disposed of by individuals and small families. Dwellings and household equipment were owned and controlled by individuals and their families. Weapons were acquired and owned by individuals. Movement out of and back to the tribal territory was a matter of individual discretion. Movement within the tribal territory was based upon the discretionary decision of herding camps and individual families. Religious observance was guided by mullas living among and supported by the tribesmen.

No internal aspect of tribal life was centrally controlled; the Sardar had virtually no hold over the resources or activities of the tribesmen, nor was there much in the way of coordination or guidance, and following the Sardar's advice about peacemaking was voluntary on the part of the tribesmen.

What centralization there was among the Yarahmadzai could be seen primarily in external relations, in foreign affairs. External groups wishing access to tribal territory, such as tinkers or herders from other tribes, had to receive sanction from the Sardar. More important were relations with other groups of political weight, such as neighboring tribes and representatives of the government. Here, the Sardar represented the tribe as a whole and acted on its behalf. Negotiations with outsiders over such weighty matters as war and peace, control of disputed resources, and political alliance and affiliation were for the most part conducted by and through the Sardar. However, the term "through" is used advisedly, for the Sardar represented the tribesmen; he did not and could not dictate to them; he led rather than ruled them. A leader whose followers refused to follow was no longer a leader, and so, even in this area, which was especially the realm of the chief, the Sardar had to be highly sensitive to public opinion, to the preferences of and constraints upon his tribesmen.

## Office

Beyond that of the Sardar, there was only one other political office in the tribal structure, the *master* of the *brasrend*, minimal lineage. As has already been outlined, *master* was a general concept of political precedence, and in any group of tribesmen—a family, a group of children, a maximal lineage, a *halk*—there was a ranking in terms of this precedence. But in most cases the status of *master* was informal and contingent. Only in the case of the *brasrend*, minimal lineage, headman was the recognition at all formal, the formality residing—in some cases but by no means all—in the explicit acknowledgment given by the Sardar. As the leader of a small constituent subgroup of the tribe, the *master* looked first and foremost to his lineage, and only secondarily to the Sardar as leader of the tribe. He was not an agent of the Sardar without a constituency of his own; on the contrary, he held his office largely by virtue of support from his lineage.

Among the Yarahmadzai, then, there was one political office, the chiefship, that represented the tribe as a whole. The second office, the *brasrend* headmanship, sometimes served to provide a link between the smaller, cohesive groups of kinsmen and the chief. There were no offices at the tribal level for agents of the Sardar: no tax collectors, legal advisers, or enforcers. Nor were there offices representing the higher levels of lineage organization that drew together larger agglomerations of tribesmen. Thus the Sardar had no protobureaucracy at his command, no functionaries whom he controlled. Nor had he a long chain of command; he had no line of officials based upon larger groupings that could conceivably carry out directives and provide political support. In consequence, the Sardar had no political apparatus on which to depend, and so had to rely upon general support from the tribesmen at large in a context of independent lineage groupings and fluid public opinion.

The relative structural solitude of the Sardar and the fluidity of his political base, while defining the limitations of his role, did not nullify the importance of his office.

The continuity and influence that the sardarship provided for the tribal level of organization clearly mark off the political system of the Yarahmadzai from those based solely upon segmentary lineage systems or other wholly decentralized structures without offices at the maximal level of organization.

## Authority

The authority of the Yarahmadzai Sardar was severely limited. As the leader of independent tribesmen, the Sardar stood for and represented the tribe, but was largely the servant of the tribe. Most areas of tribal life were in the hands of lower-level groups or individuals, as discussed above, which left little of policy or administration in the hands of the Sardar. Decisions pertaining to the tribe at large were based, as is the case at every level of organization, on discussion, consultation, debate, assessment and reassessment, and compromise or separation. One would not be far wrong to characterize the internal role of the Sardar as that of animateur, giving life to, actuating, propelling the tribe as a political unit by encouraging, bullying, inspiring, urging, and providing an example for his tribesmen.

But as with any animateur, the Sardar ultimately depended on the decisions and actions of his tribesmen, for without them voluntarily behind him, he was less than a figurehead, he was an empty symbol. In setting tribal policy—usually done in terms of specific cases rather than through abstract general pronouncements—and making decisions, the Sardar to a large extent had to crystallize and enunciate public sentiment and opinion, for to deviate too far from his tribesmen would have undermined his support and his position. The Sardar found no advantage in taking positions that would arouse resentment among his followers, which would have proven difficult or impossible to implement and which would have in the end undercut his limited authority.

For example, in a confrontation between tribes or with the state, if the tribesmen did not wish to fight, the Sardar had no way to force them to fight. If the tribesmen did not wish to suspend raiding, the Sardar was not in a position to make them do so. When General Dyer (1921:71) rebuked Jiand Han for the Yarahmadzai raids into the British Raj, "Jiand admitted the force of all my arguments, . . . but pleaded that he himself had done his best to restrain his men from interfering with the British lines of communication, warning them that is was neither safe nor wise." Dyer (1921:71) did not believe him: "He could not seriously have expected that I would swallow this excuse, as he was known to be held in such awe by his followers that not one of them would have dared to dispute his authority." Dyer (1921:64) characterizes Jiand Han as "a very notable man, with enormous power and prestige, not only with his own tribe, the Yarmohommedzais, but with all the nomad tribes of the district, and was regarded as personage by the Governments of both India and of Persia." No matter how great a "notable," and this is really a very apt term, there is no reason to believe that the Sardar Jiand Han had the authority to restrict raiding if the tribesmen were in favor of it. Dyer says that Jiand's tribesmen would not have dared to dispute his authority. I think it is more likely that Jiand would not have dared to forbid raiding because he in fact had neither the authority nor the power to restrain his supporters against their wills.

## Enforcement

The restricted nature of the Sardar's authority was clearly manifested in the fact that the Sardar had virtually no means for sanctioning. The Sardar was unable to enforce policies, decisions, and jural dispositions. There was no police arm available to the Sardar, no mechanism for bringing physical coercion to bear upon the tribesmen. Not that the Sardar had any such authority: capital punishment, corporal punishment, or incarceration were not acts that would have been deemed legitimate by his fellow tribesmen. In any case, the means of coercion were distributed throughout the tribe, and the organization of coercion was a decentralized tribewide system, the segmentary lineage system. The Sardar, like every other tribesman, was, in regard to matters of physical coercion, caught up in the lineage system; coercive action by the Sardar and members of his lineage, at whatever level of segmentation, would have simply activated the structurally equivalent opposing lineage. Physical force was not a means available to the Sardar for governance of the tribe.

Nor was the Sardar able to sanction by offering or withholding material resources. Little of the collective tribal resources—land, pasture, and water—were under his control. And, given the notoriously volatile nature of wealth in livestock and the highly restricted possibilities for cultivation in the tribal environment, the Sardar hardly had the private economic wealth to use material resources as a major means of supporting his position. The Sardar was not an economic patron; he was not able economically to support his tribal followers and thus place them in the position of clients. The Sardar was not in a position to use economic resources for sanctioning power.

However, the Sardar did perform services for the tribesmen, and these were valuable and valued. The most common service was that of acting as an intermediary, *wasta,* between individual tribesmen, between lineages, and between the tribe and other tribes, and between the tribe and government authorities. Beyond mediation, the Sardar was a war leader, responsible during conflict with outsiders for directing the disposition of the tribe and its overall military operations. These services the Sardar was able, to a degree, to offer or to withhold, and by such means tribesmen could be sanctioned, positively or negatively, at the discretion of the Sardar.

But while tribesmen could be so sanctioned, the Sardar's latitude of maneuver was not so great as it might appear at first glance. In fact, the incumbent of the chiefship fulfilled his role and maintained his status by performing these services for his tribesmen; there was little more to the role of Sardar than providing such services. And as he had to provide these services to assert his office, the Sardar was not in a position—beyond limited selectivity in application—to grant or withhold them at will, to use them as sanctions to pressure or punish his tribesmen, lest he undermine his own position. In short, with regard to enforcement, the Sardar could not impose his will upon tribesmen either by means of force or by manipulating transactions.

We can conclude that overall the Sarhadi chiefship was a highly restricted political office. The Sardars of the Yarahmadzai, Gamshadzai, Ismailzai, and Rigi led small tribes of several thousand individuals. The unity of each tribe was to a degree undercut by politically strong subgroups of a contingent nature that operated more or less independently of the tribal level of organization. Few important areas of tribal life fell under the central control of the Sardar, who had no political apparatus to assist him and few sanctions at his disposal with which to exert control. Far from being an oriental despot, a powerful ruler, or even a well-placed patron, the Sardar was a leader of independent tribesmen, a symbol and representative of the tribe and the tribesmen, and an animateur for the tribe as a maximal political entity.

## Explaining the Yarahmadzai Chiefship

In accounting for the nature of the Yarahmadzai tribal structure and its particular characteristics, we must take into account a complex of factors, some supporting a hierarchical, centralized structure, others undercutting such a structure. Thus the Yarahmadzai political structure can be seen as the consequence of conflicting pressures.

Let us begin with the factors that inhibited political hierarchy, offices, and the centralization of decisionmaking, control, and enforcement. Three factors were of major importance here: ecological adaptation, technology, and social demography.

In general, the multi-resource and nomadic adaptation of the Yarahmadzai militated against hierarchical political structures. As we have seen in detail, the environment of northern Baluchistan was harsh and erratic owing to its extreme aridity and highly variable precipitation. Both the small-stock pastoralism and the limited-rainfall grain cultivation were subject to great fluctuations of success and failure. Date palm cultivation, hunting and gathering, and predatory raiding were also subject to fluctuations. The Sarhadi tribal adaptation had a number of consequences, which in turn had important implications for the political system.

First, the volatility of the primary forms of production made it difficult for individuals and small groups to accumulate wealth. At the same time, the available extralocal forms of accumulation—perhaps most important as modes of compensation for local failures—especially predatory raiding, were open to all members of the tribe and would have been particularly attractive to those less well off. Thus differentiation in terms of material wealth, which could have supported a hierarchical structure, was not a significant characteristic of the tribal economy.

Second, the high level of spatial mobility, the ability to move easily from one place to another, guaranteed that the tribesmen were not a "captive" constituency. They and their families moved frequently in the course of the annual round of productive activities. One of the primary capital resources, livestock, was highly mobile. The technology of household living, storage, and consumption was attuned to nomadism: the dwellings were tents and the household equipment was portable. Each household had transport animals, usually camels, or access to them. Thus the tribesmen could readily invoke strategies of retreat and escape from internal despotism or external threat. A Sardar who oppressed, exploited, or even seriously irritated his tribesmen would have found his constituency disappearing into the mountains or over the horizon.

Third, the availability of natural resources, especially pasture and water, was extremely erratic and unpredictable, both in time and space. This fact, together with the sparseness of the resources whenever and wherever they occurred, made decentralized decisionmaking about the exploitation of natural resources virtually mandatory. Thus coordination of population movement and of resource exploitation, which could have been an important function of a central authority, as it was among the Zagros tribes (Barth 1961), was not useful here.

Fourth, the low population density resulting from the factors already outlined meant that the tribesmen were spread over great distances, which made it difficult to contact and keep in touch with them. This further discouraged coordination and control. In addition, the low population density meant that tribesmen seldom felt crowded or needed externally controlled organization or coordination.

Technological factors added to these considerations. First, the means of communication and transportation were primitive. Animal transport and face-to-face communication were most common and more or less the limit. Second, the means of physical coercion, that is, weaponry, were also primitive, limited to small and relatively inexpensive fire-arms at best, and were equally distributed throughout the tribe. That a small group could establish political control through superior fire-power, or enhance their power through a monopoly of weaponry, would have been inconceivable in the tribal context. Third, technological and financial means for developing agriculture, especially through the use of irrigation, were not available on a significant enough scale to provide an economic basis for political differentiation and an anchor for a nonmobile sector of the population that would have been less independent. The absence of such a development deprived the Sardar of control over a body of dependent agricultural workers and patronage that could have made independent pastoral producers more dependent.

Fifth, the social and political demography of the region inhibited tight political control by the Sardar. Tribesmen could easily retreat and escape from the Sardar if they so chose. For one thing, the region was far from crowded. The Yarahmadzai and other tribes were not pressed in on every side by other populations crowded in their own territories and loath to sustain any intruders. On the contrary, the region contained more or less unoccupied areas that could support new groups in the austere style to which they had become accustomed. For another thing, the surrounding tribes—especially the Gamshadzai and Ismailzai, which were similar in most respects to the Yarahmadzai—and other groupings were not unwelcoming. There were no serious linguistic, religious, or ethnic barriers. In some cases, there had been a history of collaboration, of affinal ties, and even of common descent. These factors contributed to the voluntary nature of participation in the tribal polity and worked against a mandatory, compulsory presence within a tribe, and thus placed constraints on the ability of a Sardar to control his tribesmen.

In sum, the adaptation, economy, technology, and demography of the Yarahmadzai and other Sarhadi tribesmen were conducive to autonomy of the household and the minimal lineage. They tended to make very difficult any concentration of the means of production, coercion, or administration, thus removing the support that any such concentration would have provided for political differentiation and hierarchy, for control and centralization.

What, then, was the basis of the political differentiation and hierarchy in the tribe, as manifested in the office of Sardar? The functional answer is that it was based primarily on the provision of an essential service: mediation between the tribe and external powers. The structural answer is that a population that is intimately and immediately engaged with a powerful external presence, but that does not erect a political organization that can compete with the external presence on a more or less comparable level, will become dependent on that external force or be absorbed by it, the only alternative being retreat and escape. Thus tribes with politically powerful neighbors take three forms: the subordinate, the politically evolved, and the no-longer-present. The Yarahmadzai, with both a chief and a permanent, noncontingent, tribal organization, was an example of the second type of tribe, one that evolved politically in response to engagement with a politically more highly organized neighbor.

The Yarahmadzai tribe did not come into being in a political vacuum. On the contrary, from its beginning, the tribe was located, if not in, at least on the borders of, a territory that was occupied by a highly organized system of formidable economic and political power. This stratified proto-state was organized and controlled by the Kords, who supplied the political and military elite, and the hakom, ruler, of the complex polity (Spooner 1969; Bestor 1979). One story of the origin of the Kords of Daptan, not universally accepted, is that the Kords were sent from Kurdistan to the Sarhad of Baluchistan by Shah Abbas the Great as part of his policy of weakening dangerous tribes by removing them from their local territories, splitting them up, and sending them to distant areas occupied by diverse, and thus not solidary, populations. Thus Shah Abbas made the Kords his agents, acting on his behalf with a mandate to establish order in the name of the crown.

In the Sarhad, the Kords established themselves at the location of the only substantial natural source of water in the region, on the slopes of the Kuh-i Taftan, and at the central, strategic location on the plains, at Khash, which was an area of good if not readily accessible water and of good soil. They gained control over the small, dispersed, and socially fragmented populations of the region, some of which were primarily settled cultivators on the mountain slopes, and others of which were locally organized, small-stock pastoralists, and all of which, as told to me by the Kords, were pagan rather than Muslim. The Kords established a tax, *rayat*, system, in which they regularly received a substantial portion, in kind, from subject agricultural producers, who were labeled *rayati*. Other groups, mainly nomads, became part-time retainers, providing additional political and military support in return for a portion of the spoils: these retainers were called *topangchini*, riflemen.

The type of system exemplified by the Kords of Taftan/Daptan, common in Iranian Baluchistan, especially in regions south of the Sarhad (Salzman 1978b), I refer to as a "hakomate," after the term used for the head, *hakom*, which means "ruler." The *hakom* and his small kin group, the *hakomzat*, was commonly based in agricultural centers, not infrequently fortified by a *kalat*, fort, while extending control throughout a region. This ruling elite was provided for primarily by dependent agricultural populations and in a more limited fashion by nomadic pastoral producers, and it was supported politically by quasi-military subordinates, usually nomads. But the hakomate was rare in the Sarhad, a region with less accessible water and with a climate unsuitable for date palm cultivation. The Sarhad was occupied, for the most part, by nomadic tribes having multi-resource economies; it was only in the Taftan/Khash region that a hakomate developed under the Kords.

The Kordish hakomate was well established by the time the embryonic Yarahmadzai—according to their own origin story—moved from the Sefid Kuh in the southeast to the Morpish mountain range on the southeastern border of the hakomate. There they stayed, increasing over the years and expanding in a relatively unoccupied area toward the east and the Mashkil drainage basin, and at the same time toward the west and highland plains area of the Kordish hakomate. Initially, as reported to me by the Kord *hakom* but stoutly denied by my Yarahmadzai informants, the latter were *topangchini*, fighters, for the Kords, having a subordinate political status but maintaining considerable autonomy and independence. In all probability, the Yarahmadzai did recognize the political ascendancy of the Kords, acknowledging it symbolically when necessary and cooperating with them when convenient and desirable. However, the Yarahmadzai and other Sarhadi tribes, unlike the nomadic populations of the hakomates in southern Baluchistan who accepted the *hakom* as their leader, either never recognized the Kord Hakom as a leader to whom they owed allegiance or at some early point withdrew their allegiance. Instead, it seems, the Yarahmadzai and the other Sarhadi tribes generated their own political leaders, the Sardars, and crystallized their unity at a maximal, tribal level of political organization.

Now although the Kords remained loyal to the Iranian crown, governed as agents of the crown, and received some encouragement and support from the crown, officials of the government and their monetary and military resources were far from the hakomate, in distant Bampur to the south or even more distant Kerman to the west. In practice, the Kordish hakomate was for the most part on its own, although it could draw for support upon alliances with other hakomates. Thus, as the Yarahmadzai tribe grew larger, more powerful, and less subservient, the Kords faced a serious challenge. In the event, the Yarahmadzai tribe expanded at the expense of the Kords and their dependents. This engagement between the Kords and the Yarahmadzai took place in fits and starts, over several generations during the nineteenth and early twentieth centuries.

During the course of the on-again, off-again conflict, interspersed with periods of settlement and peacemaking, considerable blood was spilled, and at one point the Kords were temporarily driven out of the Sarhad altogether. The final disposition, at the time of arrival of the Iranian government in 1928–35, was that the Yarahmadzai had taken control of the plains and the Kords had concentrated in the Taftan range, and that the Yarahmadzai tribe was the major political power in the region. During this conflict, the Yarahmadzai Sardars had been war leaders and peace negotiators, strategists and mediators, meeting the Kordish hakoms as independent political leaders. Here we can see positive feedback at work in political development: the Yarahmadzai were able to challenge the Kords because of, among other things, their tribal political structure, with its leadership and coherence at the maximal level, and at the same time the tribal political structure was reinforced and enhanced by the oppositional engagement with the Kords, in which the value and importance of the chiefship and tribal unity was demonstrated.

In sum, the centrifugal influences upon the Yarahmadzai lineage system, balanced by the centripetal influence of political engagement with highly organized external powers, resulted in the particular form of Yarahmadzai political structure, the restricted chiefship ingeniously fitted to a segmentary lineage system. That the lineage system was a major structure, that the chiefship was highly limited, and that the tribe was as egalitarian and decentralized as it was, were largely the effects of these centrifugal factors. That there was a chiefship and continuing maximal level of organization, that the tribal political system was as hierarchical and centralized as it was, were largely effects of that centripetal factor.

The importance of external relations in influencing the nature and development of tribal leadership is well established. Evans-Pritchard (1940:187–89; cf. Johnson 1994) attributed to new external threats the appearance of tribal leaders—"prophets," as they have come to be glossed—in the previously fragmented Nuer ethnic population:

> Powerful prophets arose about the time when Arab intrusion into Nuerland was at its height and . . . after the reconquest of the Sudan they were more respected and had more influence than any other persons in Nuerland. . . .

The only activities of prophets which can truly be called tribal were their initiation of raids against the Dinka and their rallying of opposition to Arab and European aggression, and it is in these actions that we see their structural significance and account for their emergence and the growth of their influence. . . .

For the first time a single person symbolized, if only to a moderate degree and in a mainly spiritual and uninstitutionalized form, the unity of a tribe, for prophets are tribal figures. But they have a further significance, for their influence extended over tribal boundaries. . . . They . . . were pivots of federation between adjacent tribes and personified the structural principle of opposition in its widest expression, the unity and homogeneity of Nuer against foreigners.

The importance of external relations is similarly seen in institutionalized chiefships. Barth (1961:77, 80) stresses this among the Basseri of south Persia:

Perhaps the chief's most important function is to represent the tribe in its relations with the Iranian administration, and in conflicts with sedentary communities or persons. . . .

The chief's role in mediating relations with the sedentary society, in protecting the nomadic herders' interests vis-à-vis the often formidable and always confusing organizations that structure parts of their environment and encroach on their life, is correlated with a strong feeling of respect and dependence among the tribesmen.

Among the Rwala Bedouin (Lancaster 1981:95), "the Emir has no right to negotiate on behalf of the tribe but, being the most influential man in a position to negotiate, he has an obligation to do so. If he fails to fulfil this obligation he is no longer Emir." The situation is similar in regard to "the sheikh's authority to act as a mediator with the outside" (Lancaster 1981:87).

A word remains to be said about the multiformity of the Yarahmadzai political system, about the fact that the system contained two more or less separate, almost contradictory, structures, that is, the chiefship and the segmentary lineage system. Now we have taken this juxtaposition, this combination of two seemingly incompatible structures, as anomalous, as peculiar, as requiring explanation. I have attempted to explain it both in terms of the factors and influences that gave rise to each and in terms of the ways each is fitted to the other, and how the two structures have accommodated so as to coexist and even to a degree serve one another. However, the sense of anomaly remains, because there is in our analytic models an implicit assumption of perfect integration, of structural purity, of institutional consistency.

And yet, it does not really make much sense to expect a society to be all of a piece. This is especially true if we regard society as, in some substantial measure, a set of social arrangements for dealing with needs, for coping with problems, for adapting to circumstances and external forces (Salzman 1980). Circumstances and problems are not all of the same type and cannot all be addressed by the same response, nor are the needs constant over time, but rather there is one challenge and then another quite different one. With these considerations in mind, we might consider multiformity, as in the case of the Yarahmadzai political structure, not only as distinct and contradictory parts imperfectly combined into a whole, but also as a set of organizational alternatives that could be brought to bear differentially or alternatively as different types of problems and circumstances came up, such that a particular situation could be responded to by means of the most appropriate organizational form of those available. In the Yarahmadzai case, situations most effectively dealt with by a decentralized response could be attacked through the segmentary lineage system, whereas situations most usefully dealt with by means of coordination could be responded to through the chiefship. Thus multiformity in Sarhadi political organization can be seen not as a reflection of malintegration, but as a prudent maintenance of organizational alternatives in response to the range of circumstances with which the tribesmen had to deal (Salzman 1978a).

## Tribal Polities and Their Variations

Tribal political systems are a consequence of multidirectional and sometimes contradictory influences stemming from internal forms, inherent tendencies, and local system parameters, on the one hand, and extraneous pressures, foreign influences, and external ties, on the other hand. The structural forms resulting from these influences are compromises of all the varying tendencies; sometimes these compromises can be built into a unitary structure, but sometimes they are of a multiform nature.

The internal factors—adaptation, economy, technology, demography—that drew the Yarahmadzai political system toward egalitarian, decentralized, contingent structures, would, with other characteristics than obtain among them, have exerted influence in other directions. Richer and more dependable natural resources would have provided a better basis for an extractable surplus and for hierarchical control and coordination. An economy based more upon market exchange, especially with external populations, would have been more susceptible to control and coordination. More stable means of production would have been more conducive to the accumulation of wealth and economic differentiation. Higher population density, both internally and externally, would have made the tribesmen more accessible. A less nomadic technology of production would also have made the producers more controllable, and a military technology less available to the population at large would have facilitated concentration of the means of coercion. Differentiation and concentration of the means of production, coercion, or administration would have favored increased political differentiation, hierarchy, centralization, and organizational integration. Internal factors with values in the other direction, such as lower population density, or an economy based more upon marginal resources, or the like, would have moved the political system more toward egalitarianism, decentralization, and structural contingency.

The external factors among the Yarahmadzai—especially political engagement with a more highly organized external power—that drew their political system toward hierarchical, centralized structures and institutions, particularly the chiefship, would, with other characteristics, have had influences in other directions. For example, external relations limited to decentralized tribal groups would probably not have supported the development of hierarchical, centralized structures (Sahlins 1961). External relations based upon extensive economic exchange with others, especially sedentary populations, would have required greater liaison and coordination and would have supported more elaborate and powerful offices and structures. Competitive engagement with an even stronger external power would have required greater mobilization of human and economic resources, and thus an even higher level of organization. Encapsulation within a powerful state—as happened to the Yarahmadzai after 1935, the point at which they became the Shah Nawazi—would have led to a more hierarchical, centralized, and crystallized structure as a result of a state policy of playing an indirect role and the consequent access of the tribal political hierarchy to the resources—administrative, economic, and military—of the state (Salzman 1974).

## THE YARAHMADZAI AND ITS SARDAR 1935–76

A tribe—as I define the term—is an independent, segmentary polity consisting of communities of rural primary producers. To the extent that such a set of communities loses its political independence, it ceases to be a tribe (Salzman 1996). The range of variation between complete political independence and complete subservience may, for our purposes, be recorded on a graduated continuum between tribes and peasants and extending beyond.

| POLITICAL INDEPENDENCE | | | | POLITICAL DEPENDENCE |
|---|---|---|---|---|
| autonomy | encapsulation | incorporation | assimilation | servitude |
| Tribes | | Peasants | Serfs | Slaves |

Just as there are nomadic, pastoral tribes, there are nomadic, pastoral peasants (Salzman 1996). As political circumstances change over time, a population may shift toward greater autonomy in its politics or may come under the increasing control of another polity (Salzman 1978a). Populations that were once autonomous tribes have throughout recorded history been incorporated into larger, often state, polities, just as throughout history empires and states have broken down and disintegrated, leaving local populations, especially those at the geographical periphery, largely autonomous, to operate politically as independent tribes.

In the 10 years between 1967 and 1976—during which I visited Iranian Baluchistan, residing there during three periods for a total of 26 months, primarily in the Sarhad of Baluchistan—the Yarahmadzai, along with the other Sarhadi tribes, was firmly encapsulated (Bailey 1969:chap. 8) by the *dolat*, the Iranian state apparatus of Mohammed Reza Shah Pahlavi. Iran had extended effective control to the Sarhad. I want to make it clear that at the time of my research the Yarahmadzai was not a politically independent tribe. There was an Iranian military presence in Baluchistan, and policing was carried out by the paramilitary gendarmerie. The *dolat*, Iranian governmental and administrative institutions, were represented in Baluchistan, as were various other Iranian agencies, including health, education, and social services.

## Pacification and Encapsulation

Reza Shah's "pacification" of the Sarhad began in 1928, after a series of campaigns against tribes—the Basseri and the Arab tribes of the Khamseh, the Qashqai, the Kords, the Turkmen, and the Lurs, among others. According to one of the Iranian military officers (Arfa 1964:253) involved, "Baluchistan had been one of the last regions of Iran to be pacified and brought under the control of the Central Government" and the Sarhad the last region of Baluchistan to be pacified. The military campaign in Baluchistan began in 1928, but in spite of some successes, at the end of 1934 the Sarhadi tribes continued to revolt against the government. As General Hassan Arfa (1964:254), who was the chief of staff to the general in charge and who participated in the final stage of the campaign, tells it,

> The remaining dissident tribes were subjected, with the exception of the Esma'elzais [=Ismailzai] and Yarahmadzais, who after a period of outward submission again revolted against the Government. The Chief of the Yarahmadzai, Jiand, a ninety-year-old man, had been arrested and died in Mashad, but his son-in-law, Shahsavar took the tribe into the wilderness near the British frontier, refusing all contact with the Government, while Jom'e Khan [of the Ismailzai] revolted in Shuro, west of Zahedan.

The government sent Idu Han Rigi, who had been kept in Tehran in spite of his professions and acts of loyalty, to negotiate with Sardar Jome Han of the Ismailzai, his brother-in-law. Idu Han convinced Jome Han to accept an amnesty from the government in return for giving up arms (Arfa 1964:256). "After the submission of the Esma'elzais, the important tribe of the Yarahmadzais with its allied Gomshadzai tribe, showed a desire to come to terms" (Arfa 1964:257).

What a remarkable reprise, was this confrontation, of the war some 20 years earlier between the British punitive force under General R. E. H. Dyer, supported by the Rigi tribe led by Idu Han, and the Yarahmazai under Jiand Han, supported by the Ismailzai led by Jome Han. Reza Shah's pacification of Baluchistan, however, had a much greater and longer-lasting impact. As a sign of submission, the Yarahmadzai took the name Shah Navazi, "shah stroker," and the Ismailzai took the name Shah Baksh, the "shah's pardon."

We have already reviewed some of the economic consequences of this "pacification," notably the suppression of predatory raiding and drying up of the flow of resources into the Sarhad. On the political front, the Sarhadi tribes lost—to a substantial extent—their independence of action, especially their ability to use coercion. The Yarahmadzai told me that they had fought the Persians and killed many Persian soldiers, and that the Iranian *dolat* had settled with them and had given their Sardar a handsome allowance. They were not keen to tell me that they had lost to the Persians, but they knew it and knew it well. There was no denying the effective imposition of control by Iranian military and civilian officials over the tribe, or the Iranian State's attempts—not overtly opposed by the tribesmen—to regulate certain important aspects of tribal life, such as the possession of firearms.

Whatever the economic and psychocultural dislocations resulting from pacification, there was great structural and organizational continuity within the Yarahmadzai. The Iranian government did not interfere directly with the tribal structure; its policy was to exercise external control through an indirect role. Its yearly stipend to the Sardar was both a symbol of tribal acknowledgment of Persian State suzerainty and an economic reward for past and anticipated "good behavior" by the Sardar and his tribesmen.

Within the tribe, order continued to rest in the hands of the lineages. Residence continued to be organized by herding contracts. Pastoral, arboricultural, and agricultural primary production remained much the same, except for the slow increase over decades in irrigation cultivation. The prohibition and cessation of raiding was the change that most affected daily life. The loss of the wealth imported through predation was a great blow to the economy of the Sarhad and to the standard of living of the tribesmen. And the tribesmen were no longer, and could no longer think of themselves as, daring raiders fearlessly invading foreign lands to conquer weaker peoples and capture booty, returning home enriched with wealth taken by military prowess. The human booty of raiding and trading, the slaves who had done some of the agricultural work in the Sarhad, were freed, and, although those who remained in the tribal territory were consigned to a low status, they lived independently in their own communities, engaging in primary production for their own consumption, as did other tribesmen. This, too, had a consequence for ordinary tribesmen, who now had to shoulder all of the labor required for any cultivation they wished to pursue.

The Yarahmadzai were, from 1935 on, encapsulated by Iran; the tribe was included within the government's effective field of power. At the same time, the basic organizational forms of tribal life remained as before. The actions of the Sarhadi tribes had come under constraint, but their structures maintained the capacity to operate independently, if and when the constraints were ever lifted. The daily life of the Sarhadi tribesmen remained in most respects the same as before the conquest. Cultural frames of reference and the complex of identities shifted slowly over time, more in balance and emphasis than in substance. Encapsulation of the tribes beginning in 1935 had not led, by the end of the 1970s, to incorporation, to the replacement of distinctive local institutions of the Sarhadi tribes by the national institutions of Iran.

## Adapting the Chiefship

A great change was imposed on the leadership of the tribe, not so much in the structure, in the statuses and levels of hierarchy, but in the office of Sardar, and the activities and consequent functions of that office. Previously a warrior leader and defender of tribal independence, wielding the *zur* of the tribe, the Sardar became, after the conquest and "pacification," the intermediary, mediator, and broker between the tribe and the national government of Iran. The qualities of a good Sardar were the same: strength, confidence, energy. The skills needed by the Sardar were adapted from those of mediation within the tribe and foreign relations between the tribe and opposing tribes and hakomates. But the application was new and different: for the Sardar was now a low-level middleman in a vertical hierarchy, a hierarchy that had established effective, coercive control over the tribe. The Sardar's new role was to manage the tribe for state authorities and to manage the authorities for the tribesmen. In this new role he had to wheel and deal in a bureaucratic milieu, to avoid technical legal pitfalls, and to see and take advantage of new opportunities for acquiring resources and for making innovations that used such resources. From the point of view of the government and its agents, the Sardar was responsible for the tribe, in the sense that the government demanded that he maintain successful and satisfactory control of the tribesmen for the purposes of the government.

Just as before pacification, the range of the Sardar's authority continued to be narrowly restricted. His limited judicial activity consisted primarily of mediation and was not supported by formal sanctions. Access to tribal resources, such as land and pasture, was governed by customary rights, while lineage resources, such as wells, and individual resources, such as livestock and date palms, remained in the hands of individuals and lineages; none of these were open to arbitrary appropriation and allocation by the Sardar. Movements of tribesmen in groups or as individuals, either within or outside of tribal territory, were not under the Sardar's control, nor were such matters as residence, marriage, and camp formation. Headmen of lineages had to be recognized by the Sardar but were chosen primarily by lineage elders, whose *kabul* validated the headman.

The Sardar did have the authority to make ad hoc requests of short-term labor in special circumstances. In the case of a special request for a half-day or day or even several days of work, the men complained—to each other—but said, "What can we do? The Sardar asked us." They said that he would do nothing should they refuse but recognized that there were many informal sanctions open to the Sardar—in particular, he could withhold aid in time of need. Furthermore, the Sardar was deemed to have the right to ask for help on behalf of the tribe as a whole, and tribesmen would be criticized for refusing. A request from the Sardar should be honored, it was said, as he was the representative and symbol of the tribe, but such aid and assistance should also be given to any worthy person, for only by doing such is *sawab,* credit for good works, earned, and only by having earned *sawab* can one be a "right man."

The Sardar also had the authority to request, on an ad hoc basis, monetary contributions from the tribesmen for projects that were meant to benefit the tribe as a whole. There was no set contribution, and individuals paid what they felt they were able to pay, with due consideration for maintaining status and good relations. All individuals who were living in tribal territory, whether they were Yarahmadzai proper, Ghulamzai, Luri, or members of other tribes residing there with the Sardar's permission, were subject to such requests and were expected to contribute. Requests for favors from the Sardar were sometimes accompanied by presents. And on occasion the Sardar would make a special request for a present, such as a tribesman's new wristwatch, a request that was usually not refused. In addition to material income, a wish to assert chiefly authority played a part in such cases. Other than these request-donations, there was no systematic tax or levy, as there was for the local *mulla* and tribal *maulawi.*

The Sardar's new middleman role in the postpacification context was that of intermediary, mediator, and broker—terms that I use here to distinguish different dimensions of the role—between the tribe and the Iranian national government, its agencies, and representatives. As intermediary, the Sardar acted as the channel through which information, instructions, and resources flowed between the tribe and the government. As mediator, the Sardar attempted to bring the tribe and the representatives of the government to some mutually agreeable position in regard to various policy matters and their administration. As broker, in a somewhat traditional sense of the term, the Sardar attempted to acquire advantages and resources from the government on behalf of the tribe.

## The Middleman's Dilemma

Information, instructions, and orders from the government to the tribe were given or sent to the Sardar, and the Sardar was expected to make these known to the tribe. For example, when the gendarmerie decided to crack down on unregistered arms, it was the Sardar to whom this information was directed, and he was expected to pass on instructions to the tribesmen. Material resources also were funneled to the tribe through the Sardar. During the severe drought of the early 1960s, the government sent a large amount of grain to the Sardar, and he was expected to see that it was properly distributed to the tribesmen. Aside from such temporary relief aid, more permanent types of development aid for the tribe were handled by the Sardar. The diesel-engine pump installed at Garonchin in the middle 1960s, the first for the Yarah-madzai, was controlled and administered by the Sardar, as was the first tractor in the tribal territory, which arrived in 1968.

If any disparity existed between governmental and tribal requests and demands, the Sardar had to reconcile the two sides and bring the disagreement to a satisfactory conclusion, or at least a nondestructive standoff. The Sardar's position was unlike that of a judicial mediator, for he could not stand apart and aloof from the disputants. Rather, the Sardar was the representative and highest ranking member of his group; at the same time, he was the lowest link in the hierarchic governmental chain of command and consequently faced the well-known difficulties labeled the "foreman's dilemma." Like the foreman, the Sardar represented the position of the tribe to the government authorities but nonetheless had to pass down decisions and orders issued by the authorities that were unpopular with the tribesmen, and to an extent he had to see to it that the unpopular measures were carried out, or at least were thought by the government authorities to have been carried out. This particular position of the Sardar was a result of the political subservience of the tribe to the national government since pacification. The government had overwhelming military force at its command, not to mention lesser sanctions such as the extension or retention of various kinds of aid. The Sardar was subject to government sanctions, and, like the foreman who could be fired, he was held responsible for the tribe and could be punished by withholding various positive sanctions, or by removal from office, banishment, imprisonment, or execution—these latter by no means unknown in Iran—if the tribe did not satisfactorily conform to government expectations.

A clear example of the Sardar's dilemma can be found in the gendarmerie's campaign of 1968 to confiscate what it believed to be large numbers of unregistered and consequently illegal rifles from the tribesmen. At one point in the campaign, the Sardar was sent out in a truck with a contingent of gendarmes to collect firearms from the camps in tribal territory. The Sardar, under the threat of imprisonment, asked the tribesmen in the camps that he visited to turn their rifles in. The Sardar was pained to do this but felt that he had no viable alternative choice.

The Sardar, as representative of the tribe, had a degree of access to government agencies that he used to gain concessions and extract resources for himself and for the tribesmen. He was not only the channel through which the material development aids mentioned above, the irrigation pump and tractor, were directed to the tribe, but he was at least in part an instigator of the plans of which their delivery was the fruition. This was also the case for several other diesel-engine pumps that had been promised to the tribe in 1968. In other similar matters, such as acquiring new strains of wheat from the government's agricultural service, the Sardar further demonstrated his willingness to attempt innovation and his ability to make use of government resources.

Such skills and initiative were directed not only toward material resources but also toward the workings of government agencies that affected the welfare of the tribesmen. For example, in the early summer of 1968, the customs office at Bandar Abbas confiscated a large amount of goods, mostly cloth, from some dozen or so Yarahmadzai who were bringing it into Iran from Dubai, a duty-free port in the Persian Gulf. This would have resulted in a considerable loss of money and an unfortunate precedent, and Sardar Han Mahmud was approached by some of the tribesmen involved to discuss the matter with the government and attempt to obtain a more satisfactory adjustment. The Sardar went to Teheran and spent three weeks negotiating with officials of the customs office and ultimately took his case to the minister of court, who ordered the central customs office to arrive at a compromise agreement. The order finally forwarded to customs at Zahedan, where the goods had been sent, directed that half of the goods be turned over to the tribesmen who had imported it and that the other half be returned to Dubai for refund.

The Sardar's middleman activities as intermediary, mediator, and broker provided him with a justification for political authority and with resources to be used as political patronage. Whereas the prepacification Sardar had provided military leadership, leading the tribe against helpless peasant and invading army alike, the modern Sardar provided the tribe with an expanded range of political leadership, guiding the tribe through the complex bureaucratic byways of the state that encapsulated it. In spite of the prestige of the older military function, and the remaining importance of the personal characteristics related to it, the newer middleman activities took precedence, at least temporarily. Had they not, the office of Sardar would in all likelihood have fallen into eclipse, its light blocked by informal middlemen rising to the opportunity.

Because of these middleman functions, the Sardar controlled an increasing amount of the tribe's resources, particularly those that came to the tribe from the government. One such resource was the above-mentioned diesel-motor irrigation pump at Garonchin. Out of a 336-hour two-week cycle, the Sardar himself ended up with 150 hours, more than a third of the water. Nezar Mahmud reported that his 24 hours of irrigated land at Garonchin could produce anything up to 5,000 kilos of grain. He noted, however, that even if with a harvest of 5,000 kilos, he would be able to sell only 2,000 kilos, for he needed large amounts to support the dependents of and visitors to his camp, for aside from his two wives, children, and other relatives, an evening with 10 guests was not unusual. The same was the case, but on an even larger scale, for the Sardar. In fact, generosity in hospitality was obligatory for anyone aspiring to be or to remain a tribal leader; a Sarhadi who was not a *nandeh* (generous host; literally: breadgiver) could not be a leader. Control of the irrigation pump at Garonchin, therefore, provided irrigation water that resulted in foodstuffs and monetary return for foodstuffs, at least some of which was dispensed by the Sardar and his family as patronage.

Numerous other examples of patronage by the Sardar could be cited, including the distribution of government grain during the famine of the early 1960s, the control over the new and only tractor of the tribe, and the access to government agencies in the customs confiscations. In the former cases, as with irrigation water, the patronage dispensed was based upon material possession; the Sarhadi Baluch recognize the *ru* of *mal*, the influence of property, as distinct from the *ru* of character. But the latter case was rather different, for here it was the Sardar's contacts and skills that were put to work on behalf of others, when he wished to do so. No one doubted that Sardar Han Mahmud also had personal *ru*, the power of character. These various kinds of patronage provided the transactional side of political support (Bailey, 1969:75–76) for the Sardar.

But the Sardar did not depend on transactional ties alone; moral commitment (Bailey 1969:82–83) played a part in his support as well. To an extent, moral commitment to the Sardar was based upon his position as duly acknowledged successor to the previous Yarahmadzai Sardar, and to the loyalty that any Sardar would receive as symbol and representative of the tribe. In addition, the Sardar was seen as having great *hezat*, honor and prestige, because the state recognized and dealt with him. This *hezat*, reflected in the Sardar's ongoing success as middleman between the government and the tribe, contributed to a generalized support.

The Sardar also drew on support for his leadership role through acting as a patron of religion. The Yarahmadzai were Sunni Muslims of the Hanafi rite. Before pacification, according to my older informants, only modest attention had been given to religious matters. There were few *mullas* at that time and the tribesmen, according to their own testimony, were too occupied with other things to bother. Since pacification, interest in religion and participation in religious activities had increased greatly. One reason was that Sarhadi Sunni Islam was distinct from and thus could serve as an ethnic diacritic in symbolic opposition to the Persian Shia. This development will be explored in chapter 12.

During the 1960s and 1970s, a number of Sarhadi and Yarahmadzai tribesmen were trained as *mullas*, and these *mullas* increasingly influenced various activities, the result being a shift toward orthodox practices at the expense of customary ones. Hence the 1960s and 1970s saw large collective prayer meetings on the major holidays, large collective religious propaganda and education meetings, and a number of individual and small-group sacral behaviors such as prayer and animal sacrifice, as well as life-cycle ceremonies presided over by *mullas*. Religious matters had a high status and were regarded as having priority over other matters. Deference was paid toward those of religious stature: *mullas* were said to have *hezat*, honor and standing, although it was recognized that some did not live up to the standard, being *lus*, greedy, or *badkol*, breaking their word.

Sardar Han Mahmud was said by tribesmen to be a pious man. He performed his orthodox duties, such as prayer, fasting, and the like, regularly and in spite of inconvenience; and he abstained from that which was forbidden by religious law as interpreted by the local *mullas*. Many tribesmen were pious to that extent, but the Sardar, with the resources available to him, was able to do even more. Perhaps most important, he subsidized Mulla Isa, the most learned of the local *mullas*, as was indicated by his title of *maulawi*. The Sardar arranged for the building of a four-room mud-brick building at his winter headquarters at Gorchan, which was used as a religious school by Mulla Isa, who taught some 30 tribal children there and who directed services at the small mud-brick mosque nearby. Consequently, Mulla Isa was a member of the Sardar's retinue, traveled with him when requested, and aided the Sardar to the extent possible given the limitations imposed by his calling and religious integrity.

The Sardar's resources also allowed a different but complementary sign of piety: the *haj* to Mecca. Although it is one of the five pillars, *arkan*, of Islam, the *haj* was out of the reach of most Yarahmadzai because of the great cost of making the pilgrimage. The Sardar made the *haj* in 1968, flying from Zahedan at a cost of 4,000 toman, approximately $600, or eight baggage camels. The Sardar had saved 2,000 toman for this trip and had borrowed 2,000 toman more from the bank. On his return from the *haj*, the Sardar grew a full beard and was no longer addressed as "Sardar," but as "Haji," from that time a permanent title. It is noteworthy that among, or perhaps leading, the few Yarahmadzai that had previously made the *haj* had been Han Mahmud's father, Sardar Hubyar Han. And the Sardar's half-brothers, Nezar Mahmud and Dur Mahmud, followed and made the *haj* in 1969. Piety, if not exclusive to the chiefly family, was exhibited there with good political effect. Deference to Sardar Han Mahmud as a pious man was added to that appropriate for him as the tribal leader.

With these bases for the loyalty of moral commitment, and the transactional bases of patronage, the Sardar enjoyed support from the Yarahmadzai tribesmen. He had their *kabul*. Loyalty was not, however, unanimous. In fact, most tribesmen, most of the time, were not utterly dedicated, whole-hearted supporters of the Sardar; nor were they the opposite, staunch opponents seeking his downfall. Rather, they fell on the continuum between these extremes, at the points of acquiescence, acceptance, or limited allegiance. Allegiance increased as the Sardar was effective as the representative of the tribe contra outside forces and decreased as there was competition among tribesmen over resources and the Sardar was not able to satisfy everyone, or was felt unduly to be appropriating resources for his own use. There were indications that certain elements of the tribe did actively oppose the Sardar.

Shortly after his return from the *haj*, the Sardar was called to appear in court in Kerman. He was, along with two Rigi chiefs, accused of misusing government funds that had been provided to him for the purposes of drought relief. Some of the tribesmen had complained that the Sardar had "eaten" part of the money and that consequently the tribesmen did not get their full share of grain. The members of the chiefly family denied that any of the aid money was "eaten," and said that the complaint was made by "one of the Sardar's enemies." These opponents of the Sardar were striking at a most crucial spot, the relationship between the Iranian government and the Sardar; it is clear that they meant business, for this was an attempt to discredit the Sardar with the primary source of the material benefits used for patronage and to reduce or destroy his effectiveness with the powers of the encapsulating society. In this instance, the attempt did not fully succeed, for the charges were dropped after the court appearance with legal counsel. But this was one engagement in a protracted campaign, for the Sardar's rivals for power were beginning to use resources, such as government courts, outside the traditional tribal political field in the course of their conflict (Bailey 1969:chaps. 8, 9). Such open opposition was, however, exceptional rather than usual, because of the symbolic and material resources of the Sardar.

## Shifting Balance in the Tribal Structure

Since the effective encapsulation of the Yarahmadzai tribe within the Iranian state, the balance between the tribal political hierarchy and the segmentary lineage system shifted, with the hierarchy and the chiefship coming to have relatively more weight and the lineage system somewhat less. With encapsulation, the Sardar became the reluctant bottom man in the national government hierarchy, presenting demands of the government to his tribesmen, and being responsible to government for the actions of his tribesmen. The Sardar was transformed from an independent leader of free tribesmen to a middleman: the two-way channel of information and goods, the resolver or obfuscator of differences between the tribe and government representatives, and the advocate of the tribe to the government.

The Sardar took on this new role under threat of military sanction, but also in response to financial benefits. These levers had serious consequences not only for the parameters within which the Sardar operated, but also for the relationship between him and the tribesmen. One consequence was that the chief had limited but significant external politico-military support, independent of the intentions and wishes of the tribesmen. A second was that the chief had new external sources of economic goods and services, which were used both to bolster his own economic position and also as patronage to influence his tribesmen. So the relationship shifted, with the Sardar becoming somewhat less of a leader and somewhat more of a patron, and the tribesmen becoming somewhat less independent followers and somewhat more dependent clients. Economic and political differentiation and centralization thus increased, and the egalitarian, decentralized lineage system less frequently and less effectively provided the means for dealing with political and economic concerns. The tribal political system remained multiform but was weighted somewhat more heavily than before toward hierarchy and centralization.

## A Month in the Life of the Sardar

From my first meeting in late 1967 with Sardar Han Mahmud, I crossed paths with him on numerous occasions and had had many opportunities to watch him interact with his tribesmen and with outsiders. While granting me free access and from time to time giving me the place of honored guest, the Sardar did not appear to have much interest in my work and seemed to be mainly interested in getting me to drive him around in my Land Rover, a role that I resisted, rather to the Sardar's irritation. While chauffeuring the Sardar would have put me in a good position to observe him and his activities more closely, it would have been fairly boring, and, more important, would have taken me away from ordinary tribesmen and inhibited my observation of the quotidian activities and events of herding camp and palm grove life.

But I did want a closer look at the Sardar and his works, and eventually devised a strategy other than becoming his driver. I decided toward the end of my second stint of fieldwork to move in with the Sardar. Well, not exactly "in," but "at." I decided to pack up my tent—actually the tent of Zarbonu, which she had so kindly allowed us to use—and move it from the Dadolzai camp to the camp of the Sardar. After all, I thought, why should I not make nomadism work for me? My plan was to live with the Sardar for a month, before transferring back to the Dadolzai. So we packed up at the end of March 1973 and moved to Tagazuk in Garonchin, where the Sardar was camped, remaining there until the end of April.

Although the members of the Sardar's camp knew we were coming, they teased us when we arrived. "What are you doing here? You are Dadolzai and we are Yar Mahmudzai. Why are you leaving the Dadolzai?" To which I answered, in the tribal fashion, "But are not the Dadolzai, Nur Mahmudzai? And are not the Yar Mahmudzai, Nur Mahmudzai? Well then, the Dadolzai and Yar Mahmudzai are brothers, are *yeki*, one." "Yes, yes," they said, "we are one." Everybody smiled, satisfied that I had learned the tribal idiom and could give the correct answer.

The most striking thing about the Sardar's camp was how similar it was to every other Yarahmadzai camp. There were a dozen or so tents, in various states of repair. The *ramagi pas* was small, around 140 animals. At any moment various men, women, and children were going about doing their household tasks. The women cleaned the tents and made the meals, while the girls collected wood and went to the well. Boys tended the animals. The Sardar's wife made dinner for guests, including Sardars of other tribes. The wives of the brothers of the Sardar, Haji Nezar Mahmud and Haji Dur Mahmud, cleaned and straightened their tents, milked their animals, and made bread and meals and tea. The daughters of these men went to the well and collected wood as did daughters of the black tents in ordinary camps. When the camp moved, these women packed and set up the tents, always saying, of course, that the men could not set up the tents properly.

The Sardar's camp was similar in many ways to ordinary camps, but also different in ways that indicated greater prosperity and political importance. To begin with, the tents were a bit larger than average in ordinary herding camps. This reflected wealth and the related necessity of and capability for providing hospitality. Second, the women's clothing was newer and a bit more expensive, with impressive embroidery decoration. Women also wore more of the traditional gold jewelry than would be found on women in ordinary herding camps. Third, motor vehicles, used primarily for men's business, were more frequent than in other camps. Both the Sardar and Haji Dur Mahmud owned automobiles, and they and Haji Nezar Mahmud were able to hire automobiles and motorcycle taxis when they needed transport. The Sardar had just given his oldest son—only 12 years old or so, but already introduced to leadership and expected to be responsible in his father's absence—a small Yamaha motorcycle. Others in the camp also had motorcycles. Such a density of vehicles was highly exceptional in the tribe, but understandable in terms of the need for frequent travel by the Sardar and his retinue in the furtherance of leadership activities. A fourth difference, not discernable to the eye, or to my eye at least, was the presence of an unusual number of non-Yarahmadzai women married to the men of the camp—for example, Gam Shadzai women such as Gran Bibi, the wife of the Sardar. This reflected the affinal unions among the lineages of the tribal leaders, these alliances being one of the main strategies for maintaining peace and cooperation among the tribes. A fifth difference was the frequent arrival and high status of visitors and guests in the camp. It was not uncommon for Sardars of other tribes and lineage leaders to come to the Sardar's camp. Consequently, the camp of the Sardar provided an unusual amount of high-quality hospitality, including meals and sleeping quarters.

One way of getting a sense of the density, variety, and substance of the Sardar's activities is to follow the Sardar in his comings and goings through a particular period, in this case the month in spring of 1973 during which I lived in the Sardar's camp (see table 11.2). Nothing I saw of or heard about the Sardar at other periods lead me to think that the activities recorded here were uncharacteristic, although the substantive issues that gained the Sardar's attention—such as, to use real examples, a government campaign to disarm the tribesmen, or a conflict between two tribal sections, or the building of a road between the Sarhad and Mashkil—varied over time.

The Sardar, like most male Yarahmadzai tribesmen, was frequently on the move. But he traveled more often and farther than ordinary tribesmen, and his destinations were often seats of tribal or government power. Similarly, the Sardar, like most Yarahmadzai tribesmen, was frequently called upon to help others. But the Sardar, unlike ordinary tribesmen, was often asked for help by those of high status and power, such as Sardars and Hakom of other groups, and he was asked for help in dealing with others of high status and power, either other tribal or regional leaders or government officials. This acknowledgment, by other leaders and by the government, was for his followers a sign of *hezat,* honor and prestige.

Sardar Han Mahmud was a man of action. He was literally exemplary in his energy

**Table 11.2.** Activities of Sardar Han Mahmud, March 28–April 27, 1973

| Date | Time | Place | Activity |
|---|---|---|---|
| *March* | | | |
| 28 | Day | Khash | Sent a telegram to the Ostandar, governor general, of the Province of Sistan and Baluchistan, requesting release of a truck of oranges, probably of Pakistani origin, captured by the gendarmerie and being held by customs in Zahedan. |
| 28 | Evening | Camp | Entertained Gamshadzai Sardar Halil Han and two Siahani who had come to Khash. |
| 28 | Night | Camp | Left for the camp of Sardar Halil Han. |
| 29 | Morning | Camp of H. H. | Left for the Hamuni Mashkil. |
| 30 | Day | Mashkil | Arrived at Mashkil and picked up a large truck of *dal*, dried lentils. |
| 31 | Morning | Camp | Arrived from Mashkil. Left for Khash to sell truckload of *dal*. |
| 31 | Afternoon | Khash | Tried to make arrangements for the repair of the irrigation pump motor at Garonchin. |
| *April* | | | |
| 1 | Morning | Khash | Met with Farmandar, district governor, of Khash, and also the head of local gendarmerie. |
| 1 | Afternoon | Camp | Returned to camp. |
| 2 | Morning | Camp of Nur Bik | Went to Nur Bik's tent for *patia*, mourning, and meal. |
| 3 | Morning | Camp | Left for the central Iranian city of Kerman to try to gain the release from police custody of Juda, one of the Yarahmadzai *mastair*, arrested for smuggling. |
| 5–13 | | Kerman | Met with government officials in Kerman to lobby for release of Juda and succeeded in extracting Juda. |
| 14–15 | | Khash | Lobbied with provincial officials for assistance with damaged irrigation pump motor. |
| 17 | Evening | Camp | Returned to camp. |
| 18 | Morning | Camp | Organized a welcoming party for governor general. |
| 18 | Morning | Main road and pump | Greeted governor general and his retinue. Took the governor general and his officials to see the irrigation area at Garonchin, not far from the road. Requested a replacement engine and additional pumps for other areas. Governor general agreed and promised financial assistance from the province. |
| 18 | Afternoon | Khash | Left for Khash and then Zahedan to arrange to receive new pump engine. |
| 19–24 | | Zahedan | Negotiations over new pump engine, including trips back and forth between Khash and Zahedan to arrange and pay for transport of engine. |
| 26 | Afternoon | Camp | Returned from Zahedan and Khash. |
| 27 | Morn | Camp | Met with Sardar Nawab Han of the Bameri tribe, who requested assistance in extracting a Bameri from government custody. Agreed to help. |
| 27 | Afternoon | Chahuk | Went to pay his respects to a sick uncle. |

and ambition. This is one of the main reasons that his followers chose him and continued to respect him. Sardar Han Mahmud was a tall man of regal carriage and piercing eyes, with a forceful personality and an implied menace in his manner. These characteristics helped him to carry off his role, which he did well, and to succeed at his tasks, which he did considerably more often than not. It was this that was referred to when the Sardar was said to have *ru*, influence. He was an effective and successful Sardar. (There are parallels in Beck's 1991 description of the Qashqa'i section leader Borzu.)

At the same time, Han Mahmud, like many men of action, was not a reflective man, did not have great curiosity, and did not have much patience. Many tribesmen found Joan and me to be curiosities, and they wanted to find out something about us; but the Sardar, while providing all proper hospitality, was too busy with his important tasks to expend any time or attention on us. To be fair, this was not helped by the extremely rudimentary Persian language with which we began our life in the Sarhad. Although our language usage improved and we switched to Baluchi from Persian, some people had decided early that we would never be capable of conversing and gave up trying. One woman from our camp, Pati Hartun, never could understand what I said and always asked Shams A'din or whoever else was present what I had said. One day I finally got irritated with this response and yelled at her, in Baluchi, "Pati Hartun, you do not understand what I say because you do not listen to what I say. If you listen, you will understand." Pati Hartun was rather taken aback by this outburst, but from that moment on, she not only understood what I said, but would provide unsolicited repetition to others in the vicinity. Well, I think that the Sardar, in addition to having a lot on his mind and in general not having much patience, had at some early point written us off as unintelligible and uninteresting.

Sardar Han Mahmud was thus at first rather surprised and then a bit irritated when, during the late April visit of Sardar Nawab Han Bameri, in Han Mahmud's own tent after the meal he had provided for us, Nawab Han and I settled into a lengthy conversation of two or three hours that was obviously pleasant and gratifying for both of us. Nawab Han was a patient and curious man, and rather more soft-spoken than Han Mahmud. I learned a bit about the Bameri from Nawab Han, and he learned a bit about Americans and anthropologists, or at least about this American and anthropologist. The Sardar, of whom both Nawab Han and I were guests, found at that moment that his categories were being violated and felt uncomfortable. I rather think that Han Mahmud felt a bit left out and did not like the feeling.

# 12.
# PRAYING AND PRONOUNCING

It would be an exaggeration to say that Baluchistan was a center of Islam. In fact, throughout the Middle East, tribal life has seldom been the bosom of theological, literary, scientific, or ritual concentration. Making a living with one hand and defending life and property with the other does not leave many hands for ritual and scholarly activities (Gellner 1988). Middle Eastern tribesmen have often slipped into a division of labor with sedentary religious specialists: you sedentaries pray for us; we Bedouin will fight for Islam (Evans-Pritchard 1949).

The Sarhad of Iranian Baluchistan was far from the cities that were the natural home of Islam: Kerman to the northwest was both far and, religion being in the hands of Persian Shiites, religiously alien to the Sunni Baluch; Karachi was beyond the far eastern end of Baluchistan; Arabia lay beyond the waters of the Gulf. Iranian Baluchistan itself had no cities, and its settlements were small oases. With a total population of a few hundred thousand, scattered widely and thinly over a desiccated and barren land, Iranian Baluchistan was not fertile ground for a concentration of religious specialists.

But to point to the demanding regimen of everyday life and note the absence of great centers of Islamic learning is not to say that Islam was not an integral part of the lives of Sarhadi tent dwellers or that Islam was not important and meaningful to the Sarhadi Baluch. On the contrary, during the time in the 1960s and 1970s that I spent with these Baluchi tent dwellers, Islam was a major presence, like a great mountain, that provided an ongoing frame of reference and a constant compass. Perhaps most important, the Sarhadi tent dwellers felt and believed that they were not alone in the universe, but rather that God was in heaven and looking after them. God in His wisdom might do things that were beyond their understanding, but they had a strong sense that God was in control and that God's will should be accepted and had to be accepted. But the Sarhadi tent dwellers could make their needs known to God and direct their requests to Him, with some expectation that their desires would be considered and perhaps, if they approached God the right way, granted.

The Islam of Sarhadi tent dwellers could be called "folk Islam" in the trivial sense that it was the Islam of unschooled, ordinary people rather than of religious specialists or other educated people. But I would not extend this label of "folk Islam" to include an evaluation that it was substandard in comparison with some allegedly "pure" or correct Islam of religious specialists or educated urbanites. In every religion, and perhaps every field of thought, there are broader, more inclusive formulations and narrower, more restricted, "purist" visions. The debate between these contrasting views is continual, if more intense at some moments and more muted at others, and some historical periods are characterized by catholic inclusive integration and tolerance while others are characterized by purist selectivity and exclusion.

My task as an ethnographer is to report from my observations of the Sarhadi Baluch any discourses of dispute about what is or is not legitimate belief and practice, not to participate in the debates myself. In other words, I do not intend to judge the Islam of the Sarhadi tent dwellers by measuring it against some standard; I will not be arguing that "this practice is an animistic survival" or "that belief is tribal rather than orthodox Islam." Rather, my position is that, for Sarhadi Baluch, Islam means surrender to God, and as their beliefs and practices appear to be directed toward God who is all-knowing and all-powerful, these beliefs and practices can all be recognized as part of Sarhadi Islam, which is the way the Sarhadi Baluch think of them.

## SPEAKING GOD

God's presence and importance was emphasized in the continual invoking of His name in statements and conversation. There can be no doubt that God was frequently on the lips of Sarhadi tent dwellers.

In the marvelous, conventional greeting sequence of the Baluch—somewhat variable but usually with the following elements in the following sequence—religion is not forgotten:

| | |
|---|---|
| *Salam alekum.* | Peace be with you. |
| *Jure? Hub jure?* | Are you well? |
| *Shar jure?* | Are you very well? |
| *Salamat be.* | May you have peace. |
| *Mantag mabe.* | Don't be sad. |
| *Eman darbe.* | Faith above all! |
| *Che hal?* | Are you well? |
| *Pes jure? Mas jure? Bras jure? Jure te halk?* etc. | |

After the personal questions and the injunctions of well-being comes *Eman darbe* or *Eman awanabi*, the assertion of the primacy of the faith, of religion. Nor was the content lost with conventional usage, for when I, a non-Muslim, would say *"Eman darbe,"* people would laugh or smirk or try not to.

Sometimes added to the greeting sequences was *Huda tra jure kon,* "May God make you well." This conventional phrase, along the variation *Huda hare kon,* was also used when conversing with or about someone who was ill, or not entirely well, or who was having problems.

God was also invoked when people were entering a dangerous situation, such as travel. It was conventional, but obviously also often heartfelt, to say *Huda hamrah* and *Allah te hamrah beit,* "May God travel with you," or literally, "May God be your traveling companion."

Perhaps the most common, frequently heard usage was the acknowledgment that all human actions depended upon the will of God. Whenever anyone said that they planned to do something—"Tomorrow we migrate" or "I am going to weave a tent"—they would always add *insha Allah* or *gwa womiti Huda,* "with the will of God." Not to do so was arrogantly and foolishly to claim control over future events, a control that any right-thinking person could see rests only with God.

Hypothetical statements about good or bad things that might come about were "automatically" met, respectively, by the ejaculations *Huda bakan,* "May God make it happen," and *Huda makan,* "May God keep it from happening."

In discussing future possibilities, especially desirable life trajectories, people would indicate their dependence upon God by saying *agar Huda kesmat bakan,* "if God makes it my fate," as in "I will have lots of children if God makes it my fate" or "I will go to high school if God makes it my fate."

In ruling out an activity that was deemed contrary to Islamic law or not up to the standards of a good man, people would point out that God is watching and judging by saying *sha Huda torsam,* "I am afraid of God['s judgment]."

Very important in situations of disappointment, adversity, and loss was the attribution of the situation to God's will. People commonly said, usually to explain and justify an unexplainable and unjustifiable loss, that it was *Hudai dast,* "the hand of God," that is, the decision and act of God. The comfort, and I believe that people often found comfort in it, was that God's intentions were ultimately benevolent and that, even if people could not understand the wisdom of God's acts, in the end it was all for the good. There was also the sense, of course, that the particular matters involved—stillbirths, illnesses, blizzards, droughts—were out of people's hands; humans could not control these things; only God could.

Faced with an erratic supply of nature's means, such as water and pasturage, to satisfy human ends, Sarhadi Baluch expressed their faith in God's bounty by saying *Huda don,* "God will give," and submission to God's will by saying, in contemplation of the shortfalls to come, *harchiz Huda wadont,* "Whatever God may give [is sufficient]." In the face of obstacles, whether of natural or social origin, the tent dwellers say *Huda toter,* "God is greater [than these earthly problems]."

When something good had happened, to express joy and enthusiasm, the standard response is *alhamdulelah,* "Praise God," which literally acknowledged God as the author of the benefit and thus expressed gratitude for His bounty. This expression was also the conventional response to a sneeze, which was believed to be the expulsion of a bad spirit.

The conventional reply, *Huda bebakshid,* "God forgive you," to *bebakshid,* "forgive me," was not, I hope, a sign that what one has done was so horrendous that only God could forgive one, but rather a general assertion that the ultimate judgment is that of God, not of men.

Regarding unknown matters, especially future events, Sarhadi Baluch say that they do not know, but also that *Huda zont,* "God knows." This expression may have the facetious aspect of our own, somewhat outdated expression, "God knows," but within the semantic context of Sarhadi expression, at least some of the literal content was present.

Among the Sarhadi tent dwellers, natural resources were not attributed to an abstract "nature," but rather to God. Rainwater was called *api Huda* (literally: water of God), distinguishing it from water brought—in wells, *kan,* with pumps—by human labor and technology. Significantly, among the Sarhadi tent dwellers, resources given by God could not be owned by individuals or groups, but had to be available to all and shared by all.

Other expressions used in conversation include *wallah? wallah!* and *ba Huda?* "by God?" or "really?" and "by God!" or "really!"

What is the significance of these largely conventional if frequent and pervasive references to God? Can we take them seriously as reflections of conviction and commitment on the part of the speakers, or are they little more than shibboleths with little or no content? We must be careful, I think, not take the term "conventional" to mean insignificant and lacking in substance. On the contrary, a "convention" is an established, agreed-upon practice; it is, in short, a "custom." And it thus reflects an uncontested, common basis that all participants share and upon which they express their commonality and unity. There were cultural guidelines as to the appropriate times and contexts to invoke God. As well, there were social pressures to do so. To not invoke God, to not acknowledge God's control, to not wish God's assistance, would have been a notable deviation from common practice and would have raised questions about an individual's being "right with God." It was right and proper and necessary to refer to God.

These conventional usages indicated a common if unreflective theology that was shared among Sarhadi tent dwellers. They believed in a conscious, all-powerful God who was aware of their circumstances and who might respond to their specific pleas. To be good men and women, they had to observe God's rules and to accept God's will. But at the same time they had a right to ask for and hope for God's help. In considering the impact of these everyday expressions, we might ask whether it would be baseless to suggest that "saying is believing." Does not the repeated and continual invocation of God shape thoughts and feelings according to the sentiments of the phrases? My own experience—upon returning from Baluchistan to North America and from Baluchi to English—of the desire to say "with the will of God" when stating my intentions to do something in the future, and my discomfort at leaving out such references to God's will and God's assistance, leads me to think that action, even verbal action, imprints itself upon our minds. After all, I was and am an atheist, with no belief in a personal or other God. And yet, I had a difficult time giving up invoking God and felt the discomfort of, or so it felt, violating the nature of the universe. I think that there is reason to believe that repeated and continual usage, even if based initially on imitation or even consciously feigned, comes eventually to shape feeling and thought. The influence between mind and action is not a one-way process; actions, over time, can shape the mind (Barth 1983). Thus apparently trivial actions, such as the conventional verbal invocation of God, can both represent and generate a profound level of assumption and social agreement.

## REQUESTING GOD'S HELP

Sarhadi Baluch who wished for God's intervention in resolving a particular problem could follow a number of courses.

### *Patir:* Distributing Foodstuffs

Sarhadi Baluch attempted to draw God's attention by distributing some foodstuffs—bread, dates, or candy—among the members of the local community. This was called *patir* or *sisir.* When Pati Hartun, wife of Abas, heard that Abas, during the course of trading, had been arrested and his goods confiscated, she went around the camp distributing *lawash* (unleavened bread) to support her plea to God that Abas be released from jail. Bibi Nur gave out bread so that her child would stay well.

### *Hairat:* Sacrifice and Distribution

A sacrifice was believed effective in catching God's attention. When an animal was ritually sacrificed and the meat given away in order to solve or forestall a problem, this procedure was called a *hairat.* Barkat dreamed that his wife was sick. As a prophylactic measure, he sacrificed a *trusht* and distributed the meat. When one of Monaz's camels was ailing, and the medical application of the hot iron had had no apparent beneficial effect, she sacrificed a *trusht* and distributed the meat so that God would make her camel healthy again.

Id Mahmud had a disturbing dream: He had gone crazy and had to be brought back to his tent by force. When his mother-in-law Monaz came to see him, he broke down and cried. Then his wife Bibi Nur came in, dressed all in black, including pants, dress, and *chadur*. He had asked whether she was wearing all black because he was sick. She did not answer but broke down and cried. Id Mahmud was rather shaken by this dream, and did not want to take a chance on the events portrayed coming to pass. So the next morning he sacrificed a *trusht* and distributed the meat.

Ido, too, had a frightening dream. Fully armed Iranian soldiers were coming to fight with the Ja'fari Halk. The camp members had only one rifle, and it was in Ido's hands. But the soldiers quickly grabbed him, at which time he broke up the rifle. The soldiers then beat up the camp members with sticks and rocks. Ido told everyone in the camp that they should *hairat*. The next day, Ido and Shams A'din each sacrificed a *trusht* and gave away the meat.

## *Zarat:* Holy Trees

Sarhadi Baluch also turned to *zarat,* trees with holy powers. Wishes were made at one of the special trees that were thought to grant wishes and resolve problems of various kinds, such as giving a hitherto infertile woman a child, assisting a deceased person into heaven, and the like. Commonly, animals were sacrificed at the tree and a strip of cloth, *langar,* was tied around a branch. No comments were volunteered linking the tree to God, or indicating that the tree was seen as an intermediary between the pleader and God.

Holy trees in the Sarhad were located in Garonchin, at Sangu, Shahchinal, and Malik Sah Kuh. The *zarat* at Garonchin was particular, for unlike other *zarat* it was believed to be not only efficacious, but also dangerous. Women said that some years ago two young boys broke a few branches off of the tree, and by the afternoon of the same day the boys were dead. When it was discovered by the women of the camp that Joan and I had walked to the tree, they became very agitated and asked if we had touched the tree. When we untruthfully said that we had not touched it, they were visibly relieved and expressed it verbally, *shokr,* "Thank goodness." Not everyone was convinced that the tree was dangerous. Han Bibi took the opportunity when she was alone with Joan to say that her boys had recently broken branches off the tree and that nothing had happened to them. She did not believe that the tree was dangerous and said that Joan should not worry about it. That Han Bibi preferred to relate her views in private rather than in public indicated that she did not wish to challenge publicly the prevailing view.

When I initially asked Mah Bibi about such trees, she denied that there were such things, although a *zarat* was within our sight during this exchange. Later she said that in the past people did go to such trees, but the *maulawi* had said that we should not do it anymore. So the Islamic religious specialist and highest authority in the tribal territory had condemned the practice, and as a result some people were unwilling to admit that the practices took place or even that such trees existed. But from the *langar* that Joan and I observed on the *zarat*, it was clear that people were continuing to use the trees to pursue their wishes.

Perhaps the use of *zarat* was related to the absence of religious shrines in the Sarhad. No graves, *kabre*, were deemed to have holy power, to be shrines. No remains of martyrs, *shadid*, or *adami halife*, could be found in the Sarhad. Known by some Sarhadi Baluch were the tomb of Bad Shah at Kandahar in southern Afghanistan and the tomb of Pir Sahib near Quetta, in western Pakistan. A few from the Sarhad had visited the latter shrine, where it was said that the spirit of Pir Sahib entered through the eyes of a sleeping person and cured illnesses.

### *Tiei:* Holy Pills

Consumption of a *tiei*, a pill consisting of a verse of the Qoran written on a small piece of paper, usually prepared by a mulla, was used to combat any present difficulty. The *tiei* was most commonly administered to someone who was ill or in danger.

In 1967, Ja'far's little boy Amir fell ill, and his sickness dragged on. Ja'far, desperate for help, called a Mulla who provided a *tiei*. In payment, Ja'far gave a fully grown *trusht*. Happily, Amir recovered.

In 1973, the young Lal Malik, daughter of Yelli Han and wife of Mandust, in the second quarter of her pregnancy, began losing water and blood. She had previously had a miscarriage, and so people were especially concerned. Yelli Han went to Mulla Malik Mahmud for a *tiei*, for which he gave 5 toman. But there was no improvement; the *tiei*, it was explained to me, was apparently not powerful enough to reach God. Yelli Han then went to Mulla Lal Mahmud of the Mirgolzai, who was Lal Malik's *naku*, mother's brother. Mulla Lal Mahmud wrote a *tiei*, for which Yelli Han gave a *gwarag*, a value of about 60 toman. After this, Lal Malik's condition improved. Yelli Han attributed the improvement to God and indicated that Mulla Lal Mahmud's *tiei* had been strong enough to communicate with God. In Yelli Han's eyes, the improvement was God's work, not a direct effect of the *tiei* itself; the *tiei* was a communication link. But why did the *tiei* of Mulla Lal Mahmud succeed when that of Mulla Malik Mahmud had failed? According to Yelli Han, Mulla Lal Mahmud's "heart burned" for his *gohar zad*, sister's child. Yelli Han made no reference to the general knowledge that Mulla Lal Mahmud had studied longer and was more learned than Mulla Malik Mahmud. As for the payments, Yelli Han said that the payments were required or the *tiei* would not work. He did not comment on the fact that he had paid little for the first *tiei*, which did not work, but it is likely that others did so comment, for Yelli Han was thought to be a bit tight with money and too slow to part with it.

## *Sijoss:* Holy Charms

Passages from the Qoran, wrapped in a piece of cloth, made small, light holy charms, *sijoss*, that could easily be worn—sewn onto clothes or headgear—as prophylaxis against illness in general and the evil eye in particular. Prepared by mullas and even available in stores in Khash, these amulets were widely used among the Sarhadi tent dwellers, most commonly by women for themselves and for their children.

*Sijoss* were also believed to be effective in warding off *jenn* (Arabic: *jinn*), spirits that could enter the head of a person and cause insanity. One individual was cited as an example of someone who went crazy because a *jenn* entered him, which, I was told, would not have happened if he had had a *sijoss*.

Skepticism was expressed by some Sarhadi men, who said that they were afraid of no one and nothing but God. *Jenn* and the evil eye and other alleged threats were not to be worried about, because "God is bigger than these things."

## GOD'S JUDGMENT

According to my Sarhadi informants, God's gifts to mankind are not unconditional. On the contrary, men must face God's judgment and consequent pleasure and displeasure for their acts while on earth. When the day of judgment, *adunya* or *mashari ruch*, comes and all who have died are brought back to life, they will be judged according to whether they have done God's work, *sakawat kard*, and fulfilled their ritual obligations. Those who have been good will be chosen to go to the place of God, to heaven, *jenat*, which is like a beautiful garden, cool with all kinds of fruit and other good things. Those who have not been good will be sent to hell, *duzo*, and will burn, *mesuze*, for all eternity.

## *Sawab:* Credit for Good Works

God does not himself determine ahead of time whether a man will be good or bad; rather, it is up to each man to choose his course. For good acts, men receive credit, *sawab*, which will be taken into account in the final judgment. A man with *sawab* is an *adami sahi*, "a right man." What kinds of deeds bring *sawab*? For the Sarhadi tent dwellers, being helpful and generous to others is a major source of *sawab*: a man who acts as host, sheltering and feeding others, a *nandeh*, literally "a breadgiver," brings great *sawab*. Shams A'din said that his cleaning of the Dadolzai well, an arduous and dangerous job that benefited all of his lineage mates and anyone else using the well, would be rewarded with *sawab*. Similarly, Gulap said that the midwife activities of his wife Zarbonu would gain *sawab* for her. Acting as *wasta*, bringing peace between disputing parties, would be also be a source of great *sawab*.

## Ritual Obligations

Ritual obligations for the Sarhadi Baluch, as for other Muslims, included prayer five times a day, fasting during Ramazan (Ramadan), giving alms, and the pilgrimage to Mecca. The fulfillment of ritual obligations would, it was believed, be considered in the final judgment.

Most of the adult Sarhadi tent dwellers prayed, *nomaz kort,* many the obligatory five times a day: at sunup, midday, sunset, early evening, and before bed. When there was no trained prayer leader, the men and women prayed individually in their tents. For those away from their tents, stone-outlined prayer areas by the roadside served, although one could pray anywhere. If a camp had a prayer leader, and these were always men, the men would pray as a group, which was deemed preferable. On Friday, *jome,* the Islamic sabbath, many of the male tent dwellers of the northern Yarahmadzai territory collected at the mosque in Gorchan for *jome* prayers at midday. Women always prayed individually in their tents; they did not pray as a group. Most of the Sarhadi tent dwellers did not know any Arabic, and many, especially the women, prayed in Baluchi rather than the prescribed Arabic.

Sarhadi Baluch gave alms, *pindag,* usually in the form of bread, cooking oil, milk, flour, tea, or sugar, to beggars, *pindugir,* wandering holy men, *pakir,* and to Luri, the lower-caste smiths and craftsmen. Furthermore, they contributed to the maintenance of the religious specialists, the local mullas, with gifts throughout the year: *sarsa* of three toman per person at Ramadan, *yekruchag* of cooking oil in *baharga,* spring, one-tenth of the grain harvest in the summer, and *dehyak,* dates, in the fall. In addition, there were innumerable opportunities, often taken by Sarhadi tent dwellers, to share with camp and lineage mates and to give to those who were poor or in need. There was among the tent dwellers a sense of obligation to help those in need, and they frequently and repeatedly did help, as in the case of Shams A'din's gift of money to the elderly Walli Mahmud when Shams A'din returned from trading.

Most Sarhadi Baluch observed the fast, *russe,* of Ramazan, eschewing food, drink, and smoke during the daylight hours. In 1967, Ramazan was in its last few days when we first arrived at the Ja'fari Halk. People were limiting their daily activities to the minimum and eating after sundown. Some people traveling through the camp stopped and ate during the day, as was allowed to travelers. There was a close watch of the moon, for the appearance of the new moon signaled the end of the month and the end of the fast. It was expected during the last days of December, but did not appear, leaving people muttering *dasti huda.* On the night of January 1, 1968, to the delight of all, a tiny sliver of moon appeared, and the month and the fast were over. The next day was *gwandien aid,* "the small holy day."

In 1973, Ramazan began on October 9, just as the tent dwellers had settled back on the Sarhad after their return from Mashkil. This was the period when ordinarily young and some older men would leave the Sarhad for migrant labor or trading. In fact, 12 from the Ja'fari Halk were already away working: Bahadin, Bahudur, Ghulam Mahmud, Shiruk, Mahmud Karim, Jan Mahmud, Isa, Barkat, Abdulla, Baluch, and Gemi's two sons. Of these, 6 returned to the Halk to participate with their kinsmen in the fast. Others, such as Id Mahmud, Abas, and Sabib Dad, who had been planning to leave the Sarhad for work, put off their departures until the fast had been completed.

The Ramazan fast did take its toll on those fasting. The tent dwellers tried to avoid unnecessary exertions and migrations, although the exigencies of life on the Sarhad did not always allow one to avoid exertion. The mood of Ramazan fasters has been characterized, by some observers, as irritated, with tempers on very short fuses. Burton (quoted in Von Grunebaum 1951) says:

> The chief effect of the "blessed month" upon True Believers is to darken their tempers into positive gloom. . . . The men curse one another and beat the women. The women slap and abuse the children, and these in their turn cruelly entreat, and use bad language to, the dogs and cats. You can scarcely spend ten minutes in any populous part of the city without hearing some violent dispute. . . . The Mosques are crowded with a sulky, grumbling population, making themselves offensive to one another on earth whilst working their way to heaven.

Perhaps this was true in crowded cities, although I rather doubt it, but I can attest that no such gloom or irritation was evident to me during Ramazan among the Sarhadi tent dwellers. The most one could say is that people were a bit subdued. I certainly saw no displays of bad temper or aggression among Baluch camp members.

The *haj* to Mecca had been undertaken by only a handful of Sarhadi Baluch prior to 1967. Among the Yarahmadzai, the previous Sardar, Hubyar Han, together with Di Mahmud, had gone on the *haj* around 1960, but most tribesmen had not and were not contemplating doing so. In 1968, the Sardar Han Mahmud went on the *haj*, accompanied by Abdul of Nilagu. His trip was financed partly by his personal savings and partly by a loan from the bank. Well-wishers assembled to send him off, some accompanying him to Zahedan, where he took the plane, and then gathered to welcome him back. From his return, the Sardar was henceforth addressed as Haji rather than as Sardar. He allowed his beard to grow full and long, giving him the gravitas appropriate for a *haji*. Two of the Sardar's influential brothers, Nezar Mahmud and Dur Mahmud, followed the Sardar in going on the *haj* in 1969.

In 1968, most tent-dwelling tribesmen said that they could not afford to go on the *haj* to Mecca and seemed to feel that it was within the capability of only the few. But during the next years there was an upsurge of participation in the *haj* among ordinary tribesmen. For example, in the Ja'fari Halk, Reis of the Shirdelzai, the cousin of Ja'far, went on the *haj* in the early 1970s. By 1976, quite a few tent-dwelling Yarahmadzai had gone on the *haj*, were addressed as Haji, and served as examples to others that it was possible for ordinary tribesmen to go on the *haj*.

## HOLY DAYS

There are two main holy days: *tuhein aid*, "the big holy day," called more descriptively the *aidi kurbani*, the holy day of the sacrifice, commemorating the intended sacrifice of Somail (that is, Ishmael) by Ibrahim (that is, Abraham); and *gwandien aid*, "the small holy day," signaling the breaking of the fast of Ramazan.

For these holy days, many Sarhadi tent dwellers who were away from camp or from the Sarhad returned to celebrate the feast day with their families and community. Each tent sacrificed an animal in commemoration of the event celebrated. Among the members of the Ja'fari Halk, however, participation varied in the festivities of *tuhein aid* in 1973 (see table 12.1).

There was no collective feast; each family ate its holy day meal on its own. In addition, on some holy days, male camp members went to collective prayer meetings at Gorchan, Khash, or other locations, as they did for *tuhein aid* in 1968. On that day, a number of men from Ja'fari Halk walked from Pushti Kamal to Gorchan, where Mulla Isa and Mulla Bi and several other mullas were holding a prayer service. Some 300 tribesmen, having come on foot, camel, bicycle, and motorcycle, congregated in front of the Qoranic school at Gorchan for the service, which included prayers and sermons, lasting an hour and a half. The men, having left their shoes at the perimeter of the schoolyard, lined up in eight long rows and followed the lead of the mullas. After the service, everyone returned to their camps, where they sacrificed animals. In 1973, however, the members of the Ja'fari Halk did not attend the large prayer services. The location of the camp was far from both Khash and Gorchan, 20 and 25 kilometers, respectively, and the camels, weak from the great snowfall and the absence of pasturage, were deemed not up to the trip.

## RELIGIOUS EDUCATION

Participation in ritual activities presumes some knowledge and understanding of the procedures, language, and ideas underlying ritual. This at least was the belief of those Sarhadi Baluch already educated or informed on religious matters. Thus, they concluded, socialization and training are required for people to fulfill their obligations. And this went on in several kinds of venues. Some education in Islamic matters went on whenever prayers were led by mullas, whether in herding camps, *jome* assemblies, or holy day assemblies, for prayer was usually followed by formal sermons and freer discussion. But in addition mullas organized special events specifically for educating ordinary tent dwellers.

**Table 12.1.** Participation in Tuhein Aid by Members of Ja'fari Halk, 1973

| Male Head of Household | Present in Camp | Returned to Camp | Did Not Return | Left after Holy Day | Sacrifice |
|---|---|---|---|---|---|
| Ja'far | X | | | | Gitaj |
| Reis | X | | | | Pir mish[a] |
| Dust Mahmud | X | | | | Pir boz |
| Gami | X | | | | Korus |
| Ido | X | | | | Trusht |
| Komeron | X | | | | Pir boz |
| Wali Mahmud | | X | | | Pir boz |
| Shams A'din | | X | | X | Pir boz |
| Id Mahmud | | X | | X | Pir mish |
| Ghulam Mahmud[b] | | X | | X | — |
| Mahmud Karim | | X | | X | $\frac{1}{7}$ datchi |
| Jan Mahmud | | X | | X | Pir boz |
| Isa | | X | | | Trusht |
| Baluch | | X | | X | $\frac{1}{7}$ datchi |
| Abdulla[b] | | X | | X | — |
| Karam | | X | | | Gitaj |
| Alluk[c] | | X | | X | — |
| Sahib Dad (Gami)[c] | | X | X | | — |
| Isa (zamas of Komeron) | | | X | | Pir boz[d] |
| Sahib Dad (zamas of K.) | | | X | | Gitaj[d] |
| Abas | | | X | | — |
| Barkat[e] | | | X | | $\frac{1}{7}$ datchi |
| Bahadin[c] | | | X | | — |
| Shiruk[c] | | | X | | — |
| Baharam[c] | | | X | | — |

[a]Animal had only one ear, which some said made it imperfect and unsuitable for sacrifice; others said it was not important.

[b]Recently married without children, sometimes without separate tent, sharing sacrifice with senior kin.

[c]Young unmarried men without separate tents, participating in the sacrifices with their natal families.

[d]Sacrifice arranged by female household heads, the wives of these absent men.

[e]Intended to return, but was in jail for smuggling.

## *Tabliq:* Collective Educational Meetings

In the spring of 1968, mullas held a series of *tabliq,* large gatherings for the purpose of teaching Islamic ritual and ideas. In early May 1968, for example, a *tabliq* took place at Garonchin, attended by Ja'far, Yelli Han, Shams A'din, and Gam Dad, whose adult name was to be Jan Mahmud. A congregation of some 100 men formed at 4 P.M. and for several hours were taught prayers and Muslim tradition by Mulla Bi from Khash. At night, the men ate the food that they had brought and slept under the stars in the bedding they had brought. The next morning, the congregation recited morning prayer en masse and then had another instruction session. The men returned to camp both serious and elated, saying what a good experience this *tabliq* had been and how important it was to advance one's Islamic learning, really more important than anything else. Shams A'din said that this was better than anything else he might do. Yelli Han immediately started to teach his wife what he had learned. Ja'far said that there would be more *tabliq* shortly, and that he and the others would attend. He remarked that this was only the second year such meetings had been held; this was a new thing for the Sarhad. And the reason was, he continued, that in the past there were few mullas, while now there were many.

At the end of May 1968, another *tabliq*, organized by Haji Tagazi, a Rahmatzai Yarahmadzai, who had a shop in Khash and a two-car taxi service, was held at Nugju, near the camp of the Ja'fari Halk. At Nugju, an area of ground was cleared and the area outlined by rocks, making it an open-air *masjed*, mosque. Haji Tagazi was joined by Mulla Isa, the *maulawi* of Gorchan. They began by leading evening prayers and went on for several hours into the dark. They gave sermons, taught passages of the Qoran in Arabic and other prayers in Baluchi, although Mulla Isa had been saying that prayers in Baluchi were not really good enough and that people had to learn as soon as possible to recite from the Qoran in Arabic. Members of the congregation either stayed over or returned early the next day, and the teaching began again early the next morning, with morning prayers, and went on for several hours. The congregation for this *tabliq* consisted of around 200 men, most from nearby but some from farther off, brought by Haji's taxis or having come on their own by camel, bicycle, or motorcycle.

During the spring of 1968, *tabliq* were held at Rabat, Bunzin, Poshtag, Gorchan, and Baluchibad, in addition to those at Garonchin and Nugju. Shortly after the *tabliq* at Nugju, the wedding of Mirad took place, and when the guests were sitting around the tents during the two days of the wedding, they spent much of their time reciting what they had learned and correcting one another. As well, many men practiced in their own tents, reciting for their wives and children and trying to teach their wives what they had learned at the *tabliq*.

## Qoranic School

The Qoranic school at Gorchan, the only one in the Yarahmadzai tribal territory, was built and established in the mid-1960s under the patronage of the Sardar and the chiefly family, who resided at Gorchan during the winter. The school consisted of four rooms in a line, each with a door to the outside. Two rooms were for students; one was a classroom and the other was a room for sleeping. When I visited in 1968, 10 boys from across Yarahmadzai tribal territory lived and studied there, and another 10 boys and 10 girls came daily from villages and camps in the vicinity. The 20 boys and 10 girls all studied in the same room.

The boys' preparation in Islam was a step toward going on to study away from the Sarhad and becoming mullas, although certainly not all of them would do so, and the girls' study advanced their understanding of the Qoran and their ability to pray properly. Study in this Qoranic school was said by the Mullas to be supplementary to government school, which was run by teachers from the *Sepahi Danesh,* the education corps of army recruits assigned to nonmilitary duties. Education at the Qoranic school was supplementary in two senses: Arabic and the Qoran were taught there, but not at the government school; and the secular subjects taught at the government school were not taught at the Qoranic school. So mullas encouraged students to go to both the government school and the Qoranic school.

The other two rooms in the school building were available for the use of the teachers, Mulla Isa, the learned *mulawi,* and a younger, less educated man, Mulla Abdul Karim.

## RELIGIOUS SPECIALISTS

Sarhadi Baluch were Sunni Muslims, in contrast to the Shia Persians to the north. Sarhadi Islam, along with that of Baluchistan more generally, adhered to the Hanafi school, and as such was aligned with Hanafi Afghanistan, Pakistan, and Muslim India to the east, as opposed to the Persian/Arabian Gulf and Arabia, to the south and west, which followed the Shafi'i and Hanbali schools, respectively. Consequently, Sarhadi Baluch looked to centers of Islamic learning in Afghanistan and Pakistan for Qoranic study. The mullas of the Sarhad were all trained in Afghanistan, Pakistan, and India.

It was uncertain how many mullas—men who had been educated in Qoranic schools for at least four years, actively engaged in religious leadership, and were called "Mulla"—there were in the Sarhad during the period from the late 1960s through the middle 1970s when I did my research. Even among the Yarahmadzai tribe alone, estimates varied considerably. Mulla Said Mahmud, a young man from Garonchin, said that there were 200 mullas among the Yarahmadzai. According to my calculations, if there were 5,000 Yarahmazai, of which 1,000 were adult men, the estimate of 200 mullas would have indicated that 1 in 5 was a mulla, which seems greatly exaggerated according to my observations. Nezar Mahmud, brother of the Sardar, estimated 50–70 mullas among the Yarahmadzai, which makes 10 percent or more of adult men mullas. Even this figure seemed high to me; I would have guessed fewer.

It would appear that the higher estimates of Mulla Said Mahmud and Nezar Mahmud indicated that they were using a minimalist definition, granting the title of Mulla to anyone who had studied at Qoranic school and who could lead prayers, rather than someone who was an active religious specialist on more than an occasional basis. So in the Sarhad, the title and status of "Mulla" meant someone educated, if only minimally, in Islamic knowledge and able to provide informed guidance to their fellows, but not necessarily someone primarily occupied professionally with religious matters or making their living primarily by providing religious services. And given the number of Yarahmadzai students attending the Qoranic school at Gorchan and the brief duration of education qualifying one as a mulla, the number of mullas among the Yarahmadzai was in course of swelling dramatically.

## Mulla Rustam

The mulla whom I knew best was Mulla Rustam, whose tent was part of the Halili Halk, the Ja'fari Halk's fraternal Dadolzai *halk*, with which it sometimes combined and near which it sometimes camped. In 1973, Mulla Rustam was 53 years old, married, with 6 children. He and his family resided in their black tent and owned 10 *pas*, 1 camel, 50 palms as Kindi, and owned no land and engaged in no commercial activities.

According to Mulla Rustam's account, he had received no encouragement to go to Qoranic school. He had seen mullas in the Sarhad and wanted to study religion and become a mulla himself. Mulla Rustam reported that his great-grandfather had been a mulla. His father had wanted him to stay in camp and help his family, but when he was 14 he ran away to study without his father's permission. He went to study with Maulawi Mahmud Mirad at his Qoranic school at Nushki during the winters, and with Abdul Aziz at the Madrasi Chaki in highland Quetta during the summers. While the small-town school in Nushki had 50 students, the school in the city of Quetta had 150 students. Mulla Rustam and other residential students were supported financially, receiving food, shelter, clothes, and books from local donations to the school, donations for which, as Mulla Rustam put it, the contributors received *sawab*. After 5 years, Mulla Rustam's father brought him back to Baluchistan. Later, Mulla Rustam studied at Karachi for 2 additional years. But he would have liked to have continued for the 12 or so years necessary to become a learned *maulawi*.

Mulla Rustam's studies brought him literacy in several languages, specifically the ability to read and write Baluchi, Persian, Urdu, and, above all for religious purposes, Arabic. This literacy provided the basis for his knowledge of the Qoran and of religious law. It was on this foundation that Mulla Rustam was able to act as religious leader for his kinsmen, leading prayers at the small, rustic mosque at Shagbond or in camp in the countryside. He was also able to give some instruction to the youngsters in the camp, and he encouraged youngsters to go to Qoranic school, specifically mentioning in this regard one of his brother's sons and one of his sister's sons, as well as his own older son. His younger son had been at government school for six years and Mulla Rustam planned to send him to study Islam with Rahim Yar Khan in Islamabad, Pakistan.

In addition, Mulla Rustam officiated at marriages and funerals, provided *tiei*, and prayed for sick people. Once when I was very ill, Mulla Rustam had prayed for me and ritually spit on me, with very good effect as far as I was able to tell. He was also always ready to act as a *wasta* if requested or if he felt his intervention was necessary. In return, his congregation materially supported him and his family with tithes of grain and other seasonal produce. I also provided him with a small amount of material support. During the course of my various stints of fieldwork, I took many photos, including a nice portrait of Mulla Rustam. When the *National Geographic* was preparing an ethnographic map of the Middle East, the editors asked me to provide them with a photo of a Baluch, and I sent them a portrait of Mulla Rustam. For this they gave me a small honorarium. When I next returned to Baluchistan, I gave Mulla Rustam a copy of the map with his portrait representing all Baluch. I was not sure he would be very pleased with this visual representation of himself, given the Islamic view that only God can make living things and that men should not make representations of them, so I gave him the map privately. I did not want to offend him, and, having doubts about the propriety of having let my enthusiasm carry me to using his photo in this way, was a bit embarrassed. Mulla Rustam took the map and did not really say anything, but he too looked a bit embarrassed. Then I gave him half of the small honorarium, which was somewhat less negligible for him than for me, and he seemed a bit more cheered by that.

I asked Mulla Rustam whether there had been changes in the Sarhad during the past 50 years. He answers were very definite. There had been great changes he told me. Now, he said, people pray regularly and keep the fast. The endemic raiding, killing, and stealing had ended. There is no longer music and dancing. People no longer flagellated themselves at funerals. In consequence, because people have become more religious, the work of mullas is much easier now than in the past. Now, he reported, there are a number of religious schools on the Sarhad and elsewhere in Baluchistan, for example, two in Zahedan, two in Dezak, and others at Saravan and Gosht, the latter with 100 students. In short, Mulla Rustam believed that there had been a turn toward religion among the Sarhadi Baluch, that ritual obligations were increasingly observed, that Islamic education was more widespread, and that violent and antisocial activities had declined. At the same time, Mulla Rustam acknowledged that there was little contact with Persian Shia, for example, in Khash, either in ritual activities or between religious specialists, but he did not see this as a problem.

## THE TURN TOWARD ISLAM IN THE SARHAD

From the observations reported above, I think it would be fair to conclude that there had been an upsurge in religious activities among the Sarhadi tent dwellers from the late 1960s. Ordinary tent dwellers were praying and observing ritual obligations in a more regular and determined fashion. Mullas of local origin were arriving in numbers for the first time. A religious school was built on Yarahmadzai territory at Gorchan. A learned *maulawi* was being supported by the chiefly family. Educational assemblies were being held for the first time. Tent dwellers were beginning to learn some Arabic for ritual purposes. For virtually the first time, Sarhadi Baluch were going on the *haj* to Mecca and were going in rapidly increasing numbers. Tent dwellers were regularly talking with one another about religion. Being Muslims, and being good Muslims, came to be more central in the identities of Sarhadi tent dwellers.

What accounts for this remarkable development of religious activity? Were there currents in Sarhadi society that might have encouraged this shift in orientation? If we reflect upon the historical changes in Sarhadi society from the 1930s on, two major influences appear to have provided fertile ground for the growth of Islam in the lives of the Sarhadi tent dwellers.

First, the tribal independence, military strength, and economic self-sufficiency of the Baluchi period were lost with the Iranian conquest of the Sarhad during the mid-1930s. After being in a position of independence and sometime dominance, the Sarhadi tent dwellers found themselves militarily conquered, politically subservient, and economically embarrassed in relation to the stronger and richer Persians. The Sarhadi tent dwellers could no longer raid Persian villages and caravans, no longer carry back riches to buffer the harsh Sarhadi environment, and no longer define themselves as marauding raiders and warriors superior to their opponents. They could no longer revel in tearing a living from their harsh environment, once they understood that the ingenuity of the Persians and other foreigners was economically superior to their hardiness. They could no longer rely on their tribes as the ultimate guarantors of their security, once their tribes had been conquered and subjected to the power of the state. So much that the long-haired, rifle-toting, rough, ruthless, and hardy Sarhadi tent dwellers had stood for had been wrested from them, suppressed, and negated. The proud Sarhadi tent dwellers had, with the abrupt and forced ending of the Baluchi period, less and less to be proud of and were increasingly at a loss for a positive way to think of themselves.

Second, the conquering Persians, present in the Sarhad from the mid-1930s but especially so after World War II, were represented regionally and locally by the Iranian military; the Iranian provincial, regional, and municipal bureaucracies; Persian merchants; Persian Shia clerics and teachers; and even Persian farmers. The town of Khash became a regional administrative and commercial center, and Persian irrigation-based villages sprung up on the Khash Plain. Persian, as spoken and written, was the language of government, commerce, and education, with Baluchi, only a spoken language, remaining the language of the deserts and mountains. Thus the disenfranchisement of the Baluch meant not just that Baluchi accomplishments and capabilities had been removed, but that they had been replaced by Persian accomplishments and capabilities. Baluchi losses were Persian gains. The Sarhadi Baluch had lost and the Persians had won.

The loss of stature of the Sarhadi Baluch and their overshadowing by the Persians left the Baluch with a vacuum in their values and their identities. They were not prepared to concede to the Persians and to relegate their culture, language, and identity to a lost past by assimilating to Persian society and culture. And yet they had been beaten up and shown up by the Persians. So what other course was open to them?

There was within the cultural repertoire of the Sarhadi Baluch a set of commitments, understandings, values, activities, goals, and identities that had not been devalued by the Persian onslaught. This cultural complex was Sunni Islam, which had for decades and centuries been one of the elements of Sarhadi culture and identity. It may not always have been highly prominent within Sarhadi culture, and certainly had not been the dominant feature of the tent dweller's life, but it was well entrenched.

As Sarhadi tribal independence, military prowess, and economic self-sufficiency were negated by the Persian occupation, the commitments, understandings, values, activities, and goals of these cultural fields receded. The vacuum that appeared in the cultural life of the Sarhadi tent dwellers was increasingly filled, as we have seen, by the expansion of religion, Sunni Islam becoming a greater focus of attention, commitment, and energy. Once having thought of themselves primarily as brave warriors, independent tribesmen, and survivors in a harsh land, the Sarhadi Baluch by the 1960s were emphasizing a vision of themselves as pious Muslims, men right with God. Sarhadi identity, still multiple and complex, had seen a shift in its elements, the military and political elements shrinking and the religious element expanding.

Of course, commitments and identities, understandings and activities were to a degree contingent upon the events of the day. With the heightening of the great feud between the Soherabzai and the Rahmatzai, the thoughts of the tent dwellers focused more on their political and military commitments and their identity as lineage members, and somewhat less on piety and the Islam that they all shared. During this feuding period of the early 1970s, collective education meetings and other extraordinary religious congregations dropped off. Just as the long-term turn toward Islam was driven by macro-historical events, so, too, short-term shifts in focus, activities, and identity followed micro-historical events, as some commitments, values, and goals were deemphasized for a time and others were reactivated and highlighted. The Sarhadi turn toward religion thus was not a smooth acceleration of religion at the expense of other cultural foci, but rather a series of short-term ups and downs over time, the general tendency of which was a significant increase in religion.

The Persian military, economy, and education were recognized by the Sarhadi tent dwellers as superior to those of the Sarhad, however reluctant they were to admit it explicitly, but from the Sarhadi point of view Sarhadi Islam was obviously and undeniably better than the Persian religion. The Sunni Sarhadi Baluch did not think much of the, to their minds, deviant and mistaken Shia Islam of the Persians. The Sarhadi tent dwellers were not really sure that they wanted to grant the Shia Persians status as real Muslims. The Sarhadi Baluch even expressed doubts about whether the Shia Persians would be admitted to heaven. Sunni Islam, shared by the Sarhadi tent dwellers, both distinguished them from the Persians and in their own minds manifested their superiority over the Persians. Religion thus acted as a diacritic, drawing and maintaining a line between the defensive Sarhadi Baluch and the expanding Persians. And religion not only distinguished between the Baluch and the Persians but was the one area in which the Sarhadi Baluch were able to claim superiority—even though the claim would not have been granted by the Persians—and which provided the basis for their renewed sense of cultural integrity and focused identity. The turn to religion was thus for the Sarhadi Baluch an answer to the successful Persian onslaught and a revitalization of Sarhadi vision and identity.

The intensification of religion in order to redraw boundaries around a social group, to refocus the culture, and to redefine the identity of its members in the face of external challenge is a not uncommon process. A well-documented case (Cohen 1969:chaps. 5–6) from an urban area in a part of the Muslim world far distant from Baluchistan shows suggestive parallels. The Hausa community in Ibadan, Nigeria, having had its collective boundaries and secular political authority structure undermined by changes in the wider political environment, reoriented its culture toward a religious focus, intensified ritual activities (Cohen 1969:152–53), and provided local leadership with sacred bases of legitimation:

> The 1950's brought about two major processes of change into the social organization of Sabo [the Hausa Quarter of Ibadan], one political and the other religious. The first came when the collapse of Indirect Rule began to undermine the political autonomy of Sabo. The second came with the dramatic and massive adoption by the [Sabo] Hausa of the Tijaniyya mystical order. On the surface the two processes seem to have been independent of one another, but in fact they were closely interconnected. Within a short period after adopting the Tijaniyya, the Hausa in effect transformed their community from a tribal [i.e., ethnic] polity to a ritual community. In the process, their formal political organization, which was undermined by the rise of Nigerian nationalism, became informally articulated in terms of religious ideologies, symbols, myths, attitudes, loyalties, ceremonial, and power structure. (Cohen 1969:141)

At the same time, the boundary between the Muslim Hausa and the Muslim Yoruba, which had begun to break down as members of these groups met in "modern" social and political groupings that did not recognize ethnicity (Cohen 1969:149), was redrawn by Hausa adoption of the Tijaniyya Order.

One difference between the Ibadan Hausa and the Sarhadi Baluch was that the religious differences between the Hausa and the Yoruba had to be heightened by the Hausa adoption of a special religious discipline, while the religious split between the Sarhadi Baluch and the Persians was of long standing. But the parallels are noteworthy: both the Ibadan Hausa and the Sarhadi Baluch used religion—seriously and conscientiously adopted in the case of the Hausa and enhanced in the case of the Baluch—to respond to political and cultural pressures that had undermined their group boundaries, culture, and identities. Religion redrew the boundaries between these groups and their others, filled their own cultural vacuums, and provided a new focus for the identities of their members.

# 13.
# CONCLUSION
*Reflecting on the Sarhadi Baluch*


The Sarhadi *baluch* cannot be fairly characterized, except in terms of the complexity, plurality, or multiplicity of their activities and way of life. Perhaps no people or culture can really be summed up adequately, because any such summing up requires the radical selection of one or another trait out of many, and thus the reduction of a many-faceted, many-layered way of life to one dimension and one feature. As Geertz (1979:123) has so wisely said, "Characterizing whole civilizations in terms of one or another of their leading institutions is a dubious procedure. . . ." Of course, it would be very satisfying for an ethnographer, after investigating a culture such as that of the Sarhadi Baluch, and for the readers of the ethnographer's report, to feel that we have indeed grasped the essence of that culture and could sum it up in a phrase. But should we not worry that treating cultures or societies as if they have essences may be a form of conceptual reductionism that does violence to the complexity that we would do better to respect? By this point in the evolution of anthropology, I think we can all agree that true understanding does not come from oversimplification.

After a long period of essentializing configurationalism (Benedict 1935), represented in recent versions of cultural analysis by structuralism (Levi-Strauss 1966; Sahlins 1976) and interpretationalism (Geertz 1973), an antiessentialist critique has finally been mounted from positions as diverse as radical postmodernism (Clifford 1988), empirical behaviorism (Vayda 1994), and processualism (Barth 1994). These antiessentialist authors stress diversity and variation, rather than all-encompassing cultural logic. As Barth (1994:360) puts it,

> We must turn from totalizing cultural models to generative models of processes (e.g.
> Barth 1966). I sense a welcome retreat in the newest currents within contemporary an-
> thropology from an exaggerated focus on the abstraction of culture to a more versatile

attention to the multiple levels of events, acts, experience, ranges of variation, contexts, and larger systems—all of them permeated by characteristically cultural processes, but not simply constitutive of a unitary culture.

Vayda (1994:321) argues that people do not mechanically act out a basic cultural pattern, but rather "pragmatically vary . . . their behavior and respond . . . to the different conditions in which they find themselves." In the antiessentialist view, it is futile to imagine that understanding human life can be reduced to a basic cultural model or logic from which all actions follow.

## CULTURAL MULTIPLICITY AMONG THE SARHADI BALUCH

In titling and presenting this ethnography, I have tried to avoid, or have put off as long as possible, labeling the Sarhadi *baluch* as "nomads," "lineage members," "herders," "tribesmen," "Muslims," "raiders," and the like, so as to avoid the impression that Sarhadi lives could be reduced to one crucial characteristic or underlying pattern. Indeed, the most important lesson that I learned from my field research in the Sarhad is the profound multiplicity of Sarhadi culture and life.

I had initially come to the Sarhad to study a "pastoral nomadic tribe" because I had become convinced, from surveying the anthropological literature, that nomadism greatly affected political life among such peoples (Salzman 1967), and I wanted to explore that relationship. In my initial, prefieldwork analysis (Salzman 1967), drawing on ethnographies of the Somali (Lewis 1961) and Basseri (Barth 1961), among others, I stressed differences among the tribes in political organization, especially the variation in leadership in degree of centralization and decentralization. To this degree I had broken away from ideal-typical models of "the" pastoral nomadic tribe. But my assumption of a unitary, totally integrated culture for each group remained, as did my expectation of identifying determining cultural characteristics, such as pastoralism or nomadism.

When I found myself amid Sarhadi *baluch* who were involved in a great variety of activities, and whose models of action were multiple and diverse, it took me a while to grasp that the Sarhadi Baluch were not confused, disorganized, or the victims of some kind of cultural miscegenation, and that, instead, my expectations arising from my initial conceptual framework were simplistic and that my assumptions of cultural tidiness were groundless. The multiplicity that I had "read out" of *The Nuer* and *Nomads of South Persia* in search of the cultural essence was not a bothersome deviation; it was the cultural reality. This I only understood after fieldwork in the Sarhad.

We have seen in some detail the variety of activities and conceptions that enriched Sarhadi life. During the Baluch Period prior to 1935, the Sarhadi Baluch were deeply engaged in pastoralism, predatory raiding, date palm cultivation, and dry cultivation of grain and did some hunting and gathering as well. In the succeeding Iranian Period, especially after World War II, predatory raiding was replaced by wage labor and trading, and irrigation agriculture was developed. These multiple productive activities fed together in several distinct ways.

Together they increased overall quantitative income over what any single sector could produce. The cumulative material produced in the different sectors made possible not only the support but the expansion of the Sarhadi population.

The multiple productive activities also provided a variety of raw materials for housing and transport as well as foodstuffs for both the human and animal populations. The diversity of foodstuffs—milk, grain, dates, wild vegetables, and occasionally eggs and meat—not only provided a palatable diet but a relatively balanced one.

In addition, in the highly variable and extreme environmental conditions of the region, the diversity of the sectors of production was an insurance mechanism, for conditions that led to the failure of one crop—too much wind for a good date crop, or too little rain for pasture to nourish the animals and continue the flow of milk and offspring, or the silting of irrigation tunnels and a decrease in irrigation water for crops—did not necessarily affect income from the other productive sectors.

The plurality of skills and abilities needed for prosecuting the Sarhadi multi-resource economy proved to be invaluable for the Sarhadi *baluch* in adapting to changing conditions. The audacity and mobility developed in raiding was adapted to migrant labor, smuggling, and trading. And the spatial flexibility of residence group nomadism was used to accommodate irrigation cultivation as part of the multi-resource economy.

The multiplicity of Sarhadi life was also seen in the identity of the tent dwellers. In fact, the phrase "the identity" is misleading, because rather than a single, unitary identity, we find among Sarhadi *baluch,* and probably in every other society, a number of distinct, logically discrete identities: male or female; junior or senior; dependent member or independent household head; herder, raider, trader, cultivator, laborer; lineage and tribe member, with or without solidarity; Muslim, Sunni, member of the Nakshbandi order, *haji, mulla, maulawi,* believer, nonbeliever; herd owner and employer, shepherd and employee, land and water owner, sharecropper; fighter, peacemaker; leader, follower; headman, chief; mother, father; nomadic tent dweller, sedentary house dweller. However, these identities did not form tidy packages and were not equivalent in all respects.

First, there appear to have been virtually as many identities as there were roles in Sarhadi society, and each individual partook of many.

Second, some identities were compulsory, ascribed, and permanent, such as sex and lineage membership, while some changed according to stage in the life cycle, such as dependence or independence. Some identities were optional, such as shepherd, Haji, and peacemaker, while others were virtually compulsory, even if achieved, such as parent and Muslim.

Third, individuals who shared one identity, such as sex, were divided according to other identities, such as lineage membership or seniority, occupation or residence.

Fourth, even ongoing identities tended to be contingent, depending upon the circumstances. How a woman was thinking of herself depended upon whether she was in the process of giving birth, or praying, or urging her kinsmen to avenge a death. How a man thought of himself depended upon whether he was arguing with his shepherd, going on the *haj*, defending his territory against usurpers, or mediating between conflicting parties. And whether an individual considered herself or himself a Dadolzai or Nur Mahmudzai or Soherabzai depended upon the political context. The question—Is a Sarhadi *baluch* primarily or basically a nomad, or a pastoralist, or a tribesmen, or a Muslim?—is fundamentally misconceived. For the identity felt at any given moment varied among the multiplicity of identities as the situation varied.

Fifth, over time, as circumstances changed, some identities became more prominent and others less prominent. By the 1960s, the Sarhadi *baluch* no longer thought of themselves as predatory raiders, a consequence of the long-standing suppression of raiding following the conquest and effective encapsulation by the Iranian state. Their ability to venture forth into the unknown and their willingness to face the dangers and challenges were transferred to noncoercive extraction from the wider environment. And during the same period, the identity of Sarhadi *baluch* as Sunni Muslims was highlighted and intensified in confrontation with their Shia conquerors.

Organizational multiplicity was noteworthy as well in the political system of the Sarhadi tribes. The Sarhadi *baluch* organized social control, coercion, leadership, and peacemaking by ingeniously combining two diverse structures: the egalitarian, decentralizing, democratic, segmentary lineage system, on the one hand, and, on the other hand, the hierarchical, centralizing system of political seniority and chiefship. The balance and degree of tension between these two structures was to a degree contingent, varying according to the circumstances. With the encapsulation of the Sarhadi tribes, and governance through indirect rule, the relative importance of the chiefly hierarchy in relation to the segmentary lineage system was increased. Here too, within the range of multiple elements of the Sarhadi cultural armory, there was one that was well suited to adapt to the circumstances.

Clearly, the Sarhadi tent dwellers were, to use Vayda's (1994:321) words, "pragmatically varying their behavior and responding to the different conditions in which they f[ound] themselves." However, the term "pragmatically" begs, to a degree, the theoretical questions that Vayda addresses. A "pragmatic" approach deals with finding the right means to achieve the desired ends. Cultural constructionists would ask where the ends and the means come from. Vayda (1994:320) is certainly correct in emphasizing "variations and variability" against the overemphasis of the essentialists on cultural pattern and logic. People are not automatons, ritually acting out a cultural logic. On the other hand, it is an unlikely hypothesis that people are always making up new values and goals and making up new means and techniques for achieving them. Not only would this be extremely tiring, it would quickly lead to chaos, and social life is possible only with a certain degree of order and predictability. Furthermore, in preindustrial societies (Gellner 1988), the margin of surplus is generally so small that a failed initiative could lead to true disaster.

It is more likely that people tend to be pragmatic within their cultural frame, granting that most cultural frames are characterized by multiplicity and not by unitary coherence. Rather than inventing life anew, people adapting to new conditions and even striking out on totally uncharted waters are likely to draw on their culture. In fact, would it not be most pragmatic for an individual to draw upon his or her own cultural repertoire and its range of technologies, organizational patterns, practices, and identities to adapt to new conditions?

Each culture and its repertoire of multiple institutions, customs, practices, and identities has arisen and grown in response, at least in part, to natural, demographic, social, economic, and political environmental cycles, such as drought and plenty, population growth and decline, ethnic separation and mixing, subsistence and market production, peace and war. The range of potential patterns of thought and activity in each culture provides different responses for the different conditions arising during different phases of these cycles.

The cultural multiplicity of the Sarhadi tent dwellers provided them with alternative responses to varying circumstances: during periods of political autonomy they turned to raiding; during encapsulation they turned to trading. While independent, the Baluch thought of themselves as fierce warriors; under state encapsulation by the Shia Persians, they thought of themselves as pious Sunni Muslims. Depending upon the opportunities, the Sarhadi Baluch shifted between self-sufficient, subsistence production in their territory and market-oriented activities away from home such as migrant labor, smuggling, and trading. For support in conflict, they turned to their lineage mates; for peaceful settlement, they turned to their leaders. For conflict among themselves, the Sarhadi *baluch* united with their lineage mates; for conflict with outsiders, they followed their chiefs. Sarhadi cultural multiplicity served the *baluch* in responding to the various alternating conditions of environmental cycles.

## THE SARHADI BALUCH IN COMPARATIVE CONTEXT

The nature of the Sarhadi case and its significance can perhaps be illuminated by a brief juxtaposition to other peoples similar in some respects and different in others. However, as I have argued against essentialist conceptualization, I will not make global comparisons, but rather will select particular spheres or aspects of Sarhadi life to compare with those elsewhere. Furthermore, to make the basis of comparison more explicit, I shall posit analytic continua along which the ethnographic cases to be mentioned fall.

## Environment and Demography

The high deserts of the Sarhad and of Mashkil limited pastoral and dry agricultural productivity and obliged those living by those means to spread themselves thinly across the arid landscape. In addition, human- and animal-power travel, transportation, and communication limited in practice the spatial range of social solidarity. Together, the low population density and the difficulty of travel, transport, and communication restricted the size of the Sarhadi tribes to a few thousand souls, or *musilmen*.

But not all nomadic tribesmen lived in deserts. The Basseri (Barth 1961), Qashqai (Beck 1986, 1991), and Lur (Garthwaite 1983) tribes of the Zagros Mountains enjoyed, by means of their seasonal, highland-lowland migrations, a more temperate and humid environment capable of supporting larger numbers of livestock and humans at greater density. Zagros political units were much larger than those of the Sarhad: the Basseri, one of the tribes of the Khamseh Confederacy, had 12,000 souls, while the Qashqai confederacy topped 400,000, and the Bakhtiari, the "Great Lurs," reached or surpassed a million. Furthermore, the members of each of the Basseri, Qashqai, and Bakhtiari tribes migrated together, along with their sheep flocks and other animals, on their dramatic treks over the Zagros Mountains, such a massive concentration of people and animals made possible by the richness of the environmental resources. The nomadic Yomut Turkmen (Irons 1975) *chomur,* wet-plains dwellers, numbering 122,000 at 68 per square mile, living in the southern part of the Gorgon plain, enjoyed so much rain that they engaged mainly in grain cultivation, their mobile residences and short seasonal migrations notwithstanding. The Yomut Turkmen *charwa*, desert dwellers, at 16,000 a much smaller population, who lived in the dryer, northern part of the plain, relied primarily on sheep pastoralism and at 6 per square mile were much more thinly spread across the landscape than their *chomur* kinsmen.

The largest of the Sarhadi tribes—the Yarahmadzai, Gamshadzai, and Ismailzai—at a few thousand souls were in population equivalent to the smallest tribes or to subsections of the larger tribes that together made up the Qashqai or Bakhtiari confederacies. In 1960, the 14 Qashqai tribes averaged 15,200 people each (Beck 1986:175, table 2), some tribes being as small as 1,000 and others as large as 50,000. The Qermezi section that Beck (1991) studied numbered around 1,000 persons and was only one of 44 sections of the Darrehshuri tribe of the Qashqai confederacy. So in comparison, even the largest Sarhadi tribes were small polities, and their Sardars equivalent to minor leaders among the larger tribes elsewhere.

## Nomadism

The nomadism of the Sarhadi *baluch* was territorial, free-wheeling and unanchored to a permanent residential site, and oriented primarily toward microenvironmental variations. The main tribes of the Sarhad controlled territories within which most of their members migrated and moved their residences, while smaller, politically dependent groups received permission to use the territory. Territorial control is characteristic of tribes that are by definition politically independent. In this respect, the Sarhadi *baluch* were similar to the Turkmen *charwa* of the desert region of northeast Iran (Irons 1975) and the Nuer of the southern Sudan (Evans-Pritchard 1940). The control of territory is, however, rarely found among peasant pastoral nomads, who must rent or purchase pastureland, as among the Yoruk of southeastern Turkey (Bates 1973), the Sarakatsani of northwest Greece (Campbell 1964), and the Komachi of south Iran (Bradburd 1990). The same situation is often found among Mediterranean pastoral shepherds, such as those of Sardinia (Angioni 1996) and the migratory pastoralists of Rajasthan, northwest India (Salzman 1986a).

Sarhadi pastoral nomadism was, within tribal boundaries, free-wheeling, without any home base or set direction. In this respect, the Sarhadi *baluch* differed from some other pastoral, tribal peoples, such as the Karimojong of Uganda (Dyson-Hudson 1966), who maintained permanent, riverine, horticultural settlements while young men lived in mobile cattle camps, and the Nuer (Evans-Pritchard 1940), who maintained permanent horticultural settlements on hillocks that they occupied seasonally. The free-wheeling Sarhadi nomadism differed from that of the Basseri of southwest Iran (Barth 1961), which, like other Zagros tribes, each year followed a specified migration route, the *il rah*, or tribal road, between the winter lowlands and the summer highlands, over which the Basseri had rights of access only for a certain period.

Even the free-wheeling Sarhadi pastoral nomadism was to a degree seasonal, for herding camps, while relatively stable in the fall and winter, moved around quite actively in the spring. In this respect, the Sarhadi pattern was similar to that of other desert nomads, such as the Turkmen *charwa* (Irons 1975) and the Bedouin of Cyrenaica in Libya (Evans-Pritchard 1949), who remained near wells in the summer, fall, and winter, and ranged widely in the desert during the spring, after winter rains brought spring pasture.

Sarhadi pastoral nomadism was free-ranging because it was an adaptation to microenvironmental variations, a search for the occasional presence of pasture in an unreliable and unpredictable environment. This contrasted with the pastoral migrations of the Basseri, Qashqai, and other Zagros tribes that exploited the predictable macroenvironmental variations of season and altitude between summer highlands and winter lowlands.

However, the longest migration of the year for Sarhadi *baluch* was regular and predictable. This was not a pastoral migration, but a multi-resource migration, between the pastoral area and the date-cultivation area. Unlike Sarhadi free-wheeling pastoral migrations, this multi-resource migration was seasonal, fixed in time, as well as on a fixed route, between the Sarhad and Mashkil. In this respect, it was similar to the regular Nuer (Evans-Pritchard 1940) migration between wet-season villages and dry-season riverside campsites.

## Economy

The basic means of production—uncultivated land and pasture, streams and water, undomesticated flora and fauna—were owned collectively by all members of each Sarhadi tribe. A tribesman had free access to these "resources of God," owned by no man, within the territory controlled by his tribe. Among a few tribal pastoralists, such as the Shah Savan (Tapper 1979) of northwestern Iran and many peasant pastoralists such as those mentioned above, access to land through purchase or rental was acquired on an individual or familial basis.

Production in the Sarhadi economy was diversified rather than specialized, with most Sarhadi households committed to a wide range of productive sectors, usually including pastoralism, agriculture, arboriculture, raiding/trading, hunting, and gathering. This multi-resource, or mixed, economy was and continues to be widespread among so-called pastoral tribes (Salzman 1971a). The Nuer (Evans-Pritchard 1940) may have loved their cattle best, but they worked regularly and seriously at growing millet during the wet season and fishing during the dry season. Arabian Bedouin were often involved in predatory extraction, such as providing "protection" to oases (Lancaster 1981), in soldiering (Cole 1975), and in transport and smuggling (Lancaster 1981), as well as in livestock production. The Turkmen *chomur*, living in yurts and fully nomadic, were heavily committed to agriculture in the humid Gorgon plain, extracted protection money from Persian peasants immediately to the south, produced the famous "Turkman" carpets, and slave-raided in more distant Persian regions (Irons 1975). The economy of the Tuareg (Nicolaisen 1963; Bernus 1981, 1990) rested upon a combination of pastoralism, oasis cultivation, caravaneering, trading, and raiding.

In contrast to these diversified economies, the economies of the Basseri (Barth 1961) and Qashqai (Beck 1991) were more specialized. Pastoral sheep production predominated, with only a limited amount of supplementary grain cultivation. Similarly specialized were nomadic pastoral peasants such as the Yoruk (Bates 1973), the Sarakatsani (Campbell 1964), the Komachi (Bradburd 1990, 1994), and the peasant pastoralists of India (Salzman 1986a, 1988a).

The Sarhadi tent dwellers' economy was subsistence oriented rather than market oriented; that is, most of what was produced—milk, butter oil, wool, hair, meat, grain, dates, firewood, wild greens, woven goods, embroidery—by the Sarhadis was indeed consumed by the producers. Although some products, such as grain, dates, or livestock were occasionally bartered among Sarhadi tribesmen, and infrequently some products, such as livestock or ghee, were sold in the market, most people consumed most of what they produced. The economies of the Nuer (Evans-Pritchard 1940) and Karimojong (Dyson-Hudson 1973) were totally subsistence oriented, as they did not engage in trade at all and had no markets available.

But many Middle Eastern, North African, and West African nomadic pastoralists were market oriented, as they were located in regions that had developed markets for thousands of years and in which rural production often served urban needs (Bulliet 1980). For example, camel-rearing Bedouin in Arabia and North Africa supplied camels to urban markets where they were used in the interregional and international caravan trade (Lancaster 1981). And just as the Turkmen wove carpets with their sheep's wool for sale in Central Asian markets, so, too, Persian peasants captured by the Turkmen were sold at urban slave markets in Central Asia (Irons 1975). Komachi production for sale in the bazaar of Kerman was closely attuned to export markets (Bradburd 1994). Cattle from the pastoral Fulani in northern Nigeria were sold for shipment southward to feed urban dwellers (Cohen 1969). The Bedouin of Cyrenaica (Evans-Pritchard 1949:37) in western Libya produced for the Egyptian market:

> Before the outbreak of the second Italo-Sanusi war in 1923 the normal export to the markets of Egypt was 80,000 sheep and goats a year, and it was reckoned that a settled [i.e., peaceful] Cyrenaica could produce annually for export at least 100,000 to 150,000 sheep and goats and 6,000 camels. The country used to satisfy a considerable portion of Egypt's meat requirements. It also exported clarified butter in big quantities, 91,835 kilograms being the figure for 1922 and 75,482 the figure for 1923.

## Social Organization

The Sarhadi tribes were stratified in that the tribesmen distinguished themselves from the small populations of slaves, and later from their descendants, the Ghulamzai, and from the few Luri craftsmen. Among the tribesmen themselves, who made up the great bulk of the population, there was no social stratification. Like all tribesmen, the Sardars and their families were part of the tribal lineage system, married with other tribesmen, and had a way of life and standard of living not very different from other tribesmen.

Similarly, few Sarhadi tribesmen worked for other tribesmen, and those who did, shepherds excepted, did so in an occasional way as one source of income among many in their household economies. And the resources needed for production were either collectively owned by the entire tribe, as in the case of pasture, firewood, and natural water sources, collectively owned by lineages, as in the case of wells, or individually but widely owned, as in the case of livestock and date palms. So there were no economic classes, either; tribesmen lived off their own labor and the labor of members of their households and shared labor reciprocally with other tribesmen, but they did not live off the labor of others.

Lacking the divisions of social strata and economic classes among themselves, the Sarhadi tribesmen were basically egalitarian. The lineage system favored equality, both conceptually, for lineage mates were considered formally equivalent, and substantively, for the solidarity of mutual aid and support emphasized the value of each and every lineage mate. In this regard, the Sarhadi tribes were similar to the Yomut Turkmen (Irons 1994) and the Nuer (Evans-Pritchard 1940). Likewise, among the Rwala Bedouin (Lancaster 1981:77), "All men are autonomous and equal."

In contrast, among the Zagros tribes, the differences of power, way of life, and patterns of association between leaders, *khan*, and ordinary tribesmen, *lur* among the Bakhtiari and Lur, were so significant as to be justifiably called stratification (Barth 1961; Irons 1994). In concluding his comparison between the stratified Lurs with the egalitarian Turkmen, Irons (1994:196) mildly comments, "Even within the limited range of conditions found among the tribal populations of Iran, there is room for very different types of social experiences and very different cultural assumptions."

## Politics

The Sarhadi tribes organized their politics through a balance between an egalitarian, decentralizing, segmentary lineage system and a hierarchical, centralizing chiefship. Thus there was a parity between the tendency for segmentary fragmentation and opposition, on the one hand, and unification on the other. Particularly noteworthy in this regard was the shift between segmentary conflict and unitary settlement, the latter manifested in contributions to the injured party by close as well as distant kin, by those who had sided with the injured party in the conflict as well as by those who were their opponents.

In this respect, the Sarhadi *baluch* differed from the almost exclusively segmentary Nuer (Evans-Pritchard 1940) and Turkmen (Irons 1975). But it should be noted that the political systems of the Nuer and Turkmen were not solely segmentary lineage systems. Rather, they were territorial political systems in which the lineage system structured the relations between territorial segments. Thus they, too, were mixed systems in the sense that more than one idiom—both descent and territorial residence— were combined. But in these cases both elements of the system were segmentary, and the result was pure segmentary politics, unadulterated by hierarchical, centralizing elements.

In contrast, in the Basseri political system (Barth 1961), the hierarchical, centralizing chiefly structure dominated. The tribal segments were unrelated to one another and were associated only through their common allegiance to the chief. The chief, with the support of public opinion (Salzman 2000), dictated allocation of basic resources, such as pasture, and was able to apply sanctions of corporal punishment. The other Zagros tribal confederacies, the Qashqai (Beck 1986) and Bakhtiari (Brooks 1983; Garthwaite 1983), were also strongly hierarchical, with sectional, tribal, and confederacy chiefs; many matters in their tribesmen's lives were decided by the chiefs, and they had "enforcers" to back their decisions. In these tribes, segmentary politics was constrained by the dominating hierarchical politics.

One of the main reasons for the development of strong chiefships in nomadic tribes was the spatial propinquity of state centers of power, state-controlled peasant populations, and bazaar economies. The summer quarters of the Bakhtiari were in the region of the great city of Isfahan, *nesf johan,* "half the world," while the summer quarters of the Qashqai were in the region of the splendid garden city of Shiraz. The great tribal confederacies of the Zagros range were major players in Iranian national politics; during the first decade of the century the Bakhtiari had participated actively and with force in the events of the constitutional revolution by taking control of Isfahan and then entering and "dominating" the capital (Avery 1965:138, 143– 44, 157), and just after World War II the Qashqai had rebelled against communist influence in the Tehran government, contributing to the removal of communists from high office (Avery 1965:396–97). The powerful confederacy and tribal chiefships of the Zagros developed as counters to the powerful sedentary authorities of the Iranian state and society.

If the Nuer and Turkmen can be labeled "segmentary tribes," and the Zagros tribe can be labeled "tribal chiefdoms," the Sarhadi tribes can most aptly be called "segmentary chiefdoms." They are perhaps closest in organization to the desert tribes of Arabia, such as the Rwala (Lancaster 1981), in which we find a similar balance between the fragmenting tendency of lineage segments and the unifying influence of prestigious but relatively powerless leaders. As Lancaster (1981:77) puts it, "No individual has political power, no group has political power and no family has political power; power is restricted to the workings of public opinion. . . . [T]he best that can be done is to exert influence through reputation."

All of these tribal peoples had a degree of political independence, and it was by virtue of this independence that the label "tribal" is appropriate. With the submission of a tribe to another political authority, either another tribe, or regional *hako-mate,* or to a state, they lose political independence and become less and less "tribal" in a political sense as external control increases. Effective encapsulation by a state, which governs through indirect rule, using the tribal structure for its purposes, reduces tribal independence substantially but leaves a degree of political freedom, especially with regard to internal regulation. This was the situation in which I found the Yarahmadzai, known at that time as Shah Nawazi, during my fieldwork in the 1960s and 1970s. Incorporation of a tribal people, in which tribal institutions are replaced by state institutions, removes all political independence and reduces the post-tribesmen into peasants (Salzman 1996), albeit peasants with an attitude, usually an attitude of resistance supported by ethnic distinctiveness. This was the situation of Sardinian mountain *pastori* (Angioni 1989; Salzman 1999b). The Yurok (Bates 1973) and the Sarakatsani (Campbell 1964), while remaining distinctive from their neighbors, were less bent on resistance and perhaps moving toward assimilation to the dominant population. Some pastoral, nomadic peasants, such as the Komachi (Bradburd 1990) were fully assimilated to the national culture.

## Varieties of Pastoral Nomads

Nothing would be more obvious to anthropologists, one would have thought, than the diversity of cultures, the variety of ways of life. And yet anthropologists seem inclined, when considering certain ecological or economic or political formations, to formulate ideal-typical models, a faux-Weberian type of essentialist thinking, rather than to assume variability and to compare cases in order to identify concomitant variations (Nadel 1951). This tendency toward ideal-typical models leads some students of nomadic tribes into debates about "the" basic nature of nomadic tribes that assume universal answers, such as whether nomadic tribes are egalitarian or stratified (Bradburd 1990; Mulder and Sellen 1994; cf. Irons 1994; Salzman 1999a), whether they are or are not oppressed by the sedentary power structure (Bradburd 1990), whether or not they all have charters based upon descent from a common ancestor (Wright 1994), whether they have or do not have a military advantage over sedentary society (Asad 1973), whether they are or are not merely politically dependent subunits of states (Marx 1996; cf. Salzman 1999a), and whether or not pastoral tribes must be serving the economic demands of urban populations (Marx 1996). But why must we, indeed how can we, imagine that all nomadic tribes are the same?

In opposing this essentializing and universalizing thinking, I commend a viewpoint directing attention to variability, which in our particular case would suggest that all nomads, tribes, and pastoralists are not alike, and that even nomadic pastoral tribes are not all alike. The obvious fact—still apparently obscure to some students of nomadic tribes—is that pastoral tribes differ from one another in the various ways addressed above. Consequently, the answers to all of the above questions is that some tribes are and some are not, some do and some do not, some are more so and some are less so. Certainly, the conclusion that we must draw about the comparative significance of the Sarhadi tribes is not that they can be taken as representative of all nomadic tribes, but rather that their similarities to and differences from other tribes can aid us in understanding and explaining why particular nomadic tribes are the way they are. The interesting questions are about how we can account for these differences.

I would suggest that the systematic examination of variations among tribes is the most informative strategy for understanding what nomadism and pastoralism and tribes are all about. While it has not been possible here to undertake any systematic exploration of the substantial differences among nomadic tribes, perhaps some tentative ideas might be offered.

Unreliable resources irregularly exploitable, such as desert pasture, are difficult to predict and control, and consequently are not usually subject to individual or small-group ownership or hierarchical control. In contrast, more reliable resources, such as highland summer pasture and lowland winter pasture, are more accessible to control and more commonly subject to individual ownership or hierarchical allocation.

Politically independent nomadic tribes located far from urban markets are more likely to have subsistence economies and to produce primarily or exclusively for their own consumption, while nomadic tribes spatially close to urban markets are more likely to produce for market exchange.

Subsistence producers are more likely to have multi-resource or mixed economies, while market-oriented producers are more likely to be specialized.

Social stratification among nomadic tribesmen depends upon the control of sedentary resources, such as agricultural villages, and/or close engagement with powerful sedentary forces, such as state authorities.

Equality among tribesmen is reinforced by predatory raiding, which enables those without capital resources, whether as a result of youth or misfortune, the opportunity to gain wealth rapidly without drawing on local resources.

Segmentary tribes are found far from centers of sedentary power, while centralized tribes with strong hierarchies are found close to centers of sedentary power.

Mobile members of nomadic tribes are able to avoid abuses imposed by an oppressive leader by spatially moving themselves and their capital resources beyond the reach of the leader, and by affiliating with another group led by more benevolent or prudent leaders.

Tribesmen have multiple economic strategies, political stances, and identities and shift among them according to the circumstances.

## Segmentary Politics and Political Philosophy

The great fame of Evans-Pritchard's *The Nuer* arose partly from its implications for English political philosophy. Hobbes in *The Leviathan* had argued that men in a state of nature would experience a war of all against all, and that human life would inevitably be, in the famous phrase, "nasty, brutish, and short." The only alternative, according to Hobbes, was for people to allocate their sovereignty to a ruler, who would impose order and make possible peace, prosperity, and a civil life.

What Evans-Pritchard so brilliantly showed was that people, the case in point being the Nuer, could and did live ordered lives without leaders and without a ruler, indeed virtually without any hierarchy at all. Their "ordered anarchy," in Evans-Pritchard's famous phrase, was based upon balanced, segmentary opposition of territorial units. The consequence was a democratic, egalitarian society with a restricted economic base well distributed through mutual aid and sharing. Social control was based upon collective responsibility and violent, collective self-help; as a result, all but a few men were warriors as well as subsistence producers.

For those, such as many Americans, who asserted the values of freedom, equality, and democracy, and for others, such as the British, living more of an orderly life within an established social hierarchy, the life of the Nuer had a strong appeal, either as a representation of or a challenge to strongly held values. In the 1990s of "social contestation" or "political correctness," depending upon one's sympathies, "hierarchy" is a dirty word, standing inevitably for unjust oppression based upon distinctions of gender, race, ethnicity, physical condition, body shape, wealth, age, majoritarian status, and so on. Political hierarchy is deemed in the political discourse of the 1990s inevitably to be a manifestation of and support to these oppressions. So the search is on, it would seem, for an antihierarchical alternative. Does the freedom, equality, and democracy of the Nuer or other segmentary polities such as the Sarhadi tribes present such an alternative? Before allowing ourselves to be carried away by enthusiasm for the segmentary form of polity, it would be well to note some of its conditions and consequences.

First, in segmentary societies almost all members are subsistence producers, which pretty much guarantees a very modest standard of living. There is little or no division of labor, and so no specialists: no scientists, no writers, no accountants, no opera singers, no chefs, and no anthropologists!

Second, there is really no cultural diversity—and "diversity" is another 1990s value—but rather a pressure toward cultural uniformity. Freedom was expressed within the cultural norms and did not extend to deviating very far from cultural values.

Third, peace is maintained by a balance of fear based upon threats of violence. Conflicts are expressed through violent opposition between groups. Each man is a warrior, is obliged to support all other members of his group, and fighting is an expected and honorable activity. This is equally true of many egalitarian peasant communities, such as those in northern Corsica (Holway 1978) and central Sardinia (Angioni 1989; Salzman 1999b), where violent self-help and vendetta were the basis of social order and conflict.

Fourth, outsiders were fair game for predatory violation, which included stealing and robbing subsistence property, burning habitations and other property, driving outsiders off their own land in an expansion of territory, murdering the resisters or the useless old or young, and capturing as slaves the strong or attractive to be kept or sold. Segmentary tribesmen may have been free, egalitarian, and democratic, but they were not respectful of the rights of others.

Fifth, purely segmentary polities could not respond effectively, in a unified fashion, to serious external threats. Their lack of institutions supporting unity put them at a disadvantage in defending themselves.

Therefore, although we might wish to give our approbation to some of the values and practices of antihierarchical, segmentary organization, other aspects of segmentary life seem less than attractive. Consequently, if we may draw policy conclusions from our ethnographic observations, any political ideologies and campaigns that we care to advocate, must, to be realistic, strive not to remove hierarchy, but to balance and constrain it: for complete equality must be purely segmentary, with costs that few of us would be willing to sustain.

# GLOSSARY

The following is an alphabetical list of Baluchi (and a few other foreign) terms, rendered as I have used them in the text. Sarhadi Baluchi is not a written language, so there is no standard written form. For comparison with the dominant regional language, Persian, which is a major literary language of long history, I have included some equivalent Persian (*farsi*) words, but transcribed into English letters rather than in their Arabic script.

Even when the Baluchi and Persian words are very similar, certain systematic differences in pronunciation often are present. The following are common differences. Baluch use "h" in many cases where Persians use "kh"—for example, Baluchi: Han (used in Baluchistan as a personal name); Persian: *khan;* Baluchi: *huda;* Persian: *khuda.* Baluch use "w" in many cases where Persian use "v"—for example, Baluchi: *sawab;* Persian: *savab.* Baluch often end words with consonants, while Persians often end words with vowels—for example, Baluchi: *galag, ramag;* Persian: *galle, rame.* Baluch will also use consonants at the beginning of words that Persians start with vowels—for example, Baluchi: *watag;* Persian: *otaq.* Baluch are less prone than Persians to use Arabic pronunciations—for example, using the "g" rather than the "q" in the previous example.

| | |
|---|---|
| *abadeh* | plentiful, wet years |
| *ablagon* | pots with tight lids |
| *abreshum* | embroidered cloths decorated with multiple, fine designs of many colors, used for decorating the bodice (*zi*), front pocket (*goptan*), and cuffs (*astunk*) of young women's dresses; *abreshum* is the Persian term for silk, perhaps adopted from the use of silk thread in the past |
| *abzeh* | flock of newborn lambs and kids |
| *ahouk* | gazelle |
| *aid* | religious holiday |
| *aidi buzorg* | religious celebration of the day of sacrifice; see *tuhean aid* |
| *al-tsebir* | Arabic for "big man" (Lancaster 1981) |
| *alef* | green, fresh fodder; see *duzi* |
| *api huda* | rainwater (literally: God's water), which is owned by no one |

| | |
|---|---|
| *arkan* | Arabic for the five pillars of Islam (i.e., declaration of submission and profession of faith, daily prayer, alms for charity, pilgrimage to Mecca, fasting during Ramazan) |
| *art* | flour (Persian: *ard*) |
| *babeh* | reciprocal term of address for father and children |
| *bad-e sad o bist ruz* | hot, summer wind of 120 days |
| *badkol* | someone who does not keep his or her word |
| *bagh* | garden |
| *bahar* | vegetation, pasturage |
| *bahargah* | spring, literally: "time of vegetation (*bahar*)" |
| *bak* | camel herd, i.e., number of camels herded together |
| *bakjat* | the person who herds camels, i.e., camelherd |
| *baksh, bakshist* | gift, to forgive a debt |
| *baluch* | a social category: a nomadic, tent-dwelling, livestock-herding, rainfall-runoff-microcultivating, lineage-affiliated, inhabitant of the desert and mountain |
| *baluk* | grandmother and great aunt; wife's grandmother (reference term) |
| *baluk zad* | children of *baluk* and of *tru zad* (reference term), i.e., grandmother's sister's children and aunt's children's children |
| *ban* | mud-brick hut with palm trunk and frond roof |
| *barband* | rope for securing loads on camels |
| *bari* | burden camel; see *hushtair* |
| *bastag* | yogurt (Persian: *mast*) |
| *beatopak* | lacking solidarity; see *topak* |
| *beawus* | poor, without resources |
| *behdari* | hospital |
| *bejar* | contribution |
| *bihaya* | immodest |
| *bonend* | settlements of mud-brick huts at date palm groves |
| *bonjan* | first wife (reference term) |
| *boz* | old female goat |
| *bra zad* | brother's children (reference term) |
| *bras* | brother (reference term) |
| *brasrend* | lineage of four or five generations' depth, operating as effective political and welfare solidarity group |
| *bubang* | large, metal chisel |
| *bum baluk* | great-grandmother and great-great-aunt (reference term) |
| *bum piruk* | great-grandfather and great-great-uncle (reference term) |
| *chadur* | large, half-circle of cloth, which covers head and hangs almost to the ground, used by Baluchi women as a veil; also the Persian term for tent |
| *chaharag* | wooden apparatus for hauling loads out of irrigation tunnels |
| *charki* | one fourth; a quarter share |
| *charwa* | desert-dwelling, nomadic pastoralists among the Yomut Turkmen (Irons 1975) |

| | |
|---|---|
| *chat, chart* | palm fronds |
| *chati* | young female goat |
| *chawart* | sandals |
| *chi* | tea |
| *chiluk* | rope woven from palm frond leaves, *pish* |
| *chomur* | Turkic for yurt-dwelling, nomadic cultivators among the Yomut Turkmen (Irons 1975) |
| *dachi* | mature male camel |
| *dadeh* | term of address for sisters and female cousins |
| *dadgah* | law court |
| *dal morg* | eagle; metaphorical: aggressive individual |
| *dasag* | brightly colored thread, imported, used for embroidering *abreshum* |
| *dasti huda* | God's act; literally: "the hand of God" |
| *dastur* | order |
| *dawati* | guest |
| *dehyak* | contribution of dates in the fall for subsistence of local mulla |
| *del sard* | weaned |
| *del* | heart |
| *diwan* | an assembly for deliberation (Persian: *divan*, royal court, tribunal of justice) |
| *dokal* | drought |
| *dokarch* | scissors (literally: two knives) |
| *dolat* | government, state authorities |
| *dotag* | daughter (reference term)(Persian: *dokhtar*) |
| *dozkech* | wife's sister (reference term) |
| *dramshuik* | small hut constructed inside the tent to provide shelter for lambs, kids, or chickens |
| *duro* | grain harvest, and the period of |
| *duzi* | fodder; see *alef, gedag, kah* |
| *gala* | winter wheat |
| *gala zar o bur* | the drying of the grain, and the period of |
| *galag* | flock or herd of small stock (Persian: *galle*); see *ramag* |
| *galas* | bowls for cooking and serving |
| *galfach* | thin flat bread, slightly leavened |
| *gali* | knotted pile carpets of the general "Persian carpet" type |
| *gamgine* | unhappy, sad |
| *gandom* | grain |
| *garaband* | heavy rope woven from palm frond leaves, *pish,* used to secure men working on palms |
| *gardag* | date pit |
| *garmon* | the early summer and grain harvest season |
| *gartur* | young male sheep |
| *gedag* | dried fodder; see *duzi* |
| *gedom shake* | large metal pins that hold the side mats to the tent roof |

| | |
|---|---|
| *gedom* | tent panel made of black goat hair used for tent roof; tent (Persian: *chadur*) |
| *genn* | a spirit that enters a person, causing insanity (Arabic: *jinn*) |
| *geshtar / deshtar* | female betrothed |
| *gayaban* | desert (Persian: *biaban*) |
| *gitaj* | mature female goat |
| *gohar* | sister (reference term) |
| *gohar zad* | sister's children (reference term) |
| *gosh* | flower of the male date palm, *narin* |
| *goshalak* | reproductive stem of the flower, *gosh*, of the male date palm, *narin* |
| *gusht* | meat (not including poultry) |
| *gwal* | large, heavy, wool storage sacks |
| *gwandien aid* | religious celebration at the end of Ramazan (literally: small holiday) |
| *gwang* | mature developmental stage of date palm; trunk up to 6 meters high |
| *gwarag* | lamb, newborn sheep |
| *gwarant* | mature male sheep |
| *gwarband* | low retaining wall, usually of dried mud, to hold runoff water in a cultivated plot |
| *gwash* | portion of tent occupied by *pas* |
| *gwerpat* | mats woven from palm frond leaves, *pish*, for tent siding |
| *hairat* | a sacrificial offering of an animal to God, followed by distribution of the meat to members of the community |
| *haj* | pilgrimage, especially pilgrimage to Mecca; see *arkan*, pillars of Islam |
| *haji* | pilgrim |
| *Haji* | honorific title used for those who have made the pilgrimage to Mecca |
| *haki shwaneg* | contractual payment to shepherd |
| *hakom* | ruler; a small-scale, regional ruler over both *baluch* and *shahri*, usually based in an oasis fort, *kalat* |
| *hakomzat* | the lineage of the ruler, literally: descendants of the *hakom;* usually a small, elite group, sometimes ruling a number of distinct regions; operating socially as a closed caste |
| *halk* | camping group |
| *hamin* | the late summer and date harvest season |
| *hamir* | dough |
| *hamjurad* | wives of brothers (reference term) |
| *hamsaheg* | neighbors; neighboring camps |
| *hamun* | drainage basin |
| *hapouk goharu* | co-wife (reference term) |
| *harab* | ruined (Persian: *kharab*) |
| *haram* | forbidden, used especially for what is believed to be forbidden to Muslims |
| *harguisht* | rabbit |
| *harrag* | sickle with a serrated blade |
| *hatuk* | the basic dish of Baluchi cuisine, consisting of bread broken into and |

|  | soaked with an edible liquid such as milk (*shiri hatuk*), gravy from meat (*gushti hatuk*), poultry (*morgi hatuk*), or vegetables such as lentils (*adassi hatuk*), or flavored water (*abi hatuk*) |
|---|---|
| *herr* | young camel calf |
| *herruk* | newborn camel calf |
| *hezak* | skin bag prepared for holding milk |
| *hezat* | honor and prestige |
| *hilal* | ritually sanctified, clean, allowed for Muslims |
| *hormag* | ripe dates (Persian: *khorma*) |
| *hort* | newborn lambs and kids |
| *huda* | God (Persian: *khuda*) |
| *huien* | blood (Persian: *khun*) |
| *huieni pul* | blood payment |
| *hushtair* | camel (Persian: *shotur*) |
| *hwank* | large stone serving an anvil |
| *il rah* | Persian for "tribal road" (Barth 1961) |
| *insha allah* | Arabic for "with the will of God" |
| *iwar* | the pollination of the date palms, and the period of |
| *jama kon* | come together, unite |
| *jamag* | shirt for men or dress for women, of long, loose design |
| *jan* | wife |
| *jang* | war |
| *jani adam* | woman |
| *jatk* | compressed date meat with pits removed |
| *jedmadar* | half-sibling (reference term) |
| *jird* | camel yearling |
| *jo* | barley |
| *jome* | Friday, the Islamic sabbath |
| *jube* | water channel |
| *juhan* | the period of grain allocation and storage |
| *jujuk* | sucker (new shoot) from roots of date palm |
| *kabre* | a grave |
| *kabul* | consent |
| *kach* | large transport bag woven from palm frond leaves |
| *kah* | dried, white fodder; see *duzi* |
| *kakeh* | reciprocal term of address for uncles and nieces/nephews |
| *kakian* | skilled workman on irrigation tunnels, *kan* |
| *kalat* | fort |
| *kan* | underground irrigation tunnel (Persian: *qanat*) |
| *kapt* | wild fowl, such as quail |
| *kar* | work or business |
| *karar* | contract, e.g., an annual herding contract |
| *karch* | knife |
| *katel* | small transport bag woven from palm frond leaves |

| | |
|---|---|
| *kayd* | camel hobble woven from palm frond leaves |
| *kesmat* | fate, destiny |
| *kohl* | cosmetic for darkening eyes |
| *kom* | kin (Persian: *qoum,* tribe, family, kindred; people, nation) |
| *kontak* | sharp spines of palm frond leaves |
| *kork* | soft underwool of goats |
| *kortuuk* | heavy, wooden mallet |
| *koruch* | a type of date of lower quality, from palms grown from seeds |
| *kowant* | grown female camel |
| *kuhd* | small covered hole or cave constructed inside the tent to provide shelter for lambs, kids, or chickens |
| *kuhistan* | mountainous and rocky area; literally: place of the mountains |
| *kumak* | help, assistance |
| *kunt* | flat woven rugs decorated by the "floating weft" technique, usually black and red with white designs, made by Baluchi women on horizontal looms |
| *kur karchuk* | protective pod of the flower of date palms |
| *labs* | tongue, language (Persian: *zaban*) |
| *lahb* | marriage prestation from groom and family to the father of the bride |
| *laleh* | term of address for brothers and male cousins |
| *langar* | strip of cloth representing wish tied to branch of holy tree |
| *lap* | gut, stomach, abdomen; metaphorically: mother's kin |
| *lardi* | migration of household residence |
| *lart* | wooden rod |
| *lawash* | very thin, unleavened bread (Persian: *lavash*) |
| *lira* | mature female camel |
| *lus* | greed |
| *mach* | (pronounced with "ch" as in "church") date palms; see *mok, madag, narin* |
| *madag* | female date palm; see *mok, mach, narin* |
| *madraseh* | Islamic school |
| *mahr* | obligatory Islamic agreement for compensation should a marriage end in divorce |
| *mahri rud bari* | fine riding camel; see *hushtair* |
| *mahri dashti* | good riding camel; see *hushtair* |
| *mal o maldai* | negotiation about marriage prestations; see *sang bandi* |
| *maldar* | a livestock owner |
| *maluma bi* | we will see when the time comes; literally: "it will become evident" |
| *man* | measure of weight, approximately = 5 kilos (Persian: *mand*) |
| *manah* | huts constructed of palm frond |
| *mard* | man |
| *mardi monjine* | neutral intermediary |
| *mardian adam* | man |
| *mas* | mother (reference term) |

| | |
|---|---|
| *mashk* | a skin bag prepared for holding water |
| *mashkband* | rope, *chiluk,* woven from palm frond leaves for securing water and milk bags |
| *masjed* | mosque |
| *maskom* | mother's kin |
| *master* | seniority; in the political sphere, a leader |
| *maulawi* | highly learned Islamic religious leader |
| *mayare* | at the mercy of |
| *mehudar* | horizontal loom made of wood by Luri craftworkers |
| *mesakin* | small rug on which food was placed for meals |
| *meska* | unclarified, soft, white, sour butter |
| *mish* | old female sheep |
| *misinin* | date pit gruel for kids and lambs |
| *mok* | date palm; see *mach, madag, narin* |
| *mokbur* | the date harvest, and the period of |
| *moksund* | the tying of the date bags, and the period of |
| *monjine* | neutral |
| *mud* | (pronounced: mood) hair |
| *mukay* | reciprocal term of address for mother and aunts, on the one hand, and children/nephews and nieces, on the other |
| *mulla* | educated Islamic religious leader |
| *musilmen* | humans, souls |
| *muzur* | unskilled workman on irrigation tunnels, *kan* |
| *nahal* | early developmental stage of date palm; bushlike structure, with little or no trunk yet developed |
| *naku* | uncle (reference term) |
| *naku zad* | uncle's children (reference term) |
| *nan* | bread; see *galfach, lawash,* and *wari* |
| *nan gwagh* | spatula |
| *nandeh* | host, literally "breadgiver" |
| *narin* | male date palm; see *mok, mach, madag* |
| *neshar* | wife of brother, cousin, or uncle (reference term) |
| *nomaz* | prayer |
| *nomazi* | prayer mat woven from palm frond leaves |
| *nosag* | brother's and sister's children's children (reference term) |
| *pa'dink* | a metal triangle with short legs, placed over a fire, for supporting pots or *tin* during cooking |
| *pakir* | wandering holy men |
| *pas* | small stock, i.e., sheep and goats |
| *pas, sepid (sepid pas)* | sheep (literally: white small stock) |
| *pas, sah (sah pas)* | goats (literally: black small stock) |
| *pasgah* | gendarmerie station |
| *pastori* | Italian term for "shepherds" |
| *patchenu* | mature male goat |

| | |
|---|---|
| *patir* | distribution of foodstuffs to satisfy vow given in request for God's intervention |
| *pes* | father (reference term) |
| *peskom* | father's kin |
| *pimaz* | onions (Persian: *piaz*); *pimazi kuh,* wild onions |
| *pin* | unpollinated date nodules |
| *pindag* | alms, enjoined by Islam; see *arkan,* pillars of Islam |
| *pindugir* | beggars |
| *pir* | old |
| *pir gwarant* | old male sheep |
| *pir pachen* | old male goat |
| *pira lira* | old female camel |
| *pira jurt* | old male camel |
| *piruk* | grandfather and great uncle; wife's grandfather (reference term) |
| *pish* | leaves of palm fronds |
| *pish kareh* | per animal payment |
| *pizadag* | stepchildren (reference term) |
| *plat* | mature female sheep |
| *pourap* | grown male camel |
| *pur* | stack of folded mattresses, quilts, rugs, and blankets |
| *pusht* | back; metaphorically: father's kin |
| *pust* | skin |
| *rabi* | a type of date of high quality, only from palms grown from suckers rather than seeds |
| *ramag* | flock or herd of small stock (Persian: *rame*); see *galag* |
| *rayat* | tax |
| *rayati* | those paying taxes (Persian: *raiyat,* subject, vassal) |
| *reis* | head, boss |
| *rend* | track, descent line, lineage group; children of *naku zad* (reference term), i.e., uncle's children's children |
| *ris* | heavy rope woven from goat hair |
| *rogan* | oil |
| *rogani pas* | butter oil, or ghee, from the milk of sheep and goats |
| *ru* | power, influence |
| *russe* | the fast of Ramazan; see *arkan,* pillars of Islam |
| *sah pas* | literally "black small stock" = goats |
| *sang* | stone |
| *sang bandi* | negotiation about marriage prestations; see *mal o maldai* |
| *sardar* | tribal chief |
| *sarjan* | second wife (reference term) |
| *sarsa* | contribution of cash at Ramazan for subsistence of local mulla |
| *sarsang* | stone used as hammer |
| *sawab* | religious merit |
| *Sepahi Danesh* | Persian for "Education Corps" |

| | |
|---|---|
| *sepid pas* | literally "white small stock" = sheep |
| *shadid* | religious martyrs |
| *shahri* | a social category: a sedentary, hut-dwelling, irrigation cultivator living in an oasis |
| *shalwar* | trousers of a loose, full design, secured at the waist by a draw string, worn by Baluchi men and women under long, loose shirts (for men) or dresses (for women) |
| *shaneg* | kid, newborn goat |
| *sharigdar* | relationship between lineages with multiple intermarriages |
| *sharik* | sharecropper |
| *shawarkashk* | the transport of the dates to the Sarhad plateau, the period of |
| *shekayat* | legal complaint |
| *shiakin* | heavy textile for preparing and storing bread |
| *shingiskan* | a type of date of high quality |
| *shirag* | date preserve |
| *shiri turoshp* | soured milk |
| *sholug* | disorder and confusion |
| *shu* | husband (reference term) |
| *shwaneg* | shepherd, especially of the camp herd |
| *sijoss* | a holy charm, attached to clothing, to protect the wearer against illness and particularly the evil eye |
| *silanch* | dried milk solids (Persian: *kashk*) |
| *sodayi* | commercial trading of goods |
| *sund* | large bags, woven of palm frond leaves, *pish,* used to enclose date clusters on palms |
| *suruz* | small, stringed musical instrument, played with a bow |
| *suzkumpk* | immature, green dates, and the period of |
| *tabar* | ax |
| *tabliq* | extraordinary assembly for the teaching of Islam |
| *tagert* | mats woven from palm frond leaves, *pish,* for tent flooring |
| *tajag* | milk as it comes from the animals; see *shiri turoshp* |
| *tanabi* | tent ropes |
| *tandur* | mud-brick oven |
| *tap* | injury |
| *tat* | rope fence separating tent into human and animal compartments; see *gwash* |
| *tiei* | small paper inscribed with a verse of the *Qoran,* to be ingested as protection against danger or illness |
| *tin* | a metal disk, slightly concave, on which bread was cooked |
| *toman* | unit of Iranian money |
| *topak* | group solidarity; see *beatopak* |
| *topangchini* | rifleman (Persian: *tofangci*), from *topang,* rifle (Persian: *tofang*) |
| *tru* | aunt (reference term) |
| *tru zad* | aunt's children (reference term) |

| | |
|---|---|
| *trusht* | young male goat |
| *tuhean aid* | literally: great holiday, i.e., the religious celebration of day of sacrifice; also called *aidi kurbani* (Persian: *aid-e gorbon*) |
| *wakil* | a man who had formally undertaken to ensure that the *mahr* agreement is honored |
| *wari* | thick and heavy flat bread |
| *waserk* | close male in-law, especially wife's father, uncle, or brother (reference term) |
| *wasil* | livestock |
| *wasildar* | a livestock owner |
| *wasta* | mediation, intermediary, commonly a person designated to mediate disputes or negotiate agreements |
| *wastar* | male betrothed |
| *wasu* | wife's mother or aunt (reference term) |
| *whush* | flower of the female date palm, *madag* |
| *whushalak* | reproductive stem of the flower, *whush,* of the female date palm, *madag* |
| *wond* | portion, share |
| *wonddar* | distributor of shares |
| *yakl* | capacity to reason |
| *yeki* | one and the same |
| *yekruchag* | contribution of cooking oil in the springtime for subsistence of local mulla |
| *yibor* | young female sheep |
| *yirat* | autumn |
| *zag* | son (reference term) |
| *-zai* | suffix for "descendants of . . ." |
| *zamas* | son-in-law, husband of sister, cousin, or aunt (reference term) |
| *zarat* | trees with holy powers |
| *zard o bahar* | the drying of the vegetation and pasture, and the period of |
| *zat / zad* | descent, descent line; see *rend* |
| *zek* | a small skin bag for holding clarified butter or date preserve |
| *zemistan* | winter |

# BIBLIOGRAPHY

Angioni, Giulio

   1989   *I Pascoli Erranti: Antropologia del Pastore in Sardegna.* Napoli: Liguori Editore.

   1996   On Agro-pastoral Space in Sardinia. In *The Anthropology of Tribal and Peasant Pastoral Societies,* edited by U. Fabietti and P. C. Salzman, pp. 333–342. Como, Italy: Ibis.

Arfa, General Hassan

   1964   *Under Five Shahs.* London: John Murray.

Asad, Talal

   1970   *The Kababish Arabs: Power, Authority and Consent in a Nomadic Tribe.* London: C. Hurst.

   1973   The Beduin as a Military Force: Notes on Some Aspects of Power Relations between Nomads and Sedentaries in Historical Perspective. In *The Desert and the Sown,* edited by C. Nelson. Research Series No. 21. Berkeley: University of California Institute of International Studies.

   1978   Equality in Nomadic Social Systems? *Critique of Anthropology* 11: 57–65.

Avery, Peter

   1965   *Modern Iran.* London: Ernest Benn.

Bailey, Frederick

   1969   *Stratagems and Spoils: A Social Anthropology of Politics.* Oxford: Basil Blackwell.

Barth, Frederik

   1961   *Nomads of South Persia: The Basseri Tribe of the Khamseh Confederacy.* Oslo: Oslo University Press.

   1983   *Sohar: Culture and Society in an Omani Town.* Baltimore: Johns Hopkins University Press.

   1992   Method in Our Critique of Anthropology. *Man* (n.s.) 27: 175–177.

   1994   A Personal View of Present Tasks and Priorities in Cultural and Social Anthropology. In *Assessing Cultural Anthropology,* edited by R. Borofsky. New York: McGraw-Hill.

Bates, Daniel G.

1973    *Nomads and Farmers: A Study of the Yörük of Southeastern Turkey.* Anthropological Papers No. 52. Ann Arbor: University of Michigan Museum of Anthropology.

Beck, Lois

1980    Herd Owners and Hired Shepherds: The Qashqa'i of Iran. *Ethnology* 19: 327–351.

1986    *The Qashqa'i of Iran.* New Haven, Conn.: Yale University Press.

1991    *Nomad: A Year in the Life of a Qashqa'i Tribesman in Iran.* Berkeley: University of California Press.

Benedict, Ruth

1935    *Patterns of Culture.* London: Routledge and Kegan Paul.

Bernus, Edmund

1981    *Touaregs nigeriens: Unité culturelle et diversité régionale d'un peuple pasteur.* Paris: Editions de l'Office de la Recherche Scientifique et Technique Outre-mer.

1990    Dates, Dromedaries, and Drought: Diversification in Tuareg Pastoral Systems. In *The World of Pastoralism: Herding Systems in Comparative Perspective,* edited by J. Galaty and D. Johnson. New York.: Guilford Press.

Bestor, Jane Fair

1979    *The Kurds of Iranian Baluchistan: A Regional Elite.* Unpublished Master's Thesis. Montreal: McGill University.

Black-Michaud, Jacob

1986    *Sheep and Land: The Economics of Power in a Tribal Society.* Cambridge: Cambridge University Press.

Bonte, Pierre

1990    French Marxist Perspectives on Nomadic Pastoral Societies. In *Nomads in a Changing World,* edited by P. Salzman and J. Galaty. Naples: Istituto Universitario Orientale.

Bradburd, Daniel

1980    Never Give a Shepherd an Even Break: Class and Labor among the Komachi of Kerman Iran. *American Ethnologist* 7: 603–620.

1990    *Ambiguous Relations: Kin, Class, and Conflict among Komachi Pastoralists.* Washington, D.C.: Smithsonian Institution Press.

1994    Historical Bases of the Political Economy of Kermani Pastoralists: Tribe and World Markets in the Nineteenth and Early Twentieth Centuries. In *Pastoralists at the Periphery: Herders in a Capitalist World,* edited by C. Chang and H. Koster. Tucson: University of Arizona Press.

Brooks, David

1983    The Enemy Within: Limitations on Leadership in the Bakhtiari. In *The Conflict of Tribe and State in Iran and Afghanistan,* edited by R. Tapper. London: Croom Helm.

Bujra, Abdalla S.

1971    *The Politics of Stratification: A Study of Political Change in a South Arabian Town.* Oxford: Clarendon Press.

Bulliet, Richard

1980    Sedentarization of Nomads in the Seventh Century: The Arabs in Basra and Kufa. In *When Nomads Settle: Processes of Sedentarization as Adaptation and Response,* edited by Philip Carl Salzman. New York: Praeger.

Caltagirone, Benedetto

1989    *Animali Perduti: Abigeato e Scambio Sociale in Barbagia.* Cagliari, Sardegna: Celt Editrice.

Campbell, J. K.

1964    *Honour, Family and Patronage: A Study of Institutions and Moral Values in a Greek Mountain Community.* Oxford: Clarendon Press.

Chatty, Dawn

1986    *From Camel to Truck: The Bedouin in the Modern World.* New York: Vantage Press.

1996    *Mobile Pastoralists: Development Planning and Social Change in Oman.* New York: Columbia University Press.

Clifford, James

1988    *The Predicament of Culture.* Cambridge, Mass.: Harvard University Press.

Clifford, James, and George E. Marcus

1986    *Writing Culture: The Poetics and Politics of Ethnography.* Berkeley: University of California Press.

Cohen, Abner

1969    *Custom and Politics in Urban Africa: A Study of Hausa Migrants in Yoruba Towns.* Berkeley: University of California Press.

Cohen, Ronald

1978    State Foundations: A Controlled Comparison. In *Origins of the State: The Anthropology of Political Evolution,* edited by R. Cohen and E. Service. Philadelphia: Institute for the Study of Human Issues.

Cole, Donald Powell

1975    *Nomads of the Nomads: The Al Murrah Bedouin of the Empty Quarter.* Chicago: Aldine.

Colson, Elizabeth

1984    The Reordering of Experience: Anthropological Involvement with Time. *Journal of Anthropological Research* 40:1–13.

Curzon, Hon. George N.

1892    *Persia and the Persian Question.* Vol. 2. London: Longman, Green.

Dyer, General R. E. F.

1921    *Raiders of the Sarhad: Being the Account of a Campaign of Arms and Bluff against the Brigands of the Persian-Baluchi Border during the Great War.* London: H. F. and G. Witherby.

Dyson-Hudson, Neville

1966    *Karimojong Politics.* Oxford: Clarendon Press.

Edgerton, Robert B.

1971    *The Individual in Cultural Adaptation: A Study of Four East African Peoples.* Berkeley: University of California Press.

*Encyclopaedia Britannica*

1975    Date Palm. In *Micropaedia,* vol. 3, p. 389.

English, Paul Ward

1966    *City and Village in Iran: Settlement and Economy in the Kirman Basin.* Madison: University of Wisconsin Press.

Evans-Pritchard, E. E.

1940    *The Nuer: A Description of the Modes of Livelihood and Political Institutions of a Nilotic People.* Oxford: Clarendon Press.

1949    *The Sanusi of Cyrenaica.* Oxford: Clarendon Press.

Forbes, Rosita

1931    *Conflict, Angora to Afghanistan.* London: Cassel.

Fratkin, Elliot, Eric Abella Roth, and Kathleen A. Galvin

1994    Introduction. In *African Pastoralist Systems,* edited by E. Fratkin, K. Galvin, and E. Roth. Boulder: Lynne Rienner.

Garthwaite, Gene R.

1983    *Khans and Shahs: A Documentary Analysis of the Bakhtiyari in Iran.* Cambridge: Cambridge University Press.

Geertz, Clifford

1968    *Islam Observed: Religious Development in Morocco and Indonesia.* New Haven, Conn.: Yale University Press.

1973    *The Interpretation of Cultures.* New York: Basic Books.

1979    Suq: The Bazaar Economy in Sefru. In *Meaning and Order in Moroccan Society,* edited by C. Geertz, H. Geertz, and L. Rosen. Cambridge: Cambridge University Press.

1980    *Negara: The Theatre State in Nineteenth-Century Bali.* Princeton, N.J.: Princeton University Press.

1983    *Local Knowledge: Further Essays in Interpretive Anthropology.* New York: Basic Books.

Gellner, Ernest

1969    *Saints of the Atlas.* Chicago: University of Chicago Press.

1981    *Muslim Society.* Cambridge: Cambridge University Press.

1988    *Plough, Sword and Book: The Structure of Human History.* Chicago: University of Chicago Press.

1995    Segmentation: Reality or Myth? *Man* (n.s.) 30:821–829.

Gluckman, Max

1969    *Custom and Conflict in Africa.* Glencoe, Ill.: Free Press.

Helander, Bernhard

1998    The Emperor's New Clothes Removed: A Critique of Besteman's "Violent Politics and the Politics of Violence." *American Ethnologist* 25(3):489–501.

Holway, Bradley

1978    *Adaptation, Class, and Politics in Rural Corsica.* Unpublished Ph.D. dissertation. Montreal: McGill University.

Irons, William

1972    Variation in Economic Organization: A Comparison of the Pastoral Yomut and the Basseri. In *Perspectives on Nomadism,* edited by W. Irons and N. Dyson-Hudson. Lieden: E. J. Brill.

1975    *The Yomut Turkmen.* Anthropological Papers No. 58. Ann Arbor: University of Michigan Museum of Anthropology.

1994    Why Are the Yomut Not More Stratified? In *Pastoralists at the Periphery: Herders in a Capitalist World,* edited by C. Chang and H. Koster. Tucson: University of Arizona Press.

Jackson, Michael

    1989    *Paths toward a Clearing: Radical Empiricism and Ethnographic Inquiry.* Bloomington: Indiana University Press.

Johnson, Douglas H.

    1994    *Nuer Prophets: A History of Prophecy from the Upper Nile in the Nineteenth and Twentieth Centuries.* New York: Oxford University Press.

Kennard, Coleridge

    1927    *Suhail.* London: Richards Press.

Khazanov, Anatoly M.

    1994    *Nomads and the Outside World.* 2d ed. Madison: University of Wisconsin Press.

Kottak, Conrad, and Elizabeth Colson

    1994    Multilevel Linkages: Longitudinal and Comparative Studies. In *Assessing Cultural Anthropology,* edited by R. Borofsky. New York: McGraw-Hill.

Kraus, Wolfgang

    1998    Contestable Identities: Tribal Structures in the Moroccan High Atlas. *Journal of the Royal Anthropological Institute* 4(1):1–22.

Kuper, Adam

    1988    *The Invention of Primitive Society: Transformations of an Illusion.* London: Routledge.

Lambton, A. K. S.

    1953    *Landlord and Peasant in Iran.* London: Oxford University Press.

Lancaster, William

    1981    *The Rwala Bedouin Today.* Cambridge: Cambridge University Press. (Second edition, 1997; Prospects Heights, Ill.: Waveland.)

Lancaster, William, and Fidelity Lancaster

    1996    Some Comments on Peasant and Tribal Pastoral Societies of the Arabian Peninsula. In *The Anthropology of Tribal and Peasant Pastoral Societies,* edited by U. Fabietti and P. C. Salzman, pp. 389–401. Como, Italy: Ibis.

Lévi-Strauss, Claude

    1963    *Structural Anthropology.* New York: Basic Books.

    1966    *The Savage Mind.* Chicago: University of Chicago Press.

Lewis, I. M.

    1961    *A Pastoral Democracy: A Study of Pastoralism and Politics among the Northern Somali of the Horn of Africa.* Oxford: Oxford University Press.

Marcus, George E.

    1994    After the Critique of Ethnography: Faith, Hope, and Charity, but the Greatest of These Is Charity. In *Assessing Cultural Anthropology,* edited by R. Borofsky. New York: McGraw-Hill.

Marcus, George E., and Michael M. J. Fischer

    1986    *Anthropology as Cultural Critique.* Chicago: University of Chicago Press.

Marx, Emanuel

    1996    Are There Pastoral Nomads in the Arab Middle East? In *The Anthropology of Tribal and Peasant Pastoral Societies,* edited by U. Fabietti and P. C. Salzman, pp. 101–115. Como, Italy: Ibis.

Meloni, Benedetto

   1984    *Famiglie di Pastori: Continuità e Mutamento in Una Comunità della Sardegna Centrale*
           *1950–1970.* Torino: Rosenberg and Sellier.

Mulder, Monique Borgerhoff, and Daniel W. Sellen

   1994    Pastoralist Decisionmaking: A Behavioral Ecological Perspective. In *African Pas-*
           *toralist Systems,* edited by E. Fratkin, K. Galvin, and E. Roth. Boulder, Colo.:
           Lynne Rienner.

Munson, Henry Jr.

   1993    Rethinking Gellner's Segmentary Analysis of Morocco's Ait Atta. *Man* (n.s.)
           28:267–80.

   1995    Segmentation: Myth or Reality. *Man* (n.s.) 30:829–832.

Nadel, S. F.

   1951    *The Foundations of Social Anthropology.* Glencoe, Ill.: Free Press.

Naval Intelligence Unit (Britain)

   1945    *Persia.* London: Government of Great Britain.

Nicolaisen, Johannes

   1963    *Ecology and Culture of the Pastoral Tuareg.* Copenhagen: National Museum of
           Copenhagen.

Pastner, Steven

   1971    Ideological Aspects of Nomad-Sedentary Contact: A Case from Southern
           Baluchistan. *Anthropological Quarterly* 44:173–184.

Persian Boundary Commission (India)

   1876    *Eastern Persia: An Account of the Journeys of the Persian Boundary Commission 1870–*
           *1872:* vol. 1, *The Geography. . . .* London: Macmillan.

Peters, Emrys

   1960    The Proliferation of Segments in the Lineage of the Bedouin of Cyrenaica. *Jour-*
           *nal of the Royal Anthropological Institute* 90(1):19–53.

   1967    Some Structural Aspects of the Feud among the Camel-Herding Bedouin of
           Cyrenaica. *Africa* 37:261–282.

Rao, Aparna

   1995    From Bondsmen to Middlemen: Hired Shepherds and Pastoral Politics. *Anthropos*
           90:149–167.

Ravis Giordani, Georges

   1983    *Bergers corses: Les communautés villageoises du Niolu.* Aix-en-Provence: Edisud.

Rosen, Lawrence

   1984    *Bargaining for Reality: The Construction of Social Relations in a Muslim Community.*
           Chicago: University of Chicago Press.

Sahlins, Marshall

   1961    The Segmentary Lineage: An Organization of Predatory Expansion. *American*
           *Anthropologist* 63:322–43. [Reprinted in *Man in Adaptation: The Cultural Present,*
           edited by Y. Cohen. Chicago: Aldine, 1968.]

   1968    *Tribesmen.* Englewood Cliffs, N.J.: Prentice-Hall.

   1976    *Culture and Practical Reason.* Chicago: University of Chicago Press.

   1981    *Historical Metaphors and Mythical Realities: Structure in the Early History of the Sand-*
           *wich Islands Kingdom.* Ann Arbor: University of Michigan Press.

Salzman, Philip Carl

1967    Political Organization among Nomadic Peoples. *Proceedings of the American Philosophical Society* III: 115–131.

1971a    Movement and Resources Extraction among Pastoral Nomads: The Case of the Shah Nawazi Baluch. *Anthropological Quarterly* 44:185–197.

1971b    Adaptation and Political Organization in Iranian Baluchistan. *Ethnology* 10:433–444.

1972    Multi-resource Nomadism in Iranian Baluchistan. In *Perspectives on Nomadism,* edited by N. Dyson-Hudson and W. Irons. Leiden: Brill. [Also: *Journal of Asian and African Studies* VII:60–68.]

1973    Continuity and Change in Baluchi Tribal Leadership. *International Journal of Middle East Studies* 4:428–439.

1974    Tribal Chiefs as Middlemen: The Politics of Encapsulation in the Middle East. *Anthropological Quarterly* 47:203–210.

1975    Islam and Authority in Tribal Iran: A Comparative Comment. *Muslim World Quarterly* 65:186–195.

1978a    Ideology and Change in Middle Eastern Tribal Society. *Man* 13:618–637.

1978b    The Proto-State in Iranian Baluchistan. In *Origins of the State,* edited by R. Cohen and E. Service. Philadelphia: ISHI.

1978c    Does Complementary Opposition Exist? *American Anthropologist* 80(1):53–70.

1979    Inequality and Oppression in Nomadic Society. In *Production Pastorale et Société,* pp. 429–446. Cambridge: Cambridge University Press.

1980    Culture as Enhabilmentis. In *The Structure of Folk Models,* edited by L. Holy and M. Stuchlik, 233–256. A.S.A. Monograph 20, London, Academic Press.

1983    Why Tribes Have Chiefs: A Case from Baluchistan. In *The Conflict of Tribe and State in Iran and Afghanistan,* edited by R. Tapper, pp. 262–283. London, Croom Helm.

1985    Are Nomads Capable of Development Decisions? *Nomadic Peoples* No. 18:47–52.

1986a    Shrinking Pasture for Rajasthani Pastoralists. *Nomadic Peoples* No. 20:49–61. Also in the *Journal of Sociological Studies* (India) 5:128–138.

1986b    Dates to Meet, Dates to Eat: Oasis Life in Tribal Baluchistan. *Baluchistan Studies* 3:48–62.

1988a    From Nomads to Dairymen: Two Gujarati Cases. *Economic and Political Weekly* (Bombay) XXIII(31):1582–1588.

1988b    Labour Formations in a Nomadic Tribe. In *Who Shares? Co-operatives and Rural Development,* edited by D. Attwood and B. Baviskar, pp. 233–258. Delhi: Oxford University Press.

1992    *Kin and Contract in Baluchi Herding Camps.* Baluchistan Monograph Series II. Naples: Istituto Universitario Orientale and Istituto Italiano per Il Medeo ed Estremo Oriente.

1994    Baluchi Nomads in the Market. In *Pastoralists at the Periphery: Herders in a Capitalist World,* edited by C. Chang and H. A. Koster, pp. 165–174. Tuscon: University of Arizona Press.

1995a    Comment on "Understanding Tribes in Iran and Beyond." *Journal of the Royal Anthropological Institute* 1(2):399–403.

1995b    Studying Nomads: An Autobiographical Reflection. *Nomadic Peoples* 36:157–65.

1996    Peasant Pastoralism. In *The Anthropology of Tribal and Peasant Pastoral Societies,* edited by U. Fabietti and P. C. Salzman, pp. 149–166. Como, Italy: Ibis.

1999a    Is Inequality Universal? *Current Anthropology* 40 (1): 31–61.

1999b    *The Anthropology of Real Life: Events in Human Experience.* Prospect Heights, Ill.: Waveland.

2000    Hierarchical Image and Reality: The Construction of a Tribal Chiefship. *Comparative Studies in Society and History* 42(1):49–66.

Schneider, Harold K.

1979    *Livestock and Equality in East Africa: The Economic Basis for Social Structure.* Bloomington: Indiana University Press.

Spooner, Brian

1964    *Kuch U Baluch* and *Ichthyophagi. Iran* 2:53–67.

1967    *Religious and Political Leadership in Persian Baluchistan.* Ph.D. diss., Oxford University.

1969    Politics, Kinship, and Ecology in Southeast Persia. *Ethnology* 8:139–152.

1983    Who Are the Baluch? A Preliminary Investigation into the Dynamics of an Ethnic Identity from Qajar Iran. In *Qajar Iran,* edited by E. Bosworth and C. Hillenbrand, pp. 93–110. Edinburgh: University of Edinburgh Press. Reprinted at Costa Mesa, California: Mazda, 1992.

1992    Baluchistan: Geography, History, and Ethnography. In *Encyclopaedia Iranica:* 598–632.

Street, Brian

1990    Orientalist Discourses in the Anthropology of Iran, Afghanistan and Pakistan. In *Localizing Strategies: Regional Traditions of Ethnographic Writing,* edited by R. Fardon, 240–259. Edinburgh: Scottish Academic Press.

1992    Method in Our Critique of Anthropology. *Man* (n.s.) 27:177–179.

Swidler, W. W.

1972    Some Demographic Factors Regulating the Formation of Flocks and Camps among the Brahui of Baluchistan. In *Perspectives on Nomadism,* edited by Wm. Irons and N. Dyson-Hudson, pp. 69–75. Leiden: Brill.

Sykes, Major Percy Molesworth (Later Brigadier-General Sir Percy)

1902    *Ten Thousand Miles in Persia or Eight Years in Iran.* London: John Murray.

1941    Exploration in Baluchistan. *Journal of the Royal Central Asian Society* 28:68–77.

Tapper, Richard

1979    *Pasture and Politics: Economics, Conflict and Ritual among Shahsevan Nomads of Northwestern Iran.* London: Academic Press.

Thesiger, Wilfred

1959    *Arabian Sands.* New York.: E. P. Dutton.

Vayda, Andrew P.

1994    Actions, Variations, and Change: The Emerging Anti-essentialist View in Anthropology. In *Assessing Cultural Anthropology,* edited by R. Borofsky. New York: McGraw-Hill.

Von Grunebaum

1951    *Muhammadan Festivals.* New York: Henry Schuman.

Wilkinson, J. C.

    1977    *Water and Tribal Settlement in South-East Arabia: A Study of the* Aflaj *of Oman.* Oxford: Clarendon Press.

Wright, Sue

    1992    Method in Our Critique of Anthropology: A Further Comment. *Man* (n.s.) 27:642–644.

    1994    Constructing Tribal Identity in Iran. *Man* (n.s.) 29:183–186.

Wulff, Hans E.

    1966    *The Traditional Crafts of Persia: Their Development, Technology, and Influence on Eastern and Western Civilizations.* Cambridge, Mass.: MIT Press.

Young, William C.

    1996    *The Rashaayda Bedouin: Arab Pastoralists of Eastern Sudan.* Fort Worth, Tex.: Harcourt Brace.

Zeuner, Frederick E.

    1963    *A History of Domesticated Animals.* New York: Harper and Row.

# INDEX

Abdul Karim, beating of, 258, 266, 271
Abdullak (little Abdul), as shepherd for Ja'fari camp, 98, 162, 205, 214
affines: coordinated labor activities, 199; marriages among the Baluch, 240–61; relationships among, 253–56; spatial arrangements between tents, 58–61
age(s): at first marriages, 243; status indications, 38–39
agriculture: cultivation of crops other than wheat and barley, 127; on the Sarhad high plateau, 123–29; use of products, 129–30; view of farmers as possible Baluchi spouses, 241
Alluk (shepherd), 205–6, 214
ancestor, common: defining a tribe through, 295–96; lineages constructed through, 234–35
arguments, between men and women, Baluch attitude toward, 63–64
authority: households' independence and camp authority, 300; Qoran texts as, 6; of the Yarahmadzai Sardar, 307–9

Baluchi Period, 90, 346, 351–52
Baluch Shakar, 280–82
Barkat (husband of Dur Malik), and controversy over camel meat, 61–65
Barth, Frederik, 233, 314, 350
Basseri (mountain people), compared with nomadic Sarhadi Baluch, 8, 355, 357, 359
Beadak, migrations to, 156–57, 173–74, 181
Bibi Nur (Ja'far's daughter and wife of Id Mahmud), 45, 190–91, 243
bilateral kinship, 225–30
blacksmiths, bands of (Luri): implements forged by, 22, 78, 129; roles in Baluchi weddings, 248; social position among the Sarhadi Baluch, 9, 241
borrowing/lending, of supplies and equipment by coresidents, 199
bread: amounts of grain used and monetary value, 79; soaked in various liquids as daily meals, 70–71; types of and baking methods, 72–73
brideprices, to settle disputes, 279

brothers, lineage of, 238–40
butter, clarified, 74

camel(s), 73, 115, 134, 196; conflict over a beast who ate the wrong dates, 265–77; herding arrangements, 201–2; management of, 104–5; meat apportionment incident, 61–65; pasturage for during migrations, 158–59; reproduction of domesticated animals, 105, 177, 189; transportation services of, 102–4, 170–71, 175, 181; value of as medium of exchange, 245–46
camp(s) (halk), 68–69; constitution of an annual herding group, 49–52; migrations, 152–65, 168–85; multiplex relationships within, 52–58; social makeup and lineages, 67–68; variations in sizes, 65–67; of the Yarahmadzai Sardar, 326–29. See also tents
captives, acquired by raids, 134–35
carpets, use in Baluchi tents, 32
charms, holy, 337
chickens: eggs in Baluchi diet, 76; tent areas for, 26
chiefs, Sarhadi Baluch tribes (sardar): compared with leaders of larger tribes, 355; and segmentary lineage systems, 9–10, 258–61, 294–329, 360
children: clothing worn by, 37–38; living with related families, 192–94; Persians captured and sold into slavery, 134; residency with father, 244–45; as source of family labor, 188–89, 191–95, 208–10, 251–52
clothing, Baluchi, 34–41, 51
communal eating, at feasts, 71
compensation: for injured parties in disputes, 271, 274, 275, 279, 281–85; in kind for sharecropping, 128–29, 219–20; for loss of animal through sale of meat, 82–83; payment terms for date harvesting, 200–201; for shepherds, 204–5, 217–18
"complementary opposition," relevance of individual's lineages under different circumstances, 235–37
configurationalist school, in anthropology, 4–5
containers, for food storage, 77–78
continuity of residence index (CRI), 67
contractual relationships: animal herding, 49–50, 52, 176–77; for compensated labor, 200–201